DISCARDED

D0206098

Queering Christianity

Finding a Place at the Table for LGBTQI Christians

Robert E. Shore-Goss,
Thomas Bohache,
Patrick S. Cheng, and
Mona West, Editors

PRAEGER

AN IMPRINT OF ABC-CLIO, LLC
Santa Barbara, California • Denver, Colorado • Oxford, England

Library of Congress Cataloging-in-Publication Data

Queering Christianity : finding a place at the table for LGBTQI Christians / Robert E. Shore-Goss, Thomas Bohache, Patrick S. Cheng, and Mona West, editors.

   pages cm

Includes index.

ISBN 978-1-4408-2965-9 (hardback) — ISBN 978-1-4408-2966-6 (ebook)

  1. Church and minorities.   2. Homosexuality—Religious aspects—Christianity.   I. Shore-Goss, Robert.

  BV639.M56Q44   2013

  261.8'35766—dc23   2013006776

ISBN: 978-1-4408-2965-9
EISBN: 978-1-4408-2966-6

17   16   15   14   13   1 2 3 4 5

This book is also available on the World Wide Web as an eBook.
Visit www.abc-clio.com for details.

Praeger
An Imprint of ABC-CLIO, LLC

ABC-CLIO, LLC
130 Cremona Drive, P.O. Box 1911
Santa Barbara, California 93116-1911

This book is printed on acid-free paper ∞

Manufactured in the United States of America

Dedicated to the prophetic vision of radical inclusion and human rights for all of Rev. Troy Perry

Contents

Introduction: Queering the Table

Robert E. Shore-Goss

Tony growled, "You know Troy, I learned one thing from this experience, nobody likes a queer. We're just a bunch of dirty queers and nobody cares about dirty queers."

"Somebody cares." Troy responded.

"Who?

"God cares."

Tony laughed bitterly, and said, "Oh, come on Troy, God doesn't care about me." With that, he turned and left. I knelt down and said, "All right God, if it's Your will; if You want me to see a church started as an outreach into our community, You just let me know when." And that still, small voice let me know—now!

—Rev. Troy Perry[1]

Before Stonewall, Troy Perry founded a movement that became a church, spreading throughout the United States and globally. On October 6, 1968, Troy followed the promptings of the Spirit and celebrated the first worship service of the Metropolitan Community Church (MCC) in a rented house in Huntington Park, California. Twelve people responded to an ad run in *The Advocate Magazine* and attended that service. During the first Sunday service, Troy told the attendees that he intended to develop a church that would reach homosexuals everywhere. His message was three-pronged: salvation, community, and social action.

Toward the end of the service, Perry offered a prayer over the bread and grape juice and offered those who had been excluded to come and receive communion. He dramatically and spiritually ritualized the exclusion that the gays and lesbians in attendance had experienced through their churches' politics of the table. They had been denied access to the sacrament because of their sexual orientation, for they had not been welcomed into communion with God and the church. This ritual is now repeated in many MCC churches during worship at the end of the communion table prayer with the invitation: "You neither need to be a member of MCC, nor any church nor even be a Christian. All are welcome to God's table." In that simple ritual proclamation is embodied a profound proclamation that the unconditional grace of God is available to all people. God surrounds all human beings from birth to death with inclusive, incarnational love and redemptive care. This gift of love is nothing other than God's self-communication of divine love and forgiveness. There are three notions embodied in MCC's ritual. First, God's grace is radically inclusive and without conditions. Second, no one is turned away, for the table is open. Hospitality supersedes all denominational politics of the table. Finally, the open invitation expresses a central practice of Jesus' ministry that every person is loved equally by God. Combined, this ritual invitation would become the core mission of MCC: God's radical inclusive love.

Many churches fail to recognize God's indiscriminate or even promiscuous love for all people in Jesus' table practice of meals and table companionship with sinners. The symbolic power to partake of communion by excluded queer Christians should not be underestimated. In her study of MCC, Melissa Wilcox observes how individuals, when they start attending, may take weeks or even months before they approach the communion table because of the exclusionary practices and messages within their former churches. Same-sex couples may come and receive communion as a couple, then receiving a prayer blessing from one of the celebrants. She concludes, "The *habitus* that conveys second class status to the world and oneself is thus broken during the MCC ritual."[2] Rather a new symbolic *habitus* of grace and acceptance is communicated to each participant receiving communion. The power of the open table at a queer church may have the similar significant social and religious impact upon those that Jesus invited in practice of open commensality or table fellowship. At Queer Conference of queer theologians and religious leaders at Emory University, the late feminist, queer theologian Marcella Althaus-Reid shared with me how MCC Edinburgh brought her back to Christian communion. She found communion to be an alienating and exclusive experience in many churches but found the MCC open invitation at table and the blessing meaningful.

The editors and contributors understand that the core queer theologies are based on the open invitation to communion table and that we have been comprehended as sinners. We may be sinners, but we believe that we are also companions with the risen Christ in meals remembering the inclusive grace celebrated in his first meal, his Last Supper, and his meal at Emmaus on the beach of the Lake of Galilee. The dynamics of the open communion table incarnate a dynamic of inclusionary grace.

FINDING A PLACE AT THE TABLE

The sad divisions of Christ's Church are exacerbated by rules and regulations that create barriers to the receiving of God's free grace at the table. Issues of intercommunion, closed communion, and open communion divide Christians and their practices at table. Nowhere are the divisions more realized than in a closed Church who invites a guest to the Lord's house and then dictates that the guest cannot sit and eat at the table with the family. Such behavior, at best, is rude etiquette and, at worst, a profound betrayal of the table practices of Jesus.

One of the scandals of contemporary Christianities is their politics and exclusion at the communion table. It neither expresses church unity, unless ecclesial definitions are narrowed down to a specific denomination, nor expresses inclusivity. Closed communion is the practice of restricting the serving of the elements of communion to a particular church, denomination, sect, or congregation. Although the meaning of the term varies slightly in different Christian theological traditions, it generally means a church or denomination limits participation either to members of their own church, members of their own denomination, or members of some specific class (e.g., baptized members of evangelical churches, children who have made their first communion, closeted or nonpracticing queer folks).

The Catholic Church practices an exclusionary politics of the communion table.[3] It believes that Christians from other denominations, including Orthodox Churches, who do not share the theology of the

Eucharist, are excluded from partaking communion. Those Christians, who share the Catholic doctrines around sacraments, may receive communion under specific guidelines issued by the Catholic Conference of Bishops: The person must be unable to have recourse for the sacrament of Eucharist to a minister of his or her own Church, ask for the sacrament unprompted, and manifest Catholic faith in the sacraments. This is a partial or highly qualified inclusion at the table. Divorced and remarried Catholics, on the other hand, are denied access to communion along with the parents of the RainBow Sash Movement, who display the sash as they present themselves for communion, or openly noncelibate queer and flaunting Catholics. In some churches, transgender folks are denied communion unless they dress appropriate to the gender with which they were born.

The policy of a closed Communion among churches is nothing new; in fact, it goes back to some of the practices of the earliest Christians. The *Didache*, a second-century CE book of Christian discipline states that only baptized Christians can receive the Eucharist: "But let no one eat or drink of this Eucharistic thanksgiving, but they that have been baptized into the name of the Lord."[4] So the concept of a closed Communion has its origins traced to the Church in the second century. One could claim that churches ever since are observing an ancient tradition, but nowhere does it state that Christians can deny access to the table to different believing Christians. Such historical exclusions have developed, surrounding the communion table with politics: correct beliefs, correct membership in the right church, correct loyalty, and correct moral behaviors. Many Catholic, Orthodox, and Protestant churches practice such politics of exclusions or qualified inclusions at the communion table.

Most churches that practice a closed communion table find the exclusive origin of the Eucharist in the Last Supper accounts in the synoptic gospels (Mt 26:26–29, Mk 14:22–25, Lk 14–20) and 1 Cor 11: 23–26. They dislocate the context of the final meal of Jesus with his disciples, often identifying the only participants as the male disciples present at the meal. Nowhere do the accounts of the words of institution indicate that only male disciples or only the twelve attended; but disciples, a plural inclusive of both male and female disciples. These churches decontextualize the final meal from the series of means prophetically practiced for God's reign primarily because of dogmatic considerations and ecclesial restrictions that control access to the communion table. The accounts of the institution of the Last Supper precede gospel formation as indicated by 1

Cor 11:23–26. The historical roots of the Eucharist formula at the Last Supper, however, emerged from Christian communal praxes, but the famous scholar Joachim Jeremias notes that the isolation of the Last Supper narrative from the meals of Jesus' table fellowship has led to significant theological distortions:

> In reality, the "founding meal" is only one link in a long chain of meals which Jesus shared with his followers and which they continued after Easter. These gatherings at table, which provoked such scandal because Jesus excluded no one from them, even open sinners, which thus expressed the heart of his message.[5]

Eucharist scholar Paul Bradshaw writes,

> The trend, therefore, in more recent scholarship has been to locate the source of the Eucharist more broadly within the context of other meals in Jesus' life and not merely the Last Supper . . . to take seriously various layers of meaning that can be discerned within the New Testament and the different ways that the individual New Testament writers describe those meals.[6]

This trend has had the tendency of understanding the symbolism of Jesus' final meal with his earlier prophetic meals celebrated for God's reign. Jesus practiced an alternative notion of God's hospitality by means of inclusive meals in which anyone could share. The consequence, therefore, is to contextualize Jesus' final meal in his more inclusive table praxes than exclusive politics of the communion table.

An open communion table is the opposite of exclusive ecclesial politics of the table where the Lord's Supper is reserved only for members of that particular church or others with which it is in a relationship of full table fellowship, or has otherwise has been ecclesially sanctioned for that purpose. Theologian, Michael Welker notes,

> Once we perceive how holy communion unfolds against the background of the "night of self-giving and betrayal," it becomes impossible to cast doubt upon the fundamental acceptance of sinners in the Supper. It is incompatible with Supper to have human beings sitting in judgment over each other and deciding which supposedly righteous person is admitted to the Supper and which "unworthy" is excluded. It is a total perversion of communion to turn it into a process of judgment by some persons over others, or use it to support such an undertaking. . . . It (the Supper) is not

a religious opportunity to render or refuse moral or judicial recognition to other human beings.[7]

By connecting the Last Supper to Jesus' meals of table fellowship, exclusion of particular groups, sinners, outcasts, LGBTQI folks, and others violates Jesus' central message of God's hospitality extended to sinners. It should be noted that Jesus practiced an open table at the Last Supper with Judas who betrayed him, Peter who denied him, and male disciples who abandoned him. Many churches have ignored Jesus' table fellowship during his ministry and focused on the Last Supper with their politics of exclusion at the communion table.[8] They have interpreted the Last Supper to justify their particular practices of exclusion and religious hierarchies, to determine whether a person receives communion worthily or unworthily. 1 Cor 11:27–31 highlights the misuse of the agape or Lord's Supper by those Corinthians consuming the food they brought and not sharing their food with other members in attendance, thus they violate the spirit of equality of Jesus' meal. The Lord's Supper and agape become a perversion of the intent of Jesus' meal, demonstrating social inequality and injustice.[9]

Generally, there are several contemporary churches in open and affirming congregations that open their invitations to the communion table to other Christians and LGBT Christians without requiring baptism or explicit affirmation of doctrinal beliefs. Some churches announce at the beginning of the communion rite: "We invite all who profess faith in Christ to join us at the table."

Queering the table refers to the process of exploding the cultural, theological, and ecclesial boundaries around the politics of the communion table. Marcella Althaus-Reid's work has concentrated in unmasking the fascist regimes of heteronormative theology. She and other queer theologians have intruded upon heteronormative theology with transgressive, indecent sexualities and gender fluidities to create a queeruption, creating space for theologies from queer outsiders.

One of the earliest Christian queeruptions was Rev. Tory Perry's practice and commitment to open commensality, an open communion table. From the first worship service of MCC, Troy Perry invited everyone to come to the table. I asked Troy, "What made you do this?" He told me, "It was the right thing to do."[10] The Holy Spirit was already working mischief to break out of restrictive orthopraxis of the communion table and prompted Troy Perry that day to invite everyone to the table and wanted a church that practiced once again Jesus' radical inclusiveness at the table.

JESUS' PRACTICE OF OPEN COMMENSALITY

The biblical scholar James D. G. Dunn notes that two central features of Jesus' ministry of God's reign were his table fellowship and the absence of the boundaries:[11]

> Jesus evidently saw the fellowship of the meal table as an expression of life under the rule of God (particularly Mt 22:2; 25:1); in his own social relationships he sought to live in accordance with his vision of the kingdom (cf. particularly Lk 6:20 with 14:13, 21). It was this lived-out vision of acceptability before God as expressed in table fellowship which, according to the Synoptics, was one of the major causes of complaint against Jesus among some of his contemporaries.[12]

John Dominic Crossan also underscores that Jesus' open table fellowship is a core teaching component of the reign of God and symbol of his life. He notes that Jesus' practice of "open commensality (rules of tabling and eating) is the symbol and embodiment of radical egalitarianism, of an absolute equality of people that denies the validity of any discrimination between them and negates the necessity of any hierarchy among them."[13] Crossan understands Jesus' Parable of the Feast (GThom 64: 1–2; Lk 14:15–24; Mt 22:1–13) as an expression of open commensality:

> It is the random and open commensality of the parable's meal that is the most startling element. One could, in such a situation, have classes, sexes, ranks, and grades all mixed up together. The social challenge of such egalitarian commensality is the radical threat of the parable's vision. . . . And the almost predictable counteraccusation to such open commensality is immediate: Jesus is a glutton, a drunkard, and a friend of tax collectors and sinners. He makes, in other words, no appropriate distinctions and discriminations.[14]

The banquet vision of the Parable of the Feast (Lk 14:15–24) affirms that God's reign is not about power but about nonreciprocal gifting of human beings with the abundant welcome of acceptance and forgiveness. Jesus' open commensality expressed a notion of unbrokered egalitarianism, an open access to God and one another. Marcus J. Borg also highlights that Jesus practiced "an open and inclusive table," and he writes, "The inclusive vision incarnated in Jesus' table fellowship is reflected in the shape of the Jesus movement itself."[15] Jesus invited sinners, tax collectors, prostitutes, and deviants with a mixture of poor and artisans into a fellowship meal that celebrated God's forgiveness and unconditional love.

Jesus broke the existing pattern of exclusive eating practices of his time as he redefined meal boundaries from exclusions to inclusions. When you invite someone for dinner, he said, "do not think of the rich, not even your family and friends, not the socially respectable, but the poor, who cannot reciprocate the invitation." The general scholarly consensus finds that Jesus' open commensality and his eating habits critiques the asymmetrical religious patronage exchanges, both asymmetrical and even symmetrical giving and receiving favors. His etiquette of open hospitality, service at table, unbrokered egalitarianism, and celebration of God's forgiveness of sins, around meals criticizes cultural, social, and religious hierarchies and inequalities. He replaces hierarchies for egalitarianism— proposing a transgressive religious vision of role reversals, upturning of hierarchies, and radical equality and inclusive hospitality. Jesus indiscriminately welcomes men and women of all classes and purity or impurity statuses and fosters a community in which all are welcome. Stephen Patterson indicates such an open table is table "far less manageable and far more threatening."[16] Jesus triggers a terror of open commensality to his religious critics and political opponents, whose group-centered personalities comprehended eating together without discriminations and hierarchies, but it still triggers a terror communion table. Dunn asserts,

> Jesus did not agree with the religious politics of the table at the time—
> for he drew upon the prophetic analogy of a banquet for which all were
> invited and abundance of food for all. Jesus sought to break down the
> boundaries and to create a fellowship which was essentially open rather
> than closed. His open table-fellowship, so much both constituting and
> characterizing the community which practiced it, made the point clearly
> than any other aspect of his mission.[17]

Jesus made an inclusive table practice as a central symbol of his compassionate ministry. Just as God opens the feast without boundaries, so Jesus encouraged his disciples to open their kingdom feasts to those in need and unable to repay the favor. Jesus challenged exclusive religious boundaries by practicing what Borg calls a "boundary-subverting inclusiveness," Dunn "an absence of boundaries," and Crossan an "open commensality."[18] Catholic social psychologist Diarmuid O'Murchu writes, "The commensality pioneered by Jesus was a ritual loaded with empowering intent."[19]

All these terms indicate an untamed or wild hospitality practiced by Jesus as signs of God's reign in our midst. These are signs of God's reign and are the ritual symbolics of incarnational grace. Jesus enacted a parable of God's incarnational grace through his life, ministry, death, and resurrection.

Food is much more than something material to nourish our bodies and lives, for food is a densely polyvalent symbol of encounter and communion with God and one another. Catholic theologian Angel Mendez-Montoya speaks of the incarnational dynamics of preparing a mole sauce, the blending of the ingredients that maintain their vibrant tastes and yet express richness as a whole, and culminating in a communal fiesta. His theology of food expresses a profound symbolic language of Eucharist and superabundant grace with generosity and abundance express the dynamics of God's superabundant communication of love and grace.[20] It expresses the polyvalent symbolic intent of Jesus' open commensality, perceiving the blending of a variety of ingredients as the blending of a variety of people into the body of Christ. Likewise, Leonardo Boff stresses how important a gesture at the table is to serve or pass the food to someone:

> What was not the bread on the plate placed on the table but the sharing of the bread and the passing of the bread to others. In the same way, the wine was not important, rather what was important was the cup, which was passed from one person to another, it was the cup, shared between people that was important.[21]

Meal sharing, for Boff, expresses the dynamics of communion and solidarity between people and God, for these meal sharings create the dynamics symbolizing God's love for all and justice for all. Incarnational grace takes on the symbolic of service: breaking the bread and passing the cup. The disciples at Emmaus did not recognize Jesus until he broke the bread, for they recognized him in his customary service action on their behalf and for God.

Finally, Elisabeth Schüssler-Fiorenza envisions Christian spirituality in the dynamics of Jesus' meals:

> Christian spirituality means eating together, sharing together, drinking together, talking with each other, receiving each other, experiencing God's presence through each other, and, in doing so, proclaiming the gospel as God's alternative vision for everyone, especially those who are poor, outcast and battered.[22]

Schüssler-Fiorenza expresses a notion of eating together and hospitable welcoming in alignment with Jesus' open commensality. These are all part of the incarnational dynamics of grace symbolized through Jesus' practice of an open table, and there have been a number of books that have recently stressed the untamed hospitality incarnated in the meals of Jesus.[23] The stress upon abundance and inclusivity in Jesus' meals is a metaphorical expression of incarnational theology—the presence of God in the ordinary, as revealed in the gathering of all to feast together. These meals symbolize that God's grace is wildly loose in the world.

THE WORD MADE FLESH

The symbolic language of incarnation has remained a central mode of Christian theological speech about God's immanence in Jesus the Christ. The notion of incarnation is discarded in some quarters because it no longer makes sense or because it has been used exclusively and abusively against certain social targets. Restrictive notions of God's incarnation in Christ have been specifically used to exclude sinners, LGBTQI folks, and non-Christians from salvation, create ecclesial boundaries, exclude people from the communion table, deny equal and gender access to sacraments, colonize indigenous peoples, and oppress the Earth. Wendy Farley's *Gathering Those Driven Away: A Theology of Incarnation* (Louisville, KY: Westminster John Knox Press, 2011) attempts to develop an incarnational language that includes those marginalized and erased by traditional, exclusive, and violent incarnational theologies. She inclusifies incarnational theology and its rhetoric to deflect the violence committed through incarnational exclusivity and presents trajectories of inclusive incarnational theologies for the marginalized and indecent outsider.

Traditional exclusivist incarnation language attempted to fix the divine or human nature of the incarnated Christ. Lisa Isherwood and Marcella Althaus-Reid build upon a body of recent queer explorations of God's incarnation in Christ:

> queer transformations that showed the unstable categories involved in God incarnate. It is through changes from divine to flesh, flesh and blood to bread and wine, and from human to cosmic spirit, that the full incarnation of redemptive praxis takes place? What is fixed and stable and overarchingly metaphysical about this? By guarding these stories with a protective shield of Greek metaphysics and exclusivity we made them stable and clear categories, thus negating them. Queer theology would like to take them raw and examine how we between us embody these and other forms of incarnation.[24]

Marcella Althaus-Reid explores the widening of the incarnated Christ with her interpretation of the Queer Christ as the Bi/Christ with the interpretation of John 1:14 where "The Word became flesh and pitched a tent among us."[25] Tents are analogy for the fluid nature of the incarnated God, and this allows Althaus-Reid to see the Queer Christ is incarnated in the lives of sexual and gender outsiders.[26] Thomas Bohache extends the fluidity of incarnation with a Spirit Christology into queer embodied living of Christ within us:

> Incarnation is an acceptance that we bear Christ within us—the part of God that is instilled in us to bring forth from ourselves the offspring of Christ-ness: self-empowerment, creativity, awareness of creation, joy, love, peace and justice-making . . . that God becomes one with humanity through the assurance that God has always been present and that realization of this presence will give birth to human infusion with divine anointedness as Christ.[27]

Similarly, Robert E. Shore-Goss has developed a solidarity Christology that Christ is incarnated in the suffering and oppressed in the world. On the cross, Jesus died in solidarity with all queers (and oppressed peoples): "On Easter God made Jesus queer in his solidarity with us. In other words, Jesus 'came out of the closet' and became the 'queer' Christ."[28] Shore-Goss expands his notion of the Queer Christ by dialoging with Althaus-Reid and accessorizes her model of the Bi/Christ with the Bi/Transvestite Christ.[29]

Gerard Loughlin comprehends how queer theory highlights the instabilities and fluidities of sexual or gender identities. For him, God's incarnation is thoroughly queer:

> Christian theology has always already found the body of Christ to be fungible flesh, a transitioning corporeality; never stable but always changing, becoming other, Christ's body is transfigured, resurrected, ascended, consumed. Born a male, he yet gives birth to the church; dead, he returns to life; flesh, he becomes food.[30]

Loughlin follows the lead of a number of queer and nonqueer theologians who understand the radical change of God as queer in the incarnation in Christ. It has produced some creative Christologies that are both orthodox and quite radical in their inclusivities. For example, Loughlin's, Mollenkott's, Stuart's, and Shore-Goss's queer parodies of Ephesians 5:25–27 depart from heteronormative readings of the text by traditional baptismal and incarnational theology, whereas Christ and the church become queerly embodied.[31] The authors queer a traditional text that has been used to establish binary power hierarchies of male over female and clergy over laity actually, promoting a heteronormativity. They, in process, restore a more fluid notion of gender, and I would argue, a traditional baptismal embodied theology expressed in the egalitarian formula in Galatians 3:28.

Patrick Cheng builds on previous queer Christologies to construct a Christology of radical love.[32] He recognizes the transgressive, crossing-over, erasing of boundary event of God's incarnation:

> Christian theology is fundamentally a queer enterprise because it focuses upon the incarnation, life and death, resurrection, as envision, and second coming of Jesus Christ, all which are events that turn upside down of life and death, divine and human, center and margins, infinite and finite, and punishment and forgiveness. As with the case of queer theory, it is in Jesus Christ that all seemingly fixed binary categories are ultimately challenged and collapsed.[33]

The Queer Christ as the embodiment of radical love crosses over all divine, social, gender, sexual, and racial binaries. Jesus as the incarnation of radical love undergoes continued displacements from birth, death, and beyond—erasing all binary categories, and creating a new "multigendered body" of Christ as church.[34] All the queer Christologies move toward more inclusive models and away from restrictive Christologies that exclude. They maintain that God's incarnational grace is radically inclusive and allows for pluralist explorations and expansions.

In a paper, "Theater of Bodies," at a conference on "*Queering the Church*," Harvard theologian Mark D. Jordan speaks about the rhetorical failure of churches' traditional incarnational theologies:

> When the churches fail us as queer people, they are failing the principle of incarnation. Our flight from the pain of exclusion is not assertion of our group identity. (Queer identity often comes as consolation for lost religious identity.) We flee churches because we seek a practice of incarnation that learns the divine truths in queer bodies.[35]

The crux of Mark Jordan's paper is that normative incarnational models have resulted in ecclesial exclusions of queer folks, and these failures of normative incarnational models do not understand fully the depths and fluid dimensions of God's incarnation in Christ:

> The exclusion of queer bodies from churches undoes the principle of incarnation. It is also why the toleration or acceptance or welcoming of

queer bodies is, by itself, insufficient. Queering the church means learning about church from the agency of the various queer bodies that have been banned from them. It is particularly important to learn from *queer* bodies because these bodies have, in many historical constructions, been depicted as the exact opposite of the Christian body. The sodomitic body is the antithesis, the antitype of the graced body, the sacramental body. The force of this antithesis is of course connected with the abjection of other bodies in Christian theology—women's bodies, Jewish bodies, slave bodies, pagan bodies—but the antithesis Christian/Sodomite has, for many reasons, a particular ferocity. In many traditional theologies, queer bodies are fantasized as the most defiled and defiling bodies there can be. To restore queer bodies to churches is to confront churches with their rejection of the bodily as such—with the aspects of the bodily in which they refused to recognize divine events.[36]

Queer bodies are outsider bodies: porous, malleable, ambiguous, hybrid, and transgressive. Queer Christians have frequently fled from their ecclesial communities of origin to discover the grace of their embodiments—to remember and reenact incarnation thoroughly different from mainline Christian denominations. Jordan gave some examples from pre-Stonewall history of attempts to remember incarnation. It is not enough for churches to undo the exclusion of queer bodies or tolerate us in some distorted notion of tokenism. Mark boldly states, "A queer church must rather be a church that has grieved the failure of incarnation and then re-performed incarnation differently."[37] Here Mark Jordan locates church in queer agency that re-performs incarnation, not only differently but also queerly. The process of queering for Christians is ultimately a theologically incarnational activity, participating in the bodily messiness of dismantling gender and sexual boundaries and opening new horizons of an ever-expanding understanding of incarnational inclusivities. It is similar to what Graham Ward describes as the continual displacement of Christ's body into new embodiments.[38]

WHY QUEERING CHRISTIANITY?

Grace Jantzen wrote about her profound ambivalence that she as a lesbian and many queer Christians undergo in their struggle with their religions of origin:

For many who have had the straight rule of Christendom applied in hateful and destructive ways, the answer is to slam the book shut altogether, and have nothing more to do so with this story. For some people that is surely a healthy response, not just "understandable" in a condescending way, but a very good conclusion to the particular script that have been required to read. But for me that will not do. Part of the reason is that Christendom has not only been the worst of my personal past but also the best of it; and the need to deal with the former requires a reappropriation and transformation of the latter. I will not become a more flourishing person by cutting off my roots.[39]

Almost all queer Christian theologians have experienced such ambivalence in their journeys and painful decisions to remain inside or outside of Christian institutions. Susannah Cornwall explores this precise question in her book, *Controversies in Queer Theology*, with a whole chapter entitled "Should Queer Christian People Stay Christian?"[40] This tension becomes so obvious in the chapter "Communion: Playing with Redemption" that the cast of Corpus Christi addresses religious abuse but find an unorthodox spirituality in Terrence McNally's play about a gay Joshua or Jesus figure who dies from homophobia. The play and now the documentary "Playing with Redemption" has become a ministry of MCC in the Valley and Soul Force to confront religious abuse and affording many LGBT folks to find a resolution to abusive Christian churches by reclaiming Christ as one of their own.[41]

Many LGBT theological and religious scholars have found shelter and freedom with tenure in academic institutions as they write but often remain on the margins of their churches unless they teach and participate in an open and affirming Christian denomination. Their contextual community of faith remains primarily an academic community, with various degrees of connections to open and affirming Christian denominations predominantly heterosexual and collegial queer scholarly relationships with queer groups in the Society of Biblical Literature and the American Academy of Religion.

But they also may participate in a queer contextual community that expresses a range of attitudes toward Christianity from ambivalence, apathy, partial acceptance, or to what Thomas Bohache describes as "Christophobia."[42] Even scholars from queer studies may generally see Christianity as hostile to their countercultural identities and studies or from the general queer community that views with suspicion alignments with Christianity that have oppressed them and funded propositions to oppose marriage equality. Only in the recent decade has the Human Rights Campaign realized the value of queer faith communities, queer clergy, and theologians and biblical scholars in their arguments against religious opponents in the cultural wars over equal rights.[43] Yet when the California Supreme Court on May 15, 2008, struck down the definition of marriage between a man and a woman, one of the four plaintiffs in the case, Rev. Troy Perry and his husband Philip, were not invited to speak at the West Hollywood celebration rally. There is still a range of feelings from reluctance to open resistance within the queer community to any alignment with Christianity, even queer communities of faith.

This book represents a trajectory of queer Christian contextual theologies—different from queer theologians on the margins of their denominations or who participate in churches where LGBTQI folks are a minority in the church and are the occasional focus for a sermon during queer pride celebrations or occasional ritual celebrations as blessing a same-sex union. Sermons rarely include anecdotes or stories of LGBTQI folks, for they are usually drawn from the predominant heteronormative heritage of the church. They may tone down their queer theologies to assimilate "respectably" into or fit into a homogenized ecclesial culture.[44] This does not mean that MCC as denomination is exempt from such assimilationist theological trends, for there are MCC churches that will not use the word *queer* at all but replicate heteronormative churches.

But MCC represents, on the other hand, a unique queer Christian theological community—where pastors and theologians actively participate in the Leather Community; leather groups such as Avatar and PLAY (People of Leather Among You) meet in MCC churches, or Sisters of Perpetual Indulgence groups hold their monthly meetings in their facilities. Some churches host an interfaith leather service during the festivities of the city leather contest; celebrate transgendered worship services; ritualize trans-renaming rituals; bless the motorcycles of a leather biker club; or officiate at over 100,000 same-sex unions in the history of the denomination. How many open and affirming churches experience leather-uniformed folks at service, a gaggle of Sisters of Perpetual Indulgence in white face and habits, a transgendered Dominatrix, or closeted transgendered folks coming to service in male drag and changing into dresses in the rest rooms, at worship service and welcomed to the communion the table? How are sexual identities and gender fluidities, and their life rituals and journeys incorporated and honored into worship services that are primarily heteronormative? This stretches even the most liberal of open and affirming churches.

Open table has also meant the incorporation of inclusive language for worship and the inclusive lectionary and Bible for scriptural readings. The inclusions at the table and inclusive language undermine some of the

mimetic heteronormative worship prevalent in most churches that reinforce residual patriarchal theologies. It subverts the misogyny in the traditional masculine language in the lectionaries, prayer books, and hymnals.
I have found it very strange to go to Protestant or Catholic worship where
masculine language and pronouns are used for God. This estrangement
results from years of praying, celebrating rituals, and worship in an inclusive language context.

The theologies of the contributors are shaped from such a queer worship that is inclusive and queer Christian community, whose mission is
God's radical inclusive love. All the contributors, except the authors on
"Communion: Playing with Redemption," are MCC clergy. This means
that queer theologies emerge from actual pastoral praxis where queer
identities are fluid and where sexual diversities are the norm. This mission of radical inclusion is not just the integration of LGBTQI folks into
a heteronormative Christianity (though it is the integration of LGBTQI
queer folks into a queer Christianity); rather, its mission is to include the
widest diversity of LGBTQI into a queer Christian praxis of faith as well
as the respectful inclusion of heterosexuals into a community where all
differences are welcomed because we are all the beloved children of God.
This inclusive vision breaks down binaries of heteronormative Christianity by establishing the common ground of God welcoming all equally to
the table and celebrating our unique differences as gifts brought to the
worship community.

Generally (but not always because there are exceptions), Siobhan Garrigan observes that the integration of LGBTQI folks into heteronormative churches involves a process of "covering" or an assimilationist fitting
into the church as "normal" or "straight-acting" members.[45] It mutes
LGBTQI behaviors in subtle ways in order to fit into a heteronormative culture, and this becoming the normal or straight queer is as harmful
to spiritual development and the journey to accept yourself an original
blessing in the divine image or as harmful as remaining closeted within
a congregation. These open and affirming churches attempt to integrate
LGBT Christians into heteronormative congregations, but there is no
queer flaunting. LGBTQI Christians are expected to cover over their
identities with nonqueer behaviors. If they flaunt their behaviors, it is
coded as outrageous or incorrect etiquette. Many gay men are attracted
to Anglo-Catholic rituals of high liturgy within Episcopal Churches and
participate in those churches, but they claim that such smells and bells
liturgy is already queer. This presence of gays and lesbians in the Anglican
and American Episcopal Church have transformed the Episcopal Church

in America to appoint openly lesbian and gay bishops, ordain gay or lesbian priests, and officiate at same-sex marriages.

Queering is a process defined as the contrast of the heteronormative or culturally "normal." For example, Siobhan Garrigan uses the notion of coyote, the trickster from Gordon Lathrop to understand the role of queer as transgressing borders and introduces disorder into the world of order.[46] In my chapter "The Holy Spirit as Mischief-Maker" or Kerri Messer's discussion of "jokerism" in "Innovations in Queer Theology," the theological appropriation of mischief of tricksters or jokerism introduces creativity, ceremonial breaks with traditional Christian doctrines, and practices by using camp and dramatic parody, queer play, to enrich life and create new space outside the binary boundaries of the normal (and ecclesial). Queer cultural techniques are introduced into the practice of church, which creates unique ecclesial spaces that incorporate theological explorations into a queer medium. Astutely, Garrigan observes,

> Realizing the genre as worship as a structurally queer site in human living privileges it as a legitimate site for queer theological reflection. But of course for worship to be queer it has to function not merely like Lathrop's coyote; it also has to be LGBT-cognizant.[47]

For Garrigan, queer indicates an LGBTQI need to talk about queer sexualities, fluidities, and gender diversities, topics that churches are generally uncomfortable to talk about or let to theologically reflect upon. Queer introduces, I maintain, queer play into mainstream Christian theology.

The theological context of the contributors emerges from the queer ecclesial communities of faith that read the biblical text from predominantly a queer LGBTQI perspective, incorporating their own contextual life experiences as well an interpretative queer reading and worship community. This has led to the publication of such books as *Take Back the Word* and *The Queer Bible Commentary*.[48] Yet it also led to several queer theologies and explorations of queer Christologies by MCC authors. This book represents queer theologies emerging from more than 40 years of queer, countercultural theologies that remain in dialogue with mainstream Christian theologies and engage queer academic theologies but at the same time honors queer diversities, life experiences, and queer worship communities. Gay scholar Rollan McCleary has underscored the abstract and intellectual nature of queer theory and queer theology for heterosexual Christians as well as gay and lesbian Christians who are theologically conservative.[49] However, many LGBTQI Christians in churches may not understand the intricacies of queer theology, but they do understand MCC's invitation to open commensality or the practice of radical inclusive love and hospitality. Radical inclusive love opens them to welcoming queer groups that are marginalized by some segments of the gay and lesbian community.[50] All are welcome at table means "all" is an important incarnational praxis of an inclusive church.

QUEER THEOLOGIES ENGAGING MAINLINE CHRISTIANITY

This book is neither about MCC queer theologies, nor is it about MCC as a church. It is about queer theologies emerging from thoroughly queer Christian communities and practices. It is distinguished from Gerard Loughlin's edited book, *Queer Theology: Rethinking the Western Body*, which Susannah Cornwall has observed: "the volume's essays appear to exist on a plane safely distant from grassroots struggles and homophobic violence."[51] Some academic queer theologies, aligned with queer theory and often reflected in Queer Studies in its anti-Christian prejudices, are periphery to queer movements as many segments of queer communities are at the periphery of queer churches.[52] It is closer to the recently published two-volume work, *Queer Religion*, coedited by Jay Johnson and Donald Boisvert.[53] This book has closer affinities to grassroots movements in queer culture and communities. *Queering Christianity* works out pastoral connection to the LGBTQI community and queer social movements, and it dialogues queer theologians such as Mark Jordan and Marcella-Althaus-Reid, who were deeply impacted by MCC Edinburgh and its open communion practices.[54]

The special historical context of the MCC is at the intersections of religious-social transference and countertransference of LGBTQI Christians who have suffered religious abuse and rejection, but MCC not only experiences Christian homophobia but also the Christophobia of segments in LGBTQI community which suffered religious abuse. Many queer Christians, however, also participate shoulder to shoulder with those queers who are hostile to institutional religion in the same movements for marriage equality, leather contests, transsexual days of remembrances, pride festivals, Human Rights Campaign's lobby days at state governments, and many other community movements and organizations. They find commonality in the fight for freedom against cultural and religious heterosexism, and there are pastoral moments where queer Christians can share their abuse with their colleagues and witness to the value in their lives of remaining in a queer faith community. Bohache claims nonhomophobic Christology can bridge and heal some Christophobia, and this is the particular case of the cast of Corpus Christi who perform the story of gay Joshua or Jesus to counter Christian homophobia and Christophobia.[55]

All the contributors have their own pedigrees of grassroots movements and struggles for LGBTQI human rights and freedom. All MCC clergy are required to participate in a class in Queer Sexual Theology, exploring queer theologies and sexual or gender diversities. All the clergy contributors have taken this course, and a number of the contributors have taught such courses for future MCC clergy. They have comprehended the transformative potential of queer theology for changing their lives and queer Christians in committing themselves to social justice.

Finally, *Queering Christianity* represents mainstreaming queer theologies beyond any denominational confines to mainstream a charism instilled in a denominational founder and prophet: Troy Perry. Initially, Troy Perry made it clear that MCC's mission was not forever. The original mission of MCC was to include LGBTQI folks into a Christian community. Troy Perry articulated the mission of MCC at the first worship service on October 6, 1968, held in his living room:

> I made it clear that we were not a gay church: we were a Christian church, and I said it that in my first sermon. I told them we would be a Protestant church to be an all-inclusive.[56]

They had open communion, and he knew from that worship service that MCC would be an ecumenical church, that the mission of the church would not be a ghettoized queer church, and that the church would come to an end.[57] The mission of MCC would morph into something new and unforeseeable, far more inclusive as it engaged the larger Christian denominations.

The queer audience is not just MCC members or the LGBTQI community. It includes queer theologians and theologians in mainstream churches. The symbolics of grace as expressed by the open table, queer challenges to narrow incarnational theologies, and queer ecclesial practices include a kenotic residue in MCC queer theologies to move beyond itself its contextual roots and to engage in wider conversations with Christian theologians and engage in conversations about social justice and find a commonality of Christian social practice with other Christian denominations. In doing so, a queer heterosexual theologian—Susannah Cornwall—can write these words:

Queer theology is at once a critical friend to the theological tradition, and a kernel of creative disorder right on the inside, exploding and showing forth what is within—just as popping corn does when things get agitated and heated.

Queer theology, then, is a popcorn kernel; it is a disclosing tablet; it is a conjuror who whips away the rug from beneath theological feet. It might also be characterized as a grain of sand inside an oyster's shell. The critical irritation and discomfort it produces might, like the grain of sand, be transformed, becoming prophetic harbingers of a new way of justice and peace. This new way will be something so precious that whole lands and vineyards of belief and dogma are given up and given over for its sake: a pearl of great price which makes what used to seem final and ultimate pale into insignificance in light of divine love. In this new order, justice will roll down like rivers and righteousness like an everlasting stream, as God is shown to live with those who are shut out and cast aside: a stranger at the gates whose love and mercy will not be limited by any human ideology.[58]

Cornwall uses the wonderful playful analogy of a kernel of popcorn agitated and heated to be transformed into popcorn. Likewise, MCC's queer theologies moved by grace as experienced weekly in the practice of repeating Jesus' invitation to the open table is drawn outside of the MCC ghettoes to a wider vision of inclusion of diversity, even beyond itself as church and willing to morph into new wine skins as it engages theological conversations and forges new beginnings with other Christian faith communities and beyond. As Tom Bohache asks the core question of this book with his chapter "Unzipping Church: *Is* There Room for Everyone?," *Queering Christianity* brings this theological question and practice to the greater church communities with the hope that the shared queer experiences can find resonance with other Christian communities open to the Holy Spirit who has the uncanny ability to crack open walls and tear them down to find a place at a common table.

This is not a book for Queer Christians. *Queering Christianity* has been compiled to address those churches that are open and affirming, that are addressing the heterosexism of their theologies, their ecclesial practices of LGBTQI inclusion and commensality, and their pastoral practices as they welcome LGBTQI folks into their ecclesial homes. For many years, we have been theologizing and dialoguing with Christian tradition to discover a means to accept the original blessing of being created in the image of God and find a space to practice our faith in community. We have been ghettoized, and now it is the time to engage our theological experience and faith with Christian denominations and communities that want to dialogue and learn as we will learn from wider conversations with various Christian communities.

All the contributors believe that as we dialogue with churches about creating a vision of radical inclusive love that Jesus lived and practiced and died for, we may look to a time when we all may set an inclusive table for all and welcome the diversity of each person though it may disrupt our senses of the normative and our homogenizing etiquettes to embrace the different, the queer as a site where heterosexuals and queers may find a common experience of the Queer God who has already incorporated our infinite differences and eccentricities into a divine community of love, mirrored by churches that openly practice the appreciation of personal and theological differences and still find a place for celebration that each of us carry the divine image and likeness.

NOTES

1. Chris Glaser, ed., *Troy Perry: Pastor and Prophet* (West Hollywood, CA: Metropolitan Community Church, 2005), 47–48.

2. Melissa M. Wilcox, *Coming Out in Christianity* (Bloomington: Indiana University Press, 2003), 140. Wilcox draws the term *habitus* from Pierre Bourdieu's work, meaning "a collection of learned behaviors, accents, and bodily postures that communicate both to oneself and others one's place in society" (139).

3. Patrick S. Cheng pointed out the new English translation (instituted November 2011, for the cup saying "for you and for all" has been replaced by "for you and for many.") See http://catholic-resources.org/ChurchDocs/RM3-EP1–4.htm.

4. Didache 9:10–12.

5. Joachim Jeremias, *New Testament Theology: The Proclamation of Jesus*, vol. 1 (London: SCM Press, 1971), 289–90.

6. Paul F. Bradshaw, *Eucharistic Origins* (New York: Oxford University Press, 2004), 2. See note 8 on page 2 for a list of authors. In addition, I would add to the list: James D. G. Dunn, *Jesus Remembered* (Grand Rapids, MI: Wm. B. Eerdmans Publishing Company, 2003), 599–603; Gerd Theissen, *A Theory of Primitive Christian Religion* (London: SCM Press, 1999), 130; John D. Crossan, *The Birth of Christianity* (New York: HarperSanFransisco, 1998), 423–44.

7. Michael Welker, *What Happens in Holy Communion?* (Grand Rapids, MI: Wm. B. Eerdmans Publishing Company, 2000), 73.

8. Ibid., 69–83.

9. Ibid., 76–79.

10. Conversation between Troy Perry and Robert E. Shore-Goss.

11. Dunn, *Jesus Remembered*, 599–607.

12. James D. G. Dunn, "Jesus, Table-Fellowship, and Qumran," in Jesus and the Dead Sea Scrolls, ed. James H. Charlesworth (New Haven, CT: Yale University Press, 1992), 255–56.

13. John Dominic Crossan, *Jesus: A Revolutionary Biography* (New York: HarperOne, 1994), 79.

14. John Dominic Crossan, *The Historical Jesus: The Life of a Mediterranean Peasant* (New York: HarperSanFransisco, 1991), 262.

15. Marcus Borg, *Meeting Jesus Again for the First Time* (New York: HarperSanFransisco, 1994), 55–56.

16. Stephen Patterson, *God of Jesus: The Historical Jesus and the Search for Meaning* (Harrisburg, PA: Trinity Press International, 1998), 86.

17. Dunn, *Jesus Remembered*, 605.

18. Borg, *Meeting Jesus Again for the First Time*, 142; Dunn, *Jesus Remembered*, 599; Crossan, *The Historical Jesus*, 261–54; *Jesus*, 72–75.

19. Diarmuid O'Murchu, *Christianity's Dangerous Memory: A Rediscovery of the Revolutionary Jesus* (New York: The Crossroad Publishing Company, 2011), 99.

20. Angel F. Méndez Montoya, *The Theology of Food: Eating and the Eucharist* (West Sussex, UK: Wiley-Blackwell, 2009).

21. Leonardo Boff, *Virtues: For Another Possible World* (Eugene, OR: Cascade Book, 2011), 230–31.

22. Elisabeth Schüssler-Fiorenza, *In Memory of Her: Feminist Reconstructions of Christian Origins* (New York: Crossroad Publishing Company, 1995), 345.

23. For example: Letty M. Russell, *Just Hospitality: God's Welcome in a World of Difference*, ed. J. Shannon Clarkson and Kate M. Ott (Louisville, KY: Westminster John Knox Press, 2009); Christine D. Pohl, *Making Room: Recovering Hospitality as a Christian Tradition* (Grand Rapids, MI: Wm. B. Eerdmans Publishing Company, 1999); Elizabeth Newman, *Untamed Hospitality: Welcoming God and Other Strangers* (Grand Rapids, MI: Brazos Press, 2007); Lucien Richard, *Living the Hospitality of God* (New York: Paulist Press, 2000).

24. Marcella Althaus-Reid and Lisa Isherwood, "Introduction," in *The Sexual Theologian: Essays on Sex, God, and Politics* (New York: T & T Clark International, 2004), 8.

25. Marcella Althaus-Reid, *Indecent Theology: Theological Perversions in Sex, Gender, and Politics* (New York: Routledge, 2001), 119–20.

26. See Robert Goss, *Queering Christ: Beyond Jesus Acted Up* (Cleveland: The Pilgrim Press, 2002), 170–84; Robert E. Shore-Goss, "Dis/Grace-full Incarnation and Dis/Grace-full Church: Marcella Althaus-Reid's Vision of Radical Inclusivity," in *Dancing Theology in Fetish Boots*, ed. Lisa Isherwood and Mark D. Jordan (London: SCM Press, 2010), 1–16.

27. Thomas Bohache, *Christology from the Margins* (London: SCM Press, 2008), 241–42. See pages 240–58 for a complete explanation of his Christology.

28. Robert E. Goss, *Jesus Acted Up: A Gay and Lesbian Manifesto* (New York: HarperSanFrancisco, 1993), 84.

29. Goss, *Queering Christ*, 170–82.

30. Gerard Loughlin, "Introduction," in *Queer Theology: Rethinking the Western Body*, ed. Gerard Loughlin (Malden, MA: Wiley-Blackwell, 2007), 12.

31. Robert E. Goss, "Ephesians," in *The Queer Bible Commentary*, ed. Deryn Guest, Robert Goss, Mona West, and Thomas Bohache (London: SCM Press, 2006), 636–37; Elizabeth Stuart, "Camping Around the Canon," in *Take Back the Word: A Queer Reading of the Bible*, ed. Robert E. Goss and Mona West (Cleveland: The Pilgrim Press, 2000), 31–32; Virginia Mollenkott, *Omnigendered: A Trans Religion Approach* (Cleveland: The Pilgrim Press, 2001), 110.

32. Patrick Cheng builds on the Christologies of Shore-Goss, Thomas Bohache, Marcella Althaus-Reid, Eleanor McLaughlin, Justin Tanis, and others. Patrick S. Cheng, *Radical Love: An Introduction to Queer Theology* (New York: Seabury Books, 2011), 78–83.

33. Cheng, *Radical Love*, 11.

34. Ibid., 85. See also Patrick S. Cheng, *From Sin to Amazing Grace: Discovering the Queer Christ* (New York: Seabury Books, 2012). Here Cheng expands his notion of the Queer Christ as radical embodiment of love, erasing theological boundaries between sin and grace. His Queer Christ is quite malleable and models a number of hybrid multiplicities.

35. Mark D. Jordan, "Theater of Bodies," an unpublished paper for a Conference at Boston University School of Theology on Queering the Church, April 2007.

36. Ibid.

37. Ibid.

38. Graham Ward, "On the Politics of Embodiment and the Mystery of All Flesh," in *The Sexual Theologian*, ed. Marcella Althaus-Reid and Lisa Isherwood (New York: T & T Clark International, 2005), 70–85.

39. Grace Jantzen, "Contours of a Queer Theology," *Literature and Theology* 13, no. 3 (2001): 276–77.

40. Susannah Cornwall, *Controversies in Queer Theology* (London: SCM Press, 2011), 191–223.

41. MCC in the Valley, www.mccinthevalley.com/; Soul Force, http://www.soulforce.org/. See also 108 Productions, http://www.108productions.org/.

42. Thomas Bohache, *Christologies from the Margins* (London: SCM Press, 2008), 178–83.

43. See, for example, The Human Rights Campaign, Religion and Faith, especially, its Out in Scripture program and its Scholarship and Mentoring Program, http://www.hrc.org/issues/religion-faith.

44. Siobhan Garrigan, "Queer Worship," *Theology and Sexuality* 15, no. 2 (2009): 215–23.

45. Garrigan appropriates the notion of covering from Kenji Yoshino (*Covering: The Hidden Assault Our Civil Rights* [New York: Random House, 2007], 23); "Queer Worship," 219–20.

46. Garrigan, "Queer Worship," 225–26. See also Gordon Lathrop, "Ordo and Coyote: Further Reflections on Order, Disorder, and Meaning in Christian Worship," *Worship* 80, no. 3 (2006): 194–212.

47. Robert E. Goss and Mona West, eds., *Take Back the Word: Queer Reading of the Bible* (Cleveland: The Pilgrim Press, 2000); Deryn Guest, Thomas Bohache, Robert E. Goss and Mona West, eds., *The Queer Bible Commentary* (London: SCM Press, 2006).

48. For example: Goss, *Queering Christ*; Justin Edward Tanis, *Trans-Gendered: Theology, Ministry, and Communities of Faith* (Cleveland: The Pilgrim Press, 2003); Bohache, *Christology from the Margins*; Cheng, *Radical Love*; *From Sin to Amazing Grace*.

49. Rollan McCleary, *A Special Illumination: Authority, Inspiration, and Heresy in Gay Spirituality* (London: Equinox, 2004), 105; also 340–45. McCleary uses the paradigm of "heresy," a heresy of erotic desire.

50. Some MCC churches are indistinguishably vanilla as many Protestant churches, but there are other MCCs open to the cross sections of queer diversities experienced in Pride parades and celebrations each year. A board member at MCC in the Valley joked with me that the rentals at the church should be called "kink week" because on Wednesday the Avatar (gay BDSM leather group) meeting was focused on "puppy play," Thursday hosted a leather poly-sexual bondage instruction class, Friday CMEN (California Men Enjoying Naturism) holding its monthly massage event, and Saturday having Avatar's educational practicum on safety and BDSM activities. How many churches would welcome such queer groups?

51. Cornwall, *Controversies in Queer Theology*, 244.

52. It is understandable that a number of academics in Queer Studies are hostile to religion because of the homophobic or misogynistic violence of these religious communities to LGBTQI folks. The challenge to queer theologies and communities of faith is to overcome the religious phobias of folks abused by traditional homophobic religion. This is strongly reiterated in the works of Thomas Bohache and Susannah Cornwall. See Bohache, *Christology from the Margins*, 178–86; Cornwall, *Controversies in Queer Theology*, 210–21.

53. Donald Bosivert and Jay Johnson, *Queer Religion*, vols. I and II (Santa Barbara, CA: Praeger, 2011).

54. See Robert E. Shore-Goss, "'*So Get Your High Heels on for Liberation, and Walk!*': Some Reflections in Memory of Marcella Althaus-Reid," *Theology & Sexuality* 15, no. 2 (2009): 139–45; "Nomadic Theologian: A Radical Vision of Inclusion," in *Dancing Theology in Fetish Boots: Essays in Honour of Marcella Althaus-Reid*, ed. Lisa Isherwood and Mark D. Jordan (London: SCM Press, 2010), 1–16.

55. Bohache, *Christ from the Margins*, 178–86. See the essay on "Communion: Playing with Redemption" in this volume where the cast suffered from Christophobia and overcame it through their identification of the story of love in the play. It seems to validate Bohache's model of a relational Christ with homophobic construction which can provide healing to LGBTQI people suffering from Christophobia.

56. Troy D. Perry, *The Lord is My Shepherd and He Knows I'm Gay* (25th anniversary ed.) (Los Angeles: Metropolitan Community Church, 1972), 135.

57. Ibid., 139, 247.

58. Cornwall, *Controversies in Queer Theology*, 255.

At the Open Table Café

Douglas Smith

Welcome to the Open Table,
Empty Chair,
All You Care to Eat Café

Reservations are not required,
although they are accepted,
joyful for each guest
they always have room for one more
At the Open Table Empty Chair,
All You Care to Eat Café

Crisp white walls wrap
Their arms around red booths
Silver swivel counter stools

In front of each chair
Is an empty placecard.
This invitation is an open one.
No one is turned away.

Some people gather as a family
Arriving lively and festive

Others come and go by themselves
At times the mood is somber and deeply personal

All are welcomed by J.C.
She has yet to meet a stranger
It's amazing the people she knows
She shares a soul solace
That nourishes

She's lived a lot of life
In her thirty odd years
More than hostess
She nutures needs
Warmhearted waitress
She tends deeper hungers

I've heard her say,
"Honey, listen to me.
If there's one thing I know
It's people and here's what's doing. . ."

Occasionally an ornery spirit
Will compel JC
Into giggle fits and joy spasms

All Prodigal Adams and Prodigal Eves
Eventually find their way home
to the Open Table,
Empty Chair,
All You Care to Eat
All are Welcome Café.

The menu is amazing!
They offer Forgiveness Fries,
Ritual Rice
Penitence Pot Pie
Praise Pancakes
Peace pasta
Hope Hash
Love Lasagna
Joyful Jam on Blessing Bread
Grace Grape Joy Juice

They even offer
Existential Eggs and Buddhist Bacon.

I've heard JC say
It's a wide range of all inclusive eats
Served to satisfaction

It's a feast for body and spirit
At the Open Table,

Empty Chair,
All You Care to Eat
All are Welcome Café

A philosophical Latino bus boy
Named Jesus
Quenches thirsts
He calls it
"Soul Water"
Living water is Earth's bounty
He parses out wisdom
While minding, managing and ministering
To basic needs

At the Open Table,
Empty Chair,
All You Care to Eat
All are Welcome Café

Affinity and laughter
lighten the soul
Familial feelings
of love and joy
bind all in this feast

Blessings are said.
Songs are sung
Praises raised
Sorrows shared
Comfort Granted.
At the Open Table,
Empty Chair,
All You Care to Eat
All are Welcome Café

All Prodigal Adams and Prodigal Eves
Eventually find their way home
to the Open Table,
Empty Chair,
All You Care to Eat
All are Welcome Café.

When the bill is delivered
I have seen surprise

When in JC's handwriting
The invoice states
"paid in full"

At the Open Table,
Empty Chair,
All You Care to Eat
All are Welcome Café

Part I

RADICALLY INCLUSIVE MODELS OF GOD

Patrick S. Cheng

One of my earliest encounters with the radically inclusive God occurred over a decade ago at the Metropolitan Community Church (MCC) of New York. I was a guest at the annual MCC New York Lunar New Year communion service that celebrated queer people of Asian descent. The sanctuary was awash in red and gold, East and West. I was blown away by the integration of the Asian cultural symbols of my childhood with an unapologetically queer Christian liturgy.

For me, that Eucharistic celebration of the Lunar New Year at MCC New York was a *kairos* moment[1] in which the radically inclusive Trinitarian God—that is, the triune God of (1) sexuality, (2) race, and (3) spirituality—was made visible right before my eyes. For the first time in my life, my threefold (and heretofore fragmented) identities as a gay man, as an Asian American, and as a Christian all came together. I was whole, and I had come home.[2]

Each of the five chapters in Part I of *Queering Christianity* presents a different model and vision of the radically inclusive God that can be found in MCC congregations around the world. It is ironic that most young people today see Christianity as the antithesis of radical inclusion. One recent survey showed that some of the first words that come to mind for millennials about Christianity are "antigay," "judgmental," and "hypocritical."[3]

By contrast, MCC queer theologies today are recovering a lost tradition in Christianity that affirms the radically inclusive God, whether it is Origen's notion of *apokatastasis* or universal restoration (in which all of creation—even Satan!—will be restored to God at the end of time)[4] or the Eastern Orthodox doctrine of *theōsis* or divinization (in which our ultimate destiny is not judgment and punishment, but rather to become divine).[5]

In Chapter 1, the Rev. Dr. Robin Gorsline demonstrates that the queer-acting God—which he calls the "Queer-inity"—is always up to radical inclusion.[6] Gorsline, the Pastor of MCC Richmond, describes the ways in which the God of "*extravagant* generosity" is always surprising us with radical inclusion, whether it is extending Holy Unions to polyamorous relationships, or understanding the atoning significance of Jesus Christ's body in the context of masturbation.

Gorsline gives us many powerful images of a radically inclusive God. For example, he argues that the creative power of the First Person of the Triune God can be likened to a drag queen, who applies makeup and transforms "what may be a plain male figure into a voluptuous and over-the-top female-appearing performer." For Gorsline, the queer God is "always up to something new and daring."

In Chapter 2, the Rev. Dr. Patrick S. Cheng argues for a radically inclusive God that truly honors the experiences of queer people of color.[7] According to Cheng, if we accept the definition of incarnation as the Word becoming flesh,[8] then we must also take seriously the writings of LGBT theologians of color in which the Word becomes *racialized* flesh.

Cheng, a professor at the Episcopal Divinity School, argues that the hybrid nature of Jesus Christ—that is, a God-human who occupies a third space between divinity and humanity—can be used to deconstruct the false binary of sexuality and race. That is, like Jesus Christ, queer people of color also occupy a third space (here, between sexuality and race). The religious right often tries to exploit the tensions between LGBT people and people of color, and this strategy of race-baiting must be resisted in light of our belief in a radically inclusive God.[9]

In Chapter 3, the Rev. Dr. Robert E. Shore-Goss proposes a radically inclusive God who not only redeems humanity in the incarnation, but also redeems all of creation—including the Earth and all that is in it.[10] For Shore-Goss, the Senior Pastor of MCC in the Valley, we must "go green" in our understanding of grace. That is, instead of obsessing over the red blood of atonement, we must instead focus on the greening, or *viriditas* (as coined by the mystic Hildegard of Bingen), of God's grace.

For Shore-Goss and his congregation, "green incarnational inclusivity" is not simply a matter of theory, but also of praxis. MCC in the Valley has installed solar panels and reduced its carbon footprint significantly. For Shore-Goss, God's threefold acts of creation, incarnation, and transformation of creation are "united in one act of Trinitarian self-giving or self-communication." And it is precisely this green grace that Christians need to cultivate in order to have a healthy relationship with creation and our radically inclusive God.

In Chapter 4, Megan More articulates her understanding of a radically inclusive God through her Christological reflections on the transgender Christ.[11] More, a self-identified trans-woman and a clergy-in-care intern at MCC in the Valley, understands Jesus Christ to be "fully inclusive of all variations of sex and gender." Specifically, More traces the many ways in which the transgender Christ can be seen in his birth, ministry, death, and resurrection.

For example, More argues that Jesus Christ can be understood as being intersex. This is because if we take the doctrine of the virgin birth seriously, then Jesus would have had XX chromosomes (because there would not have been any sperm to contribute a Y chromosome) along with male genitals (as traditionally understood). Similarly, Jesus' ministry can be understood as living outside of the male paradigm and expanding the notion of what it meant to be male, or female, or both. For More, Jesus Christ is the "first androgyne" who is "totally inclusive of the transgender, transsexual, and intersexed in all forms."

In Chapter 5, the Rev. Dr. Robert E. Shore-Goss writes about how the radically inclusive God can be seen in the person of the Holy Spirit as a "mischief-maker."[12] Drawing upon notions of divine foolishness as well as the mythological archetypes of tricksters and clowns (as well as Lady Gaga's video "Judas"), Shore-Goss constructs an innovative pneumatology of wild grace that cannot be contained by any person or church institution.

Shore-Goss mentions how the Holy Spirit has served as bridge for moments of discernment throughout his life. That is, the Holy Spirit has connected the many in-between moments as a continuous flow of loving grace. Shore-Goss concludes this chapter by describing the power of laughter and the work of the Holy Spirit in the ministries of the Sisters of Perpetual Indulgence, which can include the use of sex toys during the blessing of a leather contest. Shore-Goss urges MCC lay leaders and clergypersons to follow the example of these "queer spiritual tricksters."

These five chapters provide a tantalizing glimpse into the many different models of the radically inclusive God that can be found in MCC congregations around the world. Although these reflections focus on the specific themes of disruption (Gorsline), race and ethnicity (Cheng), ecology (Shore-Goss), gender identity (More), and mischief-making (Shore-Goss), many other models come to mind (e.g., themes of interfaith dialogue, disability, class, and economic justice). It is my hope that these models will be developed in future works by these and other MCC queer theologians.

It seems fitting to close these brief words of introduction with an excerpt from the eighth chapter of Romans, which is one of my favorite biblical passages about the radically inclusive God: "For I am convinced that neither death, nor life, nor angels, nor rulers, nor things present, nor things to come, nor powers, nor height, nor depth, nor anything else in all creation, will be able to separate us from the love of God in Christ Jesus our Lord."[13] Indeed, nothing can separate queer folk from the love of the radically inclusive God.

NOTES

1. *Kairos* refers to a key moment or turning point in time, as opposed to *chronos*, which describes the passage of ordinary time.

2. Patrick S. Cheng, "A Three-Part Sinfonia: Queer Asian Reflections on the Trinity," *Journal of Race, Ethnicity, and Religion* 3, no. 2.9 (2012): 1–23.

3. Robert P. Jones, "Why Are Millennials Leaving the Church?," *Huffington Post,* May 8, 2012, http://huff.to/JdNTVj (accessed March 15, 2013).

4. Patrick S. Cheng, *Radical Love: An Introduction to Queer Theology* (New York: Seabury Books, 2011), 135–36.

5. Patrick S. Cheng, *From Sin to Amazing Grace: Discovering the Queer Christ* (New York: Seabury Books, 2012), 56–57.

6. Robin H. Gorsline, "Faithful to a Very Queer-Acting God, Who Is Always Up to Something New."

7. Patrick S. Cheng, "*Cur Deus Homo[sexual]*: The Queer Incarnation." For Cheng's most recent work on the intersections of race, sexuality, and spirituality, see Patrick S. Cheng, *Rainbow Theology: Bridging Race, Sexuality, and Spirit* (New York: Seabury Books, 2013).

8. Jn 1:17.

9. John Becker, "Secret NOM Documents Reveal Race-Baiting Strategies," *Huffington Post,* March 27, 2012, http://huff.to/HbkIUL (accessed March 15, 2013).

10. Robert E. Shore-Goss, "Grace Is Green: Green Incarnational Inclusivities."

11. Megan More, "The Transgendered Christ."

12. Robert E. Shore-Goss, "The Holy Spirit as Mischief-Maker."

13. Rom 8:38–39.

1

Faithful to a Very Queer-Acting God, Who Is Always Up to Something New

Robin H. Gorsline

I remember the first time someone said to me, "God is gay." I quickly agreed, believing then, as I do now, that God incorporates all sexualities and genders. It did not seem like a big deal to me, although I know it did for others.

But even more I remember the first time it dawned on me that God might be queer—or if we don't want to name God that way, at least that God acts queer. That was, and I believe is, a big deal.

The moment involved my teaching a class at MCC Richmond using the United Methodist curriculum, *Disciple*, a comprehensive, biblical, and relatively traditional, resource. I do not recall how the subject came up, but I do remember that the group became very engaged in discussing marriage. I mentioned the struggle MCC General Conferences has had over the years in debating whether to remove the requirement from our movement bylaws that Holy Unions are only to be granted to two people.

Several participants expressed their unease with the idea, while several others indicated their agreement. I observed that I had known several triads who seemed to navigate life together relatively well. At that, another participant—a very committed member and leader—broke through all the quiet, tentative talk with a ringing declaration, "If you, Pastor Robin, or MCC, ever bless one of those '*unions*' [appropriate facial expressions and gestures indicating a judgment that not only do they not constitute *holy* unions, but also they are not unions at all] I am out of here! No questions, no discussion, no looking back!"

In that moment, I thought to myself, "We serve a God who is always messing with our all-too-human arrangements, our desire for things to be neat and tidy and easy." I had no doubt that God was enjoying Godself right then, watching the group wrestle with the conflict between social convention and church tradition on the one hand, and the realization that Jesus teaches again and again that there might be more to life than what we inherit from human sources, on the other. I especially knew God was enjoying watching this pastor wriggle my way through the moment.

Since then, I have noticed other occasions where I see the divine pushing, or pulling, or cajoling, or leading, or nudging—and other verbs that reflect God sharing God's desire for us, and God seeking change in and for us—in directions and into places we would never think to go on our own. I have come to understand God is not only a comforter and healer, but also a disruptive, unsettling presence in my life—and in the lives of others.

A note about God as used in this chapter: I am a Trinitarian, in that I accept the ancient church formulation of one God in Three Persons. Often, the word God is used when what is meant is the first person of the Trinity, what we, in the congregation I serve, call Creator or Mother or Father God. However, here God is all three, although as I explain below, there actually may be more than three (see later discussion of Queer-inity).

God often acts queerly, then, if queer means to act unconventionally or oddly, irregularly in response to the normal. Indeed, God often queers things, if we understand that use of the word as a verb meaning to interfere with and spoil the expected by acting outside normative social boundaries and rules.

What, then, does God's queerness, or God's queer behavior, mean for us, concretely? And how does the church, and specifically Metropolitan Community Churches (MCC), accommodate this queerness in our theologies and practices?

Marcella Althaus-Reid names the starting point of Queer Theology as "Queer lives and Queer relationships."[1] This is an appropriate starting point for theologizing that is liberative in character and intent. We must begin with the lives of the people whose theology we propose to articulate. Gone are the days, at least for many, when a *magisterium* in some far-off place can tell us who God is, especially when the intent of such authority is to deny relationship with a living God to those whom they appear to despise.

Queer relationships help us create the warp and woof of our lives. Queerness requires relationality. It certainly is possible to be queer, in some ways at least, by yourself, but the overall project of living queerly seems to require relating to others, sometimes in ways that are supportive and at other times in ways that are oppositional.

Queer theory, queer organizing, and queer sensibility grew up in the 1990s in response to several aspects of the various LGBT movements (and to the failure of society to respond adequately to the spread of HIV/AIDS), but two aspects are especially relevant to our present purposes. First, queer is a label that encompasses the whole little-organized, disparate gaggle of peoples of various sexual minorities often inadequately referred to as "lesbian and gay." Second, queer is an oppositional stance and way of life in relation to the normalizing tendencies of those who seek to integrate all the parts of that gaggle—but especially gay men and lesbian women—into existing social structures. It also is a reclaiming of a term that had been used to shame many, and thus it is a deliberate provocation intended to create radical rethinking and action.

As a unifying term, queer has not caught on among many. But as a self-description for many who challenge various orthodoxies—among lesbian and gay people as well as others—it is increasingly accepted. It is in this sense that queer is an especially apt theological term, if we accept the reality that God is continually engaged in disrupting the status quo.

Of course, no relationship is more troubled for many queer folk than their relationship with God. Nonqueer folks have spent, and continue to spend, considerable energy trying to break us up. For many, the relationship was broken—is broken—in church.

MCC's founder, Rev. Troy Perry, tells a typical story from his pre-MCC days. While dancing at a popular gay dance bar south of Los Angeles in 1968, his Latino friend Tony was arrested for "lewd and lascivious conduct," a catchall phrase used to harass gay men and lesbians.

When Tony was freed, he told Troy he was going back into the closet. "We're just a bunch of dirty queers and nobody cares about dirty queers!"

Troy replied, "Somebody cares."

"Who?"

Troy said, "God cares."

"No, Troy," he said, "God doesn't care. What do you mean, 'God cares.' Be serious. I went to my priest for guidance when I was fifteen and he wouldn't even let me come back to Sunday School. I guess he thought I might contaminate somebody! He said I couldn't be a homosexual and a Christian, so that was the end of church. And for me, in my religion, that meant the end of God!"[2]

Tony's Roman Catholicism equated church with God, so the church's condemnation felt like God speaking. Fortunately, Troy Perry, like others, knew one could have a relationship with God without the church.

However, even non-Catholics often experience the church's condemnation as God's judgment. Many can dismiss these statements as the ravings of people who were taught that same-gender sex and love are wrong and can't get over it. But others—certainly transgender people, bisexual people, and even others whose sexual and gender lives are more mainstream—are judged, harassed, and abused, often concluding that God does not love them, or is irrelevant to their lives.

However, despite the effort of many to merge church and God, the issue is not the church per se but rather the God with whom we seek relationship (and who seeks relationship with us).

On occasion, even MCC and other friendly folk have contributed to the denial of a full relationship among queer folk and God. MCC congregations generally consist of people from a wide range of spiritual traditions, and it is not hard to discover significant theological differences within each congregation. Some of these differences can create sharp divisions and even occasion judgmental statements about the (un)godliness of others.

Also, as MCC has tried to gain a greater toehold in mainstream religious life, some have muted parts of our queer heritage. Nancy Wilson reminds us that for much of the life of MCC, many of us have been engaged in efforts to "normalize gay sexuality for the general public," bogged down "by the necessity to do biblical or theological *apologetics*." "But what," she continues, "if we actually claimed a role in *reshaping the basic questions* concerning God and human sexuality?"[3]

Indeed. What are the contours of relationship with a God for all the folks whom church has told God condemns or does not accept them? Who is this God? Who is God for queers?

Aquinas maintained that we can only know God by what God is not. This is helpful in so far as it allows us to let God be a moveable identity, or as Gerard Loughlin says, so that God can be fundamentally "an identity without an existence."[4]

Queerness bears some relationship to that sort of fluidity that makes it possible for the term to be more than a catchall for the cumbersome constellation of LGBTQQI (and whatever new parts that are brewing somewhere). This fluidity makes room for the term to be used by all, so that no one can own it. This is good, and this is also true of God. No one owns God either.

This fluidity also makes it possible for queer to be a term that is about more than sex. But at the same time, queer, like God, cannot, and does not wish to, avoid sex (see below).

God's gender also belongs in this discussion, because queer folks, and certainly MCC people, know that God is not confined to one-gender identity.

The tradition claims that God the Creator is Father, or maybe Abba or Daddy, but that is not the limit of God's genderedness. In queer theologizing, the Creator is not only male and female but also both simultaneously transgendered and transgendering. The Holy Spirit has a history of some gender fluidity, with some writers associating it with Wisdom, often seen as a feminine character, or postulating that the Spirit's activity of comforting is a particularly feminine trait. Even the Christ, who is embodied in the male-identified body of Jesus, may be seen as more than traditionally male, especially among queer folk who understand and celebrate maleness as a wide and expandable category.

In reality, God transcends gender because God is all genders. This is a concept that is well suited to queer sensibilities, which are very open to categories being permeable, interchangeable, and fluid.

At the same time, Aquinas' postulate limits our ability to see God by God's effects, causes us to fail to see God's activity or performativity. As Loughlin says, we are left with saying only that *God is*, which is not a bad thing, but hardly adequate to sustain such an important relationship. Even so, the scholastic view helps us understand that God is not a thing. God is not an object.

Queer folks have learned that God is not a thing that anyone can take away from anyone else. We learn this because others keep trying to take God away from us. But some of us have learned a secret: When some people thought they had the inside track with God so they could deny God to us, God was still present in our lives.

Sometimes, even people in MCC try to tell others who God is and why God thinks they are wrong, but still God is present to all. Indeed, what we realize is that God is present in ways that would be very surprising and unsettling to those who think they have God all figured out. Carter Heyward has told us that "God is our relational power."[5] We find God in our relationships, all sorts of relationships.

Troy Perry knows this. His Pentecostal roots told him "it was possible to meet God anywhere."[6] Some of us met God in the bar—when we needed to be cared about by friends or when we met someone special who reminded us that we are loveable. More than one gay person found a would-be or former priest in a bar, who helped them reconnect or stay connected with God. God and God's representatives hang out in bars.

That is why MCC pastors invite drag queens to participate in worship, especially at times of celebration. They often were those over-the-top personalities that in troubled, former times held the community together, who gave us a sense of togetherness as they performed at bars, the very places that in the absence of church became our temples. The performer was not God of course, but stood in for the holy—showing that it was possible to transcend the limits of the world.

The growth of MCC testifies to the presence of God. If God does not love queer people, then why are there so many MCC congregations, and why are other Christian and Jewish groups more and more opening their doors to us?

At the same time, it is vital that we not fall into the trap of believing that things are getting better on their own, or because of the passage of time. There is one more thing God is not: God is not the agent of steady or even inevitable progress toward some future nirvana.

Still, God continuously calls us into relation, and, as Heyward says, out of that relation power emerges. God's actions, or performances, of relating create models for us, and to the extent we act relationally with God we receive power to create more relationality with others.

Much classical theological exploration seems to box God in. Definitions of who God is so often appear to try to explain God to fit into the writer's system, when what we know of God seems to indicate that God is not willing to be limited by anyone. David tried to put the YHWH God in a palace long ago, and YHWH God declined the offer, preferring to be free to wander and live in a tent.[7]

That God, the God who desires to remain free and moving, is a model for a God with whom queer folk can relate. Queers don't stay in closets anywhere, and we certainly don't want God to do so either. Increasingly, we move freely, having been released by God from our captivity so our whole, true selves can be in relation with God and each other.

Much classical exploration of the Trinity sees the Three in One as a self-contained or internal community of relationship—God seemingly relating only to Godself. When, as a child, I was first taught about the Trinity, I was told to think of it like a triple candelabra—the tall candle in the center representing God the Father, the shorter two on either sides representing the Son and Holy Spirit, respectively. There was in this view a great balance, something treasured by parts of the Greek philosophical worldview, which influenced those who developed Trinitarian doctrine, as well as my Episcopal priest and others.

But over the years, I found that image inadequate. There is no movement, no energy; just respectable, well-proportioned, stationary classical beauty.

Elizabeth Stuart offers a view of an active God—as a naturally unbalanced, triadic relationship that spills out of the church container in a lively dance. God wants all of us to join the dance, moving from one to another, being passionate and promiscuous in friendship and relationship (although that means not a lack of commitment, but rather a wide-ranging commitment to all in relationship).[8]

I have begun to think of this unbalanced, triadic divinity as a Queer-inity, meaning that at any time one or more of the three chooses to be disruptive and even playfully, lovingly disrespectful to the usual order of things. Robert E. Shore-Goss, in "The Holy Spirit as Mischief-Maker" in this book, offers a fuller exploration of this playfulness as it is enacted in and by the Holy Spirit. But such playfulness is not limited to the third person of the Holy Queer-inity. Indeed, given the infinite variations of which God is possible, the Queer-inity can enact more than three identities at the same time. The reason for this multiplicity is the divine desire for intimate, infinite, and ultimate relationality.

Indeed, the gospel accounts of Jesus show us someone given to showing up unexpectedly, being unafraid to disrespect custom, and speaking uncomfortable truths out of turn. He did not do this to create discomfort for the humans around him, but because to do otherwise would deny his relationship with the one he called "Abba," and thus deny the truth that all life is divine in origin, orientation, and creativity. This truth, and Jesus' evocation of it in his life and teaching, is the ground on which a queer and incarnational faith stands.

As Lisa Isherwood and Marcella Althaus-Reid write:

> God dwells in flesh and when this happens all our myopic earth-bound ideas are subject to change; the dynamic life-force which is the divine erupts in diversity and the energy of it will not be inhibited by laws and statutes. Far from creating the same yesterday, today and tomorrow, this dynamism is always propelling us forward into new curiosities and challenges. It does not shut us off from the world; it is the world drawing us into more of ourselves as we spiral in the human/divine dance.[9]

What Jesus performs is the unceasing divine desire for relationship with humanity, which is part of the divine desire for relationship with all parts of the divine, a desire that keeps energy unstable and moving all the time. The desire for relationship is so strong among the Queer-inity, and with all others as well, that they ceaselessly move and shift to connect, sort of like a version of the game, Twister—but unlike the conventional version, no one is ever removed from the game, and falling down is an excuse for new contact. It is a highly charged, endlessly active connecting and reconnecting and disconnecting one part in order to connect all others. The goal of the Queer-inity is total connectivity of the entire universe.

Patrick Cheng describes God as "the sending forth of radical love." Cheng says that "God reveals Godself to us because God loves us and wants to share Godself with us."[10] Cheng, along with Stuart and Heyward and others, visualizes God as preeminently relational, seeking us out in every possible way—not to tell us how we have failed, and to scare us into doing better at obeying the rules, but rather to share love and hope and joy and peace with us, that we may succeed beyond our wildest dreams in becoming all God creates us to be.

Over the past few years of serving a congregation as pastor, I have come to see this relentless relating as central to my experiencing God, and seeking to help others experience God. It is a central thread of Scripture as well, as Rabbi Heschel said long ago, "The Bible speaks not only of [the hu]man's search for God, but also God's search for [the hu]man."[11] This relentless relating is why it is so difficult for theologians and preachers to capture God in a particular definition or even a set of concepts. God is endlessly recreating Godself in order to connect. This requires God to take on every possible identity, to wear every possible costume, to become every possible gender and all genders, and colors and sexualities, and much more. God is beyond any one or more identities because God is all of them, and most important, God performs all of them.

Indeed, as Cheng says, God's attributes are not fixed, or natural or essential, but "are actually a matter of performativity."[12] This takes us back to wrestle with Aquinas and Loughlin, seeing God fundamentally as an identity without existence.

It is not God's is-ness that matters so much as God's effects or performance. It is how God lives, not who God is, that is central to being in relation with God.

For queer folk, God relates in very embodied ways. God is not a theological construct but an active body, or more properly all sorts of bodies in life-giving, celebratory, and caring relationship with each other and us. Such relation includes sex and sensuality in all its forms. Heyward speaks of God's "fluid sense of gender" that is manifested in erotic friendship among all creatures.[13] She has written much about eroticism and God, connecting desire and divinity as totally intertwined and active together.

Indeed, Christianity has a unique perspective on God's embodied relating through the incarnation of God in Christ. Alone among the three

Abrahamic religions, Christianity insists that God is embodied in the person of Jesus the Risen Christ. At least, that is the theory.

And yet, so much Christian theology and practice has actively denied the actual body of Jesus. We acknowledge that Jesus had a body, a real, human body, a male body, but really only from the waist up. Mark Jordan describes a crucifix hanging in his mother's home which, when the flimsy parchment loincloth fell away, revealed flat, smooth flesh—like an old-fashioned mannequin—in the lower abdomen.[14] The figure had realistic blood running down clearly defined muscles, the face was appropriately anguished, but the genitals were missing.

Queerness rejects such unnecessary sanitizing, especially when general Christian practice so clearly requires that Jesus be male. The ancient doctrinal arguments against ordaining women rely on Jesus (and all the disciples) having a penis, while pretending that Jesus' organ never existed. Queers not only reject such erasure, but also choose to celebrate human genitals as essential parts of human bodies.

In this, queer theologizing is very Pauline (even if Paul failed to include mention of all body parts in 1 Cor. 12). No more, but no less, than the mouth, the nose, the ears, the eyes, the limbs, the fingers, the toes, should the genitals (and even the anus) be considered worthy.

But a queer view requires more than a complete checklist of Jesus' body parts. For Jesus to be real, to be fully relational, there has to be at least the possibility, and better the reality, that Jesus had sexual feelings and dealt with them in ways that affirmed his wholeness. His choices are his own—celibate as so much of the tradition assumes; or married as others, following William Phipps maintain; or single and sexually active, either straight or gay (what about Martha, Mary, and Lazarus?).[15]

If he were an enfleshed mannequin who had no possibility of a sexual life, then his incarnation is incomplete; indeed it feels fake. If Jesus did not experience the sexual feelings we have and had to face the sexual temptations we face, he becomes less of a messiah than we need. He also is less of a messiah than we have been told he was, and is.

Yet, claiming full embodiment—and sexuality—for Jesus takes us into stormy waters. For one thing, it makes him more human. Tradition claims he was fully human and fully divine, but the former has always been subordinated to the latter. Most believers do not want to think much about Jesus' humanity, and certainly not much about his body, until he is staggering under the weight of the cross while carrying it to Golgotha and then hanging from it.

I preached a sermon series, "The Real S Word, Or Sex in the Church," in which I mentioned various "unmentionables" from Jesus' body, and I even referred to bodily functions in which he engaged. This occasioned considerable feedback, some positive, probably more negative. Here is part of one of those sermons that celebrates the embodiment of Jesus:

> But he was fully human—we have too much testimony about his life to deny that—and therefore, he had a body. First, he had a Jewish body—so it is highly unlikely that he looked like some young blonde thing from West Hollywood. He had an adult body. He had hair not only on his head, but elsewhere. He had orifices in addition to his mouth. He had male nipples. He had genitals. He peed and he pooped.
>
> He also most likely had sex. And enjoyed it. Jesus loved life, and lived it to the fullest. He wants that for us, too.
>
> The ancient authorities do not indicate he was married. If he was, I have a sense he was faithful to her. Or him.
>
> But if he was not married ... well, as he challenged the crowd to find a blameless one to throw the first stone, could he have been writing his own confession in that dirt? Was part of Jesus' willingness to challenge that crowd of self-righteous men his awareness of his own sinfulness?
>
> I love Jesus. I always have. I always will.
>
> And I love him most for how real he was, and how real he remains today, when I let the real him, the whole of him, in all parts of my life.[16]

Jesus was a sexual being. A queer view also allows for us to have sexual feelings for Jesus. Of course, this is nothing new. Mystics like Teresa of Avila were clear about their own passion for him. As I have read some accounts of mystical sexual encounters, it occurs to me that Jesus may be the object of attention, but that most likely the whole of God is engaged in the pleasure and joy. Other parts of the Queer-inity are less gender determinant, so it seems likely there is a sexual fluidity that allows for an infinite range of activities and encounters among them, and potentially with us. Thus, a queer view also allows for Jesus, and the others, to have sexual feelings for us.

It is one thing to read about an ancient mystic writhing ecstatically (in her spirit at least) in contemplation of Jesus, and another to realize that people today may experience Jesus as a sexual being, who has desires for us, too. In that same sermon series, I mentioned a time I masturbated to a representation of Jesus. It was an intensely spiritual moment in 1983 when—after divorce, being separated from my children on a daily basis, and developing a serious illness—I began to feel some recovery in my body and soul. The encounter was unplanned, a spiritual and sexual eruption that was never repeated. Jesus brought me back from an emerging depression that day—Jesus saved me by his body, not the one on the cross, not by his death, but by joining me in a mutual celebration of our sexualized bodies.

Many who heard the sermon were very angry. A few left the church. I understand their distress. I am not sure how I would have felt if I had been sitting in the pew. Others felt liberated and shared with me stories and truths about their lives they had shared with few, if any, others. I was not surprised by the anger, but I was surprised by the number of people who indicated my risk-taking—several called it "truth-telling"—had caused them to trust me enough to share deeply buried secrets and shame.

The truth for me is that I felt profoundly pushed by God to say these things, even though I knew they would upset parts of the community. I cannot be sure I heard God right—no preacher can ever make such a claim without also leaving room for doubt—but it felt as if God were begging me to tell this part of the divine story. In some ways, it felt like God was asking me to help God come out, not as gay or straight, but simply as a sexual being through Jesus.

What seems clear to me, as I have thought about the encounter over the years, is that God uses sex and sexuality just as God uses everything else in life to get through to us. In some important ways, sexuality is the model by which God shows how to live lives that are extravagantly, divinely full of joy and unconditional love. Thus, God's—the Queer-inity's—performativity includes sex, ours and God's. God seeks us relentlessly: God is constantly looking for us, wanting to hook up for a night, or a day, and, truly, for a lifetime.

This relentless relating also means that among the most important characteristics of God is generosity—as important as love because without God's generosity we would not know God's love. God lives generously. God simply performs repeated generosity in God's self-giving in order to connect.

More recently, using the word generous to describe God began to feel incomplete. Thanks to Robert Schnase, I am experiencing God's *extravagant* generosity.[17] Indeed, extravagant may be a good way of describing how God performs God-ness.

God is love, as scripture says, and God is grace as Paul and others have written. And surely God shares peace and justice, and God is generous with all. But I think the best word to describe how God lives is "extravagant."

God is extravagant in all things—God does not *god* stingily. God lives extravagantly, God performs extravagance. There is nothing half-way about God.

Experiencing God's continual performances of extravagance in my life and in the lives of others has freed me to visualize new portraits of God, what I think of as queering images of God. The freedom to have many images of God, and to insist on the preeminence of none, is a queer way to relate to God.

Many have read *The Shack*, and encountered God as a black woman who prepares big platters of food for Herself, Jesus, and the Holy Spirit—and always has ample leftovers.[18] This portrait reminds me of the feeding of the five thousand. God makes more food than we need, just for the sheer joy of doing it, of knowing that, if we want, we can be fed beyond our wildest dreams. That is extravagance, that is God *godding*.

I have another image of how God lives: as a drag queen—an aging and yet ageless, and over-the-top and fierce and yet ever-so sweet, drag queen—all dressed up in whatever finery God thinks will get us to pay attention, but who, instead of accepting dollar bills from admirers, just keeps throwing them at us, not stuffing them in her bosom but instead thrusting them into peoples' pockets and hands. That is divine extravagance, God *godding* over the top.

And God, perhaps in Jesus mode, enacts the bartender who listens endlessly to the tales of desire and woe and joy—the one who helps the shy ones reach out and comforts the bold ones when they strike out. This is Jesus, or Holy Parent and/or Holy Spirit as Confessor, Absolver, and Encourager, listening well beyond last call and night after night.

Various traditions, especially Celtic ones, have accorded Jesus the title "Lord of the Dance." I have a special fondness for the Abba song, "Dancing Queen," through which I always feel God calling me onto the dance floor to celebrate the love in my life—and the love of my life. I have no doubt that the Queer-inity dance, indeed that they dance a lot, everywhere they can, and in every way possible. When folks let go and just move together—not necessarily in step but in the spirit of joy and abandon of all that weighs them down—that is God, that is the Queer-inity having a good time.

Joyce Rupp draws upon the title Lord of the Dance to offer a short meditation in which she asks to be twirled around wildly or led in a slow glide, either way or in other ways, "heeding the gestures of [Y]our graced movement."[19] A queer view affirms the grace-filled Queer-inity, but would insist on the possibility that graced movement might range from the waltz to the rumba to salsa to wild leaping and gyrations.

And then there is another, seemingly opposite image of how God lives, this time as Mother Teresa. You may think that one really odd, because I doubt many of us think of Mother Teresa as extravagant—this small, bent-over, wizened up old woman, living so simply in and among the poorest of the poor.

And yet, she is the one who posted on the wall of her children's mission in Calcutta a version of these words entitled *Anyway Poem* (which are an adaptation of "The Paradoxical Commandments" by Kent M. Keith). They are an assertion of human agency in the face of every sort of obstacle, and begin, "People are often unreasonable, illogical and self centered; Forgive them anyway." The commandments continue through being kind, successful, honest, a builder, happy, as well as doing good and giving the world "the best you've got … anyway" because ultimately how we live is between us and God, and not between us and those who stand in our way of living full, rich lives.[20]

That is extravagance, a recipe for living extravagantly like God.

She also seems to have suffered a great dryness in her faith; in the last nearly half-century of her life she experienced a great contradiction in her life. "I long for God—I want to love Him—to love Him much—to live only for love of Him—to love only—and yet there is but pain—longing and no love."[21] Yet she did the work of God that touched millions. That is extravagance.

Mother Teresa was extravagantly faithful even when she doubted faith, which is how I imagine God is extravagant with us even when we doubt God. God gives us life even when we throw it away like so much litter on the side of the road. The extravagance with which God lives is why we are alive.

A queer understanding of a God always seeking relationship has some familiar elements for those who remember, or who currently live in, the reality of being on the prowl for someone to love. One might even say that God goes "cruising," seeking another soul with whom to be in relationship. The difference between us and God lies in the reality that every one of us is God's type.

This divine taste for all human types is a reminder of a key structure of queerness, namely that there is no one way, or one right way, or even two or three ways to *be* queer. Instead, there are many, probably an infinity of, ways to *do* queer.

It is consistent with Malcolm Edwards' claim that "Queer theology cannot be conceived as a set of answers. There is no queer understanding of God. Queer theology is a set of questions."[22]

Edwards is surely correct about the absence of one or more right ways to theologize queerly. However, I diverge from him about queer theology being a set of questions, or at least being limited to questions. It may be that, but it is more. Questions are useful in that they help us avoid dogmatism, but if theology is only questions it misses other possibilities.

One mark of queerness for many is imaginative visualization and in-your-face creativity. When I read the first chapters of Genesis and imagine God creating all the creeping things and the night sky and birds of the air I am reminded of watching a drag queen apply makeup and sequins and body enhancements—changing what may be a plain male figure into a voluptuous and over-the-top female-appearing performer.

That drag queen is not God, of course, but she is a cocreator with God of something new and fabulous. And the queer truth is that another drag queen would take the same male body and create a whole different over-the-top female-appearing person. A queer view of God understands that God does that, too, working with each of us as we are willing to be re-made again and again in God's image.

So much religion repeatedly tries to box God in—in fact, sometimes I wonder if that is the real agenda of some. By contrast, queers want to free God—of course God is free in God's reality, but not in ours—so that there are either no boxes or that the boxes multiply constantly and exponentially.

Edwards is right. There is no queer understanding of God, if by that we mean to fix on one idea. Instead, a queer view entertains them all, and like God, revels in the variety of divine creation.

This means that God, the Queer-inity of three-plus persons, is the ultimate queer—and yet, of course, there is no ultimate in a physical or classical philosophical sense, because the relationship that is God is ever-changing, never fixed, never static, or defined.

For those of us who savor the queerness of life—who see every day how inspired and inspiring the gift of unbalance in our own corners of the world is (not meaning the horror of war or poverty, but all the moments of true aliveness), let alone the entire creation—this is indeed good news.

For a long time, I have *known*—and I use that term to indicate how strongly I perceive this—that the Queer-inity did not send Jesus to die on a cross for our sins. Instead, they decided to send Jesus to lead us in the dance, the wonderfully unbalanced, promiscuous friendship with every-one, to teach the steps to us in person. That is why Jesus was completely embodied—if not, he could not truly teach us the dance routines.

However, as often happens among us humans, too many didn't know what to do with joy, and became unnerved by, and even jealous of and angry at, the fullness of the joy and the vision of a universe of complete harmony. So they arranged to end the dance. Or at least so they thought.

Of course, the dance does not end. The Queer-inity keep dancing and inviting us to join them. That is the surest sign of the divine performance of extravagance.

Queer theology, arising out of rejection and despair and HIV as well as embodied love and hope and joy, celebrates the endless dance, the perpetual amplification (and even multiplication) of over-the-top divine *personae*, and the never-ending desire for relationship.

This has enormous implications for MCC, as well as for the larger Body of Christ.

As MCC, we have the word "church" in our name, but if we understand our queer selves, we will remain open to our call to be so much more than a church. Many of us say, "We are a movement with a church." I take that to mean that we are not your typical church. You might even say we're a "queer" church, not because we are mostly (although certainly not entirely) LGBT people, but because we are not called to replicate church as an organization so much as we have been entrusted with a mission to be a freewheeling, open-ended, always-on-the-move collection of folks who want to change the world—in the name of Jesus the Risen Christ (and his friends).

It helps that we are a post-creedal church—meaning our history is not tying us down to a fixed set of beliefs. We do not have to overcome or reinterpret our founding doctrinal documents because we don't have any in the usual churchy sense—no Augsburg Confession, for example. In some ways, our founding documents only two: our bylaws, and our version of Luther's 95 Theses, Rev. Troy Perry's first book, *The Lord Is My Shepherd and He Knows I'm Gay*.[23] However, there is a difference between Perry and Luther; Luther told his story in terms of statements of belief, and Perry told his as a story. That difference makes all the difference in the world.

Because of it, we can travel light, and keep moving where God wants us to go. Of course, we may succumb to the ways of the world and actually grow up to become a church, a real church.

There is ample precedent in the biblical record for what happens when communities change from traveling light with God to gathering all sorts of baggage—think of the Israelites settling down and then deciding they need a king, or what happened to the Jesus Movement when folks started worrying too much about what the authorities thought, and certainly when the Emperor took charge.

But if we take our queer roots seriously, we will resist the siren call of respectability and normality. Instead, we will continually reinvent ourselves, putting on whatever drag fits the occasion and helps God keep the dance going.

I believe it is our call from God not to become a big powerful church, but rather to learn more and more how to be a movement that leads the whole of the church to a new sense of being faithful, not to rules, not to history, not to theological treatises—but faithful to a very queer-acting God who is always up to something new and daring.

NOTES

1. Marcella Althaus-Reid, *The Queer God* (New York: Routledge, 2003), 146.

2. Troy D. Perry, *Don't Be Afraid Anymore: The Story of Reverend Troy Perry and the Metropolitan Community Churches* (New York: St. Martin's, 1990), 33–34.

3. Nancy Wilson, *Our Tribe: Queer Folks, God, Jesus, and the Bible* (New York: HarperSanFrancisco, 1995), 231.

4. Gerard Loughlin, "Introduction," in *Queer Theology: Rethinking the Western Body*, ed. Gerald Loughlin (Malden, MA: Blackwell, 2007), 10.

5. Carter Heyward, *Touching Our Strength: The Erotic as Power and the Love of God* (New York: HarperSanFrancisco, 1989), 24.

6. Perry, *Don't Be Afraid Anymore*, 34.

7. Althaus-Reid connects this refusal of the divine to be boxed in to John 1:14, where the Word (or Verb, in her delicious formulation) "is said to have 'dwelt among us' as in *a tabernacle* (a tent) or 'put his tent amongst us,'" demonstrating the mobility of Christ. She connects this with contemporary understandings of bisexuality. See Marcella Althaus-Reid, *Indecent Theology: Theological Perversions in Sex, Gender, and Politics* (New York: Routledge, 2001), 119–20.

8. Elizabeth Stuart, *Just Good Friends: Towards a Lesbian and Gay Theology of Relationships* (London: Mowbray, 1995), 240–44.

9. Lisa Isherwood and Marcella Althaus-Reid, "Queering Theology," in *The Sexual Theologian: Essays on Sex, God, and Politics*, ed. Marcella Althaus-Reid and Lisa Isherwood (New York: T & T Clark, 2004), 7.

10. Patrick S. Cheng, *Radical Love: An Introduction to Queer Theology* (New York: Seabury, 2011), 45.

11. Abraham Joshua Heschel, *God in Search of Man: A Philosophy of Judaism* (New York: Farrar, Strauss and Giroux, 1955), 136.

12. Cheng, *Radical Love*, 54.

13. Heyward, *Touching Our Strength*, 103–14.

14. Mark D. Jordan, "God's Body," in Loughlin, *Queer Theology*, 283.

15. William Phipps, *Was Jesus Married?* (New York: Harper & Row, 1970). See also, by the same author, *The Sexuality of Jesus* (Cleveland: The Pilgrim Press, 1996).

16. http://www.mccrichmond.org/ministries/sermon.htm for audio recordings of the four messages in the series; this text is from the message given on July 31, 2011. The message with the reference to masturbation was given on August 7, 2011. The others are from July 10 and July 17, 2011.

17. Robert Schnase, *Five Practices of Fruitful Congregations* (Nashville: Abingdon Press, 2007). Extravagant generosity is the fifth practice Schnase promotes. The others are radical hospitality, passionate worship, intentional faith development, and risk-taking mission and service.

18. William Paul Young, *The Shack: Where Tragedy Confronts Eternity* (Los Angeles: Wind-blown Media, 2007).

19. Joyce Rupp, *Fragments of Your Ancient Name: 365 Glimpses of the Divine for Daily Meditation* (Notre Dame, IN: Sorin Books, 2011); see April 10.

20. See Kent M. Keith, *Do It Anyway: Finding Personal Meaning and Deep Happiness by Living the Paradoxical Commandments* (Novato, CA: New World Library, 2003). Keith describes his delight in learning that Mother Teresa had posted a version of his message on pages 190–91. The original 10 commandments, as Kent wrote them in 1968, with a check-list for using them, appear in his book, pages 170–71. Keith first wrote them, when he was 19, for a student government pamphlet for leaders, and they developed a life of their own for 25 years before he realized people from national leaders and spiritual guides to Rotarians and Boy Scouts all over the world were using them in their original form as well as in adaptations. Mother Teresa appears to have used 8 of the original 10 and had them posted on the wall of her children's home in Calcutta.

21. Mother Teresa, *Come Be My Light: The Private Writings of the "Saint of Calcutta"*, ed. and commentary Brian Kolodiejchuk (New York: Doubleday, 2007), 210. Much of the book is a record of a spiritual journey of great faithfulness during "the dark night of the soul."

22. Malcolm Edwards, "God," in *Religion Is a Queer Thing: A Guide to the Christian Faith for Lesbian, Gay, Bisexual, and Transgendered People*, ed. Elizabeth Stuart et al. (Cleveland: The Pilgrim Press, 1997), 74.

23. Troy D. Perry, *The Lord Is My Shepherd and He Knows I'm Gay: The Autobiography of the Rev. Troy D. Perry, as Told to Charles L. Lucas* (Los Angeles: Nash Publishing Corporation, 1990).

2

Cur Deus Homo[sexual]: The Queer Incarnation

Patrick S. Cheng

What relevance does the doctrine of incarnation—that is, the belief that God became human in the person of Jesus Christ—have for queer people?[1] For many queer theologians, the significance of the incarnation is centered upon *flesh*; that is, the Johannine notion of the Word becoming flesh, or "*ho logos egeneto sarx*" (Jn 1:14). In other words, the incarnation is significant because it is God's affirmation of the fundamental goodness of human flesh, or *sarx*, and this is reflected in the writings of queer theologians about the fundamental goodness of queer sexualities and queer gender identities.

One place where queer theologians have fallen short, however, is writing about the experiences of the full range of queer people, and especially queer people of color. That is, although queer theologians have been quite successful in terms of arguing for the goodness of *queer* flesh, they have been much less successful in terms of addressing the significance of *racialized* flesh. That is, the significance of queer bodies of color are largely overlooked or ignored in most queer theological writings. To this end, this chapter reviews the works of a number of queer theologians of color and examines how such works might help to create a fuller understanding of queer incarnation.

The title of this chapter is a play on Anselm of Canterbury's essay *Cur Deus Homo*, or "Why God Became Human." The purpose of this essay is to explore the queer incarnation, or "Why God Became Homo[sexual]."

The first part of this chapter focuses on the incarnation and flesh, or *sarx*, and how queer theologians have affirmed the goodness of human flesh, particularly with respect to queer sexualities and queer gender identities. The second part of this chapter focuses on the incarnation in the context of racialized flesh and the bodies of queer people of color. In so doing, it draws upon the theological and spiritual writings of queer theologians of color. Finally, the third part of this chapter concludes with some reflections on the postcolonial notion of hybridity, and how this concept might help in terms of constructing a fuller understanding of queer incarnation for all of humanity.

THE INCARNATION AND QUEER FLESH

The doctrine of incarnation traditionally involves abstract questions about the being of Jesus Christ and the relationship between his human and divine natures.[2] For example, the central theological question at the First Council of Nicaea (325 CE) was whether, in light of the incarnation, Jesus Christ was truly God; that is, whether he was in fact both fully human and fully divine. The central question at the Council of Chalcedon (351 CE) was similarly abstract; it dealt with the precise relationship between Jesus Christ's humanity and divinity. The council concluded that Jesus Christ's human and divine natures both existed in one person, yet "without confusion or change, [and] without division or separation."[3]

This movement toward theological abstraction—that is, away from reflecting upon the concrete, physical body of Christ—is particularly ironic in light of the fact that both of the Greek and Latin words for "incarnation" are literally translated as "enfleshment." In Greek, the word for becoming incarnate is "*sarkōthenta*," which is derived from "*sarx*," or flesh. Similarly, in Latin, the term for becoming incarnate is "*incarnatus est*," which is derived from "*carō*," or flesh.[4]

Queer theologians have done a particularly good job in terms of resisting this trend toward abstraction. Instead, these theologians have gone back to the original notion of flesh with respect to the doctrine of incarnation. Many of these theologians—and especially gay male theologians from a Roman Catholic background—have written about the need to acknowledge the full embodiment of Jesus Christ, including questions about his sexuality.

For example, the gay theologian and Metropolitan Community Church (MCC) pastor Robert Shore-Goss has written extensively about the tradition of homodevotion to Jesus Christ. This tradition presumes that Jesus Christ—as one who was fully human—was a sexual being. In his provocative book *Queering Christ: Beyond Jesus Acted Up*, Shore-Goss argues that "the scandal of the incarnation is not that God became flesh but that God became fully human and actively sexual."[5] Shore-Goss contends that we must ask taboo questions such as "Did Jesus have an erection? Did he have wet dreams? Did Jesus have an orgasm?" And, if so, "Orgasm with whom?"[6]

The gay Canadian religious scholar Donald Boisvert has written about the importance of uncovering the genitals of Jesus Christ in his book *Sanctity and Male Desire: A Gay Reading of Saints*. Boisvert asks, "How many Christian gay men have not glanced at an image of the crucified or dead Christ, and silently asked themselves what this penis looked like?" For Boisvert, the image of the penis of the naked crucified Christ—such as the "imposing rock penis hanging in view of all" in the Sagrada Familia temple in Barcelona, Spain—is significant because it "reaffirms, in the most visible and human way possible, the complete gift of the Creator through the Incarnation."[7]

Like Shore-Goss and Boisvert, the gay religious scholar Mark Jordan has written about the importance of affirming the full embodiment of Jesus Christ, genitals and all. Jordan notes the irony of the fact that even though Christian theology is focused on a divine incarnation, almost all depictions of the corpus of Jesus Christ on a crucifix—no matter how realistic—have erased the genitals of Christ. According to Jordan, these "alternate bodies for Jesus the Christ" are in fact "mutilated" corpses that prevent Jesus' body from being "whole, either in death or in life."[8]

Other gay men have written about literally seeing Christ in their sexual partners and/or taking on the identity of Christ themselves in their sexual encounters. For example, Jeff Mann writes about one sexual encounter in which his partner became his "Christ in the Candlelight" and how Mann "ate his smooth, perfect butt—white as a communion wafer" and "fucked him for a long time."[9] In another encounter, Mann writes about how he was the bottom and thus became "the Christos, naked, anointed with my own sweat, hands bound behind me … grunting and helpless."[10]

Gay men are not the only persons, however, who have affirmed the importance of flesh in their writings about the incarnated Christ. For example, the lesbian English theologian Elizabeth Stuart has argued that Christians should be "promiscuous with their love"—that is, "taking our bodies to other people's bodies"—in the same way that "Jesus of Nazareth gave himself bodily" in the Eucharist.[11] Similarly, the lesbian ethicist Kathy Rudy has focused on the Body of Christ and how the members of that body are called to a sexual ethic of hospitality that could include "radical sex communities" that engage in "communal living and communal sex."[12] Finally, the lesbian Roman Catholic religion scholar Jane Grovijahn has argued in her essay "Reclaiming the Power of Incarnation" that the image of God, or *Imago Dei*, must be understood as "God-between-my-legs." According to Grovijahn, if God cannot be a part of her body and sexuality, "then the Incarnation is a lie."[13]

The transgender theologian Justin Tanis has focused upon flesh by drawing parallels between the resurrected body of Jesus Christ and the experiences of trans people who have come out of sexual reassignment surgery. Like the resurrected Jesus Christ, the bodies of trans people who have transitioned are "both the same and different." That is, the transitioned bodies are not "wholly different," but are instead "transfigured and resurrected." For Tanis, sexual reassignment surgery is a way of "participating in the resurrection and of being born again."[14]

Like Tanis, the Argentinean queer theologian Martín Hugo Córdova Quero has argued that theological reflections about the incarnation must include transgender and intersex people. Córdova Quero notes that although many Christians view the incarnation in salvific terms (i.e., they profess that God has saved humanity through the incarnation), "the reality is that some humans are more worthy than others of that salvation."[15]

Finally, the queer religion scholar Virginia Mollenkott has written about the intersex significance of the incarnation. According to Mollenkott, the doctrine of the virgin birth means that Jesus Christ was conceived without any Y chromosomes (which are provided only by sperm). Thus, even though Jesus Christ is traditionally understood as having the body of a man, he lacks the usual male XY chromosomes and has instead XX chromosomes. This means that Jesus Christ can be understood as an intersex person.[16]

Interestingly, none of the foregoing reflections has affirmed the traditional theological understanding of the incarnation as the only means by which a fallen and sinful humanity is redeemed. This traditional understanding can be traced back to the 11th-century medieval theologian Anselm of Canterbury. In his book *Cur Deus Homo* (i.e., "Why God Became Human"), Anselm argued that the incarnation had to occur because no human being could ever repay the infinite debt owed to God as a result of Adam's and Eve's disobedience and Fall. In other words, the incarnation of Jesus Christ had to happen because only a person who is both divine and human (i.e., a God-human) could repay this infinite debt.[17]

Instead, queer theologians have understood the significance of the incarnation—either explicitly or implicitly—in terms of *deification*, or the process of becoming holy like God. In the words of the third-century theologian Athanasius of Alexandria, God "became human [so] that we might become divine."[18] For example, the theologian Wendy Farley, in her book *Gathering Those Driven Away*, has written about salvation in terms of *theōsis*, which is the Eastern Orthodox doctrine of deification. For Farley, the incarnation is not just about redemption from suffering, but it also "lights the path by which humanity returns to the Divine Eros."[19] That is, Jesus Christ is a compass or a guide star that directs us to our future eschatological home. And a critical part of coming home for queer people is the theological affirmation of the fundamental goodness of flesh in the incarnation.

Although queer theologians have made a strong connection between the incarnation and queer sexuality through the notion of enfleshment, it remains to be seen whether these ideas can be translated from theory into praxis by actual queer communities of faith. That is, despite the existence of a number of sex-positive practices within the queer community such as the Body Electric School and erotic genital massage,[20] or a radically sex-positive ethics as articulated in works such as *The Ethical Slut* and *Radical Ecstasy*,[21] often times a theology of incarnation is limited to less controversial issues such as equal civil rights or equal access to the sacraments and rites of the church (e.g., holy matrimony and ordination).

Despite the resistance of some queer communities of faith to broadening the range of what is considered to be "normal" sexual practices,[22] the connections made by queer theologians between the incarnation and enfleshment can be a helpful way of understanding the radically embodied nature of the incarnation.

THE INCARNATION AND RACIALIZED FLESH

Although queer theologians have done a good job over the past few decades in terms of reclaiming the goodness of sexualized flesh in light of the incarnation, they have been far less successful in terms of reflecting upon—or even giving voice to—the experiences of queer people of color. Although queer theologians of color have been writing about their experiences for nearly two decades, these writings still remain largely on the margins of queer theological discourse.

Race and ethnicity, as we have seen in the proliferation of contextual liberation theologies since the 1960s, is a central part of our enfleshed identities. Indeed, as the lesbian theologian Laurel Schneider has argued in her influential essay, "What Race Is Your Sex?," the notion of race cannot be separated from notions of sex and sexuality. That is, race, sex, and sexuality are "co-constitutive" qualities that have "utter dependence of one upon the others for meaning and existence."[23] For example, the phrase "gay man" immediately invokes images of whiteness for most people. By contrast, the phrase "gay black man" evokes images of hyper-masculinity, whereas the phrase "gay Asian man" evokes images of hyper-femininity. Race cannot be separated from sex or sexuality.

Furthermore, queer bodies of color experience a profound alienation from both the larger queer community (i.e., with respect to racism), as well as their own communities of origin (i.e., with respect to homophobia and transphobia).[24] In other words, queer people of color—and their flesh—become racialized and sexualized signifiers with respect to their communities. Some queer white theologians such as Robert Shore-Goss and Susannah Cornwall have written about the issues faced by queer people of color from a theological perspective.[25] It is unfortunate, however, that the great majority of white queer theologians have not focused on the experiences of queer people of color in their writings (whether about incarnation or other theological doctrines).

Although queer white theologies have existed since at least the 1950s—and liberation theologies have existed since the late 1960s—the theological voices of queer people of color did not start to emerge until the early 1990s.[26] In 1993, Elias Farajajé-Jones, an avowed gay-identified, bisexual black theologian, published a controversial essay, "Breaking Silence: Toward an In-the-Life Theology," which challenged the Black Church on its homophobia and biphobia, as well as its AIDSphobia during the height of the HIV/AIDS epidemic.[27] In that same year, Renée Hill, a lesbian womanist theologian, published the groundbreaking essay "Who Are We for Each Other?: Sexism, Sexuality and Womanist Theology," which critiqued womanist theologians for failing to address the issue of love between women (sexual or otherwise) in their theological writings.[28] Following the publication of Hill's essay, a number of womanist and black feminist theologians and ethicists—including M. Shawn Copeland, Kelly Brown Douglas, Emilie Townes, and Traci West—have written about the importance of challenging the sin of heterosexism in the African American community.[29]

Since the 1990s, a number of queer African American theological voices have emerged. In 2006, Horace Griffin, a gay African American Episcopal priest and professor at the Pacific School of Religion, published

Their Own Receive Them Not, a book about the homophobia that African American lesbians and gay men continue to face in the Black Church, as well as the emergence of queer black congregations and even denominations.[30] And in 2010, Roger A. Sneed, an openly gay African American religious studies scholar at Furman University, published *Representations of Homosexuality*, which documented the experiences of same-gender loving black men and the ways in which traditional black liberation theologies have failed to allow them to speak in their own voices.[31]

Queer Asian American theologians also have engaged in theological reflections on the intersections of race and sexuality. Like queer African American theologians, they have written about the ways in which they have experienced both racism and homophobia from the communities in which they are located. One of the earliest theological works relating to the queer Asian American experience was published in 1996. In that year, Leng Lim published an essay, "Exploring Embodiment," which addressed the intersections of race, sexuality, and spirituality in his life. Lim, who is an ordained Episcopal priest, wrote a series of theological works over the next decade about his experiences as a gay Asian man.[32] Eric Law, also a gay Asian American Episcopal priest, wrote about similar themes of racism and homophobia in his 1997 essay "A Spirituality of Creative Marginality."[33]

In 2001, I wrote an essay, "Multiplicity and Judges 19," which examined the queer Asian experience of racism and homophobia in light of the nameless concubine in Judges 19 who is gang-raped and then dismembered.[34] In my more recent work, such as my 2011 essay "I Am Yellow and Beautiful," I have written about the racism that is experienced by queer Asian men in cyberspace and in the larger white queer community.[35] Also, theological writings about the queer Asian experience outside of the United States have started to emerge. In 2010, the Asian feminist theological journal *In God's Image* published a special issue called "Beyond Right and Wrong: Doing Queer Theology in Hong Kong," which featured essays from 11 queer Asian writers and allies from Hong Kong.[36]

Finally, other ethnic and racial groups have started to write about the intersections of race and sexuality in the context of theology and religious studies. For example, in 2007 the gay Latino theologian Orlando Espín wrote in his book *Grace and Humanness* about the need for Latin@ theologians to break the silence about the Latin@ and black queer communities and to recognize the full humanity of such marginalized communities.[37] Despite the rapidly growing population of Latin@s and Hispanic Americans in the United States, much more work still needs to be done with respect to theological reflection upon the queer Latin@ or Hispanic experience.

As mentioned earlier, even though queer theologians of color have been writing about the intersections of spirituality, sexuality, and race for nearly two decades, the larger queer theological community has remained almost completely silent about these issues. Important anthologies about queer theology such as *Queer Theology: Rethinking the Western Body* contain few references to—not to mention contributions from—queer people of color.[38]

In sum, there is a growing body of work by queer theologians and religion scholars of color who have written about the significance of both racialized and sexualized flesh, as well as their embodied experiences of racism and homophobia. Despite the focus by many queer white theologians on the significance of flesh and the incarnation, it is troubling that, to date, few queer white theologians have written about these works or the ways in which race and sexuality are inextricably intertwined. Any queer theology of incarnation must take seriously the experiences of queer people of color, both in the United States and around the world.

HYBRIDITY AND THE QUEER INCARNATION

What can be done to expand the notion of queer flesh to include the racialized flesh of queer bodies of color as well as others who are on the margins within the larger queer community? One possibility is to broaden the understanding of queer incarnation by using the postcolonial notion of hybridity. Hybridity refers to the middle or third space between two binary poles. According to the postcolonial theorist Homi Bhabha, hybridity is akin to a landing between two floors in a stairwell. It is in this hybrid space that the two binary poles—for example, colonizer and colonized, or gay and straight—are challenged and transformed.[39]

Interestingly, the incarnation itself can be understood in terms of hybridity. That is, Jesus Christ is the third space between the two poles of humanity and divinity, as well as flesh and spirit. It is in the incarnation that this hybrid being or *"tertium quid"* is created, thus challenging the conventional wisdom that keeps these two poles separate and distinct. In light of the incarnation, Jesus Christ can be understood as a "mediator" or *"mesitēs"* (Heb. 9:15), who brings together humanity and divinity. The mediating function of Jesus Christ is particularly important with respect to Eastern Orthodox doctrine of *theōsis*, in which humanity is deified over the course of salvation history. Jesus Christ, as a hybrid being, brings the two poles together through the incarnation. To paraphrase Athanasius of Alexandria, God became human so that humans could become divine.

As I have written elsewhere, Christian theology itself can be understood in terms of hybridity. That is, Christian theology is about a love so powerful that it dissolves the natural boundaries that separate binaries such as humanity and divinity, flesh and spirit, temporality and eternity, and so on.[40] Nowhere is this seen as clearly as in the incarnation, in which the two natures of Jesus Christ (i.e., human and divine) come together in one hybrid person. Not surprisingly, this hybridity threatens the powers and principalities of Jesus' time, and it results in his torture and execution.

Queer theology can also be understood in terms of hybridity. In addition to challenging the binaries of humanity and divinity, queer theology also challenges the false binaries of sexuality and spirituality. In other words, sexuality and spirituality are not polar opposites or mutually exclusive categories. (That is, not all queer people are atheists, and not all people of faith are straight and cisgender.)[41] Rather, sexuality and spirituality come together in the experiences of queer people of faith. As others have noted, sexuality and spirituality are in fact inextricably tied together—in large part because the "rapture of sexual union and the rapture of communion with the divine are strikingly similar in their power and transcendence."[42]

Last but not least, queer theology—and the doctrine of incarnation—must challenge the false binaries of sexuality and race. A truly inclusive queer theology—that is, one that acknowledges the bodies of queer people of color—challenges the stereotypes that all queer people are white and that all people of color are straight and cisgender. We must stop seeing sexuality and race as mutually exclusive categories and start seeing them as inextricably intertwined.[43]

It is in this realm—that is, the incarnational intersections of sexuality and race—that the MCC denomination has brought forth many gifts to the broader world. Many MCC congregations are racially, ethnically, and culturally diverse. The MCC People of African Descent (PAD) group, founded in 1995, is a global network of MCC clergy and lay people of African descent as well as their allies. Over the years, PAD has sponsored many conferences and other events relating to the intersections of sexuality, race, and spirituality.[44] Queer Asian Spirit, a group that was founded in 2001 by a number of individuals with MCC ties, serves a similar purpose for queer Asians of faith and their allies around the world.[45]

There are also many MCC churches in the two-thirds world, which reflects the true incarnational diversity of queer and racialized flesh, and which also makes the Body of Christ a multiracial as well as multisexual body. In Africa, there are MCC congregations in Kenya, Nigeria, and South Africa.[46] In Asia and the Pacific Islands, there are MCC congregations in Australia, New Zealand, and the Philippines.[47] And in Latin America, there are MCC congregations in Argentina, Brazil, Chile, Colombia, Cuba, Dominican Republic, Ecuador, El Salvador, Haiti, Mexico, Nicaragua, Uruguay, and Venezuela.[48]

In sum, the notion of hybridity can be a useful metaphor for thinking about the doctrine of incarnation. Hybridity not only helps us to understand the incarnation of Jesus Christ as bridging the gap between the divine and the human, but it also helps us to recognize that incarnation is about bridging the gap between sexuality and spirituality, as well as the gap between sexuality and race.

CONCLUSION

I have argued in this chapter that, to date, queer theologians have done a good job in terms of reconnecting the incarnation with the notion of flesh. In particular, the writings by gay male theologians about the sexuality of Jesus Christ—as well as their own sexual attraction to Christ—serve a powerful purpose of reclaiming the goodness of sexuality and queer flesh.

However, I have also argued that, to date, queer theologians have not done as well in terms of acknowledging all of the dimensions of enfleshment. These dimensions include a deeper understanding of the inextricably intertwined relationships between racialized and sexualized flesh, as well as giving voice to the experiences of queer people of color with respect to racism and homophobia.

I conclude by suggesting that the postcolonial notion of hybridity can be a helpful way of thinking about the doctrine of incarnation. Specifically, hybridity challenges all kinds of binaries, including the binary poles of divinity and humanity, spirituality and sexuality, and queerness and race. Because of this, hybridity can help us better understand why God became queer, or, to paraphrase Anselm of Canterbury, *cur Deus homo[sexual]*.

NOTES

1. In this essay, I use the term "queer" as an umbrella term to describe lesbian, gay, bisexual, transgender, intersex, queer, and questioning people, as well as their allies. For a discussion of the various uses of the word queer in theological discourse, see Patrick S. Cheng, *Radical Love: An Introduction to Queer Theology* (New York: Seabury Books, 2011), 2–8.

2. For an anthology of contemporary theological reflections on the incarnation, see Stephen T. Davis, Daniel Kendall, and Gerald O'Collins, *The Incarnation* (Oxford, UK: Oxford University Press, 2002).

3. For a discussion of the theology of the ecumenical councils, see Leo Donald Davis, *The First Seven Ecumenical Councils (325–787): Their History and Theology* (Collegeville, MN: Liturgical Press, 1983).

4. Philip Schaff, *The Creeds of Christendom: With a History and Critical Notes*, 6th ed. (Grand Rapids, MI: Baker Books, 2007), 2:57.

5. Robert E. Goss, *Queering Christ: Beyond Jesus Acted Up* (Cleveland: Pilgrim Press, 2002), 119.

6. Ibid., 113.

7. Donald L. Boisvert, *Sanctity and Male Desire: A Gay Reading of Saints* (Cleveland: Pilgrim Press, 2004), 176.

8. Mark D. Jordan, *Telling Truths in Church: Scandal, Flesh, and Christian Speech* (Boston: Beacon Press, 2003), 84–87.

9. Jeff Mann, "Binding the God," in *Queer and Catholic*, ed. Amie M. Evans and Trebor Healey (New York: Routledge, 2008), 65.

10. Ibid., 68.

11. Elizabeth Stuart, *Just Good Friends: Towards a Lesbian and Gay Theology of Relationships* (London: Mowbray, 1995), 213.

12. Kathy Rudy, *Sex and the Church: Gender, Homosexuality, and the Transformation of Christian Ethics* (Boston: Beacon Press, 1997), 128.

13. Jane M. Grovijahn, "Reclaiming the Power of Incarnation: When God's Body Is Catholic and Queer (with a Cunt!)," in *Queer and Catholic*, 250.

14. Justin Tanis, *Trans-Gendered: Theology, Ministry, and Communities of Faith* (Cleveland: Pilgrim Press, 2003), 142–43.

15. Martín Hugo Córdova Quero, "This Body Trans/Forming Me: Indecencies in Transgender/Intersex Bodies, Body Fascism and the Doctrine of the Incarnation," in *Controversies in Body Theology*, ed. Marcella Althaus-Reid and Lisa Isherwood (London: SCM Press, 2008), 96.

16. Virginia Ramey Mollenkott, *Omnigender: A Trans-Religious Approach* (Cleveland: Pilgrim Press, 2001), 105–7.

17. See Anselm of Canterbury, *Cur Deus Homo* (1098), in *A Scholastic Miscellany: Anselm to Ockham*, ed. Eugene R. Fairweather (Louisville, KY: Westminster John Knox Press, 1956), 100–83.

18. Athanasius, *On the Incarnation of the Word of God*, §54, in Norman Russell, *Fellow Workers with God: Orthodox Thinking on Theosis* (Crestwood, NY: St. Vladimir's Seminary Press, 2009), 23–24.

19. Wendy Farley, *Gathering Those Driven Away: A Theology of Incarnation* (Louisville, KY: Westminster John Knox Press, 2011), 170. For a discussion of *theōsis* in the context of sin and grace, see Patrick S. Cheng, *From Sin to Amazing Grace: Discovering the Queer Christ* (New York: Seabury Books, 2012).

20. Michael Bernard Kelly, *Seduced by Grace: Contemporary Spirituality, Gay Experience and Christian Faith* (Melbourne, Australia: Clouds of Magellan, 2007), 182–86 ("Sex with soul, body and spirit").

21. Dossie Easton and Janet W. Hardy, *The Ethical Slut: A Practical Guide to Polyamory, Open Relationships and Other Adventures*, 2nd ed. (Berkeley, CA: Celestial Arts, 2009); Dossie Easton and Janet W. Hardy, *Radical Ecstasy: SM Journeys to Transcendence* (Oakland, CA: Greenery Press, 2004).

22. For a critique of normalcy within the queer community, see Michael Warner, *The Trouble with Normal: Sex, Politics, and the Ethics of Queer Life* (Cambridge, MA: Harvard University Press, 1999).

23. Laurel C. Schneider, "What Race Is Your Sex?," in *Disrupting White Supremacy from Within: White People on What We Need to Do*, ed. Jennifer Harvey, Karin A. Case, and Robin Hawley Gorsline (Cleveland: Pilgrim Press, 2004), 142.

24. Patrick S. Cheng, "Gay Asian Masculinities and Christian Theologies," *CrossCurrents* 61, no. 4 (2011): 540–48.

25. Goss, *Queering Christ*, 253; Susannah Cornwall, *Controversies in Queer Theology* (London: SCM Press, 2011), 72–113.

26. For a genealogy of how queer theology has developed since the 1950s, see Cheng, *Radical Love*, 26–42.

27. Elias Farajaje-Jones, "Breaking Silence: Toward an In-the-Life Theology," in *Black Theology: A Documentary History, Volume II, 1980–1992*, ed. James H. Cone and Gayraud S. Wilmore (Maryknoll, NY: Orbis Books, 1993), 139–59. Other works by Farajajé-Jones, now Ibrahim Abdurrahman Farajajé, include "Holy Fuck," in *Male Lust: Pleasure, Power, and Transformation*, ed. Kerwin Kay, Jill Nagle, and Baruch Gould (Binghamton, NY: Harrington Park Press, 2000), 327–35.

28. Renee L. Hill, "Who Are We for Each Other?: Sexism, Sexuality and Womanist Theology," in *Black Theology II*, 345–51. Other works by Hill include: "Power, Blessings, and Human Sexuality: Making the Justice Connections," in *Beyond Colonial Anglicanism: The Anglican Communion in the Twenty-First Century*, ed. Ian T. Douglas and Kwok Pui-lan (New York: Church Publishing, 2001), 191–203; "Rev. Dr. Renee L. Hill," in *A Whosoever Church: Welcoming Lesbians and Gay Men into African American Congregations*, ed. Gary David Comstock (Louisville, KY: Westminster John Knox Press, 2001), 189–201; "Disrupted/Disruptive Movements: Black Theology and Black Power 1969/1999," in *Black Faith and Public Talk: Critical Essays on James H. Cone's Black Theology and Black Power*, ed. Dwight N. Hopkins (Maryknoll, NY: Orbis Books, 1999), 138–49.

29. M. Shawn Copeland, *Enfleshing Freedom: Body, Race, and Being* (Minneapolis, MN: Fortress Press, 2010), 78–84; Kelly Brown Douglas, *Sexuality and the Black Church: A Womanist Perspective* (Maryknoll, NY: Orbis Books, 1999), 87–108; Emilie M. Townes, "Washed in the Grace of God," in *Violence Against Women and Children: A Christian Theological Sourcebook*, ed. Carol J. Adams and Marie M. Fortune (New York: Continuum, 1995), 65–67; Traci C. West, *Disruptive Christian Ethics: Where Racism and Women's Lives Matter* (Louisville, KY: Westminster John Knox Press, 2006), 141–79.

30. Horace L. Griffin, *Their Own Receive Them Not: African American Lesbians and Gays in Black Churches* (Cleveland: Pilgrim Press, 2006).

31. Roger A. Sneed, *Representations of Homosexuality: Black Liberation Theology and Cultural Criticism* (New York: Palgrave Macmillan, 2010).

32. Leng Leroy Lim, "Exploring Embodiment," in *Boundary Wars: Intimacy and Distance in Healing Relationships*, ed. Katherine Hancock Ragsdale (Cleveland: Pilgrim Press, 1996), 58–77. Other works by Lim include: Leng Lim, Kim-Hao Yap, and Tuck-Leong Lee, "The Mythic-Literalists in the Province of South Asia," in *Other Voices, Other Worlds: The Global Church Speaks Out on Homosexuality*, ed. Terry Brown (New York: Church Publishing, 2006), 58–76; Leng Leroy Lim, " 'The Bible Tells Me to Hate Myself': The Crisis in Asian American Spiritual Leadership," *Semeia* 90/91 (2002): 315–22; You-Leng Leroy Lim, "Webs of Betrayal, Webs of Blessings," in *Q&A: Queer in Asian America*, ed. David L. Eng and Alice Y. Hom (Philadelphia: Temple University Press, 1998), 323–34; Leng Leroy Lim, "Webs of Betrayal,

Webs of Blessing," in *Our Families, Our Values*, 227–41; Leng Leroy Lim, "The Gay Erotics of My Stuttering Mother Tongue," *Amerasia Journal* 22, no. 1 (1996): 172–77.

33. Eric H. F. Law, "A Spirituality of Creative Marginality," in *Que(e)rying Religion: A Critical Anthology*, ed. Gary David Comstock and Susan E. Henking (New York: Continuum, 2007), 343–46.

34. Patrick S. Cheng, "Multiplicity and Judges 19: Constructing a Queer Asian Pacific American Biblical Hermeneutic," *Semeia* 90/91 (2002): 119–33.

35. Patrick S. Cheng, "'I Am Yellow and Beautiful': Reflections on Queer Asian Spirituality and Gay Male Cyberculture," *Journal of Technology, Theology, and Religion* 2, no. 3 (2011): 1–21.

36. "Beyond Right and Wrong: Doing Queer Theology in Hong Kong," *In God's Image* 29, no. 3 (2010): 1–80.

37. Orlando O. Espín, *Grace and Humanness: Theological Reflections Because of Culture* (Maryknoll, NY: Orbis Books, 2007), 51–79 ("Humanitas, Identity, and Another Theological Anthropology of (Catholic) Tradition").

38. Gerard Loughlin, ed., *Queer Theology: Rethinking the Western Body* (Malden, MA: Blackwell Publishing, 2007).

39. Homi K. Bhabha, *The Location of Culture* (London: Routledge, 1994), 5.

40. Cheng, *Radical Love*, ix–x.

41. The term cisgender refers to people who do not self-identify as transgender.

42. Phil Zukerman and Christel Manning, "Sex and Religion: An Introduction," in *Sex and Religion*, ed. Christel Manning and Phil Zuckerman (Belmont, CA: Thomson Wadsworth, 2005), 1.

43. Cheng, "Gay Asian Masculinities." Some of my other theological writings on the queer Asian experience include: "A Three-Part Sinfonia: Queer Asian Reflections on the Trinity," *Journal of Race, Ethnicity, and Religion* 2, no. 13.9 (2011): 1–23; "Rethinking Sin and Grace for LGBT People Today," in *Sexuality and the Sacred: Sources for Theological Reflection*, 2nd ed., ed. Marvin M. Ellison and Kelly Brown Douglas (Louisville, KY: Westminster John Knox Press, 2010), 105–18; "Galatians," in *The Queer Bible Commentary*, ed. Deryn Guest, Robert E. Goss, Mona West, and Thomas Bohache (London: SCM Press, 2006), 624–29; "Reclaiming Our Traditions, Rituals, and Spaces: Spirituality and the Queer Asian Pacific American Experience," *Spiritus* 6, no. 2 (2006): 234–40. For my book-length discussion on the intersections of race, sexuality, and spirituality, see Patrick S. Cheng, *Rainbow Theology: Bridging Race, Sexuality, and Spirit* (New York: Seabury Books, 2013).

44. See http://www.mccpad.org (accessed March 15, 2013).

45. See http://www.queerasianspirit.org (accessed March 15, 2013).

46. See http://mccchurch.org/overview/ourchurches/find-a-church/africa-church-listings (accessed March 15, 2013).

47. See http://mccchurch.org/overview/ourchurches/find-a-church/asia-and-pacific-islands-listing (accessed March 15, 2013).

48. See http://mccchurch.org/overview/ourchurches/find-a-church/latin-america-church-listing (accessed March 15, 2013).

3

Grace Is Green: Green Incarnational Inclusivities

Robert E. Shore-Goss

The killing of Mother Earth in our time is the number one ethical, spiritual, and human issue of our planet.[1]

As the day approached for the dedication ceremony of Metropolitan Community Church (MCC) in the Valley's solar panels, I received an email from an MCC Christian: "Forget solar panels, cling to Jesus."[2] I was bothered by the email message because it typically separated Christ and social responsibility for the Earth. It was indicative of many Christians within MCC but also a majority of Christians in most denominations who separate heaven and the Earth, giving priority value to heaven over the Earth.[3] Going green is not within the educational, ministerial, or social justice perspectives of many Christian churches.

Yet as the reality of the 21st century, we are faced with an ecological disaster on this planet precipitated by human consumption, an ignorance of issues of planetary sustainability, global warming from increased carbon emissions while corporate lobbyists willfully create doubt about global warming, toxic pollution, attempts to gut environmental protections from the Environmental Protection Agency for short business gains, and so many other issues such as water shortages and climate refugees in the billions. Al Gore's *Inconvenient Truth* and ABC's graphic novel *Earth 2100* paint an apocalypse more real and horrific than we can imagine.[4] In the often repeated mantra of Christian moral theologian Daniel Maguire, "if present trends continue, we will not."[5]

Lynn White's 1967 article, "The Historical Roots of Our Ecological Crisis," laid the ideological roots of ecological crisis at the footsteps of Judeo-Christian religion, which is the most anthropocentric religion on the planet:

> In Antiquity every tree, every spring, every stream, every hill had its own genius loci, its guardian spirit. These spirits were accessible to men, but were very unlike men; centaurs, fauns, and mermaids show their ambivalence. Before one cut a tree, mined a mountain, or dammed a brook, it was important to placate the spirit in charge of that particular situation, and to keep it placated. By destroying pagan animism, Christianity made it possible to exploit nature in a mood of indifference to the feelings of natural objects.[6]

Christian anthropocentricism, arrogance, and theological disdain for nature contributed to a technological mastery of the Earth, but it also created a lack of concern for the consequences of technological advancement. To make a division between Christian practice and responsible coliving with the Earth is a major heresy that engulfs many Christians. It fails to take seriously the Genesis creation account that God said creation was good and, in addition, it falls short to give serious consideration to two central mysteries of Christian faith: (1) God's incarnation in human flesh and its relationship to created matter and the Earth and (2) the ongoing work of the Holy Spirit within creation. For too long, Christian faith communities have failed to take into consideration physical and moral degradation of the Earth as a major justice issue. In fact, Christians have lost theological focus of the incarnational and inclusional nature of Jesus that we have alienated ourselves from the rest of the natural world and have failed to perceive God's Spirit active in the world.

What I intend to cover is talk theologically about green incarnational inclusivity and the responsibility to include the Earth at the center of all inclusive worship and church praxis. For myself and my church community, the practice of open commensality necessitates a ministry of Earth care.

GREEN STIRRINGS OF THE SPIRIT AT MCC IN THE VALLEY

One of the trajectories of ecological sensitivity was the practice of open commensality at MCC in the Valley. MCC's invitation of open table has led us as a community to define our church mission as radical inclusive love. We started to comprehend that the communion table did not belong to our church, but the table belonged to God, thus removing our table hospitality from denominational polities that exclude various folks from the table. We opened our invitation to community to all who came to worship whether church members, Christian or non-Christian—regardless of sexual orientation or gender differences, race and ethnicity, age, and ability. God's open table invitation represents God's offer of grace for us at table. It is the living memory of God's self communication through the death and resurrection of Christ and the Spirit's active transformation of all things in Christ. Traditionally, God's grace is offered through the incarnation and through the Spirit, for early Christians understood Christ and the Holy Spirit as the two hands of God's offer of grace to creation and humanity.[7] God for us is a profound communication that is unimaginably wider than the communion table, the church, or Christianity. For us at MCC at the Valley, we began to perceive that God's offer and communication of grace could not be boxed, controlled, or regulated. Grace is wild, outside of the box, and in places we least imagined. God for us was not inclusive enough, for it did not include plant and animal life and the Earth herself.

The church had a communion practice of the celebrants taking communion and offering their communion for church members who could not be present. It was a wonderful practice of extending of the grace of the communion table to other members of the church. I added a new dimension to the practice from a Tibetan Buddhist meditation *tonglen* (receiving and giving).[8] I transformed the communion ritual to take in the sufferings of humanity and the Earth and giving away the communion grace for those who were suffering from violence and hunger, homelessness, and for the Earth that human beings have so ravaged and harmed.

We understood the Earth as a living being, producing and evolving diverse life forms, and how humanity had created carbon emissions to produce global warming that ravaged the Earth through deforestation, strip mining, pollution from coal power plants and petroleum fuels, and irresponsible disposal of toxic waste, the failure to recycle, and so on. We made the Earth a member of the church on one Earth Day Sunday to symbolize the great commandment that loving God and loving our neighbor included loving the Earth and taking responsibility for diversity of life. We started to reduce our energy expenditures with a tankless water heater, started to order recycled paper, cut down our paper usage, began recycling, composting in our garden, replacing our lights bulbs with compact fluorescent lamps, and replaced our toilets with high-efficiency low flush toilets, saving several thousand of gallons of water each year.

When the opportunity became affordable for installing solar panels, the board and the congregation voted unanimously to become green.

MCC at the Valley now generates more kilowatts annually than the church expends. We reduce our carbon footprint significantly and continue to proselytize other churches and faith communities to follow our lead to reduce carbon emissions and take responsibility to live green. We are now taking steps to increase water recovery for the church and the Los Angeles water table. We have joined California Interfaith Power and Light and created a green interfaith clergy group to work on transforming our communities into green centers of responsible sustainability and right relationship to the Earth as well as to pressure local city government to reduce its energy needs generated by two coal plants.[9]

GOD'S GRACE IS GREEN

MCC's theology of open hospitality at the communion table has extended its notion of grace. For myself, grace is God's gift of Godself, boundless love, and compassion and forgiveness. It is mediated through Jesus, God's Christ, and the Holy Spirit. Theologian Jay McDaniel makes the distinction between green and red grace. He asserts,

> Green grace is the healing that comes to us when we enjoy rich bonds with other people, plants and animals, and the Earth. It is a kind of grace celebrated by ecofeminists, native peoples, deep ecologists, and sacramentalists. It is green because as the green color suggests, it engenders within us healing and wholeness, a freshness and renewal that lead us into the very fullness of life. . . . In a world torn asunder by violence, forgiveness is a most precious form of green grace.[10]

McDaniel makes reference to grace as red and the Christian association of red grace with blood atonement theologies. Christian blood atonement theologies have historically been violent, if not bloodthirsty—scapegoating Jews, women, Muslims, indigenous peoples, non-Christian religions, and LGBT folks. McDaniel acknowledges this violent history of Christian blood theologies and attempts to offer a notion of grace as red, sublated into green when he states, "The cross tells us that we are not alone in our suffering, that it is shared by the Heart of the universe . . . God receives our violence without responding in kind. The blood of the cross reveals the empathy and non-violence of the cross."[11] Similar notions are expressed by Mark Wallace when he writes,

> . . . the cross is green. It is green because Jesus' witness on the cross is to a planet where all of God's children are bearers of life-giving Spirit. It is

green because the goodness of creation is God's here-and-now dwelling place where everyday life is charged with sacred presence and power.[12]

Wallace, like McDaniel, brings the green cross to planetary healing. Early Christians applied the suffering servant songs to their understandings of Jesus' redemptive healing: "By his bruise, we are healed" (Isa. 53:5). Jesus shared the sufferings of all those who are suffering, human and non-human life, the planet herself. The green cross includes all life everywhere, and all life is destined for God's coming reign. God's Christ brings healing to a broken world with compassion, love, and sustainable grace.

Grace, so much at the heart of Christian theologies of creation, incarnation, and salvation, is God's self-communication and love. Through the years, I have developed a Trinitarian theology of creation, incarnation, and the transformation of all into Christ. It starts in the superabundant love life of the Trinity—a circle or spiral of mutual loving between Creator, the Christ, and the Spirit. Greek theology speaks of *perichoresis*— each divine person empties a divine self in mutual love into each other for one another. God's love cannot be contained within the divine *perichoresis*, for it explodes and spirals into creation, an act of love emerging in the creation of the universe over 15 billion years. Traditionally, Ireneaus understood that divine activity in the world is mediated through God's two hands—the Holy Spirit and the Logos working in creation and through creation. Ireneaus' intertwining of the Spirit and Logos provides a theological matrix for a Trinitarian interweaving of the two in God's self-communication and bestowal of self in love and compassionate vulnerability to creation. The Holy Spirit breathed power, energy, and life into the evolving universe and in its physical processes and biological emergence on Earth. The 12th-century Benedictine mystic and writer, Hildegard of Bingen, wrote of about the green power of God's Spirit, coining the word *viriditas* from greening and truth. It was the divine greening power or fecundity that animates creation from the beginning, planting, nourishing, and flourishing. Hildegard comprehends Jesus as greening or greenness incarnate; she write from one of her visions, "My Only-Begotten . . . came forth into this world as the greenness of integrity."[13] Jesus himself was the greenwood empowering all human virtues. Thus, *viriditas* or greening was her language of grace for speaking of the green presence God's Spirit in humanity and creation. Veli-Matti Kärkkäinen writes, "For this spiritual mystic, *viriditas* was a key component that expressed and connected the bounty of God, the fertility of nature, and the enlivening, fresh presence of the Spirit."[14] The Spirit's greening presence

sustains and transforms all creation towards the incarnational green transformation and flourishing intended by the triune God.

Creation is not one thing and salvation something else as various theologies distinguish. Rather, they are the one uninterrupted flow of God's
communicative love. In other words, creation, incarnation, and final
transformation of creation are united in one act of Trinitarian self-giving
or self-communication, and we call that self-bestowal by the word "grace,"
gift. God freely offers Godself to creation and humanity, and for humanity God offers an invitation into conscious interrelationship. Over the
years of prayerful reflection, I have come to an awareness that incarnation
is a Trinitarian physical event. It is not only a significant bestowal of God
to us and to creation, but it also characterizes the interrelatedness of the
universe on all levels. The most creative western and Orthodox theologies
point to the fact that God is relational and that interrelatedness of the
Triune community of love is reflected in the universe, from microscopic
to macrocosmic levels. And this is the work of God's two hands. God has
become flesh and matter through Christ, and God has poured Godself as
dynamic agency of creative power and sustainable life through the Spirit.

JESUS AND HIS TEACHINGS OF GREEN GRACE

But Abba God for Jesus is also Creator God who makes the sun rise
and sends the rains, for God is intimately in the processes of the cosmos.
God is also the God for all creatures and connected to the Spirit. The
Spirit was involved in the incarnation of Jesus, for Ambrose of Milan
called the Spirit "the author of the incarnation."[15] The Spirit is present to
Jesus at his conception, with him at his baptism, leading him into the wilderness, and commissioning his message of God's reign and performing a
ministry of compassionate care for the outsider. The Spirit is present with
Christ in his death, and the Spirit raises Jesus to the resurrected Christ.

When we hear how Jesus experiences God's love for sparrows and lilies
and wild flowers, he looks at them with loving eyes and sees them as loved by
God and the revelation of God's providential care for nature. For Jesus, nature is the place of encounter with the living Spirit of Abba. When you look
at Jesus' parables, there is a sense of divineness present in the natural order.
Jesus looks at nature as gift of creation from Abba God, but it is also the
place that we as human beings can encounter and meet Abba God as Spirit.

But let's look at the greening of Jesus' teachings. It is there in the parables. For Jesus, mustard seeds are a symbol of God's spreading reign. Fig
trees that produce fruit are a sign that God is near. Growth of a seed expresses God's intention that we are to thrive. And in another place in the

gospel, the growth of a seed is God's grace. Jesus describes himself as a vine and us as the branches. Lost sheep expresses human alienation. And wind becomes a metaphor for the unseen but felt experience of the Holy Spirit. For Jesus, nature teaches us continuously about God's grace.

Jesus' message about the reign of God is thoroughly green. The kindom, not kingdom, is about our relationship or kinship to nature as well as our relationship to human beings. It is about kinship to nature and human beings, and as followers of Christ, we cannot separate our ministry to nature from our ministry to human beings. They are intertwined; they are interrelated. But Jesus also speaks about how God's activity is immanently present and active in the world.

Then Green Christians understand that if God cares about every sparrow, every insect, every creature in the seas, in the air, or on land, and those beings that prey on another, then we who are made in the image of God are called like God to love fellow creatures as God loves them. We are called into a kinship with God's creatures and the earth, not the domination of nature, the exploitation of the planet's resources, and the extinction of species. In a God-centered spirituality, Jesus teaches us that other life forms have a God-given value; they have value in themselves—a value that we as Christians are called to respect and cherish.

DUAL INCARNATIONS: CHRIST AND THE HOLY SPIRIT

Feminist theologians have underscored Jesus as God's Wisdom, using the traditional Jewish notions of Wisdom (Sophia) to explain the presence of God as Emmanuel and activity in the world. Elisabeth Schüssler-Fiorenza writes about Jesus as the Prophet of Wisdom while Elizabeth Johnson has developed a comprehensive Christology of Jesus as God's Wisdom.[16] And the Spirit Christologies of Roger Haight and Jacques Dupuis provide the metaphorical means for comprehending God's activity and immanent causality in the word.[17] Both Wisdom and Spirit Christologies have provided a foundational matrix for theological and ecological Christology that is grounded in God's embodiment in Christ. In other words, there is a profound linkage of God's incarnation in Christ and the Spirit's incarnation in the world of created life.

Long time eco-theologian Sallie McFague understands that an ecological Christology has two features: embodiment and inclusion. Both embodiment and inclusion are interrelated in her model of Christology:

By bringing God into the realm of the body, of matter, nature is included within the divine reach. This inclusion is possible only if incarnation is understood in a broad, not narrow fashion: that is, if Jesus as the incarnate Logos, Wisdom, or Spirit of God is paradigmatic of what is evident everywhere else as well. . . . Incarnational Christology means that salvation is neither solely human nor spiritual. It must be for the entire creation . . . Incarnational Christology says that God wants all of nature, human beings and all other entities, to enjoy well-being in body and spirit. Incarnational Christology, then, expands the ministry and death of Jesus, the model for Christians of "God with us" to envelop the entire universe.[18]

What McFague is speaking about is an incarnational inclusivity, that starts with the big bang and explodes the incarnated limits of God to include all matter, humanity, and all beings, to the limits of the universe. Incarnation is the initial grace of creation, made present in a specific time and place, but expanded exponentially by the death and the resurrection of Christ and through the outpouring of the Spirit. McFague continues: "An ecological Christology means that God is with us—we are dealing with the power and love of the universe; it means that God is with us—on our side, desiring justice and health and fulfillment for you, all people and all other life forms, but especially those who do not have justice, health, and fulfillment."[19]

God with us has been immanently present to the entirety of creation from the very beginning. God's agency of the Spirit results in the incarnation, and in the incarnation, God added a novelty to the creative process of some 15 billion years and gave it an incarnational direction. God so loved the universe that God became material, taking on embodiment (Jn 1:14 and 3:16). Christians have narrowly limited their understanding of world to humanity. However, the Greek cosmos was originally understood as the created order of the world. If cosmos in John 3:16 is understood not as the human world but as the entire universe, it includes the material universe, humanity, and life. Thus, the incarnation became a realization of God's self-bestowal of divine love and life not only to humanity but also to all biological life. God has transformed humanity by partaking of human nature, and we become participants in divine nature of Christ. God is embodied within creation so that creation may be brought into union with God. Thus, God's incarnation is related to creation and is immanent and fully present within it. God's incarnation remains a sublime symbol of the self-transcendence of the evolving universe into God's fullness and God's gracious and loving communication to the universe.[20] McFague rightly connects an ecological Christology to justice and the well-being of both human and other kinds of life.

Theologians such as Duncan Reid, Denis Edwards, Neil Darragh, and Niels Gregersen have creatively embedded eco-Christology in a deep incarnational model.[21] All three theologians comprehend the meaning of the incarnation, the word becoming flesh, is not restricted to human beings alone. Denis Edwards writes,

> The flesh that is embraced by God is not limited to the human. It includes the whole interconnected world of fleshy life and, in some ways, the whole universe to which flesh is related and on which it depends.[22]

God taking flesh in Christ has salvific significance beyond humanity to include the whole world of interrelated organisms. God's incarnation includes not only Jesus but also the web of interconnected life starting from the first moment of biological life on the Earth. God has embraced the whole universe of interconnected life and material existence through Christ and the agency of the Holy Spirit. In fact, God's incarnation brings incarnational change to all flesh, all biological life. New Zealand theologian Neil Darragh comments on consequences of "the Word becoming flesh" to biosphere, the web of interrelated ecological relationships that make up the Earth:

> To say that God became flesh is not only to say that God became human but to say also that God became an Earth creature, that God became a sentient being, that God became a living being, that God became a complex Earth unit of minerals and fluids, and that God became an item in the carbon and nitrogen cycles.[23]

The incarnated Christ became a part of the Earth's ecosystem. God's incarnation became a deep incarnation into the fleshy tissue of biological life on the Earth, to include human bodies but all the bodies of other creatures and plants themselves, and is now evolving within creation in a radically new way. God becomes incarnated from microscopic level to the macrobiosphere of the Earth. God communicates God's divine life to all flesh. This conforms with early Christian and orthodox theologies of divinization that "God became human so humanity can become divine."[24] God's incarnation finds its dramatic apex in the death and resurrection of Jesus, producing a profound change in direction in the material universe wherein material and spiritual agency are interconnected within a divine matrix of green grace.

Mark Wallace adds a provocative dimension to a Spirit Christology by drawing a parallel between God's self-communication of green grace through the incarnated Christ and the carnal Holy Spirit. He elaborates on the linkage:

> God incarnated Godself both in Jesus and in the Spirit—both as human and non-human animal life-forms. The full implications of this realization can be only imagined as Christianity broadens the circle of God's identity and compassion to include not only the human sphere but also the wider expanse of non-human living beings. In becoming all things—human and nonhuman—the biblical witness testifies to us that God eagerly desires the health and vitality of the whole created order, not just the human sphere.[25]

For Wallace, Jesus and the Spirit are interconnected as two "carnal expressions of God." They are interconnected in suffering and death: "The crucified Jesus and the cruciform Spirit are bound together in common affliction."[26] They both take on together the pain and bruises of suffering life, whereas Jesus suffered on the cross for the sins of the world, the Spirit suffers in the cruciform of the suffering Earth for the sins for human complicity in the degradation of the Earth. Although I am personally attracted to Wallace's dual carnal expressions of God in the world, the redemptive work of Christ and the Holy Spirit are even more integrally interconnected as the one expression of God's communication of green or life-sustaining grace. God incarnates Godself in Christ while the Holy Spirit ensouls herself or greens herself in humanity and creation.

What Wallace maintains is that the Spirit manifests herself carnally in the four elements—earth, air, fire, and water.[27] The Spirit ensouls herself with divine grace and sustaining life and creative love in human and non-human life, material reality of the universe.

GREEN INCARNATIONAL INCLUSIVITIES

"The Green Christ of Breton Cavalry" painted by French Paul Gauguin in 1989 depicts the women at the cross taking the body of Jesus down. The painting is embedded in the wild Breton landscape, Christ's body is green, prophetically signifying that his death was green—bringing life to all. I have found this painting profoundly symbolic with a human Christ within a "this-worldly" landscape. The Green Christ is interwoven with the Breton landscape, and his green coloring signifies growth and life. Women and the Earth herself accept the murdered and ravaged body of Christ. For me, Gauguin's Green Christ incorporates the multiple levels of McDaniel's notion of green grace, and it highlights Christ's death for healing and life—with a clear assertion that the cross of death is transformed into the tree of life.

The death of Jesus was a violent action, brutal and cruel death, and his death became life-giving and, in fact, inviting Christians to become peacemakers rather than warmongers and becoming loving people rather than hatemongers.[28] Thus, the cross of Jesus reveals God's identification with creation in all its complexity, struggles, sufferings, and pain. God's Spirit is with all forms of life in their suffering limitations—the cattle slain for our barbeques, the child that dies of hunger, extinction of a million species, and the gay teenager who in desperation from bullying commits suicide because he or she cannot find anyone to say it's okay to be who you are.

The Danish theologian Niels Gregersen speaks of God's coliving with all creatures that face suffering and death:

> The incarnation of God in Christ can be understood as a radical or deep incarnation, that is, an incarnation into the very tissue of biological existence, and system of nature. Understood this way, the death of Christ became an icon of God's redemptive co-suffering with all sentient life as well as with the victims of social competition. God bears the cost of evolution, the price involved in the hardship of natural selection.[29]

But the resurrection of Christ signifies that salvation is neither solely human nor merely spiritual—it must be for the entire creation of fleshly life and even all the material universe. Evolutionary theologian John Haught affirms:

> An evolutionary theology, I would suggest, may picture God's descent as entering into the deepest layers of the evolutionary process, embracing and suffering along with the entire cosmic story, not just the recent human chapters. Through the liberating power of the Spirit, God's compassion extends across the totality of time and space, enfolding and finally healing not only human suffering, but also all the epochs of evolutionary travail that preceded, and were indispensable to our own experience.[30]

The whole of cosmic history—the story of the universe, the evolution of life, and the story of humanity and the creatures that inhabit the Earth are embraced by God's redeeming love so that the whole of creation will participate in the resurrection of Jesus, God's Christ.

We are redeemed not because of Jesus' death but despite his death. Despite the murderous and evil act of crucifixion of God's Christ, God transforms what is evil and horrific in the cross into something blessed. God brings new life, freedom, and healing to the dead wood of the cross by transforming the dead wood into the tree of life. God brings new life, hope, and grace by greening the cross and the death of Jesus. The risen Christ invites us to choose life and to be for life as God is for all life. The God of life created the universe, sent the Christ so that we might have life, and the Holy Spirit to be companion to all life in its redemptive journey to God's salvation for all.

Denis Edwards claims that in Eastern Orthodox theology where God became human so that we might become divine, the resurrection of Jesus holds the inclusive promise of salvation and transformation for all creation:

> Salvation occurs because God takes humanity and the whole of creation to God's self in incarnation. The incarnation culminates in the death and resurrection of Christ, and these events promise final fulfillment. The resurrection transforms humanity and creation from within. . . . Because God embraces creaturely life in the incarnation, and above all in its culmination in resurrection, creaturely life is changed forever. Human beings and in some way the whole of creation are taken up into God. The resurrection of Christ is the beginning of this adoption and divinizing transformation of all things.[31]

In raising the crucified Jesus, God's Spirit divinizes and transfigures the creaturely humanity of Jesus, and this event is an event for the whole of creation. The resurrection of Jesus Christ is a transforming event where God's Spirit not only raises Jesus from the dead but also adopts the physical matter and begins the divinization process of humanity, all living creatures, and universe. Anglican bishop and biblical scholar Tom Wright sums up the early Christian view of transformation: "They believed that God was going to do for the whole cosmos what God had done for Jesus at Easter."[32] In other words, Christ is the pledge and beginning of the perfect fulfillment of the world—Jesus risen from the dead is the representative of the cosmos yet to be perfected—the beginning of the transformation of all things in God.

Roman Catholic theologian Karl Rahner understands Christ's resurrection as the beginning of universal deification: he writes that resurrection is "the embryonically final beginning of the glorification and divinization of the whole of reality."[33] God for us is resurrection love that breaks into the universe and continues to become sustainable within the universe and all life as the Spirit immerses herself into material reality. In other words, resurrection love means that God's incarnation becomes embodied in all matter and life, and God's incarnation is further expressed in the outpouring of the Spirit into life as divine presence and agency. Jürgen Moltmann speaks of God's Spirit as the "unspeakable closeness of God in creation."[34] This closeness means not a God for us, but a God for all—to envelop the entire universe with abundant green grace. The resurrected incarnation is at work, expanding and active through the Spirit in the physical universe. The Holy Spirit is the green face of God in the universe, and together with Christ's incarnation, the Spirit greens the universe.

EASTER: GRACEFULLY GREENING THE GARDEN

In one of the beautiful scenes of mistaken identity, Mary Magdalene's epiphany deepens into a Christophany of the risen Christ. Jesus says to her, "Woman, why are you weeping? Who are you looking for?" She mistakes the risen Jesus as the gardener that Easter morning. Mistaken identity in appearance narratives is found in Luke's account of the disciples on the road to Emmaus (Lk 24) and the extracanonical Johannine chapter 21 where the disciples fishing only recognize the risen Christ when he tells them to cast their nets and were unable to haul in the fish because they were too numerous.

Supposing that the risen Jesus is the gardener, Magdalene pleads, "Sir if you have carried him away, tell me where you have laid him, and I will take him away." What if in her misperception of the garden Christophany of the risen Christ, Mary spoke prophetically that the risen Jesus is indeed the gardener? Eco-theologian Edward Echlin writes, "Mary's initially mistaking Jesus for the gardener is profound irony with many connotations. Jesus in fact is the Gardener, the New Adam, as the open side on the cross intimates, Master of the garden earth, the One in whom, with whom, and under whom all human gardeners garden."[35]

Jesus appears to her in the garden, symbolic of Eden restored to a new fullness and the cosmos coming to life fully within God. She recognizes the gardener as her teacher only when he calls her by name. She is the disciple that Jesus predicts in John 16:20 who will "weep and mourn" and have pain turned into joy. Her inclination is to touch or to cling onto Christ. She holds onto Jesus but Jesus tells her that she cannot continue to hold this way as his resurrection transformation is not completed until his body becomes transformed from one plane of existence into the entire ecosystem. The Jesuit mystic and poet, Teilhard de Chardin. comprehended grace as the seed of resurrection.[36] The resurrection of Jesus is not only the radical transformation of the crucified Christ, but also the "green" transformation of all things in God. All things become interconnected through the risen Christ as he is the vine connected to the branches (Jn 15:1–5) and God is the vine-grower. This strengthens the irony of the mistaken identity of Jesus as the gardener. The risen Christ now assumes the divine position of vine-grower and the vine, and the resurrected Christ now permeates all the universe through the Spirit.

Easter is the final green event, a transfiguration of all things—an incarnational ripening and greening of human life and the cosmos. But the Johannine resurrection narrative is connected to the bestowal of the Spirit in the upper room that Easter evening. The metaphors of the garden and gardening communicate life transformation, new growth—fragrant smells, and exuberant colors. God loves to create gardens, and the resurrection garden is not far from Golgotha, the place of death and execution. God transforms the cross into a resurrection garden. For John's community, there was no doubt that what God was doing for the whole cosmos and humanity had been done to Jesus in the dark hours before Easter dawn. In other words, gardening is a resurrection activity of God's Spirit, for what God did to Jesus that Easter morning, God has been doing from the beginning—saving and bringing and sustaining life from death. God calls Jesus back into God's life to green the world. Mark Wallace with his ecological pneumatology notes that the Spirit is named the "Lord, Giver of Life," who encompasses a biocentric role as the power of healing and renewal within all creation. He writes:

> Could it be that the most compelling response to the threat of ecocide lies in a recovery of the Holy Spirit as a natural living being who dwells and sustains all life-forms? Could it be that an earth-centered re-envisioning of the Spirit as the green face of God the world is the best grounds for hope and renewal at a point of human history when our rapacious appetites seemed destined to destroy the earth?[37]

Wallace's notion of the Holy Spirit as "the green face of God" comprehends the incarnational inclusivity of the green Christ and the ongoing green work of the Spirit in the traditional notions of the two hands of God active in the world. Just as God incarnated in the human flesh of Jesus as life-giving green grace, so God continues to be enfleshed through the Spirit in life on earth.

Magdalene and the other disciples were called to follow in the steps of the gardening Christ. They were invited to participate in the important job of cocreating, coparticipating, and coliving with the Spirit in giving life to the garden and bringing that garden to the fullness where God intends. MCC at the Valley gardeners have jack-hammered the asphalt in the back of the church to create a meditation garden while allowing rain waters into the water table and not run off into the Los Angeles drainage system into the oceans. Water is precious in this semiarid climate of the city. But our gardening reminds us that God loves and creates gardens and reminds us of responsibilities to Earth ministry and care.

But our garden, the Earth, is dying, and human beings are responsible for killing the garden. All resources are required to heal, nurture, cultivate, and restore health to God's garden. Humanity in its drive for overconsumption and reckless disregard for long-term consequences of carbon emissions to the atmosphere have impacted our fragile ecosystems with global warming. There are fore-signs with shifting weather patterns, oceans warming and coral reefs dying, intense storms and floods, and rapid melting of the polar ice cap. In watching the ABC graphic novel *Earth 2100*, my congregation was horrified by the possibilities of billions of climate refugees with sea level rising 7 1/2 meters above current sea levels if we do not change our overconsumption of fossil fuels, develop alternative green technologies for power, and modify our lifestyles. Our church became one of the totally green churches in Los Angeles, with enough solar panels to cover more than our energy needs, an active recycling program, a green model to other faith communities, a pet friendly and welcoming church, and activist community for saving the Earth.

We are called to heal the wounds of the Earth—making amends for our sins of consumptive greed, rapacious appetites, and ecclesial heads in the sands. It starts with a personal conversion that began on Easter Sunday when Christ appeared to Magdalene in the Garden and invited us to the mission of gardening the Earth. Resurrection is about gardening the Earth and nurturing life on the Earth for God. Resurrection inclusivity is released into creation and life through the raising up of the green Christ and the release of ongoing incarnational green grace within life itself through the spirit. God's green grace is fully enfleshed in life, and God's green face is the ever-present and enfleshing Spirit. The Spirit is alive wherever human beings and faith communities bring healing and sustainability to the web of life on the Earth.

I appropriately end with an insight from Jürgen Moltmann about the Spirit: "So experience of the life-giving Spirit in the faith of the heart and the sociality of love leads beyond the limits of the church to the rediscovery of the same Spirit in nature, in plants, in animals, and in the ecosystems of the earth."[38] Incarnational inclusivity and spiritual enfleshment are for a single flow of green grace of love and life (*viriditas*) from the threefold community of divine love that reaches out to extend abundant life and unending love to all. It is the greening power—the life energy or force deeply embedded in the Earth that allows life to grow and flourish. And it is this green grace that Christians need to cultivate to participate in a healthy relationship within the Earth community.

NOTES

1. Matthew Fox, *The Coming of the Cosmic Christ* (San Francisco: Harper & Row, 1988), 144.

2. I responded: "Your theology is flawed. Ecology, in fact, is at the heart of Christian faith, starting with creation, enfleshed in the Incarnation, and culminating in the resurrection that impacts all the universe."

3. Synder and Scandrett maintain the Christian separation of heaven from the Earth has contributed to the ecology of sin. Howard A. Synder and Joel Scandrett, *Salvation Means Creation Healed: The Ecology of Sin and Grace* (Eugene, OR: Cascade Books, 2011).

4. ABC's Graphic Novel, Earth 2100. Global Warming Effects. Part 1 on YouTube. (All 9 parts are on YouTube). http://www.youtube.com/watch?v=bjmWivCTcvE.

5. Daniel Maguire, *The Moral Core of Judaism and Christianity: Reclaiming the Revolution* (Philadelphia: Fortress Press, 1993), 13.

6. Lynn White, Jr., "The Historical Roots of Our Ecological Crisis," http://www.earth talktoday.tv/earthtalk-voices/historical-roots-ecological-crisis.html.

7. Ralph Del Colle, *Christ and Spirit: Spirit-Christology in Trinitarian Perspective* (New York: Oxford University Press, 1994), 8–29.

8. A good explanation of tonglen practice, see: http://www.naljorprisondharmaservice. org/pdf/Tonglen.htm.

9. See: California Interfaith and Power: http://interfaithpower.org/ CIPL and its IPL (Interfaith Power and Light) provide practical resources for assisting congregations to go green and educate congregants. For those communities of faith that want to move into advocacy, they provide opportunities for writing and lobbying politicians.

10. Jay B. McDaniel, *With Roots and Wings: Christianity in an Age of Ecology and Dialogue* (Maryknoll, NY: Orbis Books, 1995), 44.

11. Ibid., 53.

12. Mark I. Wallace, *Green Christianity: Five Ways to A Sustainable Future* (Minneapolis: Fortress Press, 2010), 38.

13. Hildegard, Scivias, 2.6.26.147.

14. Veli-Matti Kärkkäinen, *Pneumatology: The Holy Spirit in Ecumenical, International, and Contextual Perspective* (Grand Rapids, MI: Baker Academic, 2002), 51.

15. Ambrose, *The Holy Spirit*, 2.5.41 (FC: 44:110).

16. Elisabeth Schüssler-Fiorenza, *Jesus: Miriam's Child, Sophia's Prophet* (New York: Continuum, 1994). Elizabeth Johnson, *She Who Is: The Mystery of God in Feminist Theological Discourse* (New York: Continuum, 1992).

17. Roger Haight, *Jesus Symbol of God* (Maryknoll, NY: Orbis Books, 1999). Jacques Dupuis, *Who Do You Say I Am?* (Maryknoll, NY: Orbis Books, 2002); *Toward a Christian Theology of Religious Pluralism* (Maryknoll, NY: Orbis Books, 2006). (I would also point out that Dupuis also develops elements of a Wisdom Christology.)

18. Sallie McFague, "An Ecological Christology: Does Christianity Have It?," in *Christianity and Ecology: Seeking the Well-Being of Earth and Humans,* ed. Dieter T. Hessel and Rosemary Radford Ruether (Cambridge, MA: Harvard University Press, 2000), 37–38.

19. Ibid., 34.

20. Karl Rahner, "Dogmatic Questions on Easter," *Theological Investigations,* vol. 4, (New York: Seabury, 1966), 126–28; "Christ Within an Evolutionary View of the World," *Theological Investigations,* vol. 5 (New York: Seabury, 1966), 157–203.

21. Denis Edwards, *Ecology at the Heart of Faith: The Change of Heart that Leads to a New Way of Living on the Earth* (Maryknoll, NY: Orbis Books, 2007). Neil Darraugh, *At Home in the Earth, Auckland* (Auckland, NZ: Ascent Publications, 2000); Niels Hendrik Gregersen, "The Cross of Christ in an Evolutionary World," *Dialog: A Journal of Theology* 40 (2001): 197–207. Duncan Reid, "Enfleshing the Human," in *Earth Healing: Ecology and Christian Theology*, ed. Denis Edwards (Collegeville, PA: Liturgical Press, 2001), 69–83.

22. Denis Edwards, *Ecology at the Heart of Faith*, 58.

23. Darraugh, *At Home in the Earth*, 124.

24. Ireneaus, Adversus haereses, book 5, preface. Athanasius also affirmed this notion of divine filiation, the transformation of human nature by God's grace in the incarnation: Archibald Robertson, ed. *Select Writings and Letters of Athanasius, Bishop of Alexandria.* Nicene and Post-Nicene Fathers, Second Series, volume IV. 1891. Reprinted by Grand Rapids, MI: Wm. B. Eerdmans Publishing Company, 1957, 65.

25. Wallace, *Green Christianity*, 44.

26. Ibid., 45.

27. Ibid., 39–41.

28. Rita Nakashima Brock and Rebecca Ann Parker, *Saving Paradise: How Christianity Traded Love of This World for Crucifixion and Empire* (Boston: Beacon Press, 2008), 254–307.

29. Niels Hendrik Gregersen, "The Cross of Christ in an Evolutionary World," 205.

30. John Haught, *Christianity and Science: Towards a Theology of Nature* (Maryknoll, NY: Orbis Books, 2007), 92.

31. Denis Edwards, *How God Acts: Creation, Redemption, and Special Divine Action* (Minneapolis: Fortress Press, 2010), 97.

32. N. T. Wright, *Surprised by Hope* (London: SPCK, 2004), 104.

33. Karl Rahner, "Dogmatic Questions on Easter," 129.

34. Jürgen Moltmann, *The Spirit of Life: An Universal Affirmation* (Minneapolis: Augsberg-Fortress Press, 1992), 12.

35. Edward P. Echlin, *The Cosmic Circle: Jesus and Ecology* (Dublin: Columba Press, 2004), 125–26.

36. Teilhard De Chardin. "Cosmic Life," in *Prayer of the Universe* (London: Collins, 1977), 82.

37. Mark Wallace, *Fragments of the Spirit: Nature, Violence, and the Renewal of Creation* (New York: Continuum, 1996), 4.

38. Jürgen Moltmann, *The Spirit of Life*, 9–10.

4

The Transgendered Christ

Megan More

Throughout my life, I have been searching for a religious community, a church home, where I could feel free in my own self-awareness and understanding of who I was. Throughout my youth and young adulthood, this was seriously lacking. I always felt at odds, not with God or Christ, but in the doctrines of churches which were exclusive and limiting in who they felt worthy or acceptable within their church families and walls. If you didn't fit their standards of piety or behavior, or mold yourself to their image of what was proper or normal, you couldn't belong. I rebelled against this concept, always believing in my heart that this was not Jesus' way, and that God created each of our souls as intended for a purpose and worthy of God's love, no matter how diverse we are.

My own personal journey in both my faith and social life has been fraught with many stumbling blocks, some of which were of my own making in an effort to conform to the wishes of others, who I later discovered didn't have the same concern for my social, emotional, or spiritual welfare. It was in my great effort to preserve what I had, and thought I loved, and loved me, is what led to my own epiphany. I learned that if you can't be honest with yourself, and honestly love who and what you are, you can never make another person truly happy. This awareness of life was a major renewal of my love of God and Christ, and an increased awareness of Christ's role for all of humanity, and especially the transgendered individuals around the world. For Christ to truly be all things for all people, especially in the resurrection, that ideal of the transformation, that all encompassing completeness in both the physical form as well as the spiritual, was necessary.

After many years of searching, and much spiritual and personal growth, I discovered the Metropolitan Community Church in the Valley. Ironically, when I was going through some of my darkest times of self-discovery, this church was only a short walk away, and I never knew it. When I finally did walk through those doors in the fall of 2006, I discovered something profound in a church. I discovered what real inclusive love in a church community, through Christ, really was. This was a church body that didn't just claim to be Christians. This was a church body that were Christians, displaying a level of love that welcomed the stranger, regardless of how different that stranger might be, with Christ's inclusive love. Here also was God's table, the Eucharist, offered every Sunday, but here it was not limited to members, or the baptized, or even the believers and pious, but to everybody, without limits or restrictions. Here it was truly presented as God's meal, God's gift, and something that no church or faith or dogmas has the right to own or control. Never in my life had I encountered a church that felt like home, until that Sunday. While that has not changed, it has profoundly changed me.

Seeing Christ as the whole expression of all that is human was a key factor in my eventually answering my own call to ministry, and seeking to awaken others like myself to the inclusive image of a transgendered Christ. It is in that fullness of completion of humanity, both male and female, man and woman, in body and spirit, that I understood my own part in life. We are a part of God, no matter who we are or what we are. That divine spark which is our soul is that connection to our creator, who is all things and everything at once. As such, our spirits, created in God's image, must also be all things and everything at once, and that includes all sexes and gender expressions. To be just male or just female is to limit the spirit and to deny a full half of who we are in God. As Susannah Cornwall states, "This is particularly interesting in thinking through visions of a society where sex and gender do not work as a binary but rather as a continuum or a multiplicity, and where anatomy (particularly genital anatomy) is not unproblematically used as a cipher for identity."[1] The very image of gender linked with the completeness of spirit must consider gender expression not as a static binary, but as a total vision of our spiritual selves. Jesus showed us this in the resurrection, in his very transformation. That understanding has driven me to my own mission in life.

My experience in discovering a more inclusive Christ, a transgendered Christ, provided me with the means to more fully explore my own faith journey and religious awareness, which has led me through seminary and the realization that I have a voice that needs to be heard, and a story worthy of being told. My understanding and relationship with God and Christ in my life, and being transgendered, which is something I began discovering at a very young age, has also helped shape an image of a very inclusive Christ, in a very special relationship not only with his disciples, but also with all of humankind through both the flesh and the spirit. The following is a result of that discovery.

THE BIRTH OF JESUS

In our more modern world, as the greater diversity of humankind is coming of age and increased awareness, more expansive and enlightened viewpoints of Jesus needs to be addressed. This more radical, but pragmatic understanding of a more expansive Jesus looks into all elements of God as well. Looking at scripture from a less dogmatic or patriarchal perspective, Jesus is seen not as the quintessential male image in human form of a dominant male God, but of a Jesus who is the true child of a complete and unlimited God, thus being equally unlimited in all expressions of the spirit as well as sexual and gender expression.

But in a newer look at Jesus, something else must be addressed. Statistically, the world's population in any culture will be composed approximately one half by women, and yet throughout most of history, women are either absent from the written record, only marginally mentioned when absolutely necessary, and even then, often denigrated or diminished in their capacity relating to world events. Seldom are women given the full recognition of their achievements in history. In scripture, this is clearly seen when women in the Old Testament are given marginal roles or even deprived of names. In the New Testament, early church writers have also, with some great success, removed women from prominent positions in the early church. It is this "silence of scripture," as explained in some depth by Elisabeth Schüssler-Fiorenza[2] that begs the question of the contributions in all of history by women, and what is missing from the patriarchalization of the written records. While this systematic silence regarding the historical and religions contributions of women has been major, there is another segment of the population that has been totally ignored until recently, even though their mention in scripture has always been with favor: the transgendered element of society.

The birth of Jesus has always presented questions for both religion and science to reconcile. With Mary being "impregnated" by the Holy Spirit, which Christian tradition reflects as feminine, Jesus is born with no male interaction,[3] giving question to the chromosomal nature of Mary as intersexed, born with a female body but with XY chromosomes enabling her to reproduce without outside male influence. This could also account for Jesus' apparent transgendered nature, since Mary could have been born of a genetic and chromosomal anomaly with elements passed on to her son. While this condition is very rare, testicular feminization syndrome (TFS) is not unknown in current medical science. Virginia Ramey Mollenkott considers this in *Omnigender*, and therefore also presents the idea that Mary, and consequently Jesus, were both intersexed. Because of TFS, Mary could have been an XY female, with the Y factors feminized resulting in her total appearance being female. While this condition would have made Mary intersexed, it does not necessarily presume this condition would also fall in Jesus. Even with the anomaly of his mother, Jesus would still have been born XY, displaying all the physical attributes of a male. Nevertheless, this also does not negate the assumption that in Virginia Mollenkott's book *Omnigender*, she cites Edward Kessel's[4] suggestion that since Jesus would also have been born without any male influence in the egg, he would have to have been born female, and needed to transform physically into male after birth. Kessel argues for the concept of parthenogenesis, but this condition is only known in lower animal life forms, and not as yet in humans, even though it could be possible. Either that, or Jesus could have been born intersexed, possibly even with TFS, and it went undetected in his childhood. Whether Jesus was intersexed, transgendered, or both, all of Jesus' earthly life clearly demonstrated this blend of the masculine in form and the feminine in behavior.

Even though Mary's conception and pregnancy can be explained through science and medicine, this does not detract from the miracle. The very rarity of this condition which resulted in Jesus is miracle enough, but when coupled with the man Jesus was to become and the impact he would have on all of humanity, the divine was surely present in this birth.

Jesus of Nazareth is the perfect embodiment of God's image of humankind, in total and complete communion with God's divine will and vision. By this, Jesus does not equate with the traditional concept of the son of God who was seen as both a king and a warrior, but rather the true image of God in humankind, being of all genders and sexes, presenting the feminine as well as the masculine in one body, and all variations in between. This presents Jesus as transgendered, or polygendered, since all gender expressions are known in the image of God. Jesus is the Logos of God in the spirit, incarnate in human form. As human, Jesus was therefore in intimate understanding of God in all of God's variations. As for the divinity of Christ, the Spirit of God was infused in Jesus, forming a bond of human and divine, and through God's power did Jesus perform the wonders credited to him. In his ministry, Jesus, as part of God's vision, was here to show humankind how to live within the Word of God, and not just by the words of law, knowing that in his direct defiance of the church and state, such a ministry could cost him his life.

Through God, Jesus was also given power over men and men's minds, to heal and work miracles, and through these acts, to let people know that surely it was God who spoke through Jesus and worked in God's name and with God's blessing.

MINISTRY OF JESUS

It is through the life lessons and parables that Jesus revealed, first to his followers and then to all of humankind, how we should live our lives in relationship with God, and through God, with all of humankind and creation. In that example of Jesus' life, the tools for conquering sin and needless suffering are presented to us. Forgiveness of ourselves and others helps us cleanse our own souls, as well as the concept of doing no harm to others. Ultimately, when we treat others with the same dignity and compassion and love we in turn would desire, evil itself is driven out into the abyss. But that compassion and love must be freely given to everybody. "Love your neighbor as yourself" does not have a qualifier after it. Jesus does not say "love your neighbor as yourself as long as they look just like you," or have the same income bracket, or dress a certain way, or have a particular political philosophy. Even Jesus freely went among the marginalized, the poor, the helpless, the crippled and sick, and all those whom the powerful and the church and the Roman state had rejected. These people were Jesus' flock, the ones whom he loved most, and the ones who loved him back without conditions. In this ministry, Jesus even broke with every tradition, even in the rejection of all traditional male models of behavior and custom, all in an effort to show that the love of humankind carried more weight than the letter of the law. This is what it means to be a Christian. Here, Jesus even assumes the role of female and servant by this act of humility and feet washing. Such an action was not that of a Jewish male to perform under any circumstances, but relegated to that of a woman, or a slave. His actions demonstrate his breaking with gender normative behavior, whether it was willingly engaging in an action or a behavior that was strictly for women, or in his rejection of a normal, acceptable Jewish male lifestyle.

In *Putting Jesus in His Place*, Halvor Moxnes describes Jesus as an ascetic, engaged in a lifestyle that defied the social norm of the day for both Jews and Romans, and challenged a new way of thinking. He was living outside of the male paradigm as defined by the social normative and expanding the notion of what it meant to be male, or female, or both. Moxnes also goes on to give some justification that Jesus' statement in Matthew 19:12, where Jesus remarks, "For there are eunuchs who have been so from birth, and there are eunuchs who have been made eunuchs by men, and there are eunuchs who have made themselves eunuchs for the sake of the kingdom of heaven. He who is able to receive this, let him receive it." (RSV) was in reference to himself and his disciples, who had voluntarily become eunuchs for the sake of the kingdom of God, meaning they had voluntarily rejected the standard, dominant male lifestyle for one without sex, rather devoting their whole lives to God. In this manner, Jesus is also taking the word eunuch and claiming it as his own, removing any derogatory sting from the term. Whether Jesus was in fact intersexed, or an eunuch by birth or choice, the fact remains that his rejection of the recognized dominant male role in his day was clearly apparent. Tertullian, a third-century writer, also makes claim that Jesus was *spado*, the Latin term for eunuch, in which Tertullian uses to mean both by choice and by birth in the case of Jesus.[5]

It was in this kind of behavior that Jesus was showing us God's grace in order to help drive us forward to do good works in Christ's name. Through those good works, and in doing Christ's work on earth, grace and salvation was and is present among us. But this is a constant behavior, living our lives in Christ daily, monthly, and yearly. It is essential to live in and through Christ all day, and every day, for salvation and grace demands this of us.

In this transgendered nature of Jesus' life, there is also the question of his love relations for his beloved disciple, as well as his relationship with Mary Magdalene. Although the beloved disciple is not directly named (but could possibly be John, Thomas the twin, or even Lazarus), the intimate, almost sensual and sexual indicators by using the term "beloved" leave open questions to the free expression of Jesus' physical love. There is also the question of the youth who is present when Jesus is taken in the Garden of Gethsemane, who flees while leaving his robes behind, which is possibly an analogy to his body falling as he dies in the flesh,[6] and then appears again as the pure angelic youth in the tomb to announce that the Christ Jesus is not present. Could this youth be that beloved disciple? We already know from Luke that the term disciple extended well past the original twelve when Luke speaks of the two, one of them named Cleopas, whom Jesus meets on the road to Emmaus after his crucifixion and resurrection. This coupled with his attitude towards Mary Magdalene, whom he treats as an equal in status, gives additional weight to the feminine qualities of Jesus' character.

In addition, there is Jesus' rejection of the traditional Hebrew male role in all aspects of his life, and how Jesus defies all cultural convention. He treats women as equals, including Mary and Martha and Mary Magdalene. He calls a follower, probably male, his beloved, and faces his final fate with a woman's strength of sacrifice for her children. All of these actions provide support for the XY chromosomal nature of Mary, and the transgendered nature of Christ Jesus.[7]

In the Greco-Roman world in which Jesus grew up, custom and culture had long divided the responsibilities of males and females, men and women, into distinct groups. There was also a model of what a man should be in society and what a woman should be. As presented in Jerome Neyrey's article, *Jesus, Gender, and the Gospel of Matthew*, this division is well defined.[8] It was this clearly divided world of gender roles which Jesus also violated repeatedly in his life. It was not just his breaking with his own Hebrew traditions of the male role in community and family, but also in violation of the Greco-Roman models, when Jesus would readily assume the feminine model of behavior in society, both public and private.

This theology of Christ Jesus truly places Jesus in an intimate relationship with God, a God who transcends all aspects of the spirit in gender and sexual expression. Such a God, who is all things in all ways in creation would not be bound by any human constructs of limits. Therefore, neither would Christ Jesus be limited in spirit as the intimate reflection of God in human form. It would require Jesus to be all genders and sexes personified in that image. This would also not limit Jesus in his physical and emotional love as human, being free to openly express all aspects of this love. Thus, intersexed and transgendered by birth, polysexual by nature, Christ Jesus is the total human expression of the spirit of an infinite God. To deny this complete and unlimited nature of Christ Jesus is to also place human limits upon an infinite God, which is theologically unsound when we accept God in the infinite, and this is the core of all Judeo-Christian belief.

The human spirit has always been male and female, man and woman, but we have become polarized in our sexual gender and expressions, self-imposed by human convention, thus losing the complete nature of self. It has become an issue in culture to know what is male and what is female, and gender must express that sexual relationship. This is not how our spirits are. We are living in the spirit, and since we are living, we are an expression of God itself. Through God, in God, we are therefore all gender expressions and sexual expressions within us. When we reject one in favor of the other, when we subvert one nature to allow the domination of the other, we become a fraction of ourselves. We are no longer the complete image of God in spirit through our outward expression. It is because of this we lose our humanity, our compassion toward others, and increase our self-centered and self-serving natures. When left to our own devices, we think only of ourselves first and foremost.

It is only in the reincorporation of all elements of our spirit that we expand beyond ourselves, understanding more of our connection with God's divine nature. Accepting such a transgendered model for God is therefore essential for understanding Christ Jesus. This is also the argument presented by B. K. Hipsher in "God Is a Many Gendered Thing."[9] To limit God to just one gender and sexuality, or to limit God to only the male or man and female or woman image, is to in fact impose limits on an unlimited God. God must, by all understanding, be all things, all sexes and all genders, and likewise, so must Jesus. For humanity to progress to where we can become fully inclusive of all variations of sex and gender, and in doing so, to more fully understand and embrace God through Christ, accepting the transgendered spirit within all of us is necessary. We are, in the spirit, made in the image of God, and God is transgendered and transsexual.[10]

THE DEATH OF JESUS

Given over to outsiders, the pagan Romans, by the religious authorities, Jesus was put to death by an extremely efficient and brutal patriarchal empire, using the most painful and degrading of execution devices. Designed to prolong suffering and extreme agony, the cross not only made breathing nearly impossible, but there was also no possibility of relieving this torture because of a spike situated at the rectum which would also gouge and penetrate the victim, thus adding to the suffering and degrading humiliation. The cross was not meant for men as it were, but those the Romans had set apart from their image of what was masculine and manly.

In this manner, Jesus did die on the cross, and through the power of God, was raised up from the grave, to show humankind that in God there was both salvation from our sins and an existence with God beyond death. This was also a clear indication that God in Christ Jesus was greater than all of Rome, and the spirit was stronger than the flesh. Thus, it is in the risen Christ and the salvation and the forgiveness of our sins by God's grace that forms the cornerstone of Christian belief, and the driving force that should be behind how Christianity should be practiced. It was through this intimate connection between God and Jesus in all moments of time, in perfect response, that God was totally intimate with humankind, experiencing life through Jesus. It was through the life of Jesus the Christ that God experienced humankind in the flesh.[11]

Jesus is the example of everything in humanity that is good and positive, that ideal worth striving for. Jesus showed humanity in his brief earthly existence the pathway to God's love and grace, but also that in faith and belief in God, salvation beyond death can be achieved, and that our past and future sins were forgiven. Jesus displays this from a non-masculine, feminine perspective, rejecting what is traditionally male and what that male position and power brings.[12] Jesus openly challenges the very nature of male life at the time, voluntarily surrendering his social position for a lesser one, a station dominated by women, slaves, and eunuchs.

Viewing God as both father and mother also provides that transgendered image of God, which Jesus also demonstrates as transgendered spirit of self, male in body and female in heart and mind. It was through this feminine-based teaching of Jesus that we come to understand more of God's divine nature and infinite love as a loving parent figure, and intimate connection to all creation. As one born of only the female egg with no male sperm donor, incarnate of the power of the Holy Spirit, Jesus might have been female in chromosome, but male in outward appearance, thus being intersexed and transgendered.

By his dual nature of the masculine and feminine, Jesus clearly demonstrated in his lifestyle and behavior the equality towards both men and women, and the transgendered, intersexed nature of Jesus is clearly defined. This is compounded by his own ultimate willingness, in spite of his plea in the garden, to have this cup pass from his lips, to sacrifice himself for all humanity in a manner such as a mother sacrificing herself for her children's salvation, with quiet determination. Jesus goes to his fate with a woman's resolve knowing her actions saves what she loves most.

THE RESURRECTION

Jesus, totally in tune to God's call, that still small voice of process, was in complete harmony with God. Even when Jesus wanted to do the other, and always had the option of doing the other, he still followed God's call, even unto death. Nevertheless, Jesus was not ordained to die upon the cross. While Jesus knew this was a real possibility from his actions and ministry, being in such open defiance of the Roman State and culture, and even in opposition with the established Jewish church of the day, Jesus was not preordained to this. Jesus, as human, still had free will, even to the point of asking God to take away this cup when he was in the garden. Still, upon the resurrection, Jesus and God become one, complete, joined in flesh and spirit. It is here that God unlocks the gates of Hades and conquers death (of the spirit), raising all up with God to the heavens. It is also here that God, through the Christ, the risen Jesus, cements that mission of Love, that call to salvation in a life beyond life, and a reunion with the spirit of God.

When Christ physically leaves the tomb on the third day, reappearing on the pathway in the Garden to Mary Magdalene, he had undergone a transformation, both in spirit and in body. Even those closest to him did not recognize him until he reveals himself in full. Was Jesus now complete in body, male and female, as it always was in spirit and soul? It was Jesus, the Christ, with the spirit of God within, who was sent with a dual purpose for humanity and God. As Virginia Ramey Mollenkott[13] and Justin Tanis[14] suggest, through the new "Adam," the androgyne, who is both "Adam" and "Eve" in spirit, Jesus is showing humanity that it was necessary to reintegrate the human spirit, embracing inside the male and female and everything in between, and in the resurrection to show the new human model, or the first born in the resurrection, the total human androgyne bringing together again all aspects of sex in male and female.

How does this speak to humanity, and especially the transgendered, in salvation? In life, while Jesus seems by all biblical accounts transgendered in nature, and therefore in spirit, like all transgendered, there is still the question of the physical form, in this case male with Jesus. This struggle of self though does not seem to come into play with Jesus. Body and spirit do not seem to be in conflict in Jesus' life. But for the transgendered today, this is not much in the way of comfort beyond the understanding that scripture does not condemn those who are transgendered. It is in Jesus' resurrection that the question of salvation is addressed. Here is a vindication of the transgendered life in Christ Jesus' transformation of body. The risen Christ, the resurrected Christ, is now more than just joining of a man and a woman, but also of a male and a female, providing a restoration of wholeness in the *imago dei* within human beings. Created in the beginning in God's image, humankind was designed as a union of all gender expressions, as well as sexual expressions in the soul. Our *imago dei*, our image of God, is just that; the completeness of God's spiritual self within us. This must mean we are born man and woman, male and female, and yet still divided, only to be rejoined as complete in our own resurrection. This is our salvation in Christ and God, our reawakening of our complete nature as created.

While Jesus, in life, was transgendered in spirit, born of the spirit of God incarnate, it was in the resurrection that Jesus now becomes the transgendered or transsexual, or as Mollenkott describes it, omnigendered also in body. It is this example of life, through Jesus, of living fully in all of the spirit of God, that we see the complete nature of our own genders within us, working as one in harmony, not competing or seeking dominance over the other. In his transgendered nature, Jesus is showing us the harmony of the spirit and a way for all humankind to live. With the transformation of the resurrection, Jesus further shows us the completeness of humanity in the flesh with the spirit, being both male and female, not as intersexed, but omnigendered and omnisexed in unison. It was thus the mission of Jesus Christ to bring the transgendered nature of God back to humanity, and humanity in spirit, the total and complete transgendered spirit, back to God. It is also in this transformation of Christ Jesus in resurrection that the concept of equality of all genders and sexes is actualized in totality. Jesus showed us that neither man nor woman is above each other, but joined in equal union.

Christianity since its founding has worked hard to undo much of what Jesus has taught, by creating divisions, subjugating groups and classes, and marginalizing again those whom Jesus worked to liberate. It has been a religion of control and power, rather than healing and love. As Rev. Dr. Shore-Goss points out, "Christian theology . . . is the product of people with power and privilege, influence and wealth."[15] This dogma of power has resulted in centuries of oppression and negation of many who had needed loving access to God and Christ the most, not the least of which are transgenders. The tragedy is that this dogmatic wall has also rejected the very transgendered and transsexual nature of Christ and God, seeing God only as a male figure, stern and dominating, rather than as also the mother figure, loving and nurturing. If God is to create humankind from God's image, how could God create the feminine as well as the masculine in humanity without being both within and of God? We need to seriously reimagine God, both as mother or father, and all shades in between, as well as the nature of the human spirit. The transgender in society is nothing more than the full expression of the *imago dei* in humanity, unlocked from the binary prison of our bodily expression as dictated by society.

This very freedom must also be recognized in the truer expression of the androgyne, that original Adam in the intersexed, who not only can display that freedom of full gender expression, but also presents the union of the physical.

It is the binary human being that is not in balance with God, limited in awareness of the total image of the divine within us. Even the nature of Jesus was limited in the Hellenistic world of the first few centuries of Christianity through the theologies of Tertullian, Jerome, and Augustine. In an effort to spiritualize Jesus, they in fact neutered Jesus.[16] All sexuality in Jesus was negated, including all notions of intimate love. Jesus was no longer male or female, man or woman, but simply Jesus, pure and virginal. Even when Mary Magdalene sees Jesus in the garden on that day of resurrection, there is no reference to the nature of his transformation, of his complete union of gender and sexuality. The gospel text neutralizes this by simply saying that Mary didn't recognize him until he acknowledged her. Unless Jesus had been substantially transformed in his resurrection, how could she not have known it was him on sight? Mary loved Jesus as no other in her life. In truth, there is nothing in scripture to virginalize Jesus in life, with either men or women. His love for Magdalene is well indicated, as well as frequently mentioned remarks of his beloved disciple whom he loved. This polyamorous nature of Jesus only gives greater credence to his transgendered nature and completeness of the *imago dei* of spirit.

In life Jesus was the personification of male and female, man and woman, without being effeminate or masculine, soft or aggressive. Jesus in life showed to humankind what it meant to be a total human in spirit, even while being male in the body. All aspects of the female spirit were present in the softness and compassion of women, and with the leadership mastery of purpose as the male spirit. Jesus was the reincorporation of the first androgyne in the spirit. It is in the resurrection that Jesus then completes the spirit and body transformation, giving birth to the new Adam, total and full in the image of God.

In resurrection there is salvation. In Christ Jesus' conquest of death he showed all of humanity God's love and compassion for everybody, no matter whom or what they are, or where they live, or the life they have. Rich or poor, sinner or saint, Hebrew or Gentile, man or woman, male or female, and all variations of humankind were given both the promise of salvation in God through the life and death, and resurrection of Jesus, and God's own promise of total love. But it was that nature of resurrection, the form of Jesus himself, in rebirth as the first androgyne which speaks to the transgendered the most. This is a validation of life, and an acknowledgement of God's love through that completeness of Christ. All of humankind finds salvation through Christ and being born also in the *imago dei* (image of God), but for the transgendered, salvation is not just told to them, but it is shown to them in the resurrection of the androgyne Christ himself. In this the transgender finds that salvation is direct and personal, totally inclusive of the transgender, transsexual, and intersexed in all forms. Here Christ shows all transgenders that in resurrection, he also is fully transgendered in body and spirit.

That radical inclusiveness of Christ, both in his life, and in showing us how we should live or own, is not an easy thing for many to accomplish. Surrounded by our own barriers of protection, sheltering us from the potential harms of the world we live in, we exclude what we don't understand, both in experiences and people. This potentially can also exclude Christ from our lives as well, limiting how we understand the Gospels and the life of Jesus. For any real understanding of Jesus and his affect upon humanity to be viable, that element of total and radical inclusivity must be accepted as paramount to all Christian theology. In Christ Jesus are all things, all people, and all experiences in gender and sexual awareness. Anything less is to systematically limit Jesus, and in doing so, limit God.

As I said in the beginning, my search for Christ and a church ended when I found a place where such radical inclusive love was present, where the unconditional love of God through Christ Jesus was a lived reality, and where anybody, no matter what their gender, sex or sexual expression, ethnic background, race or abilities, or even creed, would find no barrier. This was a church home where the concept of God's table and the Eucharist was open to everybody, with the only limiting factor as their own willingness to receive. This was not an idle remark in passing, but a lived creed, a statement of faith repeated every Sunday so there was no confusion. Anybody seeking God's love in Christ Jesus walking through those doors would find a home filled with accepting love, just as anybody approaching Jesus with the desire to be saved in the spirit would discover the overflowing well of Love. The transgendered Christ is all things to all people because Jesus is total and unconditional love for all people. There can be no other explanation.

As I continue in my own ministry as transgendered clergy, it is a multi-faceted goal. It is necessary for all people to have a healthy spiritual foundation, free from doubts and prejudices, and this is what I hope to teach others who are transgendered—that they reflect image of the transgendered Christ and are an original blessing. It is also important to open the eyes and minds of those who are not transgendered, to see us for what we are without hate and fear, as children of God and reflecting the image of Christ, no less than anybody else. God is within us all, in total love.

NOTES

1. Susannah Cornwall, *Sex and Uncertainty in the Body of Christ, Intersex Conditions and Christian Theology* (Oakville, CT: Equinox Publishing, 2010), 73.

2. Elisabeth Schüssler-Fiorenza, *In Memory of Her: A Feminist Theological Reconstruction of Christian Origins* (New York: Crossroad Publishing, 2002), 41–64.

3. http://www.guardian.co.uk/science/blog/2008/dec/30/virgin-birth-mary.

4. Virginia Ramey Mollenkott, *Omnigender: A Trans-Religious Approach* (Cleveland: The Pilgrim Press, 2001), 105.

5. Halvor Moxnes, *Putting Jesus in His Place: A Radical Vision of Household and Kingdom* (Louisville, KY: Westminster John Knox Press, 2003), 84.

6. Gregory Riley attributed to lecture at Claremont School of Theology.

7. http://www.medterms.com/script/main/art.asp?articlekey=14430.

8. Jerome H. Neyrey, "Jesus, Gender, and the Gospel of Matthew," in *New Testament Masculinities*, ed. Stephen D. Moore and Janice Capel Anderson (Atlanta: Society of Biblical Literature, 2003), 49–51.

9. B. K. Hipsher, "God *Is* a Many Gendered Thing: An Aphophatic Journey to Pastoral Diversity," in *Trans/formations, Controversies in Contextual Theology Series*, ed. Lisa Isherwood and Marcella Althaus-Reid (London: SCM Press, 2009), 99.

10. Ibid., 100.

11. Jurgen Moltmann, *The Crucified God* (Minneapolis: Fortress Press, 1974), 3.

12. Moxnes, *Putting Jesus in His Place*, 73.

13. Mollenkott, *Omnigender*.

14. Justin Tanis, *Trans-Gendered, Theology Ministry and Communities of Faith* (Cleveland: The Pilgrim Press, 2003).

15. Robert E. Goss, *Jesus ACTED UP: A Gay and Lesbian Manifesto* (San Francisco: HarperCollins, 1993), 61.

16. Ibid., 64–65.

5

The Holy Spirit as Mischief-Maker

Robert E. Shore-Goss

People are paying attention to the spiritual dimension of their lives and often seem to experience the Spirit in ways and places that often challenge traditional theologies and Church structures and sometimes have little connection with traditional religious practice. The Spirit is present and active beyond the official structures and ordained ministries of the Church.

—John R. Sachs[1]

The Holy Spirit is part of God's communication in the universe; the Holy Spirit is God's agency in and through the evolution of universe from the very inception of the big bang until now into the future. The Spirit is the most underdeveloped theologically, and most theological conversations and explorations through history have always been focused on the perichoretic Triune being of God. When Christians talk about the conception of Christ as God Incarnate, the Spirit was involved. When Christ was raised from the dead, the Spirit was active in the resurrection. Often, the Spirit is comprehended as an extension of Christ, creating the possibility to hear and receive the Word. Yet the Spirit is present at creation and remains intimately present as God, active in the world of material universe and in all life.

There are no central doctrinal topics of Christian faith that do not include the presence and activity of the Spirit. God, Christ, Trinity, sanctification, grace, salvation, the evolution of life, personal transformation, and prayer; the Spirit is everywhere in Christian theologies, yet the Spirit is the most underdeveloped theologically. Gregory of Nazianzus speaks of the Holy Spirit as *theos agraptos* ("the unwritten of God"), or Veli-Matti Kärkkäinen speaks of the Holy Spirit as the "Cinderella of Theology" and "pneumatological deficit."[2] I suggest a possible hypothesis: The reason for its underdeveloped theology of the Holy Spirit is because it is a dangerous theology, full of novelty, mischief, laughter, creativity, and marginality.[3] The Spirit troubles theologically and ecclesially since the Spirit continues to reveal the wildly gracious nature of God. A second reason is that we cannot speak about the Spirit without talking about Christ and other people's responses because the Spirit is thoroughly relational. Human existence, as well as all life, is a story of grace, and we are born into a world of grace, God's self communication of love to every human. The language of the Spirit has a grammar of spirituality, making possible an interplay between human and divine, between creation and fulfillment, between Good Friday and Easter, between Easter and the fulfillment of resurrection in the entire universe. Language and reflection about the Spirit must focus on human experience of the Spirit, but experience of the Spirit is not sufficient since it needs to be tested and examined to discern that it is the Spirit, not yourself.

When I look at the particular moments of in-between or transitions in my life, I have discerned the presence of the Holy Spirit. Traditionally, one of the gifts of the Holy Spirit is discernment, the ability in prayer to discern the origin and motions of graces or divine communication in prayer. Discernment has been the gift often relegated to conversations between spiritual mentors and their companions. It is, however, where I first encountered God's gracious wildness in the story of Jesus, in personal prayer and between experiences in my own life. Reflectively, I can look back over the decades of my spiritual journey from entrance into the Jesuit community, ordained as a Catholic priest, falling in love with another Jesuit and leaving the Society of Jesus, becoming a Bodhisattva Christian, my involvement in the LGBTQ community, my doctoral dissertation on the mad saint movement and the Tibetan saint Milarepa, transferring into MCC, my theological writings, and returning to the priestly vocation as Pastor of a Church Alive MCC in the Valley, falling in love again, and becoming a queer and green activist.[4] These are many discrete moments of in-between, and the Spirit provides a bridge for comprehending the many in-between moments as a continuous flow of loving grace.

I can hear one of my former Jesuit spiritual mentors stressing that God always works within the Church and citing Ignatius of Loyola's principles of "thinking with the Church." I always thought these rules were precipitated by the Inquisition's investigation of Ignatius of Loyola. Mystical and religious experiences are threatening to institutional control and orthodoxy. Thinking with the church has been thinking with authoritarian orthodoxies. This can be viewed in all institutional forms of Christianity that use violence and all sorts of rhetorical strategies to discredit theological dissent and novelties. Clear examples can be seen in Christian polities that exclude LGBT folks from the communion table or demonize same-sex marriage. Have these churches taken the time to pastorally listen to the faith life and stories of LGBT folk? Have they witnessed heroic acts of compassion and charity in their lives? Have they witnessed the love of God and one another in the married lives of same-sex partners and for their children? Have they listened to God's Spirit with an ear of discernment? The failure to listen to the faith lives of LGBT Christians has been a fundamental failure to listen to the promptings of the Holy Spirit and discern genuine love of queer Christians. Thinking with heteropatriarchal or even LGBT institutional orthodoxies can block discernment of the actions of the Holy Spirit. Dorothee Söelle writes the following words as part of her creed:

> Every day I am afraid that he (Christ) died for nothing because he is buried in our churches, because we have betrayed his revolution in our obedience to and fear of the authorities.[5]

I intuited as a pious young Christian college student that the energy of the Holy Spirit breaks us open to new ideas, creative possibilities, thinking differently, and things unimagined. I was involved in the Catholic charismatic movement, and I watched how the Holy Spirit broke me open from my narrow dogmatisms of life to a greater vision of openness, compassion, and love. I went around as a student wishing everyone the unrest of the Holy Spirit. That was a thoroughly mischievous wish because the Holy Spirit happens to play tricks on us to get ourselves to laugh at ourselves when we take our religious beliefs too seriously and are dogmatically rigid or when we create obstacles to the channel of God's grace. People love to throw road blocks for other people trying to find their way to God. And the Holy Spirit has a full-time job trying to undo with mischief and laughter the human roadblocks to God.

THE SPIRIT

The Spirit is a coequal partner in God's nature as threefold community of inclusive love. She is spoken as the communion of love between God and Christ and us. She is the passionate glue of the Trinity; she is passionately connected to God's and Christ's mission to include humanity, all life, and the universe into the divine love life.

The Spirit of God is immaterial without form or substance. We have imaged her as tongues of fire, a dove descending upon Jesus, and as feminine principle with the triadic community of God. The Spirit is immaterial, a dynamism or potential power to be unleashed but never controlled. Christ speaks of the Spirit "blowing where she blows." The Spirit hovers over the chaos of pre-matter before the Big Bang of creation some 15 billion years ago, and she remains immanent in creation as an inner dynamism connecting the universe and ourselves to God.

The Spirit is the dynamic love of God touching, empowering, and transforming material reality. In the Scriptures, we hear how the Spirit is involved with the embodiment of God in Christ; Mary becomes overshadowed by the Holy Spirit and pregnant with Jesus. The Spirit is present at Jesus' baptism, where Spirit descends upon Jesus and reveals that he is God's beloved child. The Spirit leads Jesus into the wilderness for 40 days and transforms Jesus into charismatic prophet and agent of God's kingdom. The Spirit leads Jesus from the wilderness to preach in his home synagogue when he proclaims, "The Spirit of the Lord is upon me, because the Spirit has anointed me to bring good news to the poor. The Spirit has sent me to proclaim release to the captives and recovery of sight of the blind, to let the oppressed go free" (Luke 4:18). The Spirit was active throughout Jesus' ministry, preaching, and healing. The Spirit was there on the cross, connecting Jesus and Abba God in his passion and death. And the Spirit was there in the tomb that Easter morning, raising Jesus from the dead to the glory of God. The Spirit transformed Jesus' dead body to a risen, glorified body. The Spirit is always there within material reality of the universe, all life, and within us.[6]

The Spirit makes sense only when we speak about bodies: the body of Jesus, our bodies, bodies in sacraments, bodies in prayer, and the body of Christ—God's spiritual body in the world. What the Spirit did for Christ on Easter, the Spirit does for us, all life, and the universe. The Spirit mixed God's desires and human desires in the incarnated Christ. God took material fleshliness in order to divinize humanity and the universe, and the process of divinization is from within the material universe and within us. From the very beginning, Christians understood the Spirit as operative within our intimate longings for God and in our prayer communication with God. The Spirit creates a divine or material ontology of relationality, and we cannot discern the Spirit or speak of the Spirit apart from specific bodies with desires and participating in a divine or human co-creativity that incarnates the Spirit within a transformative milieu—called grace. Early Christians spoke about the Spirit as "the hand of God" in the world. In my own words, I would like to add that the Spirit lifts us and all living beings into the gracious life of God. The Spirit will work outside the Christian churches, outside of Christianity with people of faith and love. For the Holy Spirit continues to overshadow human beings, impregnating within us the Christ and divine image of God as an inclusive community of love.

DIVINE FOOLISHNESS AND THE HOLY SPIRIT

It is no secret in my congregation that I am a Lady Gaga fan. I love her video release "Judas," wherein Jesus leads a gang of hunky biker disciples, and Lady Gaga, of course, plays Mary Magdalene. I love the refrain, "I am just a holy fool, oh baby, it's so cruel, I am still in love with Judas." It is a haunting refrain that speaks profoundly to my spirituality, the path of compassion and peacemaking, and the mischief-making of the Spirit. Let me foolishly juxtapose Lady Gaga with a quotation from St. John Chrysostom, the fourth-century Archbishop of Constantinople:

> Only a fool would attempt to change the world with a simple message of love and peace. So we can conclude that Jesus was a fool. Only fools would agree to follow such a man . . . . So we can conclude that all of us are fools . . . . So let all happily admit that we are fools. Then we will happily commit ourselves to change the world.[7]

I want to suggest to you that holy foolishness of Lady Gaga and John Chrysostom, an intertextual chimera for Roman Catholic hierarchs, is part of the divine nature. There is divine foolishness in God as Creator, as the Christ, and the Holy Spirit. For some Christians, Jesus was a holy fool, and those who follow him genuinely are fools. Jesus was a holy fool to many Jews and intra-Jewish holiness groups such as the Pharisees, the Sabbath fundamentalists, and the Temple priestly leadership. There have been several portrayals of Jesus as a clown figure from the portrait of Christ the Clown by Georges Rouault, Jesus in *Godspell*, and the short movie *The Parable*.[8] These artistic Christian presentations figure Jesus the holy fool as a clown. Harvey Cox discusses the significance of clown and Christ the clown:

> The clown represents different things to different people. For some he is the handy butt of our own fears and insecurities. We can jeer at his clumsy failures because they did not happen to us . . . he reveals to us our stubborn

human unwillingness to be encaged forever within the boundaries of physical laws and social proprieties. The clown is constantly defeated, tricked, humiliated and tromped upon. He is infinitely vulnerable, but never finally defeated.[9]

Jesus breaks many culturally religious laws and conventions with such comic intensity that warns that such foolhardy behaviors that will lead to defeat and humiliation.

One of the many foolish and troublesome things about Jesus was his pursuing of sinners and his radical hospitality in welcoming them in the name of God.[10] It was unheard of behavior, for he showed a radical acceptance of ragged and sinful people outside of mainstream institutional religion. His meals with sinners not only meant inclusivity but also fellowship in the eyes of God. He proclaimed the wild grace of God that stepped outside the ghettoized boundaries of his religious community that the exclusivist gatekeepers so violently protected. Jesus' revolution of inclusive grace was based on compassion, forgiveness, peace, and love. If it were really carried out, it would, I am convinced, cause a chain reaction that would shake the world. God's divine foolishness aims to renew and transform the hearts of all peoples, and it stands against the tribal boundaries of Jesus' religious community then and now. Jesus invited his disciples to take up their crosses and follow him, and his invitation to discipleship defies all conventional common sense of ego-centeredness. It expresses a divine mystery that in weakness is the strength of God.

The Holy Spirit continues the expression of divine foolish originating from Christ and located in the ministry of Jesus and Easter. However, theological writings about the Holy Spirit are the most underdeveloped branch of theological reflection, except in the area of the modern rediscovery of Trinitarian notions. Christian churches have turned the Holy Spirit into a mere Comforter and Guide, never disturbing ecclesial orthodoxies and communal boundaries, always affirming orthodoxies and authority, but the Holy Spirit often colors outside boundary lines, outside churches, transgressing orthodoxies and flaunting authority.

In John's Gospel, Jesus speaks about the Spirit, "she blows where she blows" (3:8). She cannot be pinned down; she is impossible to contain (though that does not stop church leaders from trying to domesticate her or ignore her promptings). Spirit is translated from the Hebrew word *ruah*, meaning breath or air in motion, thus a blowing wind. It can be gentle as a spring breeze, refreshing, or the blowing wind of a violent storm. Spirit in the scriptures and in theological traditions is always in relation to the material world and its evolution, people and their activities, or church sacramental actions, and church reform and change.

If we focus on individuals upon whom the Spirit rests, we see that her manifestations in people include unpredictability, spontaneity, rashness, selflessness, creativity, resourcefulness, foolishness, unorthodoxy, mischief, and apparent drunkenness. The Spirit is God's dynamic work in the world; it is wild, mischievous, and so transforming. The liveliness of God means that God is lively and active in the world and in people following the way of Christ the fool. And the Spirit is just right in the midst of this lively action.

From the Pentecost story in Acts 2, the primary image of the Spirit is the Intoxicator. The presence of the Holy Spirit is an intoxicating presence. When the Spirit descended on the disciples in the upper room, those in the market thought the disciples were intoxicated. The Holy Spirit induces amazingly intoxicated strange and foolish behaviors. I want to talk about several fools of God who have created mischief as they imitated the foolish wisdom of Christ. Imitation of Jesus is the willingness to meet him wherever he is to be found in his holy foolishness. Meeting Jesus through the Holy Spirit is to allow the Spirit to intoxicate us with the foolishness of Christ—this means to change ourselves to be transformed into a holy fool. Mischief is defined as a playful action or actions that cause annoyance. It has a playful but troublesome quality. It is the job of the Holy Spirit to raise up holy fools in history to bring an authentic voice of God's wild grace that brings challenge and change with disturbing play. The mischief of the Spirit can be retrieved hermeneutically in religious tricksters, mad monks, holy fools, religious clowns, and jokers. The focus of the essay will look at the enfleshing of the Holy Spirit in religious fools and look at contemporary queer religious clown nuns.

TRICKSTERS AND CLOWNS

In many religious cultures and stories, the trickster is a creator, a crossdresser, a joker, a truth teller, a storyteller, a clown transformer linked to the spiritual frequency that changes humanity by stretching people beyond their comfort zones or challenges them to openness.[11] Tricksters can be cunning or foolish or both; they are often very funny—like clowns—even when considered sacred or performing important cultural tasks. In many cultures such as the First Nations stories, the trickster and the cultural hero are often combined in the same story. The trickster is often a teacher, a survivor, a cultural hero, a spiritual guide, always traveling, outrageous and cunning, foolish and wise, mischievous, and often doing good despite obstinate humans. As I study comparative religions, I am convinced that the trickster is a metaphor for the action of grace in the alchemy of time.

Many Native American traditions hold tricksters such as Coyote and Raven as essential to any contact with the divine. Coyote assumes many disguises and is gender variant in forms. Coyote may function as a clown, creating laughter. Stories of the mischievous antics of coyote taught the Navajo or Dine to laugh: "Native American traditions held Coyote's clownish, trickster ways as essential to any contact with the sacred. People could not pray until they had laughed, because laughter frees us from rigid preconceptions."[12] How much better would Christians be if they learned to laugh before they learned to pray! There might be a lot less Christian hatred, prejudice, and violence. Humorless Christianity is a real problem. For example in 1960s, *Playboy* magazine printed a cover with a laughing Jesus. There was an outcry not because Jesus was on the cover of the magazine but because Jesus was laughing. Humorless Christianity is a toxic spirituality, centered on judgmentalism, shame guilt, and orthodox dogmatism.

Humans need tricksters in most sacred rituals, or they might forget that the sacred comes through upset, reversal, parody and campiness, and surprise. The trickster in most Native American traditions is essential to creation, birth, the significant events in life, and death. Frequently, the trickster figure exhibits gender variability, changing gender roles, cross-dressing or bizarre garb, and engaging in same-sex practices.

The concept of the trickster is as much a part of humanity's history as the concept of God. The trickster awakens us to question who we are—allowing us to explore the true purpose of our soul's journey in the holographic experience of the spiritual world. The trickster's energy allows us to break out of old conventions and regulations, whether these have been imposed by ourselves, our families, our culture, or religion. This is the energy to create laughter and thinking outside of the box, and it opens us to a world of limitless new possibilities.

Another specific example might help us understand that the trickster can express resistance to oppression. When I was a kid, Disney's "Song of the South" took countercultural stories of Brer Rabbit from its American slave context—the stories of Brer Rabbit, Brer Fox, and Brer Bear. According to Riggins Earl, Brer Rabbit is the "creative way that the slave community responded to the oppressor's failure to address them as human beings created in the image of God."[13] He is the metaphoric representation of the African American slave community—figurative, vulnerable yet outwits the

Fox and Bear who can kill him and eat him, for he succeeds through his own ingenuity and transgressing the rules. Slaves created their own symbols of narrative resistance by turning upside the oppressive meta-narratives of slavery, just as queer theology has overturned and challenged dominant Christian theological narratives with their own narratives of perversion.

MCC AND THE SISTERS OF PERPETUAL INDULGENCE

As I mentioned above, the Holy Spirit is connected to physical bodies and often out of bound actions. So my bold exploration of holy foolishness and tricksters explores the Holy Spirit as Mischief-Maker. It also simultaneously suggests that one of the late 20th and early 21st centuries' incarnations of the mischief of the Spirit are the Sisters of Perpetual Indulgence (SPI). The founding chapter describes the Sisters as:

> The Sisters of Perpetual Indulgence is a leading-edge Order of queer nuns. Since our first appearance in San Francisco on Easter Sunday, 1979, the Sisters have devoted ourselves to community service, ministry and outreach to those on the edges, and to promoting human rights, respect for diversity and spiritual enlightenment. We believe all people have a right to express their unique joy and beauty and we use humor and irreverent wit to expose the forces of bigotry, complacency and guilt that chain the human spirit.[14]

The Sisters, in my assessment, are a burst of incarnational energy that MCC leaders and clergy might imitate in their ministries. MCC churches, working with the Sisters, will attest to the spiritual values that they represent: the fundraising events to benefit various LGBT and non-LGBT causes, and provoking social and even spiritual mischief in the LGBT and greater community. Some may believe my equation of the Holy Spirit working through the sisters as blasphemous, but I will hold from my experience that these queer tricksters most align with the mischievous and challenging values of the Holy Spirit.

MCC and the SPI have a strong connection in some of the western states of the United States. The Sisters have sainted Rev. Jim Mitulski, Senior Pastor of New Spirit in Berkeley, and the founder of the MCC movement, Rev. Troy Perry.[15] The Sisters meet in several MCC churches, and my husband Rev. Joe Shore-Goss holds the unique dual position as a current MCC clergy and a Sister of Perpetual Indulgence, Sister Attila D'Nun. MCC clergy, Rev. Clinton Crawshaw, found his ministerial vocation as clergy in MCC starting as a Sister of Perpetual Indulgence in the

United Kingdom. My own church awarded the Los Angeles Sisters our Justice Love Award for the chapter's raising hundreds of thousands of dollars for AIDS, the Trevor Project, LGBT youth, Children's Hospital, and many more social causes. The Sisters of Las Vegas and MCC Las Vegas work together to raise hundreds of thousands of dollars for Sisters ADAP (AIDS Drug Assistance Program) for those HIV folks who fall outside the federal guidelines of the ADAP assistance.[16]

According to the San Francisco Sistory (Sister History), Sister Hysterectoria designed the sisters' habits after 14th-century Flemish women in waiting and French cloister nun wimples, with "ear brassieres" or hoobie-doobies with veils.[17] The Sisters of the Perpetual Indulgence are queer spiritual tricksters, holy clowns or fools, who use outrageous behaviors and flashy bejeweled and rhinestone garb, white-face makeup, glitter and sparkling face paint, to tweak the seriousness of homophobic and erotophobic religion. I have found myself calling the Sisters with the endearing term "clown-Sisters," and the association came from Catholic spirituality writer Henri Nouwen's description of clowns as a powerful image for those involved compassionate care and ministry:

> Clowns are not in the center of the events. They appear the great act, fumble and fall, and make us smile after the tension created by the heroes we came to admire. The clowns don't have it together, they do not succeed in what they try to do, they are awkward, out of balance, and left-handed, but . . . they are on our side. We respond to them not with admiration but with sympathy, not with amazement but with understanding, not with tension but a smile . . . . The clowns remind us with a tear and a smile that we share the same weaknesses.[18]

Humor is one of the key weapons of the Sisters in combating heterosexism and guilt or shame complex created by Christian erotophobia. Many churches perpetuate guilt and shame to control people's sexuality and gender conformity, and they exclude those who are sexually different or gender variant. The Sisters utilize camp, parody, and vulgar humor to help us laugh ourselves and those institutions that have been toxic in conditioning people to guilt and shame, especially over their sexual and gender nonconformities. They are devoted to expiating guilt and shame and promoting a pro-sex, pleasure ethic. The Los Angeles Sisters of Perpetual Indulgence (LA SPI) articulate their mission:

> Our mission is to make people happy, stamp out guilt brought on by a judgmental society and help various organizations and charities, etc.[19]

The SPI parodies Roman Catholic demonization of queer bodies as "intrinsically evil" and "objectively disordered" by sacralizing queer embodied sexualities and gender diversities. Melissa Wilcox writes about the Sisters:

> To bring queer bodies into sacred roles is to bring sexuality into the Church. To bring predominantly male queer bodies into the Church is to draw attention to the rampant presence of homoeroticism within the culture of the Church, to boisterously shatter the glass closet the Church has been trying so hard to paint over the past decade . . . .[20]

The Sisters aptly call themselves "avant guard activist guerrilla theatre nuts."[21] However, they are more than guerilla theater nuts, for they are queer ritualists, who transform the abominable and profanely sinful, queer bodies into graced bodies.

Similar to Catholic nuns, the Sisters have stages in the formative process of future sisters moving from aspirant, to postulant and the novice, and finally a full professed black-veil sister. A novice sister has to propose a community or fundraising event and lead the event before the vote to full profession. Unlike Catholic nuns, the Sisters are inclusive order of nuns that opens its membership to men and women, LGBT and straight, and intersexed. There is the growing phenomenon of heterosexual female and male Sisters developing. This is particular of the Russian River Sisters where I spent an evening meeting the Sisters, many of whom are female, heterosexual, or bisexual. I met Father Bertha De Zoot, a heterosexual male whose brother is gay and who found spirituality in the practice of promulgating universal joy and expiating stigmatizing guilt. He was attracted to the Sisters because of their fundraising for the LGBT and non-queer community as well as the community service of the Sisters.

In early debates about whether to white-face, some sisters refused to wear white-face because nuns did not wear white-face. The Australian and English orders do not wear white-face because they see themselves as real nuns.[22] Although the Sisters parody Catholic nuns, they incorporate spirituality and ritual traced back to the Radical Faeries. In an article on the spirituality of the Sisters, Sister Aura Scortea Beneficia wrote:

> The ideas of the Radical Faeries to redefine queer identity through spirituality and to constantly reconsider personal development seem to have influenced the Sisters strongly during and after their first appearance in 1979. The origin of the Sisters would not have been the same without the aspect of spirituality; the idea of queer nuns not focused on a religious

community but spiritually dedicated to a queer community, in my humble
opinion, was the key to success of our movement.

From the very beginning the Sisters (just as the Radical faeries) ignored
religious uniformity but did not throw their spiritual facets overboard.
Thus we practiced (and a lot still practice) all the spiritual things without
being attached to religious commandment: We meditate and we pray in
order to come to a deeper understanding about our own development and
about the nature of the world.[23]

An LA Sister, when asked by myself, "how she understood being a clown-
nun?," Sister Rosario Hala Peno told me that in her Hispanic Catholic culture, she grew up in the Catholic Church to respect nuns because nuns were
respected for their service. She takes her vocation as a clown Sister as serious
as she respects Catholic nuns, for it is about community service.[24] Service to
the queer community is one of the principal hallmarks of Sister spirituality.

Cathy Glenn notes that the Sisters embody their own sense of camp.[25]
Glenn writes, "The Sisters appropriate—through a subversive, discursive
aesthetic—and embody the sign 'nun,' bending it, twisting it, distorting
it, and ultimately, making it amazingly their own."[26] The Sisters queer
the signification of nun and give a novel and queer re-signification with
its own mission of community service. Harvard theologian Mark Jordan describes the Sisters as "a group that would use ecclesiastical drag to
promote pleasure but also for fundraising and protest."[27] They parody
Catholic nuns with veils that few Catholic nuns would dare to wear, and
they produced safe-sex pamphlets that few church folks would ever dis-
tribute. Jordan notes that some of the sisters had previous vocation to
Catholic religious life, and that they have become post-Stonewall icons
of queer spirituality, promoting joy and fighting shame and guilt from
religious erotophobia.[28] From the Sisters' perspective, they are not mock-
ing nuns, they are embracing the ideal of nun in albeit thoroughly queer
fashion and reflect a level of commitment to community and care for the
needy generally not found with many LGBT service organizations. What
it means for a Sister to be a white-faced nun is to serve the pressing needs
of the wider LGBT and non-LGBT communities. At the heart of their
dedication is a commitment and vow to service. As a queer order of nuns,
the SPI have spread to many of the major cities around the world and
have grown to become an international order dedicated to fund raising
around AIDS/HIV, fighting drug use, LGBT causes, and frequently fundraising for mainstream charitable causes.

The SPI have received negative reactions allegedly because of Catholic
bashing and parody of Catholic nuns from the extremist Catholic League

for Religious and Civil Rights. They objected to the Sisters' "Condom Savior Mass" when John Paul II came to visit San Francisco in 1987. President William Donohue of the Catholic League has tried to persuade the Internal Revenue Service to revoke the SPI's nonprofit exempt status.[29] The same Catholic League and president attempted to close down Terrence McNally's play *Corpus Christi* when it opened up at the Manhattan Theater Club in 1998.[30]

Mark Jordan aptly calls the Sisters "post-Christian ritual specialists for gay spaces." The Sisters, in general, perform the role of religious or spiritual mischief-makers, and their "theatricalization of experience" is certainly gay camp.[31] Their public displays of ritual outrage and mischief create what Marcella Althaus-Reid describes as a "libertine theater of passions."[32] Their public performances or queer rituals have a definite political camp dimension, parodying heterosexist cultural norms and undoing the damage of homophobic and erotophobic religion. In a press release of the Third Annual LA Queer Posada, the LA Sisters join with Mama Pancha Queer Performance Collective to reenact a queer Posada:[33]

> The Posada is traditionally a community performance that reenacts the pilgrimage taken by Mary and Joseph as they search for shelter leading to the birth of Christ. . . . This year in particular we call attention to the closing of Le Barcito, formerly the Black Cat, a landmark gay bar the Advocate out of pre-Stonewall protests against LAPD raids. . . . Not only had Le Barcito become a sanctuary for the gay Latino community, but they also hosted the previous two Queer Posadas and tons of other queer life rituals.[34]

The Posada started at the Eagle Bar, a leather bar, with a mile-long procession with performance of a Gospel Choir, queer street performers, and ending with a dance party. It is advertised as a LGBTQ "inclusive and intercultural spiritual happening."[35]

They are appropriately post-Christian, though a fair number of the Sisters are Christian, including my husband who is a sister and an MCC clergy, and a number of others from a variety of religious traditions. The San Francisco Sisters led the first candlelight vigil and procession in response to AIDS in 1982. And more recently, the LA Sisters staged a nontraditional Hispanic "posada procession" with a pregnant Mary portrayed by a lesbian and a lesbian Joseph. Their reenactment underscored that queer married folks were not welcomed and given hospitality in the manner Mary and Joseph could not find accommodation. The Sisters are invited to lead Pride festivals, bless leather contests, major LGBT events, and the final arrival of the

AIDS Cycle Run from San Francisco to Los Angeles. Their ritual blessings are salacious, outrageous, and scandalous to the puritans in a crowd; for instance, they may use sex toys in their blessings of a Leather Contest or incorporate blessings from various interfaith contexts. But when compared to the erotic Catholic Easter fertility ritual of dipping the "phallic" paschal candle into the "vaginal" baptismal waters, there is a Catholic amnesia on the fertility origin of the Holy Saturday symbolic rite. The Sisters' ritual of sex toys is more overtly erotic and thus scandalous, and their rituals frequently integrate sexuality and spirituality in ways that few religious communities do.

The Sisters are more popular than other clergy within the LGBT community because they parody institutional religion to those excluded, harmed, shamed, and abused by churches. The Sisters have an uncanny way of ministering to the spiritual needs of LGBT bar attendees and folks generally abused and shamed that not even an MCC clergy can do without a great deal of psychological transference.[36] One novice project "Confess Anal" at the Los Angeles Eagle, a leather bar, was organized by the heterosexual woman Novice Sister Edna; it was a night of confession, a camp performance and storytelling about sexual experiences with absolution. The ritual parody of Catholic confession and guilt about queer sexuality was subverted in an explicit ritual celebrating non-heteronormative sex. Instead of regulating sexuality through confession, the Sisters free the erotic as part of spirituality. Or, the San Francisco Sisters revalorizes Easter with the Hunky Jesus contest and Easter bonnet competition in Dolores Park.[37]

The Sisters can help LGBT folks to laugh at themselves: their religion, guilt, and shame. Thus, LGBT people begin to distance from their religious guilt and shame about themselves. Or Sisters may use their rulers or a small colorful whip to punish those with residual guilt and shame about sexuality. They use humor and buffoonery to mock compulsory heterosexism and erotophobia by denying them, thus affirming a positive ethic of pro-sex pleasure. Harvey Cox notes that the clown affirms by denying:

> The clown does affirm by denying. But in denying, he is also affirming. He enables us to laugh at our failures and successes, at our fears and also our faith. By involving you in his denial, he lures us into affirming after all.[38]

The Sisters have frequently chased fundamentalist ministers and their followers from queer spaces or laughed and parodied them. When Burbank High School kids performed the *Laramie Project* about the death of Matthew Shepard in 2009, the toxic fundamentalist Christian brigade of Fred Phelps' family protested the performance. What was wonderful was the counter protest of the Sisters staged on the opposite corner, bringing laughter and spoofing their Christian hatred with their own outrageous mockery. The Phelps clan knows how to play victim all too well and expect public antagonism for their extremist and hateful protests, but it does not know how to handle laughter and satirical humor directed at themselves. Laugher and comic parody are weapons to counter religious hatred, gender fundamentalism, and a variety of erotophobias.

When the Sisters get us to laugh at such protesters and their hatred, we develop a comic distance from the hurtfulness of the protesters and see it for what it is—human foolishness to restrict God's love and mercy. We might even feel a pang of compassion for their hateful obsessions and lack of freedom as we laugh at them. And one healthy consequence is that we let go our anger against their religious violence.

Another example of the Sisters' public foolishness and mischief is the following report of the novice project of Sister Glory Hole-Elujah that would elevate her to a fully professed black veil sister:

> I am so happy to report that the Sisters were well received both on the bus and at the Santa Monica Pier. We met so many wonderful tourists visiting from such places as Idaho, Colorado, New York, England, Australia, and a HUGE crowd from China, to name a few. We met local families who were Armenian, Jewish, Hispanic and also African American, to name a few. If they weren't watching the Fish Dance or receiving a Communion from the Glorious Holy Fish Blessing, they were talking to us, asking for brochures, Sister stickers, fortune reading fish, or to have their pictures taken with us. One female downloaded an App for her smart phone to read the QR Code, which I had designed for the Sisters to wear, and was instantaneously connected with the Sisters website, while we were on the Pier! When taking our group photo, a huge group of people gathered around to take pictures of us with their own cameras. While performing our Fish Dance, the viewers were laughing so hard and so loud that you can hear them laughing in the videos which were taken of our performance (to be posted online soon!). The bubbles we had blowing behind us, while we performed, reached well across the street and led more people to our ritual. In closing, right before we left the pier, the Park Ranger paid us an enormous compliment by inviting the Sister to return every Saturday as he was pleased with the positive energy which he noticed from the crowds. In short, we had a safe journey both to the beach and back and an immeasurable amount of joy and laughter was spread and shared by all.[39]

Another Novice Sister project was Sister Lucy Furr staging the "red heel party" and silent auction to raise monies for HIV in Long Beach.[40]

The philanthropy of the Sisters worldwide outdistances most queer and open and affirming churches. This alone attracts new recruits to the Sisters who want to help in generous fundraising for queer causes often ignored. Many sisters are committed to fundraising monies because of compassionate care and service to the community and not necessarily just for queer causes.

SPIS AND THE SPIRIT

The Spirit of God is surrounded in humor—creating mischief and spiritual anarchy to the over-institutionalization of Christianity. When we honestly look at ourselves, we realize how odd we are or how we do not fit into male-stream churches. The SPI function as a clown mirror to ourselves and make us laugh. And by laughing, we become more sane and more wholesome, for laughter and humor are essential ingredients for spiritual and human balance. It can bring life, events, and relationships into a more clear and healthy focus. Just as Coyote brought laughter for first Nation peoples so that they could learn how to pray, the Holy Spirit teaches us how to laugh so we can pray and have faith. Clown SPI provide a lot of laughter and joy in their zany ministry and outreach to the LGBT community, but in doing so, point to another world breaking in from the future and with the hope of change and freedom from the bonds of the past. In others, the SPI have an eschatological, spiritual function of transgression of the present moment by spreading erotic joy and offering parodies of dogmatic religion.

Try tracking the Spirit—it is like what Jesus said to Nicodemus, it is like tracking the wind; it is indeed hard to accomplish! "The Spirit blows where she wills . . ." (Jn 3:8a). You can harness the wind but you can't catch the wind and box it, market it, or sell it. Likewise, the Spirit of God cannot be harnessed and never controlled despite all human and ecclesial efforts. She is thoroughly unpredictable, and she endows us with a spirit of radical freedom that makes suspect any absolute or dogmatic claim that "this is exactly the way it always happens." The Spirit has a way of comically moving not according to our best-made plans and theological schemes but according to her own inspiration as a part of triune community of unconditional love, radical freedom, laughter, playfulness, and radical inclusive outreach. So the dynamic movement of the Holy Spirit cannot be charted but occurs in an unlimited number of open ways and possible routes. All theological and ecclesial blueprints are out, for the only way that we can deal with the Holy Spirit is through openness in prayer—an openness that may change the course and directions of our lives or a new call to reinvent ourselves to serve a ministry of life-giving love. This can be accomplished on individual, communal, and denominational levels.

For centuries, Christians have often been toxically serious; that is, they banned laughter from their lives as religious duty. Clement of Alexandria questioned laughter as a disruption of rational humanity, and others Christian leaders questioned whether if Jesus ever laughed since it was linked to carnality and the body.[41] The asceticism of the Greco-Roman syncretistic movements was imported into Christian asceticism and monastic practice, and Christian asceticism became suspicious of laughter in the religious quest to tame bodies. Throughout Christian history, there has been a deep ambivalence over laughter and its role in the spiritual path. Laughter was viewed at best ambiguous and often negatively because it threatens the spiritual order of the church.

Medieval Christians were divided on the issues of laughter because it was connected to embodiment and carnality. Hildegard of Bingen comprehended that laughter was one of the consequences of original sin and the fall.[42] Peter Cantor raised the question whether Christ ever laughed, and he answered that Christ could have laughed but that there is no scriptural evidence of his laughing.[43] In a more contemporary setting, *Playboy* magazine ran a cover image of the laughing Jesus that upset the Christians not because Jesus was on the cover of the magazine but laughing.

As the poet Patrick Kavanaugh describes, Easter is a "laughter freed forever and forever."[44] The mischievous event of Easter expresses God's anarchic and creative response of wild grace—grace outside the conventions, grace beyond all expectations. For myself, the Sisters incarnate the Holy Spirit in such a mischievous aesthetic public performance that represents what I imagine the intoxication of the Spirit at that first Pentecost. Christians intoxicated with the Spirit get along with the Sisters.

The Sisters resurrect a longstanding trajectory of humor, embodied clowning, and foolishness within Christianity. Theologian Elizabeth Stuart points out medieval English Christianity performed mystery plays with a great deal of incarnational humor at the Feast of Corpus Christi.[45] There was the French Feast of Fools, residual tradition from the Roman Saturnalia, staged as a New Year celebration with its topsy-turvy reversals of power wherein those without status and power assumed social positions of power and status. The feast started with a procession to the church or cathedral, the celebration of mass, and continuance of carnivalesque performances outside the church. It was celebrated with carnivalesque humor and buffoonery to the dismay of serious ecclesial hierarchs.[46] In 1400, Gerson, the Rector of the University of Paris, wrote "Deforming the Lord's Supper and Elevating the Ass," referring to the Feast of Fools:

> A detestable mockery is made of the service of the Lord and of the sacraments, where things are impudently and execrably done which should be done only in the taverns and brothels, or among the Saracens and Jews.[47]

The objection registered could as well be leveled against the SPI's seemingly blasphemous behaviors. Gerson and the Christian critics operate out of purity code that radically separates the holy from ludicrous parodies.

Many medieval churches practiced a custom on Easter Sunday: *risus paschalis*, God's joke or Easter laugh. It became banned by institutional Churches. On the morning of Easter Sunday the churches were filled with jokes and laughter over the most incredible of all, that the crucified Jesus had come back from his death, and life had prevailed over death. God fooled the devil, felled him using his own trick. This is the most laughable of everything laughable, the most incredible of all unbelievable things, and the most joyous of all pleasant things. You cannot help but laugh at the wonderful amazement and surprise of Easter. Some orthodox and Protestant churches still celebrate God's joke on the Monday after Easter.

Fundamentalist Christians (from Vatican fundamentalists in the Catholic Church to Evangelical Christians) have no sense of humor, none at all. Life is burdensome to them while they wait in suffering to go to heaven. As the American journalist and satirist H. L. Mencken wrote, Christian Puritanism suffers from "the haunting fear that someone, somewhere, may be happy."[48] How many Christians are humorless and hyperserious? They mask and cover, I suspect, over a shallow spirituality, based on rigid and judgmental expressions of Christianity. The idea of Holy Spirit as Mischief-Maker evolved over a period of time, study, and writing. But the catalyst came as I encountered the SPIs and their joyous spirituality, remembering a former spiritual mentor telling me: "where there is authentic joy, the Holy Spirit is there."

"WE ARE JUST HOLY FOOLS"

As I am writing this chapter, Troy Perry is scheduled to be canonized as a Queer Saint for his decades as civil LGBT rights activist by the Los Angeles Sisters at MCC LA, the founding church.[49] The LA Sisters recognize the values that they hold most dear have been reflected in the visionary leadership and foolish ministry of Founder Rev. Troy Perry. In his study of charismatic religious leaders, Max Weber incorporated sociological and psychological processes in his definition. He defined charisma as a "certain quality of an individual's personality by virtue of which he is set apart from ordinary men and treated as endowed with supernatural, superhuman, or at least specifically exceptional powers or qualities."[50] Weber's notion of charisma is pivotal concept for comprehending religious movements and the attempts at routinization of charisma into institutional religion. In an earlier book, I wrote about the continuing bonds with the religious founder (Buddha, Jesus the Christ, Mohammed the Prophet, and Chogyam Trungpa):

> With the passing of a charismatic religious leader, charismatic authority is routinized by the successors. "Routinization" is the transfer of charisma and charismatic authority from the religious teacher or founder to followers who use it to stabilize social relationships, religious visions, and social values. The process of routinization is not just about succession of authority but the institutionalization of the teacher's vision and his social movement. For Weber, the charismatic religious figures bring a vision of the world and ideal values that are adapted to the everyday social world and have consequences for future development.[51]

The next generation of leadership in religious movements such as Buddhism, Christianity, and Islam, or the Christian religious orders such as the Franciscans or the Jesuits, institutionalized the movement, but they functioned as interim leaders preparing the way for future leadership. The third- and fourth-generation leaders often had the flexibility to restore charismatic visions of founders by keeping the presence of the founder's mission and vision after the process of institutionalization. They reincorporated some of the mischief of the original charisms of the founder. This notion was the heart of my doctoral dissertation as I investigated the spiritual renewal of the mad saint movement by Tsang-Nyon Heruka when he attempted to renew the Tibetan monastic movement, in particular, to the Kagyu school with unorthodox behaviors challenging Buddhist monastic dogmatisms.

The holy foolishness of Troy Perry, recognized by LA SPI's sainting, is the recognition and celebration of the founder's original charisma of being "a holy fool" as Lady Gaga sings. Rev. Troy Perry incarnates many of the virtues that the SPI practice worldwide—a crazy wisdom or holy foolishness or Spirit-led mischief that led to prophetic demonstration, founding a counter-church, hunger strike to protest the Briggs Initiative in California, marrying thousands of same-sex couples in Washington, DC, or asking for marriage license and being denied a license to marry at the Beverly Hills Courthouse. In MCC, due to recent multiple restructuring attempts in the past decade and the retirement of Troy Perry, the denomination faces the challenge how to restore the original charismatic vision and foolish wisdom of its founder. If MCC is founded by the mischievous action of the Holy Spirit, it has to be an open system that allows novelty, creativity, and imaginative reinventing of the Spirit. In other words, MCC (and all other Christian churches) is an open system that can be defined not from within but from the outside experience and transgressive experience of the Holy Spirit. A Spirit-filled or mischievous church remains open to the promptings of the Holy Spirit, placing those promptings under discernment (not institutional regulation or suppression), but gives primacy to the Spirit over the structures and entrenched ministries, allowing for theological pluralities and searching for ecumenical or interfaith connections and unity brought about through the outside and inside work of the Holy Spirit.

The idea of MCC's leaders and clergy putting on white face, hoobie-doobies, and colorful veils and becoming clown sisters is a thoroughly camp and entertaining notion, but it does not produce the mischief of the SPI within a church. It is primarily the question of spiritual renewal and prayerful awakening that MCC (and many mainline denominational churches) faces in the second decade of the 21st century, and the Holy Spirit has the habit of inspiring holy fools and foolish movements to break open structures that confine original charisms and separate people so that churches can come to appreciate new understandings and respond to the challenges of the postmodern American society. For MCC, spiritual renewal is a breaking open of structures and involves reigniting the charismatic vision and holy foolishness of Troy Perry of Jesus' radical inclusive love. Spiritual renewal is not all about ecclesial restructuring but about genuine spiritual leadership and awakening in the midst of prayer and changed lives; it is transferring the mischievous charisms of the past into the present and making the mission real and alive once more for the future. It is about an open mission, fearlessly wide and inclusive, rather than the focus of organization restructuring, for the early Christian followers of Jesus, intoxicated with the Spirit, concentrated on the mission by following Jesus the holy fool. The mission renewed will require the bold energy of visionary mischief-makers who bring the playfulness and the camp of the Holy Spirit into the world and incarnate its energy into the church through bold reinvention and reawakening of the mission of radical inclusive love. These visionary mischief-makers will bring an end to the old, prepare the way for the new, and reinvent new mischief-making in the lineage of Jesus, Francis of Assisi, Teresa of Avila, Ignatius of Loyola, Dorothy Day, and Troy Perry. Living lives of profound mischief in the Spirit will always come back to a widening and specific detailing of the church vision and mission of the church for the 21st century's requirements of a compassionate engagement with the world with all its endemic challenges. The SPI are the "queer John the Baptists," heralding the new mischief-makers of the Spirit, who will renew the vision of Jesus' message of radical inclusive love. Tim Morrison writes about the holy fool:

> But in accepting the danger and asserting joy in its face the fool wins the kind of freedom from constraints of normal society that makes life glorious, livable, and fun. To be foolish is to live in the reality of the resurrection.[52]

The holy fool lives resurrection in the present moment through the promptings of the Holy Spirit the Mischief-Maker. And finally to theologians and me, Robin Meyers writes a cautionary tale about the Spirit:

> The real problem is that the Holy Spirit cannot be controlled by the pen of any theologian. Or to use a metaphor, we often assume that we can write about God and Jesus only by using a "justified" left and right margin. But then after we turn out the lights, confident that that the shape of our sentences will be preserved overnight, the Holy Spirit will appear to dance outside the block of the text, or to scramble it. It will write itself into the margins as poetry, jumbled and asymmetrical like an E. E. Cummings poem.[53]

NOTES

1. John R. Sachs, "'Do Not Stifle the Spirit': Karl Rahner, The Legacy of Vatican II and Its Urgency for Theology Today," *Catholic Theological Society Proceedings* 51 (1996): 15.

2. Veli-Matti Kärkkäinen, *Pneumatology: The Holy Spirit in Ecumenical, International, and Contextual Perspective* (Grand Rapids, MI: Baker Academic, 2002), 16–18.

3. Just look at the reaction of mainline denominational churches and their suspicions of the charismatic wings and the rise of Pentecostal churches globally.

4. Robert E. Goss, "The Hermeneutics of Madness: A Literary and Hermeneutical Analysis of the Mi-la-ras-pa'i-rnam-thar by Gtsang-smyon Heruka" (unpublished dissertation, Harvard University, 1993).

5. Dorothee Söelle, *Against the Wind: Memoir of a Radical Christian* (Minneapolis, MN: Fortress Press, 1999), 40.

6. There are numerous writings about the Spirit immanent and enfleshing herself in Nature, other kinds of life, the Earth, and the universe. My retrieval of the Holy Spirit is focused within human beings and outside and transgressive behaviors.

7. St. John Chrysostom, *Six Books on the Priesthood* (New York: St. Vladamir's Seminary Press, 1996), 52.

8. Ingrid Saelid Gilhus, *Laughing Gods, Weeping Virgins* (New York: Routledge, 2009), 116–20.

9. Harvey Cox, *The Feast of Fools* (New York: Harper and Row, 1970), 141–42.

10. Some good books on Jesus as holy fool: Elizabeth Anne Stewart, *Jesus the Holy Fool* (Franklin, WI: Sheed & Ward, 1999); Matthew Woodley, *Holy Fools: Following Jesus with Reckless Abandon* (Carol Steam, IL: Tyndale House Publishers, 2008).

11. Georg Feurstein, *Holy Madness: The Shock Tactics and Radical Teachings of Crazy-Wise Adepts, Holy Fools, and Rascal Gurus* (New York: Arkana, 1990).

12. Rick Heffern, "Creation and the Trickster Coyote," National Catholic Reporter, November 2, 2010, http://ncronline.org/news/spirituality/creation-and-trickster-coyote.

13. Riggins Renal Earl, Jr., *Dark Symbols, Obscure Signs: God, Self, and Community in the Slave Mind* (Maryknoll, New York: Orbis Books, 1993), 131. See also Ruth Anne Leslie, "Brer Rabbit: A Play of Human Spirit: Recreating Black Culture Through Brer Rabbit Stories," *International Journal of Sociology and Social Policy* 17, no. 6 (1957): 59–83.

14. San Francisco Sisters of Perpetual Indulgence, http://thesisters.org/.

15. U.K. Lesbian Theologian Elizabeth Stuart has been sainted as well. In San Francisco, the Sisters have canonized such figures as Harry Hay, Armistead Maupin, and Harvey Milk. The Sisters have redefined sainthood within a queer context.

16. http://www.sinsitysisters.org/sadap.html.

17. San Francisco Sisters of Perpetual Indulgence, Sistory, http://www.thesisters.org/content/sistory. The term "hoobie-doobie," a Sister term, refers to the headdress or wimple under the veil.

18. Henri Nouwen, *Clowning in Rome: Reflections on Solitude, Celibacy, Prayer, and Contemplation* (New York: Doubleday, 2000), 3.

19. http://www.lasisters.org/index.php?option=com_content&view=article&id=171:our-mission&catid=34.

20. Melissa Wilcox, "Queer Theory and the Study of Religion," in *Queer Religion: LGBT Movements and Queering Religion*, vol. II, ed. Donald L. Boisvert and Jay Emerson Johnson (Santa Barbara, CA: Praeger, 2011), 246.

21. http://www.lasisters.org/index.php?option=com_content&view=article&id=171:our-mission&catid=34.

22. Grand Mother Vicious Power Hungry Bitch (aka Sister Vish), "A History of White-Face in SPI," http://brewcitysisters.org/SPI-whiteface.html.

23. Sister Aura Scortea Beneficia, "Spirituality of the Sisters," One Veil, March 2012, http://1veil.tumblr.com/.

24. Conversation with Sister Rosario at the Preliminary Mr. LA Imperial Court Leather contest at the Bullet Bar, August 19. Sister Rosario was competing in the leather contest in her male persona.

25. Cathy B. Glenn, "Queering the (Sacred) Body Politics: Considering the Performative Cultural Politics of the Sisters of Perpetual Indulgence," in *Sexualities & Communication in Everyday Life: A Reader*, ed. Karen Lovaas and Mercilee M. Jenkins (Thousand Oaks, CA: Sage Publications, 2007), 251. See also Mark Jordan on camp and theology: Mark D. Jordan, "Notes on Camp Theology," in *Dancing Theology in Fetish Boots: Essays in Honour of Marcella Althaus-Reid*, ed. Lisa Isherwood and Mark D. Jordan (London: SCM Press, 2010), 181–90.

26. Glenn, "Queering the (Sacred) Body Politic," 250–51.

27. Mark D. Jordan, *Recruiting Young Love: How Christians Talk About Homosexuality* (Chicago: University of Chicago Press, 2011), 183.

28. Ibid., 184, 188.

29. Catholic League for Religious and Civil Rights, "IRS Asked to Revoke Tax-exempt Status of the Sisters of Perpetual Indulgence," October 25, 2001, http://www.catholicleague.org/release.php?id=418.

30. Cathy Che, "Offending Catholics," *The Advocate*, July 7, 1998, http://books.google.com/books?id=f2MEAAAAMBAJ&pg=PA49&lpg=PA49&dq=Catholic+League,+Corpus+Christi&source=bl&ots=kdj-huDJCT&sig=tgHz1YYUQMRAtqvN-BdgA9Ey9Nc&hl=en&ei=K6A5ToXTJePmiALXwbTDDg&sa=X&oi=book_result&ct=result&resnum=7&ved=0CE0Q6AEwBg#v=onepage&q=Catholic%20League%2C%20Corpus%20Christi&f=false.

31. Susan Sontag, "Notes on Camp," in *Against Interpretation and Other Essays* (New York: Farrar, Straus and Giroux, 1966), 287. Jordan notes that the "theatricalization of experience" sounds like a definition of religious ritual. Jordan, "Notes on Camp Theology," 187.

32. Marcella Althaus-Reid, *The Queer God* (New York: Routledge, 2003), 47.

33. Posada means accommodation in Spanish. It is a mid-December Mexican/Aztec candlelit procession with songs that reenact Mary and Joseph seeking shelter in Bethlehem, going from house to house.

34. Email from Sister Medusa Love Forbid, "Los Angeles Performance Art Presents: LA Queer Posada," December 20, 2011.

35. Ibid.

36. As an openly queer MCC clergy, I can engage in conversions with individuals in bars who have had shame-filled and abusive experiences within their past religious communities, but my husband, Sister Attila D'Nun, is able to release LGBT folks from guilt and shame that most MCC clergy are unable to do so because of their institutional connection to Christianity.

37. See http://www.sfgate.com/news/article/SF-Easter-celebrations-blend-indulgence-reverence-3467468.php; http://www.youtube.com/watch?v=eu7kGzl3fjI; http://blogs.sfweekly.com/exhibitionist/2012/04/photos_the_sisters_of_perpetua.php.

38. Harvey Cox, *The Feast of Fools: A Theological Essay on Festivity and Fantasy* (New York: Harper and Row Publishers, 1969), 155.

39. Sisters Pilgrimage to the Sea Report, email July 24, 2011, from Novice Sister Glory Hole-Elujah.

40. See the photo essay: Sisters of Perpetual Indulgence Raise $ to Help HIV Positive, *LA Weekly*, July 25, 2011, http://www.laweekly.com/afterdark/slideshow/sisters-of-perpetual-indulgence-raise-to-help-hiv-positive-1330970/8/.

41. Ingrid Saelad Gilhus, *Laughing Gods, Weeping Virgins* (New York: Routledge, 2009), 64–69.

42. Ibid., 79.

43. Verbum Abbreviatum, 60; Gilhus, *Laughing Gods, Weeping Virgins*, 79.

44. Patrick Kavanagh, "Lough Derg," in *Jubilate* (London: Darton, Longman, and Todd, 1984), 73.

45. Elizabeth Stuart, "Camping Around the Canon," in *Take Back the Word: A Queer Reading of the Bible*, ed. Robert E. Goss and Mona West (Cleveland: The Pilgrim Press, 2000), 25. Stuart provides a good brief history of humor and Christianity on 23–33. See also Gilhus, *Laughing Gods, Weeping Virgins*, 87–96.

46. Gilhus, *Laughing Gods, Weeping Virgins*, 80–87.

47. B. Swain, *Fools and Folly during the Middle Ages and the Renaissance* (New York: Columbia Press, 1932), 207.

48. H.L. Mencken, in *The Oxford Dictionary of Quotations*, ed. Elizabeth M. Knowles (New York: Oxford University Press, 1999), 504.

49. See Scott Bloom's documentary, *Call Me Troy*, which traces the life of Troy Perry and his struggle for LGBTQ civil rights and, in particular, marriage equality in California.

50. Max Weber, *On Charisma and Institution Building: Selected Papers*, ed. S. N. Eisenstadt (Chicago: University of Chicago Press, 1968), 49.

51. Robert E. Goss and Dennis Klass, *Dead but Not Lost: Grief Narratives in Religious Traditions* (New York: AltaMira Press, 2004), 150.

52. Tim Morrison, "Bodies, Sex, Wholeness, and Death," in *Religion is a Queer Thing: A Guide to the Christian for Lesbian, Gay, Bisexual and Transgendered People*, ed. Elizabeth Stuart et al. (London: Cassell, 1997), 123.

53. Robin Meyers, *The Underground Church: Reclaiming the Subversive Way of Jesus* (San Francisco: Jossey-Bass, 2012), 66.

Part II

OPENING THE BODY OF CHRIST

Thomas Bohache

The essays contained in Part I demonstrate that an important part of *Queering Christianity* is to explore radically inclusive images of God. In order for Christianity to be properly queered, God's very self must be queered so that we may dream beyond the narrow confines of heteronormativity. God is not the only concept or Being that must be queered, however. From its inception, the Metropolitan Community Church (MCC) has insisted on a radical (re)development of what it means to be church.

Elsewhere I have suggested that the Queer Movement might be the new Pentecost[1]: If Pentecost was the day when the Holy Spirit blew the doors off of the first Christians' comfortable domicile and forced them out into the streets to gather others, speaking to them in their own languages, then in the same way today's queer theologizing and church-making blows the doors off the Church universal and urges its congregants to move outward, to open up, and embrace all people in their own languages, idioms, cultures, and lifestyles. This is a further type of inclusivity that goes beyond discussion of who God is; it gets to the very heart of Christianity, for it examines who is entitled to worship that radically inclusive God. MCC has been on the forefront of this type of inclusivity, and the eight essays that comprise Part II describe eight different ways of thinking about this dimension of inclusivity.

Scripture calls the Christian community "the Body of Christ." Indeed, St. Paul suggested to the church at Corinth that their gatherings should be inclusive because each member of the Body of Christ has a function that makes it essential to the whole (1 Cor. 12:12–27), while to the Galatians he asserted that in Christ the categories this world holds dear (race, gen-der, class) were dissolved (Gal. 3:26–28). Alas, the history of Christianity has failed to perpetuate these notions. A cursory inspection of any church history book reveals how almost from its inception the Christian Church's story has not been one of inclusion, but rather exclusion based upon char-acteristics those in power have deemed unacceptable and unembraceable.

Thus, an essential part of queering Christianity must be to turn it back (pervert it?) to its roots (Latin *radix*, from which we derive "radical"). MCC has been about this task for over 40 years, sometimes with success, but not always, for there are still people kept out—even in MCC. The following essays, each in its own way, describe facets of what it means to open the Body of Christ to include more and more people in Jesus' radical vision of the Reign of God. For if the Church *is* the Body of Christ, then any/every *body* must be welcome. Theologian Wendy Farley puts this well when she writes that Jesus "sees persons, not social types. He sees in society's throw-aways beings to cherish, enjoy, befriend. . . . What is most invisible to us is what is most visible to him: we are all bearers of the divine image."[2]

Activist pastor Robin Meyers has recently asserted that today's church must be a place of radical hospitality, reaching beyond doctrines and poli-tics and even denominations, in order to form what he calls "the Un-derground Church"—a place that is truly the Body of Christ because it embraces all bodies without expecting them to convert to one acceptable image or way of being.[3] This Underground Church enacts Jesus' policy of inclusivity, especially his radical notion of the open table—the place where all *become* the Body of Christ because they are fed *with* the Body of Christ. In this way church communities once again begin meeting people's daily needs of subsistence, because at the table everyone is recognized as a sis-ter or a brother, no matter where they come from, what they believe, or whom they love. In its early days, MCC captured this subversiveness as it moved from place to place, eluding homophobic landlords and police forces[4]; most recently, in this author's opinion, MCC has dialed back on this subversiveness as it has strived to assimilate to the dominant society and take its place as a real church—what Meyers points to as the begin-ning of the early church's downfall, when it "got in bed" with Empire.[5]

The authors whose essays comprise Part II, "Opening the Body of Christ," embody the unquenchable hope that still resides in the MCC that one day the Body of Christ will be truly opened—penetrated, as it were—to include all those who have been driven away. This will not come without effort, intentionality, and, yes, even pain. For whenever we open our bodies (whether in a surgical procedure or in an act of sexual intercourse) there is some pain involved; we give up something in order to gain something; we let something be taken out of us in order to make room for something more; we hurt in order to heal. When it comes to opening the church universal, this pain means confronting and striving to overcome racism, sexism, classism, and homophobia. When it comes to opening MCC, this pain might come in the form of dealing with erotophobia caused by our internalized homophobia or our desire to just fit in and be like everybody else. This healing pain might consist of embracing and dispensing with what I have called the "Christophobia" implanted in us by noninclusive faith communities, who have led us to equate Jesus Christ with hatred, intolerance, and exclusion.[6] Each of these authors, in her or his own way, has sought to transcend ecclesial exclusion by envisioning a truly open, inclusive, and hospitable Body of Christ.

In Chapter 6, the Rev. Dr. Thomas Bohache *opens doctrine* by suggesting that Christians must continue to explore and celebrate, rather than mute, our sexualities.[7] This means empowering the Erotic Love that is God and is within each of us. To this end, Bohache, the Pastor of MCC Christ the Liberator in central New Jersey, presents an alternative view of the Trinity, based upon the three Greek words for love, and concludes with a proposal for a new sexual paradigm that would open our churches beyond narrow moralizing about acts and point us toward discussion of what we really do/mean/think/say when we open ourselves to others (and God!) through our sexuality.

The next four chapters *open the sacraments* beyond traditional interpretations. In Chapter 7, Bryce E. Rich first presents a historical analysis of the sacrament of baptism.[8] After examining how baptism has been viewed as a boundary-marker in both Catholicism and Protestantism, Bryce, a member of MCC and a doctoral student at the University of Chicago, then discusses how MCC in its diversity as a postdenominational church movement might contribute to breaking open the sacrament in order to include even more diverse beliefs and practices. Can MCC transform baptism from a mark of exclusivity to a means of extending hospitality to Christ's table?

In Chapter 8, the Rev. Dr. Axel Schwaigert, Pastor of the MCC in Stuttgart, Germany, broadens the notion of Christmas to include more than the December holiday of gift-giving sentimentality.[9] Noting that the meaning of Christmas is incarnation—when Christ joined the human race in an act of divine/human reciprocity—Schwaigert suggests that everything we do in our churches, especially communion, must be a recapitulation of this radical inclusion of the human in the Divine. Thus, he asserts that when MCCs practice open communion, we are practicing radical incarnation/inclusion: Our invitation mirrors God's own invitation through the embodiment of Jesus Christ.

In Chapter 9, the Rev. Rachelle Brown, MCC clergy and a doctoral student at Chicago Theological Seminary, queers the sacrament of Holy Communion as she likens the church to a kitchen, the altar to a dining table, and theologies of communion to recipes that come together from diverse places to cohere into the one Body that is offered to all.[10] She concludes that the queer communion offered in MCC embodies abundance and decadent hospitality because of its mixture of ingredients, spices, and flavors, all of which combine to present one dish that can be served in a variety of ways.

In Chapter 10, the Rev. Kerri Mesner, former Pastor of the MCC in Scotland and now a doctoral student at the University of British Columbia, explores how Latin American Theatre of the Oppressed might be transplanted beyond its origins to enrich our ideas of how communion works.[11] When read in combination with Robert E. Shore-Goss's pneumatological essay in Part I,[12] Mesner's contribution of a Joker Christ calls us to an appreciation of how the sometimes over-the-top nature of our communities can embody the Christ in ways that other parts of church cannot, thus providing a broader and more inclusive invitation than is found in traditional churches.

In Chapter 11, Nic Arnzen and others associated with a recent production of Terrence McNally's *Corpus Christi* show us what it means to be *open beyond church settings* in order to embody Christ's inclusive love.[13] The voices in this powerful essay explore through autobiography and poetry how they were able to (re)connect with the Body of Christ by telling his story on stage, even amid controversy and threats from so-called Christians. Just as McNally's play is a parable about inclusion, likewise these participants' experiences become a parable about the costs of truly following Jesus into the world.

In Chapter 12, the Rev. Dr. Robert E. Shore-Goss, Senior Pastor of MCC in the Valley, discusses *opening to other spiritual practices* as a way of opening the church itself.[14] He describes his hybridity as a Buddhist Christian in order to show how each of us can (re)claim the disparate parts of our life journeys in order to galvanize today's church into becoming more inclusive of the many paths that lead toward the Divine.

In Chapter 13, the Rev. Dr. Thomas Bohache calls for an *opening of community*. Drawing upon nearly 25 years as pastor and theologian in MCC, Bohache suggests that we "unzip and let our junk fall out,"[15] by which he means be(com)ing totally honest about who we are and whether we really mean to welcome everyone in MCC or not. Provocatively beginning with a theophany in a sex club, he sets the stage for realistic talk about what church could be if we dared to include every part of our selves. When we are open, the church becomes open; when the church is open, others will come inside and open themselves in a constant spiral of divine/human hospitality that knows no bounds.

These eight essays excite me not only because of their diverse views on how we might open the Body of Christ, but also because they are able to ask difficult questions without the assurance of nice, neat answers. Today's Body of Christ needs to reflect the messiness of the human situation, as well as the eschatological uncertainty of an assured outcome. Whether the Body of Christ is opened depends upon the willingness, assertiveness, availability, and perseverance of *all* of us to participate in "the dream of God"[16] for which Jesus lived, died, and rose again. When we queer Christianity, we embody this dream.

NOTES

1. Thomas Bohache, "Acts of the Apostles: Pentecost Queered," in *The Queer Bible Commentary*, ed. Deryn Guest, Robert E. Goss, Mona West, and Thomas Bohache (London: SCM Press, 2006), 569.

2. Wendy Farley, *Gathering Those Driven Away: A Theology of Inclusion* (Louisville, KY: Westminster John Knox Press, 2011), 194.

3. Robin Meyers, *The Underground Church: Reclaiming the Subversive Way of Jesus* (San Francisco: Jossey-Bass, 2012), passim but esp. ch. 6.

4. See Troy D. Perry, with Thomas L. P. Swicegood, *Don't Be Afraid Anymore: The Story of Reverend Troy Perry and the Metropolitan Community Churches* (New York: St. Martin's Press, 1990).

5. Meyers, *The Underground Church*, ch. 3.

6. Thomas Bohache, *Christology from the Margins* (London: SCM Press, 2008), ch. 8.

7. Thomas Bohache, "Can We Sex This? Eroticizing Divinity and Humanity."

8. Bryce E. Rich, "Reinterpreting Baptism: An Ongoing Dialogue."

9. Axel Schwaigert, "Toward a Church of Radical Christmas: The Open Communion in MCC and Its Ecclesiological Consequences."

10. Rachelle Brown, "Beyond the Open Table: Queering Holy Communion."

11. Kerri Mesner, "Innovations in Queer Theology: Embodying Open Communion through Theatre of the Oppressed."

12. Robert E. Shore-Goss, "The Holy Spirit as Mischief-Maker."

13. Nic Arnzen and Cast and friends of *Corpus Christi*, "Communion: Playing with Redempton."

14. Robert E. Shore-Goss, "Bodhisattva Christianity: A Case of Multiple Religious Belonging."

15. Thomas Bohache, "Unzipping Church: *Is* There Room for Everyone?"

16. Verna J. Dozier, *The Dream of God: A Call to Return* (Cambridge, MA: Cowley Publications, 1991).

6

Can We Sex This? Eroticizing Divinity and Humanity

Thomas Bohache

Holy Spark

What is Eros
but a
Burning Coal
deep within My Self—

The Spark
of the Divine Presence
that is
    Creativity
    Authenticity
    Passion

The Fire
that
enlivens my Life
but must be
st(r)oked constantly

The Flame
fragile in its power
and
so easily
quenched?[1]

This poem expresses what I have come to believe about the intersection of God and humanity during 20 years of theological study and ministry to the queer community. I believe that human and divine, natural and supernatural, coalesce in the Erotic. Genesis 1 tells us that in the beginning God's Spirit was soaring over the waters of chaos; then God's dynamic Word was spoken and living things began to come forth. These living things—vegetative, animal, and human—had bodies that differentiated them from God, who has no body but whose body is all of creation. Each of us is a part of the body of God; thus, our bodies express the Divine. When bodies coexist in harmony with God and with one another, *shalom* occurs: wellness, well-being, wholeness, health—the peace that passes understanding. When disharmony among bodies disturbs this peace, there is a rupture in the creation. Theologians call such disharmony "sin" or "brokenness," a dis/ease in God's intention.

Erotophobia is the fear or hatred of the integration of body, mind, and spirit that Eros accomplishes when it is allowed to flourish. While not listed among the seven deadly sins, it is perhaps the deadliest of sins, for it involves hatred of and disdain for God's creation as manifested in sexuality. I believe that sexuality—the capacity of relating to other beings as bodies, whether genitally or aesthetically[2]—must be a gift from God, for who else could fashion something so marvelous and complicated, so capable of bearing joy and pain at the same time? Consequently, theologies that see sexuality only as a result of humanity's fall from grace are bound to become erotophobic and counterproductive to the work of replenishing God's *shalom*.

Over the years, the various groups that make up the broader LGBTQI community(ies)[3] have struggled over issues of sexual behavior. For example, the lesbian community has strenuously debated pornography, sadomasochism, the use of sex toys, and the propriety of role-playing.[4] Likewise, members of the gay male community have asked one another, in the context of HIV/AIDS, whether sexual exploration is a good or a bad thing and whether so-called promiscuity resulted in a death sentence for an entire generation of gay men.[5] These discussions have at times been quite confrontational, employing judgmental taunts rather than informed conversation. Because traditional churches have failed to nurture their congregants as sexual beings, religious and spiritual voices have—until recently—been relatively absent from these struggles.

Further complicating matters is an overarching heterocolonialism that silences much meaningful discussion of sexuality because of its expectation that society and interpersonal relationships must be ordered according to a heteronormative paradigm, to deviate from which involves ostracism and judgment. By heterocolonialism, I mean the assumption of heterosexuality as default category in any consideration of daily life. In the same way that people of other races and cultures have been led to believe that they must mute their ethnic particularities in order to be acceptable to their Euro/American neighbors (even though in actuality they still are regarded as Other, simply by virtue of being non-white or speaking with an accent), LGBTQI people have been subjected to an indoctrination process from our earliest memory that tells us to change, suppress, or hide a core part of our being—our relational, affectional preference— in order to be worthy of tolerance by the heterosexual majority. I do not say acceptance, inasmuch as true acceptance of LGBTQI people exactly as we are is difficult to find; it is much more commonplace to encounter tolerance, that is, the mind-set that the queer person may coexist with the majority if he or she does or does not do a particular thing and/or does or does not speak honestly about who he or she is.

This heterocolonialism requires that sexual minorities keep our identities and our activities secret and shameful. Gays and lesbians have become adept at shifting pronouns during the most innocent or innocuous conversations because we do not feel safe speaking openly and without self-censorship. Indeed, I believe that this is why many gays and lesbians have begun to refer to their significant others as their partners (rather than lovers, which was prevalent before the 1980s), for partner is deliberately nonsexual and ambiguous; this term caters to the heterocolonial mind-set that does not want to be confronted with any notion of same-sex physicality even if one is forced by liberalness and/or political correctness to coexist with queer people.

Included in the overall muting of the Erotic in church and society is the facet of heterocolonialism that makes sexual minorities believe that when appropriate sexuality is defined it must never be our sexuality but only that of the heteronormative majority. In this regard, our situation is similar to other postcolonial people who exist at the crossroads. However, as postcolonial theologian Mayra Rivera points out, the people who inhabit crossroads, borderlands, and margins (*los atravesados*) are perhaps the best situated to construct a more inclusive theology.[6] I contend that it is precisely queer people's ostracism from the center that is constitutive and productive for a theology of sexuality and spirituality. Thus, we must not assimilate or strive to adhere to decent, safe views of the Divine, but must, with the late queer postcolonial theologian Marcella Althaus-Reid, indecent the entire theo-ethical process.[7]

In this chapter I propose the Erotic as a corrective both to the sexual battles that have plagued gays and lesbians and to heterocolonialism itself, for Empire facilitates the colonization of bodies, while Eros involves the empowerment of bodies. I begin by describing how some scholars have already begun to view the Erotic as a salvific category and conclude by presenting my own constructive theology of Eros as it impacts the Trinity and anthropology.

GLIMPSES OF EROS

The late queer sexologist Eric Rofes is to be commended for introducing the theme of spirituality into the queer community's dialogue on promiscuity, sexual safety, and recovery from AIDS decimation. In examining queer post-AIDS lives and lifestyles, he suggests that we do this is by integrating—perhaps for the first time—the Erotic into our sexual behavior:

> The erotic is a source of tremendous knowledge and power. It is of the mind, yet it goes beyond the mind; one with the heart, yet greater than the heart; rooted in the soul, yet branching beyond the soul. Many gay men know that the erotic is a force for metamorphosis; our lives provide indisputable evidence of its transformative powers. Sexual desire springs from deep and complex sources and tapping into it unleashes energy and creativity which makes us stronger, clearer, and more engaged in the richness of life.[8]

Rofes, like some feminist and queer theologians, attributes his appreciation of the Erotic to the late black lesbian feminist poet and theorist Audre Lorde, who believed that Eros was "the bridge" between the spiritual and the political.[9] Lorde saw the Erotic as that ingredient which adds color, texture, and taste to our lives; it engages the five senses in a holistic way that binds together the components of our beings: In this way Eros is able to assume its rightful place in religion (from *religare*, "to bind back or again"). Rofes has asserted that we should (re)turn to the Erotic as a bridge between our sexual lives and our political consciousness and has even gone so far as to demand that we begin to talk more about sex— what we do, why we do it, how it feels, and what it means erotically and spiritually.[10]

Sexual theologians have also called for more open discussions about sexuality and the spiritually erotic meaning of sexual behavior. Thus, Marcella Althaus-Reid has pointed out how crucial a theology of sexual storytelling becomes when sexual minorities try to overcome heteronormativity.[11] In answer to those who would claim that the sexual be strictly relegated to the private realm, she insists that this is impossible to do with authenticity, inasmuch as sexuality, rather than being confined to one's own home or a friend's bedroom, goes with us wherever we go and "permeates our economic, political and societal life."[12] Moreover, because sexual stories are always unfinished, they mirror our very lives and theologies which, of necessity, must remain unfinished to be truly authentic.

Gay theologian Mark Jordan, trained in the Roman Catholic tradition, has also called for greater openness in discussions of sexuality and spirituality, suggesting that those of same-sex affinity may have a special ability for teaching others through our sexual dialogues, not only through what we say but also how we say it.[13] He points out the irony that much mystical language in theology concerning the Godhead is erotic, yet everyday churchgoers have been discouraged from bringing their erotic selves with them on their faith journeys.[14] I believe that in making this point, Jordan demonstrates how a heterocolonial Christianity has arrogated the power of Eros to itself and kept the common person away from this power, when, in reality, whenever we talk about the Erotic we are talking about the Deity,[15] in whom we live and move and have our being.

One of the first to engage the Erotic as a theological category was lesbian feminist theologian Carter Heyward, who named it as "the deepest stirring of our relationality, our experience of being connected to others."[16] When we divorce this power from our relationships, we experience the alienation that is sin. Thus, Heyward names as sin the sort of homophobia on the part of gays and lesbians that I would call "internalized heterocolonialism"; for, instead of embracing the Erotic as what might give them a window into the Divine, they divorce themselves from it out of fear (erotophobia) that engenders desperation and despair instead of the wholeness and empowerment that an erotic and embodied spirituality can provide.[17] Heyward believes that God has given us guideposts for our becoming in the form of our sensuality: "If we learn to trust our senses they can tell us what is good and bad."[18] In this way, by championing our senses as a way of accessing God, Heyward disempowers the heterocolonial scripts that tell us our senses are evil and misguided when they reveal to us anything other than heteronormativity and what Althaus-Reid calls decent behavior.

Queer activist-theologian Robert E. Shore-Goss has also been vocal and explicit about the eroticization of sex, encouraging queer faith communities to attempt to undo Christianity's ongoing suspicion of sex. For Shore-Goss, our sexual activity reclaims the beauty and holiness of the body at the same time that our sexual pleasure combines joy, sexual justice, and spiritual practice.[19] Moreover, he has suggested that we not demonize sexual practices such as barebacking (condomless intercourse) without trying to understand what it means to the parties involved.[20] Queer theorist Michael Warner agrees, noting that a sex panic seeks to "put sex in its place," which is always a place of secrecy and shame that does no one any good. Instead, he suggests that through conversation and understanding we acknowledge that we "all have contradictory desires"; demonizing certain activities or people does nothing more than confirm people in their shame-based or rebellious activity.[21]

Gay liturgical theologian Scott Haldeman, in a deeply personal essay, describes his erotic journey from "topping" (insertive anal intercourse) to "bottoming" (receptive anal intercourse), boldly asserting that for him bottoming is not just sexual desire but a "physical need" like hunger or thirst, through which he opens himself to another man and receives (from) him. In this way a sexual role that has been vilified throughout time becomes for Haldeman a life-giving activity, erotic in its engagement of sensuality as a window into spirituality.[22] He injects a deliberately ethical nuance into the discussion, which I believe is crucial for a new understanding of the Erotic, for he insists that "we must consider our practices in terms of their effects and choose, without ignoring real constraints, what will make us better neighbors and friends, more attuned to the needs of others and our world."[23] Haldeman describes the erotic reclaiming of acts that have been forbidden or despised as transgression, which breaks down barriers and upsets heteronormative notions of what is physically and religiously appropriate at the same time that it reintegrates the Erotic as a spiritual component of our sexual behavior.[24]

African American theologians have also been active in reintegrating the Erotic into spirituality in the black church tradition, since non-white people, like queers, are often stereotyped as sexually voracious and rapacious,[25] leading many black churches to embrace an antibody dualism when it comes to appropriate expressions of Christian spirituality.[26] Thus, Anthony Pinn insists that black people reclaim Eros as sexual but more than sexual, since it is an "energy of connection-making [which] opens us, draws us out, moves us beyond ourselves into sustaining relationships with things, ideas, and beings."[27] He agrees with Althaus-Reid that often, in reclaiming the Erotic, we will be perceived as indecent, but this does not mean that we abandon the theology of eroticism, since it involves the very survival of our embodied selves.

Womanist theologian Karen Blaker-Fletcher concurs, asserting that blacks—women especially—must overcome the messages that were ingrained from childhood about not "speaking everything you think," lest the white majority be confirmed in their misconceptions about black sexual preoccupation; these messages, while well-intended, have resulted instead in black people's hatred of their own bodies and sexuality, "compartmentalization" of their lives into the private and public spheres, and a mistrust of their own creative (erotic) power.[28] She invokes the historical image of the hush harbor, a private place where black slaves would go to pray away from their masters' prying eyes; similarly, many contemporary black men and women have created metaphorical hush harbors for private discussions of sexuality and spirituality. However, Baker-Fletcher cautions that "Black women must take care not to turn our hush harbors of sacred wisdom and mystery into closets of shame and internalized oppression."[29] The private realm, while necessary for personal growth and healing, may become a prison if it is one's only option, enforced by the churches' dualistic message of body versus spirit and private versus public. Her discussion in this regard mirrors queer activists' lament that many so-called respectable gays and lesbians seek to assimilate into mainstream heteronormative society so that the majority will believe that gays and lesbians are just like normal people.[30]

Nevertheless, disagreements within the queer communities regarding sexual behaviors seen as controversial or inappropriate have brought up issues of safety, risk, and propriety. This is where mutual understanding and interpersonal dialogue become important. We must begin to hear one another regarding what acts mean to the actors themselves, rather than develop disembodied theories that universalize and essentialize what constitutes true eroticism. Thus, lesbian religious leader Nancy Wilson, Moderator of the Metropolitan Community Churches (MCC), questions the very meaning of what it means to be safe sexually and instead suggests that what is most important in queer sexuality and spirituality is the creation of the beloved community in which people intentionally work together to forge solidarity across differences in the interests of creating a just world.[31] Shore-Goss concurs, advocating a position of negotiated risk in which sex partners make informed decisions about whether they will engage in an activity typically considered unsafe; he shares his own decision-making process about whether to engage in unprotected sex with his HIV-positive partner, courageously pointing out that in life and death situations we cannot presume to inject ourselves and our moralities into the involved parties' minds or hearts.[32]

Lesbian ethicist Kathy Rudy has contributed to this discussion by suggesting that we must think more about what moral sex looks like.[33] Thus, as both Rofes and Shore-Goss have pointed out, the morality of a sexual act will not always equate strictly with mere survivalism, safety, or propriety.[34] For Rudy, the crucial ethical question becomes, "Is the sex we're having pleasing to God?"[35] Only we as individuals can answer this question (often in combination with our sex partners), for what makes an act moral are the surrounding conditions and overall context.[36] Thus, Rudy and Wilson stress hospitality as a criterion for ethical sexual behavior, while Carter Heyward sees mutuality as crucial for all acts, sexual and otherwise, between persons.[37] Heyward's recent work about therapeutic horseback riding, although written for another context entirely, nevertheless draws some conclusions about making quick moralistic judgments concerning safety that are germane to our discussion. In discussing whether horseback riding is safe or risky and dangerous, Heyward asks why people take "such calculated risks" and wonders, "Could it be to see the face of God? Is this what people are yearning for when they risk even their lives for experiences of right relation . . . ?"[38]

I have personally lived this type of risk-taking:

For Tony

All these years later
I remember
Walking down the corridor
Seeing you seeing me:

"Hey," you said,
"Want to come to my room?"
Of course I did!
You were gorgeous
Brown skin against white towel
Tall and thin

And you had chosen me . . .

We got there
And who knows what happened?
The years
    have injected
      / Barriers
    of
    Romanticism /

I know that I submitted to you
(You wanted me!)

and even though
I didn't usually give myself
That Way . . .
I thought, "Why not?"

Now I say I guess I wasn't thinking fully
But then I had just One Thing on my mind . . .
Only later
After we had come to know each other
Did you let me in on your little secret—
That even though I hadn't asked
You still had sheathed your Love—
For you prided yourself on being
A Safe Player.

How ironic:
You were the one to choose safety
And yet
You were the one to die.
I on the other hand
Live on,
Even though I wanted you so much
That I was willing to risk everything . . .

Now decades later
When others debate and shout
I know in the secrecy of my heart
And the silence of my hypocrisy
There are no easy answers
There are no easy judgments
There are no quick fixes:
It's more than we know
It's more than we can describe
That feeling
Inside
When we'd do anything—
    To feel connected
    To feel whole
    To feel desirable
    To see the face of God.

The scholars I have discussed have dared to think beyond heteronormative—what I would call heterocolonial—parameters; nevertheless, much work remains to be done in order to craft an erotic theology of sexuality and spirituality. What is most important, in my opinion, is for all of us involved in these communities to foster the willingness to openly and honestly discuss our sexual natures by promoting safe spaces within the margins, where shame is not admitted and the Erotic is the gatekeeper. Elsewhere I have called this spiritual dialogue on the Erotic (Althaus-Reid's sexual storytelling) a "politics of holy voyeurism."[39] Indeed, if, as I pointed out at the beginning of this chapter, God has no body of His or Her own, but rather depends upon us to embody the Divine through our bodies, God may be the ultimate Holy Voyeur! Therefore, it becomes all the more important to continually ponder how what we do with our bodies might be a window into the Divine. In understanding the Divine better, we understand ourselves better; and in embracing our authentic selves, we embrace the Divine and all that He or She intends for creation. Womanist ethicist Katie Cannon, in discussing black women's eroticism, expresses this sentiment well: "All of us must take personal risks associated with growth and change if we are going to be our best erotic selves."[40]

THINKING EROS: AN/OTHER('S) TRINITY

Unfortunately, however, much Christian God-talk has centered on categories and images that do not include Eros. While most would agree that it is biblically warranted that God is Love (1 Jn 3), theologians and church pronouncements have concentrated almost exclusively upon divine love that does not mention Eros, thereby implicitly excluding it from consideration as indicative of God/Love. Students of New Testament *koiné* ("common") Greek are familiar with the classification of three types of love: *Philia* is friendship love that is often predicated on reciprocity, while *Agape* is the unconditional outwardly directed love that is of the Spirit (translated in older Bibles as charity) and not of the flesh; this fleshly sexual love is *Eros* (often narrowly interpreted as passion), which has been downplayed in Christian theology beginning as far back as the patristic period.[41] However, as theologian-psychologist Lee Butler has noted, "Splitting spirituality and sexuality has resulted in our having deviant perceptions about embodiment and how we are to achieve holiness."[42] Some of these deviant perceptions have included a body/spirit dualism that has not only produced defective beliefs regarding women, non-whites, and non-heterosexuals, but has also resulted in some deviant Christological and soteriological propositions.[43] Moreover, sexuality divorced from spirituality (what I would call "eros thwarted") ceases to be erotic and becomes pornographic, which is a true perversion of God's intention for humankind as revealed in Genesis 1–2.[44]

But what would happen if we were to inject Eros into the Christian Trinity itself? Ecofeminist theologian Sallie McFague has proposed as an alternative Trinity "God the Mother," "God the Lover," and "God the Friend" with the Earth as "God's Body"[45]; while Elizabeth Johnson, in imaging the Godhead as Sophia/Wisdom, has offered the Trinity of "Spirit-Sophia," "Jesus-Sophia," and "Mother-Sophia."[46] Both of these suggestions are extremely helpful and provocative within the contexts for which they were written—ecological and feminist concerns. However, in the context of theology for those oppressed by Empire's erotophobia and body colonization, I believe another Trinitarian proposal is appropriate.

My notion of the Christian Trinity involves a Godhead that has three aspects yet is one. It is organic, dynamic, cyclic, mutual, and nonhierarchical. There is interchange and flow between the three who are one. Rather than being equidistant *from* humanity, each one is equipresent *for* humanity. These aspects are contained in created beings but are not exhausted by them, thus retaining traditional theology's notion of the transcendent and the imminent, the apophatic and the kataphatic.[47] I would name the three parts of this Trinity after the three Greek words for love, for God is Love[48]:

- *Agape* is God/Love the Source—originate and unconditionally loving, from whom everything comes forth (the subject of theology);
- *Philia* is God/Love the Savior—a reciprocal part of God imparted to all so that we too may become agapaic (the subject of Christology);
- *Eros* is God/Love the Sustainer—the com/passionate One who is Many through physical manifestation of passion in relationship (the subject of pneumatology).

I call this an/Other('s) Trinity because it is another version of the traditional Trinity, yet it comes from an Other, that is, one who has been othered by traditional Christianity. Undoubtedly, those who have devoted their careers to theologizing about the Godhead would find much to critique in this suggestion; nevertheless, I believe it is a place to start because through it disenfranchised others may see themselves in God. *Agape/God* is what we come from and to which we return; our life is a journey back to this original Source and its unbounded love. *Philia/God* is that part of the Divine that became one of us in Jesus, demonstrating God's reciprocity and fellow-feeling and through emulation of whom we journey further toward completion by becoming other Christs.[49] *Eros/ God* is Deity present in each of us, who are the Body(ies) of God; the use of our bodies in sexual passion gods the creation. The Erotic empowered in creation's sensuality and sexuality not only births the spirituality that changes the world and softens hearts; but this Erotic also fortifies us with the passion to be community and church for one another precisely because it works through our bodies and not in spite of them. Furthermore, by eliminating some of the nuances of patriarchal theology, this love-centered Trinity imagines a more holistic, mutual Deity who nurtures us, fortifies us, and partners with us; because the persons of this Trinity interpenetrate and penetrate us with love, no one person is able to withhold love in top-down fashion, as many queer persons have been taught God the Father does when we do not behave according to heterocolonial expectations.

TALKING EROS: AUTHENTIC HUMANNESS AS THE RESPONSIBILITY OF EROS

If, as I have contended, each of us embodies Eros, we are entrusted with an awesome responsibility, for by our very love/making we can choose whether or not to manifest Eros: For example, a sexual act between two people of the same sex that is mutually empowering and fulfilling, thus directing the parties toward wholeness, embraces the Erotic and human authenticity; whereas a sexual act of nonconsensual violence between people of any gender would not be erotic at all. Similarly, I differentiate between pornography and nonpornographic erotica: The former portrays violence and nonmutual or nonholistic sex, while the latter depicts playful, unitive sex that titillates but does not harm or objectify. Historically, many of the interactions between the lesbian and gay male communities and within the lesbian and gay communities themselves over issues such as S/M, leather, use of sex toys, and pornography have revealed a great deal of misunderstanding and judgment concerning sexual behavior.[50] Of course, a wonderful suggestion would be if we learned to listen to one another in better and more helpful and healthful ways. Nevertheless, as a realist, I recognize that the process of communication must begin one individual at a time, with each person dialoguing with himself or herself about the meaning of sex and what brings each person toward wholeness and authentic humanness as the erotic *imago dei*. This will require a revision of the culture of sexuality in society and in churches and a reformulation of how we look at *sexual feelings*, *sexual behavior*, and *sexual ethics*.

I therefore propose an anthropology that blends these elements into a self-conscious and other-conscious theo-ethics of eroticism.

The Traditional Paradigm

Perhaps from our Augustinian legacy, Euro/American society seems to follow a linear sexual paradigm that looks something like this:

- *Sexual ethics* are propounded from above, based on a general morality and code of behavior rooted in tradition and culture, including religion and sacred texts.
- *Sexual behavior* derives from these principles and is labeled either appropriate or inappropriate according to the ethical norms.
- *Sexual feelings* depend upon how one's behavior is judged. It is here that one experiences shame or comfort, guilt, or completion.[51]

An Outlaw Paradigm

Some queer people have rebelled against this traditional paradigm. This could be due to shame, anger, or despair, and manifests itself in a lack of concern for society's norms. Since these persons are, in John Rechy's words, "sexual outlaws,"[52] they do not prescind from society's sexual ethics because they have rejected them. In any case, these outlaws seem to have followed a different linear paradigm that looks something like this:

- *Sexual feelings* are accepted as given and sometimes unexamined.
- *Sexual behavior* results from these sexual feelings; if unexamined, they may result in behavior that is risky, dangerous, and unhealthy physically, emotionally, and spiritually.
- *Sexual ethics*, largely situational, are developed (if at all) out of sexual behavior. (In my own experience, my sexual ethics have sometimes been to embrace none at all, while at other times to determine these ethics in combination with a sex partner.)

An Erotic Paradigm

I suggest that both of the above paradigms are problematic. The first makes the mistake of imposing sexual ethics from above, without considering the sexual person's feelings or behavior, while the second formulates sexual ethics after the feelings have been engaged and the activity performed. Perhaps the difficulty is that they are both linear in structure, whereas what is called for—and how this really works—is more cyclical in nature. Thus, I would suggest the following as a way of addressing anew our construction of our sexual lives and the ensuing discussions:

- *Sexual feelings* are examined for how they nourish the entire person, taking eroticism and holistic passion into account.
- *Sexual ethics* are derived from these sexual/erotic/passionate feelings; these ethics are other-oriented *and* self-oriented, rather than strictly self-oriented.
- *Sexual behavior*—or lack thereof—is derived from the sexual ethics that have grown out of reflection upon our sexual feelings; this may mean that there is no sexual behavior at all in a given situation because the ethics and the feelings counsel otherwise.
- *Sexual behavior* (or lack thereof) leads back to *sexual feelings*, sometimes resulting in a re-examination of *sexual ethics*, as the process continues without cessation.

Because these three aspects of sexual life coexist in a circle, they constantly inform one another, for they are in a dialogue of mutuality. While I recognize that this alternative paradigm requires further examination and discussion, I believe that, in order to curtail the prevailing atmosphere of mistrust and disrespect, this is a place to start in our communities and our churches for the following reasons: (1) The paradigm I envision does not require or promote any particular level of sexual activity (i.e., celibacy, monogamy, or polyamory); (2) it does not forbid controversial sexual activities (i.e., barebacking, rimming, fisting, use of sex toys, or nonpornographic erotica); because (3) it encourages individuals to develop from their own sexual needs, desires, and feelings their own criteria for sexual ethics that lead to more carefully considered sexual behavior.

Overarching and empowering this entire dialogue process would be God/Love, requiring at the outset that we agree that for any feelings, ethics, or behavior to be representative of God/Love they must be reflective of the two great commandments of Judaism and Christianity—love of the Divine as revealed in both ourselves and others. By employing self-love, love of others, and love of God as the ultimate criteria for an erotic ethical paradigm, we are able to minimize the central criticism that has been made of erotic theology, that it is eschatological, idealistic, and essentialist in its exclusive empowering of the goodness of Eros and its outright dismissal of perversions of Eros such as sexual violence and pedophilia.[53] Both an erotic view of the Trinity and an erotic anthropology acknowledge that Eros/God has been perverted by human sin, especially patriarchal logic and heterosexism.

A turn to the Erotic need not remain theoretical or postponed to the future, *if* we are willing to allow Eros to come to church with us. Any movement toward an erotic spirituality would require that community and church leaders educate themselves in all aspects of sexuality, including the way the Divine expresses Itself through the Erotic—even if this makes us uncomfortable—through openness and the telling of our sexual stories. In this way, attitudes of judgment might give way to gospel values of justice-love, inclusion, and understanding for all people, including oneself. Mark Jordan reminds us that redeeming sex is a "rhetorical challenge"[54]; who better to take up such a challenge than those who have labored under heterocolonialism and fought long and hard for validity, dignity, justice, and a place at the theo-ethical table? Eros just might be able to come to church if faith communities would demonstrate a willingness in thought, word, and deed to become places of erotic hospitality, openness, and inclusion.

My two decades as a pastor in the MCC has demonstrated to me that there could be a willingness among some LGBTQI people, but that this willingness is often asphyxiated by an erotophobia which has been learned and internalized. Coupled with this erotophobia is a yearning within many LGBTQI people to be "just like everybody else" (whatever that means!), leading them to assimilate to heteronormative paradigms and focus narrowly on issues such as same-sex marriage at the expense of other issues of sexual becoming. The seed of erotic questioning that remains hidden must be watered and nurtured by creative and prophetic leaders who are willing to open themselves to queer theories both inside and outside the church in order to find that empowering kernel of Eros/God's love that, in the words of novelist Toni Morrison, is "lying in wait to show us the splendor."[55]

NOTES

1. The poems in this chapter were written by the author during the preparation of his doctoral thesis at the Episcopal Divinity School, entitled "Heterocolonialism Queered: When Eros Comes to Church" (2007); this chapter is a reworked version of Chapter 3 of that thesis. I wish to acknowledge the mentoring of my thesis supervisor, Kwok Pui Lan; her words and witness continue to inform my own.

2. By aesthetically I mean a nongenital sort of sexual relating that, while not traditionally sexual as our society has come to understand it, is nevertheless sexual in that it includes passion, sensuality, and eroticism. For example, I have never had sexual intercourse with a woman, yet, in the course of preparing this chapter, have realized that I have had relationships with women that were indeed sexual, in that they involved intense affection, engagement of the senses, and erotic appreciation for the women's bodies. It is in this sense that I agree with queer theorists that the terms gay and lesbian can become unnecessarily confining.

3. This unwieldy anagram stands for gay, lesbian, bisexual, transgender, intersex, and queer. I note that these groups are not one homogeneous community but rather several heterogeneous communities that are sometimes grouped under the umbrella term queer. For an excellent discussion of the problematics of queer as umbrella term, see Patrick S. Cheng, *Radical Love: An Introduction to Queer Theology* (New York: Seabury Press, 2010), esp. ch. 1.

4. Dorothy Allison, *Skin: Talking About Sex, Class and Literature* (Ann Arbor, MI: Firebrand Books, 1994); Lisa Duggan and Nan D. Hunter, eds., *Sex Wars: Sexual Dissent and Political Culture* (New York and London: Routledge, 1995); Sheila Jeffreys, *Anticlimax: A Feminist Perspective on the Sexual Revolution* (London: Women's Press, 1990), and *The Lesbian Heresy: A Feminist Perspective on the Lesbian Sexual Revolution* (Melbourne: Spinifex Press, 1990); Carole S. Vance, ed., *Pleasure and Danger: Exploring Female Sexuality* (Boston and London: Routledge and Kegan-Paul, 1984).

5. Larry Kramer, "How Can We Be Gay Now?" *LGNY*, July 6, 1997: 1, 28–29, and "Sex and Sensibility," *The Advocate*, May 27, 1997: 59–70; Gabriel Rotello, *Sexual Ecology: AIDS and the Destiny of Gay Men* (New York: Penguin/Dutton, 1997); Michelangelo Signorile, *Life Outside: The Signorile Report on Gay Men: Sex, Drugs, Muscles, and the Passages of Life* (New York: HarperCollins, 1997).

6. Mayra Rivera, "God at the Crossroads: A Postcolonial Reading of Sophia," in *Postcolonial Theologies: Divinity and Empire*, ed. Catherine Keller, Michael Nausner, and Mayra Rivera (St. Louis, MO: Chalice Press, 2004), 187.

7. Marcella Althaus-Reid, "Queer I Stand: Lifting the Skirts of God," in *The Sexual Theologian: Essays on Sex, God and Politics*, ed. Marcella Althaus-Reid and Lisa Isherwood (New York: T & T Clark International, 2004), 101.

8. Eric Rofes, *Reviving the Tribe: Regenerating Gay Men's Sexuality and Culture in the Ongoing Epidemic* (New York: Haworth Press, 1996), 105.

9. Audre Lorde, "Uses of the Erotic: The Erotic as Power," in *Sister Outsider: Essays and Speeches*, ed. Audre Lorde (Trumansburg, NY: Crossing Press, 1984), 54–55.

10. Rofes, *Reviving the Tribe*, 106–9, 264–74.

11. Marcella Althaus-Reid, *Indecent Theology: Theological Perversions in Sex, Gender and Politics* (London: Routledge, 2000), 130–31.

12. Ibid.

13. Mark D. Jordan, *Telling Truths in Church: Scandal, Flesh, and Christian Speech* (Boston, MA: Beacon Press, 2003), 56.

14. Ibid., 74.

15. Ibid., 76.

16. Carter Heyward, *Touching Our Strength: The Erotic as Power and the Love of God* (New York: Harper & Row, 1989), 55.

17. Ibid., 60, 104.

18. Ibid., 93.

19. Robert E. Shore-Goss, "Gay Erotic Spirituality and the Recovery of Sexual Pleasure," in *Body and Soul: Rethinking Sexuality as Justice-Love*, ed. Marvin Ellison and Sylvia Thorson-Smith (Cleveland: Pilgrim Press, 2003), 202, 204, 208

20. Robert E. Goss, *Queering Christ: Beyond Jesus Acted Up* (Cleveland: Pilgrim Press, 2002), 79–80.

21. Michael Warner, *The Trouble with Normal: Sex, Politics, and the Ethics of Queer Life* (New York: Free Press, 1999), 195–96, 215–16.

22. Scott Haldeman, "Receptivity and Revelation: A Spirituality of Gay Male Sex," in *Body and Soul*, 221–23.

23. Ibid., 219.

24. Ibid., 225. Goss articulates transgression as the very meaning of queer. *Queering Christ*, xiv–xv.

25. Dwight N. Hopkins, "The Construction of the Black Male Body: Eroticism and Religion," in *Loving the Body: Black Religious Studies and the Erotic*, ed. Anthony B. Pinn and Dwight N. Hopkins (New York: Palgrave/Macmillan, 2004), 182–88.

26. Victor Anderson, "The Black Church and the Curious Body of the Black Homosexual," in *Loving the Body*, 299–302.

27. Anthony B. Pinn, "Embracing Nimrod's Legacy: The Erotic, the Irreverence of Fantasy, and the Redemption of Black Theology," in *Loving the Body*, 163–64.

28. Karen Baker-Fletcher, "The Erotic in Contemporary Black Women's Writings," in *Loving the Body*, 204–7.

29. Ibid.

30. Urvashi Vaid, *Virtual Equality: The Mainstreaming of Gay and Lesbian Liberation* (New York: Anchor Books/Doubleday, 1995), 3, 37; Warner, *The Trouble with Normal*, 59.

31. Nancy L. Wilson, "Queer Culture and Sexuality as a Virtue of Hospitality," in *Our Families, Our Values: Snapshots of Queer Kinship*, ed. Robert E. Goss and Amy Adams Squire Strongheart (New York: Haworth Press, 1997), 30, 33. Queer AIDS activist Douglas Crimp asserts that absolute safety is a fantasy. *Melancholia and Moralism: Essays on AIDS and Queer Politics* (Cambridge: MIT Press, 2002), 300.

32. Goss, *Queering Christ*, 74–86. Shore-Goss concludes, "The exchange of semen is often experienced as a vital expression of intimacy; . . . [t]he intimacy of ejaculating in a partner leaves tangible, albeit transient, evidence of intimacy, connection, and a profound exchange. . . . I would argue that the taboo of theological silence must be broken. . . . There is room for much more theological exploration of anal intercourse . . . " (80–81).

33. Kathy Rudy, *Sex and the Church: Gender, Homosexuality, and the Transformation of Christian Ethics* (Boston: Beacon Press, 1997), 78, 97.

34. Goss, *Queering Christ*, 83; Eric Rofes, *Dry Bones Breathe: Gay Men Creating Post-AIDS Identities and Cultures* (New York: Haworth Press, 1998), 226–27.

35. Rudy, *Sex and the Church*, 83.

36. Ibid., 110, 126.

37. Carter Heyward, *Speaking of Christ: A Lesbian Feminist Voice*, ed. Ellen C. Davis (New York: Pilgrim Press, 1989), 21.

38. Carter Heyward, *Flying Changes: Horses as Spiritual Teachers* (Cleveland: Pilgrim Press, 2005), 66–67.

39. Thomas Bohache, "Pentecost Queered," in "Acts of the Apostles" in *The Queer Bible Commentary*, ed. Deryn Guest, Robert E.Goss, Mona West, and Thomas Bohache (London: SCM Press, 2006), 570.

40. Katie G. Cannon, "Sexing Black Women: Liberation from the Prisonhouse of Anatomical Authority," in *Loving the Body*, 17, quoting one of her graduate students.

41. Recently some patristics scholars have begun to explore some queer readings of the Church Fathers which go against the grain of previous understandings of the early church. See, Virginia Burrus, "Queer Father: Gregory of Nyssa and the Subversion of Identity," in *Queer Theology: Rethinking the Christian Body*, ed. Gerard Loughlin (Malden, MA: Blackwell, 2007), 147–62; and Morwenna Ludlow, *Reading the Church Fathers* (New York: T & T Clark International, 2011).

42. Lee Butler, "The Spirit Is Willing and the Flesh Is Too: Living Whole and Holy Lives Through Integrating Spirituality and Sexuality," in *Loving the Body*, 118.

43. Patrick S. Cheng, *From Sin to Amazing Grace: Discovering the Queer Christ* (New York: Seabury Press, 2012).

44. For an erotic, non-normative reading of Genesis 1–2, see Phyllis Trible, *God and the Rhetoric of Sexuality, Overtures to Biblical Theology* (Philadelphia: Fortress Press, 1978), chs. 1 and 4.

45. Sallie McFague, *Models of God: Theology for an Ecological, Nuclear Age* (Philadelphia, PA: Fortress Press, 1987). See also Sallie McFague, *The Body of God: An Ecological Theology* (Minneapolis: Fortress Press, 1993).

46. Elizabeth A. Johnson, *She Who Is: The Mystery of God in Feminist Theological Discourse* (New York: Crossroad, 1992).

47. Susannah Cornwall, "Apophasis and Ambiguity: The 'Unknowingness' of Transgender," in *Trans/Formations*, ed. Marcella Althaus-Reid and Lisa Isherwood (London: SCM Press, 2009), 13–40.

48. For another type of Trinity focusing on God as "Radical Love," see Cheng, *Radical Love*, chs. 3–5.

49. Meister Eckhart, quoted in Matthew Fox, *The Coming of the Cosmic Christ: The Healing of Mother Earth and the Birth of a Global Renaissance* (New York: Harper & Row, 1988), 121. See also my queer Christology in Thomas Bohache, *Christology from the Margins* (London: SCM Press, 2008), esp. chs. 10–11.

50. See the works cited in notes 4 and 5, above.

51. Of course I recognize that these steps are not this discrete and separate; I have listed them in this way strictly for heuristic purposes of description.

52. John Rechy, "The Outlaw Sensibility: Liberated Ghettos, Noble Stereotypes, and a Few More Promiscuous Observations," in *Beneath the Skin: The Collected Essays of John Rechy*, ed. John Rechy (New York: Carroll and Graf Publishers, 2004), 155. See also John Rechy, *The Sexual Outlaw: A Documentary* (New York: Grove Weidenfield, 1977).

53. Kathleen M. Sands, "Uses of the Thea(o)logian: Sex and Theodicy in Religious Feminism," *Journal of Feminist Studies in Religion* 8, no. 1 (1992): 7–33; Alyda Faber, "Eros and Violence," *Feminist Theology* 12, no. 3 (2004): 319–42.

54. Mark D. Jordan, *The Ethics of Sex* (Oxford, UK: Blackwell Publishers, 2002), 156.

55. Toni Morrison, *Paradise* (New York: Alfred A. Knopf, 1998).

7

Reinterpreting Baptism:
An Ongoing Dialogue

Bryce E. Rich

What if we could see baptism as inclusively as we see communion, and really made it our own, got comfortable with it, reinterpreted it with the authority and power with which we celebrate communion week after week?[1]

In 2006 UFMCC Moderator Nancy Wilson preached a sermon in which she called our denomination to a dialogue around our understandings of baptism:

Wouldn't it be wonderful and amazing if in MCC we were able to have discussions about spirituality and what we believe about baptism and other things in safe spaces in our local churches, at our Regional Gatherings, at Conferences? What if we deliberately created safe spaces where we did not judge each other, or try to "convert" each other to our point of view, but where we just listened and learned and allowed ourselves to be amazed at the depth and breadth of our feelings and thoughts about our faith—so that it might unite us more than it divides us?[2]

The following essay is offered in the spirit of fostering just such a discussion.

Members of Metropolitan Community Church (MCC) are drawn from practically every corner of the Church, bringing with us a wide array of beliefs and teachings concerning the nature and function of baptism. For this reason any discussion around reinterpreting baptism would profit from an overview of the rich foundational heritage that continues to inform our development on a number of levels.

BIBLICAL WITNESS

Each gospel tells the story of John the Baptist who preached by the Jordan and practiced a baptism of repentance. By one account some of Jesus' disciples were baptized by John the Baptist and were on the lookout for Jesus' coming. In the synoptic tradition, Jesus too came before John and presented himself for baptism. But the baptism of repentance was transformed into a new baptism of the Holy Spirit when Jesus came up from Jordan's waters. The accounts vary as to who saw the Spirit as it descended from the heavens and came to rest on Jesus, but the synoptics tell us that a voice from heaven announced that Jesus was God's own beloved son. It is from these accounts that MCC has derived its foundational understanding of baptism as a sign identifying the recipient as God's own child.[3] It is with this baptism that Jesus commissions his followers to make disciples of all peoples.[4] The Luke–Acts narrative continues to develop the understanding of baptism by making a distinction between John's baptism of repentance and the baptism of the Holy Spirit, which appears as a sign of God's presence in the phenomenal growth of the early Church (Acts 1:5, 8; 8:6; 19:2). Within the Pauline corpus, baptism takes on the additional symbolism of being buried and raised into new life with Jesus Christ (Rom 6:4), a washing and regeneration (Titus 3:4–7) and a putting on of Christ, eliminating boundaries of class, nationality, and gender (Gal 3:27–28).[5]

HISTORICAL DEVELOPMENTS

Beyond the biblical witness, baptism is mentioned in the *Didache*, a document widely believed to be of Syrian origin from the late first or early second century. The text includes instructions concerning ritual fasting before baptism, the use of the Trinitarian formula, and several modes of baptism in order of preference from running water to still water to the pouring of water over the head of the one receiving baptism (*Didache* 14). Later, around 160 CE, Justin Martyr wrote in his explanation of Christian practices to Emperor Antoninus Pius that those wishing to be consecrated to God and regenerated through Christ first underwent instruction, fasted, and asked God to forgive their sins. Afterward they were led to water where they were baptized using the Trinitarian formula.[6] Within the Eastern Orthodox and Roman Catholic traditions (representing two of the oldest and most widespread forms of Christianity), baptism is considered a sacrament—an act by which God's grace is communicated to the recipient, bringing about a spiritual change. This understanding already appears as far back as Justin Martyr's apology and continues without challenge until the rise of the Protestant Reformation in the 16th century. Martin Luther and John Calvin also affirmed the sacramental nature of baptism—an understanding that is still embraced by the Lutheran and Reformed traditions today. However, it was also during the Protestant Reformation that Ulrich Zwingli broke with the sacramental understanding of baptism to advance a new line of thought. For Zwingli baptism was not a sacrament, but a sign. In this formulation, baptism conveys no special grace from God, nor is it what saves a person. Rather, as an analog to circumcision within the Jewish context, it is a sign of membership within the community. It is from this understanding that we receive the common description of baptism as "an outward sign of an inward change."[7] Several groups of modern Christians still espouse Zwingli's understanding of baptism as we shall see below.

PEDOBAPTISM AND CREDOBAPTISM

Within the discussion surrounding baptism, Christian churches can also be divided into two major categories: those who baptize infants (*pedobaptism*, from the Greek word *pais*, meaning, among other things, "child") and those who baptize only those who can profess Christian faith (sometimes known as *credobaptism*, from the Latin *credo* meaning "I believe"). Both theologies claim biblical authority for their practice.

For those who practice pedobaptism, scriptural passages that describe the baptism of entire households (e.g., Acts 16:15, 31–33; 1 Cor 1:16) are interpreted as including even infants and small children.[8] The writings of Irenaeus of Lyons (ca. 130–200) provide evidence of the baptism not only of catechumens, but also of infants and small children.[9] While Tertullian (d. ca. 225) advised against the baptism of children, his *De Baptismo* ("On Baptism") describes the practice of sponsors taking baptismal vows on behalf of children, thereby risking the possibility of bringing death upon themselves should the children not grow up to fulfill that which had been sworn on their behalf.[10] Origen of Alexandria (ca. 185–254) also mentions infant baptism as a matter of course in three separate homilies and commentaries (Lev 158; Lk 58–59; Rom 367). Furthermore, the *Apostolic Tradition*, which has historically been attributed to antipope Hippolytus of Rome (d. ca. 236) provides instructions to baptize the little ones first, letting them speak for themselves if they were able, but having parents or relatives speak for them if they were not.[11] Although a growing number of scholars have questioned the authorship of this document, it appears that pedobaptism was a widespread practice among Christians by the third century.[12] Contemporary practitioners of pedobaptism include the Eastern Orthodox churches, the Anglican Church, the Reformed Tradition, and Roman Catholicism, the last of which is strongly represented within MCC.

The Radical Reformers of Switzerland, arising contemporaneously with the broader Protestant Reformation, preached against the practice of pedobaptism, instead espousing a believer's baptism.[13] Like their contemporary, Ulrich Zwingli, the Radical Reformers viewed baptism not as a sacrament, but rather as a sign. However, unlike Zwingli, who accepted infant baptism, they believed that only a person who had achieved the ability to reason should undertake baptism. Proponents of this understanding of baptism were often baptized a second time of their own volition, believing that their infant baptisms were invalid because they were received without their conscious understanding or confession of faith.[14] Within a short time believer's baptism spread from these original reformers to English dissenters who had fled to Amsterdam, Holland to avoid persecution by the Anglican Church. Led by John Smyth and Thomas Helwys, these dissenters sought to reconstitute what they perceived as New Testament church patterns. Their adoption of believer's baptism and subsequent return to England led to the spread of what would within a short time be known as the Baptist movement. Modern groups practicing credobaptism include various Anabaptists groups (including the Mennonites, Brethren, and Amish), Baptists and Pentecostals, with the latter two groups being strongly represented within MCC. In addition, a greater emphasis has been placed on believer's baptism in Roman Catholicism as an element of the Rite of Christian Initiation of Adults since the Second Vatican Council.[15]

BAPTISM WITHIN THE ECUMENICAL MOVEMENT

In 1982, the World Council of Churches released a document entitled *Baptism, Eucharist, and Ministry* (from here forward referenced as *BEM*), an ecumenical report embodying the fruit of 50 years of dialogue between practically all the major church traditions, both Eastern and Western. The purpose of *BEM* is not to lay out a complete systematic theology, but rather to concentrate on areas of teaching where differences prevent mutual recognition and unity within the Church.[16] As ecumenical dialogue has been a longstanding priority of MCC, the recommendations found within *BEM* are of considerable import to the internal MCC discussion around reimagining baptism. What follows is a summary of major points in the conversation:

- Baptism is the sign of new life through Jesus Christ, which unites the recipient with both Christ and the Church. It is participation in the life, death, and resurrection of Jesus Christ.[17]
- Baptism implies confession of sin and conversion of heart, effecting pardon, cleansing, and sanctification by Christ, together with a new ethical orientation under the guidance of the Holy Spirit, which is bestowed on the recipient's life and nurtures the life of faith.[18]
- Baptism incorporates the recipient into the Body of Christ (the Church) and initiates the reality of the new life given in the midst of the present world.[19]
- Baptism is accompanied by a profession of faith, made by the recipient or by sponsors in the case of pedobaptism. Infants confirm this confession at a later time. For both believers and infants alike, understanding of baptism continues to develop over time. The difference between these types is a matter of age. "The differences between infant and believers' baptism become less sharp when it is recognized that both forms of baptism embody God's own initiative in Christ and express a response of faith made within the believing community."[20]
- Baptism is an unrepeatable act and any practice which might appear as re-baptism is strongly discouraged.[21]
- Baptism is administered with water, using the Trinitarian formula. Immersion is encouraged for the symbolic dimensions of death, burial, and resurrection.[22]
- Baptism is normally administered by an ordained minister and as a part of public worship.[23]

As MCC continues its own internal dialogue around baptism, it is helpful to keep the larger ecumenical conversation in mind. As we appropriate baptism, working out our own theological understandings and practices, we do so in relationship with the larger Christian community. While we may choose to formulate our own unique practices and beliefs, doing so with an awareness of the framework presented in *BEM* allows us to make intentional decisions, cognizant of the potential consequences of our actions for our relations with other Christian churches.

BAPTISM WITHIN MCC

Over the 40 years of our shared history, MCC has had remarkably little to say about baptism. In part this may be due to the nature of our first congregations, which primarily comprised LGBT Christians who had already received baptism in other denominations before coming to our churches. As Moderator Nancy Wilson has pointed out, MCC is "all over the map about baptism" and "our theology and teaching about it is underdeveloped."[24] Our 2007 Bylaws contain a mere three lines dedicated to the topic:

> BAPTISM by water and the Spirit, as recorded in the Scriptures, shall be a sign of the dedication of each life to God and God's service. Through the words and acts of this sacrament, the recipient is identified as God's own Child.[25]

Although not explicitly stated within the Bylaws, Kittredge Cherry has noted that "[MCC] has always recognized all three forms of baptism (emersion, pouring and sprinkling) which may be administered to people of any age."[26] MCC is somewhat unique within the larger Christian Church as a group that espouses both pedobaptism and credobaptism.

Although our Bylaws define baptism as a sacrament, a quick survey of any local congregation will show that we do not all accept this tenet or even know what is stipulated in our foundational documents. Many MCC members come from nonsacramental Christian traditions (e.g., Baptists, Pentecostals) that embrace a Zwinglian view of baptism as a sign, while still others enter MCC with either a Christian cultural identity that does not include a theological awareness regarding baptism or with no previous Christian experience at all. For this last group, discussions around the communication of particular graces most often bear no particular significance. As of 2007 we estimate that roughly 80 percent of MCC members come from evangelical Protestant (including Pentecostal) and Catholic backgrounds.[27] Between these two groups exists a gulf separating their understandings regarding baptism, with the former group often rejecting pedobaptism completely.

Until recently, those choosing baptism within MCC have primarily been LGBT youth and adults, thus postponing the imminent necessity for theological education and reflection around pedobaptism. Finally, anecdotal evidence suggests that some MCC members are rebaptized by their own request upon coming to MCC. This reality is addressed further.

WHAT MCC THEOLOGIANS HAVE SAID

Although MCC theology concerning baptism is sparse, a review of available sources turns up three interesting voices within the conversation. What follows is a brief overview of the contributions made by Robert Goss, Marcella Althaus-Reid, and Nancy Wilson, followed by observations regarding areas for expansion or unique contributions that MCC can make in furthering the conversation. As our discussion progresses we should remember that these authors' contributions, while helpful to our work in constructive theology, were never intended to address all aspects of the questions at hand. In fact, only Wilson's comments were offered with a broader constructive theological discussion concerning baptism in mind. As such, the descriptions that follow and the observations offered are in no way meant to imply deficiency in the original contributors' comments.

In his seminal work *Jesus Acted Up*, Robert Goss describes Jesus' own baptism as both an event of disclosure and a rite of initiation.[28] Prior to his baptism, Jesus had spent 40 days in the desert, a liminal space at the margins of his society, where he received a vision of the reign of God in which social boundaries are broken down and society's outcasts are invited to participate fully in this new way of being. Following what Goss characterizes as a shamanistic vision quest, Jesus' status as beloved child of God was revealed at his baptism. In the symbolism of being immersed in water, Goss sees "eroticism, purification, liminality, death, and rebirth."[29] Following Jesus' example, we too are initiated through our baptism into this new vision of God's reign. Joining the struggle for God's justice, we take on a new identity and help to usher in Jesus' vision of the *basileia*[30] of God by creating new social boundaries in the margins. Goss further suggests that this baptismal symbolism is inclusive of our queer sexual identities.[31] Not only are we making a stand as followers of Christ, but also as queer[32] followers of Christ. Through our baptism we come out of the illusion that our sexual being is incompatible with the message of the gospel. We are incorporated into this reign of God with our sexuality fully intact.

This powerful claim of integration between sexuality and spirituality continues in the MCC trajectory begun by Troy Perry when he claimed that God's love encompasses all of our being, including our sexuality.[33] In drawing together all marginalized people, this vision pushes past MCC's original concerns with sexuality, while blazing a trail for the 2005 Strategic Plan in which inclusion is cited as an MCC Core Value.[34] The embrace of sexuality within our spirituality and the call to overturn systems of exclusion, drawing all marginalized people into Jesus' vision of the reign of God are two important contributions to our reimagining of baptism.

It is interesting to note that though he was raised Roman Catholic and ordained as a Jesuit priest, Goss's appropriation of baptism does not explicitly convey a sacramental understanding of the act.[35] Furthermore, by narrowly defining baptism as initiation into the *basileia* practice of

Christ, this understanding falls squarely into the camp of believer's baptism, practiced within this context by queer Christians as a coming out ritual. However, since this formulation of initiation for queer folks was first proposed in 1993, MCC has witnessed an explosion in the number of children within our denomination. Our families of choice have grown to include our children from previous opposite-sex relationships, adopted children, and children born into a variety of family configurations that defy traditional definitions. This development brings to the fore two realities of baptism that are not included in Goss's definition. First, pedobaptism becomes a more prominent issue as parents present their children for inclusion in the Church. Second, both infants presented for baptism, as well as our older children and youth, are no more likely to self-identify as LGBT than the general population. We have long asserted that we are not a church organized around either homosexuality or the legitimatization of a certain type of behavior.[36] Thus, while Goss's inclusion of queer sexualities within the reign of God is a positive contribution to our constructive theology, it is not necessarily the primary focus of our opposite-gender-loving children or others who come to Christ through the ministries of MCC. To make it so would be to repeat the exclusion many of our members have faced in other quarters of the Church. While it is incumbent upon us to model *basileia* practice that is inclusive of all sexual orientations and gender identities, overemphasis does not serve the next generation well.

Moving to the work of Marcella Althaus-Reid, we find a critique of a certain understanding of pedobaptism as a washing away of original sin (Roman Catholicism) or total depravity (Reformed tradition). Drawing on the work of Bloch and Guggenheim, Althaus-Reid notes that in some societies, the idea of original sin and rebirth has been co-opted into power structures of empire,[37] insinuating that the work of the mother bringing a child into the world is imperfect and in need of supplementation that only the Church can provide. "Baptism implies that newborn children are incomplete in some respect. It asserts that the creative power to complete this humanity lies not with the mother . . . but with the church."[38] As a result, motherhood is devalued and women are seen as contaminating their children with the stain of original sin which can be ignored only at the risk of eternal damnation. Such understandings breed misogyny, as well as a strong dualism between flesh and spirit and a deep suspicion of the body.

While tracing the development of the baptismal liturgy through the ages, Aidan Kavanagh describes Augustine's doctrine of original sin as a consequence of changes that were taking place in liturgical practice. Originally, reception into the Church was predicated on a series of liturgical acts performed over the course of several years: catechesis, the administration of salt, the laying on of hands, exorcisms, examinations (or scrutinies), anointing with oil, consignation (making the sign of the cross on the forehead), and culminating in baptism and participation in the Eucharist. However, by the beginning of the fifth century when Augustine was formulating his doctrine of original sin in response to Pelagius' teachings, infant baptism had become commonplace within Christianity and the liturgies that had marked the preparation and baptism of adults were being applied to infants as well. Exorcisms that were originally formulated as a renunciation of evil by adults who recognized their own culpability for sinful acts were applied in the same manner to infants. As a result, the idea of personal guilt originally embodied in the liturgy was transferred to the concept of original sin.[39]

Perhaps from the richness of our theological diversity and shared experience around the issue of baptism MCC can offer a corrective to this view. For example, the pedobaptism which Althaus-Reid describes takes on an urgency that is not shared by those who espouse believer's baptism. Although many among the evangelical Protestants of the MCC also acknowledge a fallen world that shapes us from our earliest experiences, they also believe in a measure of grace given to those who have not yet reached the age of accountability. This grace, extended by God, allows us to rest in the assurance that we do not serve a capricious, vengeful Deity who metes out an irrational punishment of eternal damnation to little ones who are incapable of choosing whether to participate in God's work on the Earth. Although we have lived with some tension over these questions, the relationships within our intentional community have allowed us to see the value in differing views held by sisters and brothers within our Fellowship. In this way we challenge the folk understanding of original sin and provide a corrective for deep-seated suspicions of the body.

While the doctrine of original sin is of lesser importance in many MCC contexts, Althaus-Reid's critique of power dynamics that exalt the power of the institutional church and its sacraments at the expense of motherhood and bodily incarnation highlights a reality whose undercurrents can be detected in most church settings. As a result some parts of the Church today react by denying any doctrine of original sin, and by extension, any kind of sin at all. While the folk conception of original sin as a trait passed from parent to offspring has failed as a tenable metaphor for the condition of humanity and the world, it is also patently ridiculous from a theological perspective to assert that there are no problems in the world and that humanity is capable of rising above past mistakes through our own devices, independent of the power of the living God. MCC enjoys a unique position in the Church today as a denomination that has grappled intensively with incarnational theology. One gift that we may offer to the rest of the Church is an understanding of physicality (including the eroticism attendant to our bodies) as a gift from God to be embraced and used within our work in the world. How might we enter into the conversations around original sin and rebirth in a way that balances the need for transformation in our lives with an acceptance of God's good gift of sexual bodies, closing the gap between flesh and spirit?

Finally, Althaus-Reid's comments raise our awareness of the potential perversion of baptism when it is used as an instrument of control by nation states or the institutional church. Our shared experience and living memory of being turned away from Christ's table in other denominations serve us well in the discussion of baptism. Just as our theology around Holy Communion has opened the invitation to the table to all who wish to approach, our collective memory of exclusion can also inform our understanding of baptism, ensuring that this sacrament would never be withheld as an act of domination or exclusion from Christ's new vision of humanity and the world.

Having explored these earlier contributions to the conversation surrounding baptism, we now turn our attention to the framework presented by Nancy Wilson in 2006. In her sermon "Baptized and Beloved," Wilson suggested three points from her personal beliefs as discussion starters:

- Baptism is invitation to follow Jesus, joining our hearts to the heart of God and claiming our "Beloved-ness";
- baptism is identification both with a new community of liberation as well as with the suffering and pain of our Christian sisters and brothers around the world; and
- baptism is alignment or coming out with a public commitment to the will of God. It is a willingness to let go of those things in our lives that do not fit with our new commitment to the heart of God and God's way.[40]

Within Wilson's articulation we find principles that closely match other historical proposals regarding baptism. Without resorting to traditional formulations including "the Body of Christ," she has pointed beyond the act of baptism itself to the wider reality of incorporation into a unity with other baptized believers, sharing our joys and our suffering as we work together to bring about God's way of restoration and harmony. For sacramentalists baptism is the gateway through which believers enter into the Church, becoming mystically united with Christ. While those with a more Zwinglian understanding view baptism as a public commitment of a life to the corporate life of the Church. Whether this commitment is undertaken by the guardian(s) (as with pedobaptism) or the individual believer, nonsacramental Christians have traditionally understood baptism as a confession of alignment and an initiation into God's work in the world through the Church.

CHURCH PRACTICES AND INDIVIDUAL BELIEFS OR FAITH COMMITMENTS

Although MCC has existed for four decades, we have only recently begun the work of a systematic survey of the practices of our various churches and the individual beliefs of our congregants. In Summer 2011 MCC released a survey which seeks to map the baptismal practices of our congregations along with a second survey for individuals which explores personal experiences with baptism, what congregants have been taught, and what their current beliefs and faith commitments are concerning baptism. The latter survey includes responses from the entire range of MCC participants, from clergy to members to friends of our local churches.[41] Responses to this survey are invaluable in our further constructive theological endeavors.

TOPICS FOR FURTHER REFLECTION AND DIALOGUE

As we move from review of our current situation into the constructive phase of our theological discussion, several open questions of both faith and practice have been posed within MCC. Although this essay will not attempt to come to a single answer, it will offer commentary on what is at stake in each of these questions within the dialogue.

The Importance of *BEM*

As previously noted, throughout our history MCC has placed a high value on ecumenical dialogue. Although we are no longer seeking membership within the National Council of Churches USA (NCC),[42] we have remained in cooperation with the World Council of Churches and continue to offer ministry within this context.[43] As we continue our reimagining of baptism, we must also wrestle with the question of the importance of our ecumenical work and the ramifications of *BEM* within our own context.[44] The major traditions of the Christian faith have jointly invested over 75 years in the ongoing ecumenical dialogue around a unified understanding of baptism. While it is incumbent upon us to work out our own understanding of baptism within MCC, we must also consider how our conversations affect our involvement with the larger Christian community. One avenue of reflection must address our commitment to ecumenical dialogue and our reasons for pursuing relationships with the NCC and other ecumenical bodies. If our original intention was to seek validation of our existence through the recognition of ecumenical bodies, then perhaps ecumenical dialogue is no longer of particular importance to us. From humble beginnings MCC has grown into a worldwide movement. We are regularly mentioned in the media and consulted in questions related to the intersection of religion and LGBT affairs. If our intention was ever to receive validation from the larger Christian community, then perhaps it is time to reevaluate that desire to see whether it is still valid.

However, if our desire for ecumenical fellowship extends beyond matters of validation to a genuine desire to participate in the larger work of the Body of Christ, then perhaps *BEM* remains an important factor within our own internal dialogue around baptism. Any denominationally sanctioned practice falling outside the agreed upon framework of this document has the potential to complicate our efforts in the larger ecumenical community. While ecumenical unity should not necessarily become a *sine qua non* guiding MCC's formulation of our theology and practice around baptism, we should nonetheless be clear about the far-reaching implications of adopting any practice at variance with this historic document.

Pedobaptism and Credobaptism Redux

While MCC has long accepted both infants' and believers' baptisms as valid practices within our denomination, a certain tension still exists between adherents of these respective traditions. At stake in theological discussions that center on the tensions between pedobaptism and credobaptism are three central issues: (1) the role of baptism in salvation; (2) the role of faith in baptism; and (3) the teaching of baptism as sacrament.

As previously noted in the discussion of Althaus-Reid's critical reflection on baptism, most Christian traditions that practice infant baptism do so with an understanding of baptism as an act that washes away the stain of original sin. Following this line of theological reasoning, baptism is a prerequisite to salvation and those who withhold it do so at the peril of their children's eternal souls. While official Roman Catholic teaching leaves room for God's grace, folk understandings of the relationship between baptism and salvation can generate great anxiety for those who fear that their children will face eternal damnation if they die without having received baptism.[45] Members arriving in MCC from various pedobaptist contexts, in accordance with their own traditions and theological understandings, may request that their own children be baptized as infants. In this way MCC goes beyond acknowledging extradenominational pedobaptism, but also provides pastoral care by continuing the practice within our own churches.

Among members whose previous faith journeys include evangelical or Anabaptist traditions in which credobaptism is the established norm, an understanding of conscious faith accompanies the decision to seek baptism. From this perspective, infants are neither capable of comprehending the proclamation of the gospel nor of making a profession of faith in Christ in response to the message. Furthermore, credobaptists deny that faith can be either imparted or transferred from one person to another, excluding the possibility that parents or other sponsors can make vows on behalf of the child. In the worst case scenario this conflict of interpretation can lead to the questioning the validity of pedobaptism celebrated by sisters and brothers in Christ from other traditions.

Finally, most credobaptists within MCC see baptism as a sign pointing to a change that has already taken place in the life of the new Christian. In opposition to the pedobaptist view of baptism as an outward sign that communicates a sacramental grace; those who espouse believer's baptism often attribute no sacramental value in the practice, but rather see it as the first act of obedience in the life of a Christian who has already received the gift of salvation. From this perspective, withholding baptism from infants is of no particular consequence. Stauncher critics may even suggest that from this perspective, providing baptism to those who have not already made a profession of faith is tantamount to offering the hope of a false salvation. With this in mind it becomes clear that the tensions between pedobaptists and credobaptists within MCC are a reflection in microcosm of this age-old controversy.

Finally, a smaller group of pedobaptists espouse a Zwinglian view in their practice. For these believers, baptism is not a sacrament either, but is rather a sign as it is for most credobaptists. However, in contrast to their credobaptsist sisters and brothers, they view the act of baptism not as the first sign of obedience to Christ's decrees, but rather as the sign of the community's covenant to raise the child in the church, providing spiritual instruction and preparation for the day when the child will confirm the vows taken on his behalf by the community. In this way, baptism is a sign of covenant for Christians in much the same way that circumcision was a sign of covenant in Judaism.

Through co-labor and fellowship in our churches, practitioners of both infants' and believers' baptism have grown to appreciate the signs of transformation evident in one another. Faced with the same fruits of the Spirit and dedication to both Christ and the mission of the Church in the world in people who embrace opposing doctrinal understandings of baptism, the differences in baptismal belief often become less of an issue. However, there is room for further reflection and constructive theological work within MCC.

The Bylaws state that MCC define baptism as a sacrament.[46] However, for a significant portion of the denomination, especially those coming from nonsacramental traditions such as Baptists, Pentecostal/Charismatics, Anabaptists, and many evangelical Protestants, this is not the case. In fact, an informal poll of any given congregation within the movement would easily find that most members do not know the definition of a sacrament or particularly endorse it once it is explained to them. This presents a clear inconsistency between the Bylaws and the actual faith and practice of our local churches. Furthermore, while the current formulation begins by declaring baptism a sacrament, it continues, as previously mentioned, with the characterization of baptism as a sign, thereby mixing theological language of two views of baptism that are traditionally considered mutually exclusive. While MCC is characterized by such tensions on many levels, education around the meaning of sacrament and intentional conversation around what we mean as a denomination when we use the language of *sacrament* and *sign* is in order. This will become clear as we examine further topics including confirmation and rebaptism.

Catechesis and Confirmation

In other traditions practicing infant baptism the religious education and spiritual preparation of a baptized child continues through a process of catechesis (religious instruction) and culminates in the rite of confirmation during which the previously baptized person affirms the commitments made on her behalf by parents or other sponsors. However, while MCC acknowledges the validity of infant baptisms performed either within our own congregations or in other Christian contexts, there is no consistency in our approach to subsequent religious instruction. As a result, we run the risk of raising new generations within our ranks who have received baptism, but are unprepared for the obligations of membership in the local church or participation in the work of the Body of Christ. Such a failure not only bodes poorly for the future of our denomination as young people rise to positions of service within our local churches, but also—more importantly—does a disservice to the children entrusted to our care. As we continue to discuss new avenues for constructive theology around baptism within MCC, catechesis should enjoy a high priority on our list of concerns.

However, catechesis is not only for children and youth. In churches with adult rites of Christian initiation, a period of catechetical instruction before baptism is also commonly observed. During this period of preparation for full incorporation into the Church, catechumens are often taught church history, polity, denominational practices, theological positions, and the significance of being incorporated into the larger Church through baptism. Although Christians from evangelical traditions are often quick to act on a request for baptism, perhaps one lesson we can take as a denomination from the experiences of our more liturgically minded sisters and brothers is the value of a period of instruction and preparation to ensure that the person seeking baptism is reasonably aware and in agreement with the purposes for baptism and the obligations incumbent upon the baptisand.

In most traditions practicing infant baptism, a later ritual of confirmation often serves to finalize the process of initiation into the church. Children or youth who have reached an age of understanding and undergone a period of catechetical preparation are presented with the opportunity to confirm the vows taken earlier on their behalf. Within Roman Catholicism and Anglo-Catholicism, confirmation is viewed a sacrament, while other major denominations practicing pedobaptism, including Lutherans, Anglicans, Methodists, and members of various Reformed traditions, refer to confirmation variously in nonsacramental terms.[47] In each of these contexts, confirmation provides the opportunity for those who were previously baptized on the pledge of their sponsors to make public affirmations of belief in the faith into which they were previously initiated through baptism.

Although MCC has long practiced infant baptism, we have not agreed upon understanding of confirmation. As a result, we provide no denominationally coordinated process by which our youth may acknowledge their upbringing within the Christian faith and affirm their own commitments to Christ and the church. Many within the Roman Catholic, Anglican, and mainline Protestant traditions have raised concerns about the phenomenon of casual baptism in which parents bring their children for baptism out of tradition or perceived obligation with no intention of raising these young ones within the church and taking part in religious education and spiritual formation. Yet through our failure to create opportunities for systematic religious instruction of our young and to set aside a specific time and space for the reception of young people into full participation in the life of the church, MCC creates perfect conditions for young people to simply slip through the cracks.

Ecclesiology: Baptism, the Body of Christ, and Church Membership

From early in the history of MCC, the Bylaws have stipulated that in order to attain good standing as a member of an MCC congregation, one must be a baptized Christian.[48] At the same time, anecdotal evidence suggests that individual MCC churches have begun to dispense with this requirement, accepting members without baptism,[49] raising the question: Should baptism be required for membership in MCC? Before proceeding to a response, some background history and personal stories may prove helpful.

The 1991 General Conference in Toronto redefined the requirements for membership in an MCC congregation. While previous requirements regarding instruction in MCC polity and doctrine were abrogated, the baptism requirement was upheld. A second attempt to remove the baptism requirement was made at a 2006 Regional Conference by lay and clergy delegates of MCC Portland. Their proposal included a rationale statement that explained: "In the spirit of our core values of inclusion, community, spiritual transformation and social action, we want to open our hearts and community to all who desire to live in spiritual community within MCC. Therefore, we welcome those who's [*sic*] spiritual seeking and practice includes other traditions to journey with us."[50] However, the proposed amendment did not pass in a sufficient number of Regional Conferences to be presented at the 2007 General Conference.

Two different lines of thought can be found within the movement to church membership without baptism. The first recognizes the reality of people who profess Christianity, but for whatever reason do not wish to be baptized. In some instances these are Christians from traditions such as the Society of Friends (Quakers) who eschew the sacrament of water baptism in lieu of a view that recognizes all of life as sacramental. In the case of MCC Portland, Rev. Glenna Shepherd, who pastored the church during the events described, recalls that the question of the relationship between baptism and church membership arose when regular attenders from the Assemblies of God (AOG) tradition did not see a need for baptism. AOG churches do not recognize baptism as being sacramental in nature, nor do they believe it necessary for salvation.[51]

Parishioners have had other objections to water baptism as well. Sheri is culturally Jewish, but was raised in a nonreligious household. When she came out, she found community in her local MCC. While exploring membership she learned that baptism would be required to become a member of the church. Although this was not a problem for Sheri, her father strongly objected, insisting that baptism would wipe away her Jewish heritage. So Sheri chose to remain a Friend of the congregation. Later she met her partner, Sarah, who had been baptized prior to their acquaintance and who subsequently became a member of the congregation. Sheri and Sarah celebrated their Holy Union in their church and later adopted a son who was baptized there as well.[52] When Sarah died unexpectedly, the church community gathered around Sheri and her son. For the next year members of the congregation brought the family food, prepared meals, and ate together with them.

Sheri identifies as culturally Jewish and religiously Christian. She was okay with not being a member of the church as long as Sarah was alive because she felt that her family had a voice in the church through Sarah's vote. But in losing Sarah they had also lost this connection. Yet as Sheri thought again about baptism, she decided against it. She felt that she had already lost so much in losing Sarah that she could not bear to lose her identity as a Jewish person as well. Sheri believes in Jesus as the Son of God, but over time has grown to agree with her father's position that baptism would amount to a repudiation of her Jewish identity. In Sheri's case, her local MCC made a choice to accept her as a member without baptism after hearing her heartfelt testimony, in which she recounted her years of service to the congregation, her Holy Union, her son's baptism, her partner's funeral, and the fact that, regardless of all of this, she could not be a member.

In the preceding examples parishioners have professed belief in Christ and self-identity as Christians. However, the second line of thought in the conversation around dispensing with baptism within MCC as a requirement for membership is connected with a larger question regarding the inclusion of non-Christians as full members of our local churches. MCC ecclesiology has always had a strong emphasis on social justice. And over time, this focus has shifted for many to the creation of a space that upholds not only marginalized peoples of various sexual orientations, gender identities, ethnicities, races, socio-economic classes, and so on, but also embraces as equally valid various non-Christian religious traditions and spiritual movements. In the process, some churches within the denomination appear to be shifting from an embrace of theological diversity within the Christian tradition to a religious pluralism that acknowledges Christianity as one path among many that may be accepted within the Fellowship. At issue for these is the role of hospitality. For many, this quote from the current survey describes the importance of an inclusive welcome: "Though things are getting better, [MCC] is still often a home for people of many backgrounds, who've been rejected by where they're from. No theology, or theological reconciliation, however well intentioned, should be allowed to interfere with our being that to people who desperately need it."[53] While some of these individuals were rejected in other Christian traditions, not all are. Recent documents from MCC headquarters have emphasized the fact that Muslims, Jews, Buddhists, Wiccans, and other non-Christians regularly participate in Communion within the MCC while remaining within their own faith traditions.[54] In some instances it is these people to whom some of our local churches wish to open membership without the requirement of baptism.

New Spirit (Berkeley, California) provides another interesting example. An ecumenical church that affiliates with MCC, the United Church of Christ (UCC), and the Disciples of Christ (DOC/CC), New Spirit offers an annual baptismal service at a nearby river and baptism by sprinkling in other services. They also practice *asperges* (the sprinkling of the entire congregation using palm branches or another instrument to disperse water broadly). In each case they refer to these acts as both baptism and renewal of baptism. However, baptism is not required to be a member of New Spirit, nor is there any theological affirmation. They ask only one question: "Do you wish to become a part of New Spirit Church?" A value of the congregation is summed up as "Everything by volition, nothing from coercion"—a phrase that encapsulates their commitment to theological diversity.[55]

These examples move us to the broader corporate identity of MCC. In the case of MCC Portland, Rev. Shepherd began to ponder the question of whether salvation had become a checkbox on a list of requirements for church membership: our Bylaws bar an unbaptized, self-professing Christian from MCC membership, while an individual previously baptized but without subsequent identification with the Christian faith (e.g., infant baptism or an initial faith later repudiated) would be technically eligible to join the local church. Such an example, in Rev. Shepherd's view, highlights a conflation of administrative policies and matters of faith. The 2010 *Holy Conversations* resource published by the MCC Theologies Team offers a similar scenario in a discussion question:

> If Baptism were a requirement for Membership in MCC, would there be any difference between receiving a member who was baptized as an infant but who would not voluntarily choose to be baptized as an adult, and receiving someone who did not wish to be baptized as an adult but whose parents did not baptize them? What would make one more or less 'qualified' for Membership in MCC?[56]

Sheri professes Christ as the Son of God and has attended her local church for 15 years, celebrating important events and mourning losses with her congregation. She has contributed of her time and financial resources and even pondered serving as a board member. However, she could not serve in this capacity without membership. Finally, New Spirit welcomes anyone who professes a desire to be a part of the local church.

While historically MCC has professed that the Church serves to bring people to God through Christ,[57] the current trend towards incorporation of other faith traditions has created a tension between traditional ecclesiology and the perceived need to express hospitality through full inclusion in the administrative life of the local church. In most cases one might suppose that Friends of the Church of other faith traditions are drawn to MCC because of our ministry to the LGBTQ community. However, as previously stated, MCC has long asserted that we are not a church organized around either homosexuality or the legitimization of a certain type of behavior. If this is still the case, then sexual orientation and/or gender identity are insufficient criteria for full membership within the local church. It would appear that our current tensions arise from a shift away from an emphasis on the local church as an expression of the Church universal, headed by Christ, with baptism as the act of incorporation into Christ's body. In Sheri's case, when asked what her local church membership signifies, she reported that she feels like she is a member of her local community; however, she has no sense of membership in MCC as a denomination, nor had she given any thought to how participation in her local church might be related to the larger concept of incorporation into the spiritual Body of Christ.

Within MCC, membership bestows the right to vote in church business meetings and the capacity to serve as a lay delegate at denominational gatherings or as a board member within a local church. All other rights and privileges are already open to "Friends of the Church" as designated in Section VIB of the Bylaws.[58] Furthermore, it is common custom within MCC to practice an Open Table, which has come to be commonly understood as issuing an invitation to all people to participate in Holy Communion, regardless of baptism or personal religious convictions. Thus, the participation in the sacramental life of the local church is open to all. Other MCC rites such as Holy Union/Holy Matrimony, Funeral or Memorial Services, the Laying on of Hands, and Blessing are also open to all without requirement of church membership. But during our discussion, Rev. Shepherd voiced a concern shared by several other pastors: full inclusion requires a voice in shaping the direction of the church. For Rev. Shepherd, a certain hypocrisy rings through when a church claims full inclusion of its Friends, but denies them a vote in church decisions. She suggests that the administrative life of the church should be viewed as separate from the question of an individual's baptismal status.

Although the question of church membership has been formulated with the sacrament of baptism at the fore, baptism has become for some a handy euphemism for the deeper issue of whether one professes the Christian faith. As such, in the question of baptism as a prerequisite for local church membership, what is at stake appears to be our understanding of ecclesiology. If MCC still holds to the traditional formulation of the Church with Christ as the Head of the Body in which we participate, then profession of Christ follows as a necessary element of incorporation. We cannot simply join others into the Body of Christ who have not made the decision for themselves to come to God through Christ. However, if we have moved to a position in which the local church may be understood as an administrative body, a social gathering, or a place of support for marginalized peoples, devoid of an understanding of Christ as Head, then church membership without a profession of the Christian faith seems plausible.

With a number of our churches reporting open membership in their ranks without the traditional prerequisite of baptism, it is clear that this question will not simply go away. In a recent discussion, Rev. Kharma Amos compared the situation to the former situation of "Don't Ask, Don't Tell" policy observed in the U.S. military. In the name of preserving the peace, we have made a (largely unspoken) pact not to raise tough questions. Ministers who disagree with current ecclesiology feel immense pressure to remain in a closet of heterodox belief, even as they may quietly, without open discussion, choose to receive nonbaptized people (with or without a commitment to historic understandings of Christianity) into their local churches. With the publication of this essay and the unprecedented denominational survey of baptismal practices at the local church level, MCC is presented with an opportunity to continue a further conversation in response to Rev. Elder Nancy Wilson's invitation. As this conversation begins, I suggest the following two paths for consideration.

While MCC has begun with a clean slate on a number of theological issues in its 44-year existence, there are at least two models in existing denominational movements that might prove useful in our current situation. In the first case, the Society of Friends serves as a model of a group with historically Christian origins that has, in recent times, openly acknowledged those in their ranks who do not share an explicitly Christian path. Friends' theology has long embraced the sacramental nature of all of life. And while the majority of Friends still self-identify as Christians, a growing number embrace the spiritual practices of Quakerism without a profession of Jesus as the Christ. As one Quaker site puts it: "Unprogrammed meetings [traditional Quaker gatherings where Friends gather in expectant waiting for leading from God, often without any explicit pastoral leadership as recognized in other churches] are often characterized by great theological diversity, while still experiencing profound spiritual community."[59] Tacking even further away from an explicit commitment to their European, Christian origins, the Unitarian Universalist Association (UUA) has grown into a noncreedal religious community that embraces a plurality of spiritual paths, encouraging individual theological discernment among its members. Unitarian Universalists share a set of seven principles that explicitly value individual dignity, equality in relationships, individual responsibility for spiritual discernment, and an acknowledgement of the interrelatedness of all life. The UUA also consciously embraces the insights of various world religions in a way similar to a small number of MCC churches.

Moving in the opposite direction, MCC has also set precedents for the acknowledgement of religious diversity while maintaining its own commitment to historic Christian belief. MCC founder Rev. Troy Perry is fond of telling the story of the first MCC worship service held in his living room on October 6, 1968. Twelve people gathered in Troy's living room. "Among them were nine friends and three strangers, one person of color, one Jew, and one heterosexual couple. It was a view of things to come for the Metropolitan Community Churches."[60] By 1972, when MCC Los Angeles (MCC LA) had secured its own building, the congregation had grown to include several Jewish people, estranged from their own heritage and finding a home in the local church. Rev. Perry encouraged the group to start their own congregation and offered use of MCC LA's facility—a kindness to be returned in 1994 when the Northridge earthquake damaged MCC LA and Beth Chayim Chadashim, a Metropolitan Community Temple, opened their doors to MCC LA. On the American East Coast, 1975 saw the birth of Metropolitan Community Temple Mishpocheh[61] in Washington, DC, aided by the original MCC congregation in that city. Before either group had its own building, the MCC congregation helped to arrange space for MCT Mishpocheh with their own hosts, the First Congregational Church. The two congregations share a long and fruitful cooperation in the planning of the annual LGBT Pride service in DC. The spirit of interfaith cooperation within MCC continues up to the present as we work together with a gay Muslim group in Kuala Lumpur, Malaysia. Such interfaith work provides a second model of inclusion by which our denomination would be able to identify opportunities for collaboration on common interests while acknowledging and celebrating our religious distinctives.

Rebaptism

Many people have requested and received rebaptism within MCC churches. Anecdotal evidence suggests that some wish to embrace vows taken on their behalf while they were yet infants, unable to speak for themselves. Others have sought, as people more fully integrated through their own coming out experiences, to take on an identity as an openly lesbian, gay, bisexual, or transgendered Christian. Still others have requested rebaptism as a public profession of their commitment to MCC. While rebaptism is not unique to our denomination, this particular practice requires careful reflection.

BEM includes an unequivocal pronouncement regarding avoidance of any act that may be interpreted as "re-baptism."[62] The directive is intended to avoid the devaluation of any one Christian tradition's practice of baptism by another, but also to acknowledge the special, unrepeatable nature of baptism that is embraced by most sacramental traditions. A brief exploration of both points follows.

One of the first historical situations giving rise to demands for rebaptism is known as the Donatist controversy, which occurred in the fourth and fifth centuries when the claim was advanced that the effectiveness of sacraments depends on the character of the one administering them. In a time of persecution, some Christians had fallen away from their faith rather than face hardship. The Donatists claimed that anyone baptized by lapsed clergy was not truly baptized and consequently neither truly Christian nor a member of the Church. However, in time the Church came to recognize that it is not the agency of the baptizer which effects the sacramental change inherent in baptism, but rather the grace communicated from God. With God as the active agent, once baptism was administered the change was effected regardless of who the baptiser was. This understanding is carried forward today in ecumenical dialogue that emphasizes the work of God in baptism rather than the denominational affiliation of the baptizer.

Within sacramental traditions, the act of baptism is a one-time event, imparting a particular grace that may not be repeated. This understanding traces its roots to some of the earliest theology of the church, but is now commonly associated with medieval scholasticism and the application of Aristotelian categories of substance and accident. Although a person may have no change in her appearance (accidents) after baptism, this sacramental theology claims that an ontological change (or change in her very substance or being) has occurred independent of any changes that may be perceived through human senses. Later theology following this understanding refers to this as the indelible mark that God places on the baptisand. Once the change has been effected there is no further need of additional baptismal acts.

With these two points in mind, even less inclusive groups such as Roman Catholics or the various Eastern Orthodox jurisdictions recognize baptisms which have been performed with water, using the Trinitarian formula.

Yet MCC has long provided opportunities for rebaptism in our churches and in our regional gatherings. Thus, if MCC continues a practice of rebaptism, we should do so by conscious decision and with an understanding of how it might impact our ecumenical efforts. Moreover, as our own Bylaws state that MCC embraces baptism as a sacrament, any act of rebaptism carries with it additional interdenominational implications, which may be inconsistent with our stated understanding of the unique nature of the baptismal act.

One option for consideration by those wishing to reclaim their baptism is the renewal or reaffirmation of baptismal vows. This particular practice is common in many Christian traditions, including Eastern Orthodoxy, Roman Catholicism, Anglicanism, and Methodism. Such a practice would allow the previously baptized to own that which has already transpired, recognizing that it is Divine agency rather than human initiative which communicates the grace of baptism, regardless of the intentions of parents or sponsors. Such a renewal or reaffirmation allows space for internalizing the previous baptismal act without raising the issue of rebaptism specifically proscribed by *BEM*.

This is not to say that there might not be reasons within the experience of individual members for requesting baptism anew within MCC. For example, previously closeted people have described such a profound disconnect between the people that they were and who they have become upon openly accepting their sexual orientation or gender identity that they have come to understand themselves as an entirely new person, completely separate from the false identity of their former existence. Perhaps such a profound distinction between the former, externally constituted self and the new person may be viewed not as rebaptism, but rather as baptism of a wholly other person? From a sacramental perspective such a question cannot be evaluated solely on the basis of a feeling or an emotion, as neither has any bearing on the spiritual efficacy of the baptismal act. However, a certain compelling logic may be no less present in the profession of faith of an openly integrated human being who has become utterly separated from an identity imposed by family or culture.

On the other hand, if we follow Pauline principles of baptism in which the old person is put off and a new person is put on, then distinctions around whether a person is gay or straight, closeted or open, or even male or female, are vested with much less consequence. In Christ there is neither Jew nor Greek, no slave nor free, no male and female (Gal 3:28). As such, gender identity would not appear to be sufficient reason for rebaptism.[63] What appears to be at stake for many transgendered people in this conversation is the opposite-gendered name they received during their original baptismal celebration.[64] From a purely pastoral perspective, I suggest that rather than rebaptizing a person, MCC could instead institute a policy by which churches may issue a new baptismal certificate with the baptized's newly chosen name. All other details such as the minister performing the baptism, the date of baptism, and any witnesses listed would be faithfully transcribed, adding only at the end an attestation from an MCC clergy member as a witness attesting to the original event by way of the cloud of witnesses whose observations are recorded in the original document. Such a solution acknowledges the new name chosen by the baptized while avoiding the complications that rebaptism could introduce.

The Trinitarian Baptismal Formula and Inclusive Language

From early in our collective tradition, Christians have baptized using the Trinitarian formulation "in the name of the Father, (and the) Son and (the) Holy Spirit."[65] However, with the rise of feminist consciousness this traditional wording has become a stumbling block for many who hear within this formulation a devaluation of women and a claim of an exclusively masculine nature of God. But attempts to soften the patriarchal ring of the Trinitarian vow have resulted in the rejection of some baptisms as illegitimate.[66] Individual MCC pastors and congregations have introduced a variety of liturgical substitutes for the traditional formulation, inadvertently raising obstacles to the ecumenical recognition (and sacramental validity) of our baptismal practice. As Horace Allen has pointed out, at the heart of the matter is a liturgical "meta-question" regarding the verbal exactitude required for ecumenical recognition.[67] Beneath the surface of this discussion lies a difference in understandings of the very nature of the Trinity between Eastern Orthodox and Western Christianity.

Formulations such as "Creator, Redeemer and Sustainer" are commonly used not only in MCC congregations, but also in other denominational settings around the world. However, this seemingly straightforward substitution neglects historic understandings of the Trinity. Known as an *economic model* (based on the idea of job descriptions within a household), this and other descriptive reinterpretations of the Trinity have the unfortunate consequence of isolating particular functions to a unique person of the Trinity, suggesting that only one person creates, while another redeems, and the third sustains. However, traditional understandings of the Trinity profess the co-creative, co-redemptive and co-sustaining activity of the three persons, each of whom is of one being with the others. Furthermore, such utilitarian descriptions of the Trinity deprive the Godhead of the relational understanding of *perichoresis* found in the traditional formulation. Rather than simply coworkers, the ancient formulation of Father, Son, and Holy Spirit implies relationships that cannot exist in isolation—a prerequisite of parenthood is the presence of children, while the designation son does not exist in the absence of a parent. Although the relational aspect between Father and Son can be encapsulated within modern discourse through combinations that may substitute Mother and Daughter, the equally important understanding of authorized agent, deputy, or substitute is more troublesome. In the worldview of early Christians who formulated the Father–Son model, a father's authority is bestowed upon his adult son, allowing the son to make legally binding agreements in the father's stead. Furthermore, as all Christians were known as brothers of Christ, the authority of this Father God was also understood to be a part of the inheritance of all Christians working to usher in the reign of God. Thus, a more fundamental problem of language appears as modern concepts of family within many cultures no longer recognize proxy representation of a father as the sole right of a son, nor is legal authority to create binding contracts any longer the sole purview of men. While education regarding the polyvalent nature of the original metaphor can help us to appreciate the authors' intent, a tension remains between the presuppositions of these originating cultures and our modern understanding of family dynamics and legal rights. Clearly the dialogue within MCC surrounding this particular issue has only just begun. Like many other faith traditions within the Christian milieu, we must continue to seek a balance between our understanding of metaphorical language, the changing nature of our social realities, and our desire for continuity within the rich stream of our shared Christian heritage.

Creating new baptismal formulae, while preserving ancient understandings of Trinitarian doctrine, is a daunting task. Because of the multiple relationships embedded in the original metaphor of Father–Son language, it is difficult to conceive of new images that capture both relationality and delegated authority without introducing problematic divisions in activity and an attendant feeling of tritheism as the persons of the Trinity become more delineated. At the other extreme, simplifications such as baptism in the name of Jesus only as in the Pentecostal Oneness tradition have raised charges of modalism, suggesting that the work of God takes place throughout history in only one Trinitarian person at a time. With these problems in mind, I suggest that augmentation of the original formula may be our best recourse.

In her examination of the problem of inclusive language in the baptismal formula, Ruth C. Duck offers the so-called Riverside solution developed by The Riverside Church of New York during the tenure of William Sloane Coffin. Inspired by the meditations of Julian of Norwich, James F. Kay suggested a formula that was slightly modified to become "In the name of the Father and of the Son and of the Holy Spirit, One God, Mother of us all." This formulation preserves ecumenical essentials while adding elements that both reinforce the single essence of God and add gender parity. The use of the Riverside solution or similar formulations that augment the traditional Trinitarian baptismal formula would allow MCC congregations to honor our commitment to inclusive language in the worship life of our churches while retaining historical understandings of Trinitarian theology and avoiding the creation of impediments that could unwittingly complicate our ecumenical discussions.[68] However, such formulations cannot simply stand without education regarding the work of Christians who came before us. If MCC members do not understand the imbedded meanings in Nicean metaphors, then there is no incentive to preserve them. Furthermore, we cannot undertake a thoughtful endeavor of developing counterproposals if our ignorance overshadows the mysteries at which the metaphors hint.

Baptism and the Open Table

Since the first worship service held in Troy Perry's home, MCC has practiced an Open Table which has grown to include an explicit invitation to all people, regardless of baptismal status or religious beliefs and practices. Yet since the early church, the Eucharist has commonly been reserved for baptized believers. This tradition can be traced back as far as the *Didache*, which quotes Matthew 7:6 as a justification for denying Eucharist to the unbaptized, who are, by inference, "dogs" who are not to be given what is sacred.[69] In the early church, catechumens participated in a three-year preparation process during which they received instruction and were observed by the congregation. In a time when Christianity was still considered an illicit religion by Roman authority, catechumens were dismissed from the liturgy before the beginning of the Eucharist. This practice is still reflected in some Eastern Orthodox churches today during the Divine Liturgy at the cry, "Catechumens, depart!" at the conclusion of the prayer for the catechumens. Moments later, before the recitation of the Nicene Creed, a further cry, "The doors! The doors!" still marks the point at which the ancient church closed the doors so that no outsiders would witness the holy mystery of the Eucharist.

A common question among MCC members, as well as our conversational partners outside the Fellowship, concerns the theological support for our innovative practice of commensality that makes no distinction between Christian and non-Christian, baptized and nonbaptized. What follows are two constructive theological suggestions that may provide starting points in our continuing conversation.

To answer questions for himself and his congregation, Robert E. Shore-Goss has developed a theology of the relationship between baptism and Eucharistic practice that relies on traditional Roman Catholic understandings of baptism to include baptism by water, by spirit, and by blood—or the baptism of martyrs who have not yet received water baptism when they suffer death for the sake of faith.[70] During periods of persecution the early church sometimes canonized as saints and martyrs people whose baptism falls into the latter category. Shore-Goss suggests that faith is central of all forms of baptism, including pedobaptism where the faith of the parents or sponsors comes into play.[71] He then goes on to ask, "If baptism is a sacrament or sign of faith of our relationship with God, then could we understand that there is an implicit notion of implicit faith in a person presenting themselves for communion at MCC when he/she may not be officially baptized[?]"

Shore-Goss answers this question in the affirmative, suggesting that it is the Holy Spirit that moves a communicant to come forward, linking this action then with an implicit form of baptismal faith. He goes on to suggest the faith displayed in the communicant's acceptance of invitation to the table is analogous to the Catholic teaching that leads him to believe that the Holy Spirit is operative in other religious traditions.

In evaluating Shore-Goss's proposal, it might be helpful to introduce a fourth category of baptism from Roman Catholic teaching known as the baptism of desire: "For catechumens who die before their Baptism, their explicit desire to receive it, together with repentance for their sins, and charity, assures them the salvation that they were not able to receive through the sacrament." Rather than suffering for the faith (martyrdom), this expression of baptism indicates a desire (that has yet to be consummated) to follow the leading of the Holy Spirit in receiving baptism—an idea that seems to align more closely with Shore-Goss's thought. However, the Roman Catholic teaching requires an explicit desire for baptism which is not central to Shore-Goss's proposal. Thus, we might speak of an *implicit* desire for baptism, recognizing that this presses beyond the original intent of the Catholic teaching.

Such a teaching, however, leaves open the possibility of a great many questions. For example, might there be cases where a person participates in communion based on a desire for solidarity with a friend, a partner or partners, or perhaps the community as a whole? Can we justify the claim that anyone approaching the table does so in response to the call of the Holy Spirit? Do we deny individual agency if we claim that there are no cases in which a person approaches the table outside of a response (explicit or implicit) to the invitation of the Spirit? Because answering these questions seems a heavy task, I offer a second theological understanding for our open table practice.

We might ask why traditional mystagogy declares baptism as initiatory, with Eucharist being reserved for those who have successfully completed catechesis, culminating in baptism. Teachings from the *Didache* about giving holy things to dogs appear to be based more on an *us-versus-them* mentality that often characterizes situations of marginalization. It also imposes standards that the original Last Supper cannot meet, with participants such as Judas who handed Jesus over to his death, Peter who denied Jesus three times, and the rest of the disciples who all fled in the face of persecution. The disciples' witness to the faith through evangelism and martyrdom occurred only *after* their invitation to the table to taste and see.

In the early church careful preparation of the catechumen was of two-fold importance. On the one hand extended catechesis provided time for the catechumen to live into the experience of the Christian community. However, of no less importance was the probationary period during which the congregation made its own determinations about the sincerity of the catechumen and assessed the risks of betrayal by a spy or one who might fold under persecution. Such concerns have been obviated for most of us since the Edict of Milan in 313 CE when Emperor Constantine declared Christianity a licit religion. With these insights in mind, I offer the following alternative to the traditional mystagogy of baptism before communion.

Our experience in MCC for more than 40 years witnesses to the power of the invitation to the Open Table. By modeling the gracious hospitality of Christ, the Head of the Church, we have played the role of servants dispatched into the streets to invite all who will come to the wedding feast prepared by our master.[72] As a result, those who never would have made the A list have found a place at Christ's table, sharing in a tradition founded by Jesus himself who thought nothing of dining with those whom others considered to be traitors, sinful, ritually impure, or unholy. This is nothing new to us. What I further suggest is that while all are welcome to eat at Christ's table, it is the particular duty of the baptized members of the Body to serve as stewards of the table. Having made the commitment to follow Christ through the symbolic death, burial, and resurrection and incorporation into Christ that come with our baptism, we act as the mouth that gives thanks to God, remembers the words of institution, and offers the symbols of Christ's body and blood to those who gather for the feast. This is a more fitting division between the baptized and the unbaptized, marking the responsibilities of celebrant and acolyte as roles properly fulfilled by the servants of Christ, while proclaiming the open invitation to the wedding feast of, symbolized in Holy Communion and pointing to the eschatological promise of the feast of Revelation.

CONCLUSION

From the early Church until now, Christian understandings of baptism have enjoyed a certain fluidity, allowing for constructive theology in response to the pertinent issues of particular communities in particular circumstances. Having briefly touched upon many of the key moments within our shared history, perhaps we may continue our dialogue about baptism with an appreciation of the overarching narrative in which MCC finds itself today. As a denomination with 40 years of phenomenal growth and a message of inclusion to all who would choose to align themselves with Jesus, MCC undoubtedly has many other contributions to make to the Body of Christ. May we undertake our constructive theological task with a sense of respect for those called before us and the contributions they have made, while stepping with humility and assurance into our call as a new prophetic voice in the ongoing ecumenical work of the Church. The writer of Ephesians tells us that there is one body, one Spirit, and one hope of our calling, one faith and one baptism, and one God who is above all, through all and in all (Eph 4:4–6 paraphrase). Wherever our conversation leads us, may we keep these words close to our hearts.

NOTES

1. Nancy Wilson, "Baptized and Beloved," *Metropolitan Community Churches* (2006), http://mcchurch.org/AM/Template.cfm?Section=Search&template=/CM/HTMLDisplay.cfm&ContentID=2042 (accessed January 8, 2010).

2. Ibid., para. 14.

3. Universal Fellowship of Metropolitan Community Churches, "The Universal Fellowship of Metropolitan Community Churches Bylaws" (2007), http://www.mcchurch.org/BylawsandGovernance/December07/Bylaws07eng.pdf (accessed June 17, 2009).

4. The Matthean account specifies that baptism should be performed in the name of the Father and the Son and the Holy Spirit (Matt 28:18), perhaps suggesting the origins of the later Trinitarian liturgical formulation (see W. F. Albright and C. S. Mann, *Matthew: Introduction, Translation, and Notes* (Garden City, NY: Doubleday, 1971), 362–63). While the gospel of Mark is generally considered older, the analogous baptismal directive (Mk 16:16) is located within the second ending, commonly believed by biblical scholars to have been appended to the original text as late as the middle of the second century. In light of its late addition and absence of the Trinitarian formula, it is plausible to suggest that the Trinitarian liturgical formula derived from the Matthean passage did not appear until later.

5. Gal 3:27–28 is believed to be an ancient baptismal formula quoted here by Paul.

6. Justin Martyr, "First Apology," in *Documents of the Baptismal Liturgy* (Collegeville, PA: Liturgical Press, 2003), 3.

7. This phrase, commonly used among MCC members coming from the Baptist tradition, is not to be confused with Augustine's formulation, "an outward and visible sign of an inward and invisible grace," used in reference to sacraments.

8. For the exhaustive Protestant conversation regarding infant baptism, see the works of Lutheran theologian Joachim Jeremias and biblical scholar Kurt Aland. Jeremias first made an argument that New Testament accounts of converts being baptized with their households (Greek, *oikos*) would have included children. See Joachim Jeremias, *Infant Baptism in the First Four Centuries*, trans. David Cairns (London: SCM Press, 1960), 19–24. Aland's

counterargument focused on the baptism of infants. While both agree that references to infant baptism can be traced with certainty to the third century, Aland argued that references from the second century would appear to support the novelty of pedobaptism. See Kurt Aland, *Did the Early Church Baptize Infants?*, trans. G. R. Beasley-Murray (Philadelphia, PA: The Westminster Press, 1963), 10. Jeremias's response to Aland clarifies his own arguments regarding the baptism of children (vs. infants) and further examines the relevant a sociohistorical case for infant baptism from the beginning of the early Church based on Jewish customs of baptizing the entire household of proselytes and Greco-Roman mystery cult practices. See Joachim Jeremias, *The Origins of Infant Baptism: A Further Study in Reply to Kurt Aland*, trans. Dorothea M. Barton (Naperville, IL: Alec R. Allenson, Inc., 1963), 11. For a contemporary collection of essays regarding the ambiguous history of infant baptism, see David F. Wright, *Infant Baptism in Historical Perspective* (Waynesboro, GA: Paternoster Press, 2007).

9. Irenaeus of Lyons, "Against Heresies," Christian Classics Ethereal Library (2005), http://www.ccel.org/ccel/schaff/anf01.ix.iii.xxiii.html (accessed July 13, 2009).

10. Tertullian, "De Baptismo," in *Documents of the Baptismal Liturgy* (Collegeville, PA: Liturgical Press, 2003), 10.

11. Hippolytus of Rome, "Apostolic Tradition," in *Readings in World Christian History*, ed. John W. Coakley and Andrea Sterk (Maryknoll, NY: Orbis Books, 2004), 18.

12. Until recently the *Apostolic Tradition* was viewed as Hippolytus's own record of the practice of the Roman church; however, contemporary scholarship now suggests that this text may very well be a synthesis of materials from several faith communities, ranging over a much broader period of time. See Paul F. Bradshaw, Maxwell E. Johnson, and L. Edward Phillips, *The Apostolic Tradition: A Commentary* (Minneapolis: Fortress Press, 2002), 2, 13–14.

13. Believer's baptism is sometimes referred to as *credobaptism*, from the Latin *credo*, meaning "I believe."

14. From this practice arose the term *anabaptist*, a pejorative meaning "rebaptizer," coined by those who believed in the unrepeatable, sacramental nature of the initial infant baptism. Today Anabaptists have co-opted this originally negative term as a part of their own identity.

15. Aidan Kavanagh notes that the earlier Roman baptismal liturgy was written with adults in mind, but over time the liturgy was both compressed and truncated as it was adapted for use in the baptism of infants. Although the lengthier liturgy for adult baptism remained in the *Roman Pontifical* in 1595, its use was displaced by the liturgy originally intended for infant baptism. See Aidan Kavanagh, *The Shape of Baptism: The Rite of Christian Initiation* (Collegeville, PA: Pueblo, 1991), 104–5.

16. *Baptism, Eucharist, and Ministry* (Geneva: World Council of Churches, 1982), ix.

17. Ibid., 2.

18. Ibid.

19. Ibid., 3.

20. Ibid., 4–5.

21. Ibid., 4.

22. Ibid., 6.

23. Ibid.

24. Wilson, "Baptized and Beloved."

25. Universal Fellowship of Metropolitan Community Churches, "The Universal Fellowship of Metropolitan Community Churches Bylaws," Metropolitan Community Churches (2010), http://mccchurch.org/download/mccbylaws/UFMCC%20Bylaws%20as%20of%20 June%202010.doc (accessed September 19, 2011). This formulation has changed very little since the first draft of the Bylaws, published by UFMCC in 1970, in which baptism was also defined as one of two Holy Sacraments of the Church: "Baptism by water and the Spirit, as

exemplified by Christ at the hands of John the Baptist. This baptism shall be a sign of the dedication of each life to God and His [*sic*] service. Through the words and acts of this baptism, the words 'God's own child' shall be stamped upon the recipiant [*sic*]." See Universal Fellowship of Metropolitan Community Churches, "By-Laws of the Universal Fellowship of Metropolitan Community Churches," In Unity, August 1970, 3. The reference to John the Baptist was subsequently removed, perhaps in acknowledgement of the minority report in the Johannine tradition, which does not follow the synoptic tradition.

26. Kittredge Cherry, " MCC's First Quarter Century," Scribd (1993), http://www.scribd .com/doc/6338248/MCCs-First-Quarter-Century (accessed June 15, 2009).

27. Nancy Wilson, "The Moderator's Report to General Conference," Metropolitan Community Churches (2007), http://mccchurch.org/events/gc2007/business/modrpteng .pdf (accessed July 3, 2010); ibid.

28. Robert Goss, *Jesus Acted Up: A Gay and Lesbian Manifesto* (San Francisco: Harper-SanFrancisco, 1993), 128.

29. Ibid., 129.

30. Goss avoids the problematic translation "Kingdom" of God by instead leaving the original Greek *basileia* untranslated. This original word, derived from the Greek word *basileus*, translated as "king," was used within the period of Jesus' life by the Romans to describe their territorial holdings. Its appropriation by the early Christians to describe the "Empire" of God was in itself a subversion of the word's common usage.

31. Goss, *Jesus Acted Up*, 130.

32. Here the term queer is used not only in relation to sexual activity, but more broadly, including other boundary transgressors and liminal people as well.

33. Troy D. Perry, *Don't Be Afraid Anymore: The Story of the Reverend Troy Perry and the Metropolitan Community Churches* (New York: St. Martin's Press, 1990), 38.

34. Universal Fellowship of Metropolitan Community Churches, "Mcc Core Values," Metropolitan Community Churches (2005), http://www.mccchurch.org/AM/Template .cfm?Section=Search&template=/CM/HTMLDisplay.cfm&ContentID=1154 (accessed December 12, 2010); ibid.

35. In correspondence on this point, Shore-Goss (his married name) indicates that even in 1993 when he wrote *Jesus Acted Up* that his understanding of baptism was sacramental, Robert Shore-Goss, "Email Correspondence," ed. Bryce E. Rich (2010).

36. Nancy Wilson, " MCC & NCC: The Ecclesiology Issue," Scribd (1987), http://www .scribd.com/doc/6339277/MCC-NCC-the-Ecclesiology-Issue (accessed August 14, 2011).

37. This has been true since shortly after the Constantinian adoption of Christianity when baptism became a sign of national identity and allegiance to the state.

38. Marcella Althaus-Reid, *The Queer God* (London: Routledge, 2003), 136.

39. Within Roman Catholicism this idea continues to the present as is evidenced the 2006 *United States Catholic Catechism for Adults*, which states, "Infants need to be baptized because through this Sacrament, they are freed from Original Sin and are welcomed into the community of the Church, where they have access to the fullness of the means of salvation." *United States Catholic Catechism for Adults* (Washington, DC: United States Conference of Catholic Bishops, 2006), 189.

40. Wilson, "Baptized and Beloved."

41. Preliminary results of this survey are found at http://mccchurch.org/mcc-individual-baptismal-experiencesbeliefs-snapshot/ (accessed August 21, 2012).

42. In 1993 MCC withdrew its application for membership within the NCC. However, Stan Kimer, chair of the MCC's Ecumenism & Interfaith Ministry, now serves as president of the North Carolina Council of Churches. Furthermore, in November 2010, Rev. Elder Nancy

Wilson, Rev. Pat Bumgardner, and Kimer attended the national assembly of NCC in New Orleans, rekindling connections.

43. "Ecumenical & Interfaith History," Metropolitan Community Churches (2007), http://www.mccchurch.org/programsinitiatives/ecumenical/timeline.html.

44. MCC enjoys a unique position in that we are in ourselves an ecumenical body of Christians who have come together from many traditions.

45. The *United States Catholic Catechism for Adults* quotes the *Catechism of the Catholic Church* as saying, "the Church and the parents would deny a child the priceless grace of becoming a child of God were they not to confer Baptism shortly after birth," while at the same time pointing to the *Code of Canon Law* as dictating that, "Baptism of an infant may be postponed if there is not a 'founded hope' that the child will be brought up in the Catholic Faith". (See *United States Catholic Catechism for Adults*, 189–90.) Such seemingly contradictory statements add to the anxiety of Christians who view baptism as integral to salvation.

46. Universal Fellowship of Metropolitan Community Churches, "Bylaws."

47. The Eastern Orthodox practice of chrismation is parallel to confirmation in the Western churches. Considered a sacrament, chrismation is generally performed following baptism as part of a single rite for both infants and adults. [See Michael Pomazansky, *Orthodox Dogmatic Theology: A Concise Exposition*, ed. Seraphim Rose (Platina, CA: St. Herman of Alaska Brotherhood, 2005), 274.] Recognizing the greater frequency of adult conversions, some Orthodox jurisdictions have also begun developing chrismation liturgies for converts previously baptized in other Christian contexts.

48. In the 2010 Bylaws this long-standing requirement is found in Article III.C.2, Universal Fellowship of Metropolitan Community Churches, "Bylaws."

49. At the writing of this essay, a systematic survey of baptismal practices in local congregations is underway. Twenty-one percent of early respondents indicate that they do not require baptism for membership.

50. From the unpublished Regional Conference 2005 minutes.

51. My thanks to Rev. Shepherd for her willingness to share this information in an unpublished phone interview. It should be clearly noted that while the Assemblies of God (AOG) do not consider baptism necessary for salvation, it remains one of two ordinances practiced within AOG after repenting of one's sins and receiving Christ's gift of salvation. It would appear that there is some variance between the official AOG position and the beliefs held by individuals attending MCC Portland.

52. At her request, I have omitted the last names of Sheri and her deceased spouse, Sarah, as well as the details of their congregation and their son's name.

53. A response submitted in the current MCC Descriptive Theologies survey regarding baptism.

54. Universal Fellowship of Metropolitan Community Churches, "Mcc: A Call for Proposals in New Theologies Project Book," Metropolitan Community Churches (2008), http://www.mccchurch.org/AM/Template.cfm?Section=Search&template=/CM/HTMLDisplay.cfm&ContentID=4711 (accessed July 19, 2011); ibid.

55. From the author's electronic correspondence with Rev. Elder Jim Mitulski who pastors New Spirit Church.

56. MCC Theologies Team, "Holy Conversations: A Resource for Local Congregations," (2010), http://mccchurch.org/download/theology/spiritualtransformation/HolyConversations.pdf (accessed September 19, 2011).

57. Universal Fellowship of Metropolitan Community Churches, "Bylaws."

58. Ibid.

59. Quakerfinder.org. Information in brackets added for clarification.

60. Troy D. Perry, "Imagining the Church's Ministry Based on Luke 4:18–19," Lancaster Theological Seminary (2008), http://www.lts-allies.org/index.php/lgbt-week-resources/11-other/54–2008-convocation-troy-perry-imagining-the-churchs-ministry-based-on-luke-418–19 (accessed November 4, 2011).

61. Now known as Bet Mishpachah.

62. *Baptism, Eucharist, and Ministry*, 7.

63. This understanding follows from David Kelsey's theological anthropology in which he states that the *imago dei* is not based, as Barth suggested, on Gn 1:26–27, where gender complementarity appears to figure into the divine image. Rather, he suggests, the proper understanding of the *imago dei* is portrayed in the image of Christ in the New Testament. Rather than asking "what" is the image, Kelsey suggests that we ask "who" which is answered "Jesus Christ." David H. Kelsey, *Eccentric Existence: A Theological Anthropology* (Louisville, KY: Westminster John Knox Press, 2009), 938..

64. While not an issue within MCC, the problematic of gender and baptism is real within the Roman Catholic tradition. For example, see the story of Sally Gross, an intersex Roman Catholic priest who subsequent to ordination decided to live her life as a woman. Not only was Gross laicized by order of Pope John Paul II and further denied communion, but her baptism was also called into question by Christian acquaintances who argued that because she was neither determinately male or female, she was also not human and as such "not the kind of thing which could have been validly baptized." See the retelling of Gross' story in Susannah Cornwall, *Sex and Uncertainty in the Body of Christ: Intersex Conditions and Christian Theology, Gender, Theology and Spirituality* (Oakville, CT: Equinox, 2010), 11, 69.

65. "Didache," in *Readings in World Christian History*, ed. John W. Coakley and Andrea Sterk (Maryknoll, NY: Orbis Books, 2004), 14. Also BEM, 6.

66. For example, in 1993 the Roman Catholic Archbishop of Boston declared a group of baptisms performed by Paulist Fr. William Larkin in the name of "God our creator, through Jesus the Christ in the power of the Holy Spirit" to be invalid. Fr. Larkin had removed the father–son language from the baptismal formula in an attempt to use vocabulary he felt would be "more sensitive to women." (See "Inclusive Language Invalidates Baptisms, Church Tells Priest," *National Catholic Reporter*, October 22, 1993.

67. Thomas J. Scirghi, *An Examination of the Problems of Inclusive Language in the Trinitarian Formula of Baptism* (Lewiston, ME: The Edwin Mellen Press, 2000), i.

68. Recent baptismal formulae containing augmentations include several from the Disciples of Christ (Christian Church) and the Presbyterians of the Reformed Tradition. DOC formulations have included, "According to the commandment and promise of our Lord and Savior Jesus Christ," "By the authority of the Glorified Head of the church, I baptize thee [my brother, my sister, my child]," "In obedience to the Great Commission, and upon profession of your faith in the Lord Jesus Christ," "Upon the confession of your faith in Jesus as the Christ," and "Upon your profession of 'repentance toward God and faith in the Lord Jesus Christ . . .'" The Presbyterian Church (USA) until recently included the formulation, "(Name) _____, child of the covenant, I baptize you. . . ." See Peter Ainslie, *A Book of Christian Worship for Voluntary Use among Disciples of Christ and Other Christians* (Baltimore: Seminary House Press, 1923).

69. "Didache." Dogs are again referenced in Rv 22:15 in relation to practitioners of the magic arts, those involved in sexual immorality, murderers, idolaters, and those who love and practice falsehood.

70. Eastern Orthodox Christianity also recognizes these three forms.

71. In Luther's own understanding of pedobaptism, the faith of an infant is considered the purest in form, unadulterated by the doubts that often beset the faith of those who are capable of more mature thought.

72. Matt 22:1–14.

8

Toward a Church of Radical Christmas: The Open Communion in MCC and Its Ecclesiological Consequences

Axel Schwaigert

SOME PRELIMINARY REMARKS

I write this article as a theological thinker who had to rethink his theology several times on several levels during his life. I was originally trained in a very strict form of German theological thinking, represented by the theological school of the University of Tübingen, Germany. I was trained in systematic theology, which is mainly based on the work of Karl Barth and is a consequent application of the historical critical method to the biblical texts. In this school of thinking every dogmatic sentence has a specific place in a larger system. Ecclesiology was understood as thinking about the nature of the church. Liturgy is part of practical theology that describes the correct way to conduct a service.

Early on in my theological education I made the experience that those distinctions were not as clear as I had thought. In one lecture I had invited

This article was originally written in 2008 for the class "Queer Incarnation" by Mark Jordan at Episcopal Divinity School (EDS), Cambridge, Massachusetts. I thank Mark Jordan and EDS for giving me the opportunity to develop these thoughts.

my fellow students to a service that included a display and dedication of a part of the NAMES Project, the so-called AIDS Quilt. This invitation developed into a huge argument with my then professor, about the involvement of LGBT people in the church. In this heated argument he loudly stated the following: "I know, Mr. Schwaigert, that you think that the Holy Supper is the meal of Jesus with the tax collectors and the sinners. But it is not! It is the esoteric meal of communion of Jesus and his disciples!" In this sentence I understood that the way we understand and practice our main sacrament has deep implications on the way we understand what our church is and for whom our church is. In other words: Our sacramental practice determines our ecclesiological understanding of the nature of the church. Therefore we have to ask about the consequences the practice of open communion in Metropolitan Community Churches (MCC) has not only as a liturgical question but also as an ecclesiological question. Open communion is not only a special way of wording the celebration of a specific sacrament but it also changes the whole church.

INTRODUCTION

In MCC we celebrate an open communion. In this chapter I want to argue that this is an expression of radical Christmas in MCC. In the incarnation Jesus Christ became radically available for humankind. This availability was proclaimed by the heavenly hosts to the poor, and in praising God peace was declared to all, not only to a particular group. I want to show that we can understand the open communion as a radical theological reflection of Christmas.

I then want to reflect on the consequences this understanding of open communion has for MCC's understanding of her rites and sacraments from both behind and in front of the altar. "In front of the altar" means that one has to rethink one's understanding of the church itself, of blessed or holy unions, and of baptism. "Behind the altar" means that one has to rethink ones understanding of the priesthood of all believers and of ordination. For this I want to use the image of the Temple in Jerusalem to think about the relationship of the different rites and sacraments with each other.[1]

THE SITUATION IN MCC

"At MCC We Celebrate an Open Communion"

"In Metropolitan Community Churches around the world we celebrate an open communion. With this we mean, that we do not ask, if you belong to this church or any other church at all. We know that this table is God's table, and this invitation is God's invitation. If you hear or feel this invitation to experience God at this table, you are welcome." With this or similar words MCC around the world invites people to God's table. There is no set wording in our liturgy[2] or bylaws[3] and therefore the exact words can differ from church to church. The bylaws of MCC state that "All who believe, confess and repent and seek God's love through Christ [...] may freely participate in the communal meal [...]."[4] It is clear that MCC declares and confesses God's love through Christ to the world and invites people to participate in this love. But it is also clear that there is no described set of beliefs one has to subscribe to, in order to participate in Holy Communion in MCC.

Being an Accessible and Available Church

In celebrating an open communion MCC places itself in the very spot of availability and vulnerability as the infant Jesus who was placed in the manger in Bethlehem. It becomes a church of radical Christmas. In the birth in the manger in Bethlehem God made god-self totally available to the people. The stable and the manger were not surrounded by doors, walls, guards, rules, or regulations, but quite contrary by angels singing God's invitation to humankind.[5] Those angels did not ask, if anyone they spoke to belonged to a certain group, recited a certain creed, or followed a certain theological understanding. They announced God's gift and God's presence to all on whom God's favor rests. The shepherds in the fields did not have to prove that they lived or existed in God's favor, but the invitation sung by the angels announced this favor to them. The three wise men did not have to discuss theology, but the invitation that the star shone upon them, announced this invitation to them.[6] God's favor was not the prerequisite for the invitation, but the invitation itself was the manifestation of God's love. And this love God had already shown in giving God's only son to humankind. On Christmas God offered an open invitation to the world.

In being born in a stable in a manger as human among humans, God made Godself available to the people. Christ lived as an ordinary person available and accessible among the people. In his birth, in his life and in his ministry, Jesus was always available and accessible to everyone who had a need, a question, or just the desire to be close to Jesus.[7] Jesus did not ask about a certain understanding of theology, but was available to all, outside of his own part of Judaism and even outside of Judaism itself.[8]

In his ministry we often see how Jesus had to struggle to limit the access people had, when he needed time for himself. He had to go to great lengths to have his own space and never stayed unavailable for long. He even rebuked his disciples, when they tried to limit the accessibility and availability people had to him.[9]

Even after Easter the risen Christ did not make himself only available and accessible to a small group of especially initiated followers, but came to many, and in the experience of Pentecost became available to all, who wanted to be part of the new movement.

To celebrate Holy Communion as an open communion is one step toward living the accessibility of the newborn Christ of Christmas in the world and the availability of the ministering Christ before and even after Easter.

Being a Vulnerable Church

In becoming a helpless child, placing himself at the mercy and unmercifulness of humanity; God made god-self not only available and accessible, but also totally vulnerable. "Your attitude should be the same as that of Christ Jesus: Who, being in very nature of God, did not consider equality with God something to be grasped, but made himself nothing, taking the very nature of a servant, being made in human likeness."[10] In other words, in Jesus, God gave up all heavenly power, and placed god-self not only in the form of—compared to God—a powerless human being, but even became—compared to other human beings—a powerless servant. With this God became extremely vulnerable, vulnerable to the point of humiliation, torture, and death.

The task of the church, as the incarnated body of Christ in the world today, should be to place itself in the very same situation. It is therefore the task of the church to not consider the church's equality with God as the body of Christ something to be grasped, but something to transform herself into the very nature of a servant.

This means not only to be humble and accessible, but also to give up power and control. This not only applies to the actual power of the *ecclesia visibilis* as an organization within the world, who as an organization can decide on structures, organizations, and rules, but it also means to give up the power to determine the *ecclesia invisibles,* the invisible and undeterminable and mysterious body of Christ. In giving up the secular power over the access to Holy Communion, MCC also has to give up the theological power of describing a certain understanding of Holy Communion and ultimately of a certain understanding of Christianity itself.

In doing so MCC makes herself vulnerable on a lot of levels: By celebrating an open communion, MCC cannot develop a theology that determines every aspect of an MCC theology, therefore cannot answer every question from within and from outside the church. MCC also has to live with the fact that there is a constant potential of misunderstanding and conflict around theology. I believe that ultimately MCC has not only to live with this situation but also celebrate this fact.

To celebrate Holy Communion as an open communion is one step toward living the vulnerability of the newborn Christ of Christmas in the world.

Being a Struggling Church or Struggling with Mary

Of course the infant Jesus was not totally helpless and without defenses in the manger. In his mother Mary Jesus had a guard and protector. She nursed him and together with Joseph fled into exile to protect the infant. She tried to control Jesus to perform certain miracles (the miracle at the wedding in Cana[11]), or tried to control Jesus in telling him what company to keep, or who should be the people he affiliated with (the question of the real family of Jesus[12]). In all those cases Jesus rebuked her. But still, it was his mother Mary who was with him until the end, struggling and suffering with her son.[13]

In many traditions Mary is seen and understood as a symbol and example for the church.[14] I believe that in our move to be an open, available, and vulnerable church, Mary can serve as such an example for us too. Like Mary we want to protect Jesus from those we see as a threat. Like her we want to regulate, when Jesus does or does not do things in the world. Like her we want to take Jesus away from the strangers and want to keep him in our family. Like Mary we have to learn that Jesus is going his own way. And ultimately we have to stand with Mary at the cross, witnessing the cruel reality of human unmercifulness and injustice and suffering deep pain from it. Mary had to learn, perhaps as every mother does, that her beloved child would go his own way that she could not protect and regulate him forever. I am sure that hers were the best intentions. Still, Jesus rebuked her and her attempts to control who he gathered with in the clearest ways. This means that with Mary we have to learn that we do not have control over Jesus, cannot control where he goes, with whom he walks, and to whom he makes himself available.

To celebrate Holy Communion as an open communion is one step toward living the lifelong struggle of Mary in the world; a struggle of a loving, caring mother with her son, who just walked his own path.

Consequences for Our Understanding of Communion

The tradition in the church was usually very clear: The Eucharist and communion was the innermost sacrament, so to speak the holiest of holies. In the architecture of the Temple in Jerusalem this inner sanctum was surrounded by walls and outer yards. Those yards gave access to a certain degree depending on certain rules and regulations. There was the area in the Temple that was accessible to all (as the court of the Gentiles). Within this area were further courts, where only members of the Jewish people could enter (as the court of the Israelites). Within that was the court of the priest, and ultimately the Holy of Holies, which only the High priest of the year could enter for one ritual on Yom Kippur. Only the most initiated were allowed to participate or even be present at that moment. The degree of holiness grew depending on the proximity to the center.

The early church functioned in a similar system of growing holiness. In the early church the non-baptized even had to leave the room before the celebration of the Eucharist. So those candidates had to first go through an extensive period of learning and preparation (similar to Court of the Gentiles) before they were, through the ritual of baptism, allowed into the group of those who were allowed to be part of the Eucharistic feast (gaining access to the Court of Israelites).

A further step toward the very center of the Christian sacrament was then the rite of ordination. With this rite the candidate was allowed to actually perform the Eucharist. In performing the Eucharist, rather than only participating in it, the person (who in that time in history already was limited to men), was even closer to the Holy. This closer proximity to the Holy became only possible after even more education and several promises and vows concerning the restrictions on life. The candidate was, so to speak, allowed into the court of the priests.

All this served to control the access of the sacrament. The intention was that only people, who had learned what Christian life and the sacrament meant and signified, were allowed to have access to it. With this the church tried to prevent people without knowledge, understanding, and worthiness from participating in this inner ritual of the church.

In celebrating an open communion MCC breaks this system of different levels of proximity to the Holy. One does not need to go through the different stages of growing proximity to reach the innermost sacrament, the Holiest of Holies. But one can gain the close contact to Jesus in Holy Communion directly. This has deep consequences for the understanding of all other rites and sacraments in MCC.

Coming to the Altar or How to Understand Baptism?

In the traditional understanding baptism is the rite that separates those, who are part of the church from those, who are not in the same way part of the church. Baptism can be understood as something that is a sole action of God, which can be celebrated by the church even to an infant, who was not able to make his or her own decision. Baptism can also be understood as the end of a conscious process and decision, in which an individual gives his or her life to God. Both of those understandings deal with a soteriological dimension. The question here is: Who is saved?

If we practice an open communion as equal access to Christ this individual soteriological dimension of baptism is less important than a communal ecclesiological dimension. The question here is then: Who belongs to the church? Or even more: Who belongs to *this* church to which *I belong*? Under these questions baptism is not a personal soteriological decision or experience but serves only as the deciding sign of membership.

In the image of the Temple, baptism allows the individual to enter a court that is closer to the center than the one this individual used to belong. In this new court the individual then was allowed to participate in a communal experience of closeness to God, the Eucharist.

In celebrating an open communion MCC reverses that situation. Everybody is welcomed to receive Holy Communion, regardless of belonging or non-belonging. This leads to at least two problems.

First, the category of belonging becomes unclear. Why and how should someone want to belong, if he or she can participate in the most important sacrament? In other words: Why should someone want to be baptized?

Second, baptism is an instrument of power. This means that receiving baptism always happens in a power structure. One has to confess a certain creed, agree to certain dogmas, or uphold a certain way of living, in order to be allowed to receive baptism. In this aspect baptism serves a wall that separates the different courts in our temple. In celebrating an open communion MCC negates this function of baptism.

Within a theology of open communion I see one possible theological solution: MCC would have to understand the invitation of God to all, as we celebrate it, radically. It would mean that baptism could not be the defining sign of membership. So, instead of seeing baptism as a guarding rite that protects Holy Communion (first baptism, then Communion), we would have to see Holy Communion as the low-level entrance into the body of Christ. This entrance would then lead to a closer relationship with God, who then could be celebrated, if the individual wishes so, in the rite of baptism. This would effectively reverse the traditional understanding: first communion, then baptism.

Serving at the Altar or How to Understand Ordination?

In being radically open and vulnerable to those who hear the invitation to come to the table, we have to be equally open to those who serve at this table. The same very low level of control we exercise toward those who come, we have to apply to those who serve. This means that we cannot rule out people on grounds of race, gender, age, ability, sexual identity or orientation, or other human categories to serve at the altar. If we want to live an open invitation at the altar, we have to live it on both sides of the altar. My experience in MCC is that this does not seem to be a problem in our churches. It may be a surprise and an unfamiliar view for first-time visitors, depending on their personal experience and tradition to see, for example, a woman or a person in gender transition serving at the altar. But for those who are willing to live this openness these sights become very quickly a common view, and more often than not a sign of liberation and of living the gospel.

More difficult is the issue of ecclesiological status. Being open means also being open to the fact that MCC needs to rethink the categories of clergy and laity. MCC believes in the priesthood of all believers, but still maintains a clerical group with special rights and responsibilities. The challenge therefore would be to develop a theology of ordination that values training and knowledge, but makes sure that there is no special sacramental power involved. MCC would have to understand that ordination does not lead into an even more central court of the temple of our theology. But much more is only a reflection of secular necessities that do not exist in a church of radical Christmas at all.

The further challenge would therefore be, not to understand ordination as an instrument of power, where individuals are examined spiritually and intellectually, but see it as the celebration of the community welcoming a new, open, vulnerable, and struggling servant in radical Christmas. It would mean that we not only avoid the questions of different theologies, but also celebrate them.

Further Consequences or How to Understand Marriage and Holy Union?

There are further consequences following the open communion. If we celebrate an open communion, meaning that we do not limit the access of people to the Eucharistic sacrament (how to understand baptism) and meaning that we do not limit the group of people who are allowed to celebrate communion (how to understand ordination), we also have to question our understanding of marriage and holy union. This is the question of how to live. So far MCC understands and practices marriage as the joining and blessing of two people of different gender and holy union as the joining and blessing of two people of the same gender. As far as I know there is no conflict around joining and blessing of two people with different gender identities. (There might exist legal problems around this issue in different states which I am unaware of, but as far as I know there are no spiritual problems around these issues.) There is a conflict, though, to open up marriage and holy union to groups larger than two. Should MCC bless unions of three or more?

Here we find the same problems: In a protective theology one wants to make sure that there is a common agreement of a certain way of life. Only groups of two have a place in the Temple of our theology. In an open and vulnerable church MCC would have to learn to live with different ways of life, seeing in them not a threat, but a theological possibility to bring people closer to God. In an open and vulnerable church MCC could find theological value to open a path to God for people who did not have this path before.

CONCLUSION

To celebrate an open communion is a move away from a protective theology of a Temple toward an accessible and vulnerable theology of Christmas. A protective theology builds spiritual and intellectual barriers around the sacramental core of the faith. An open and vulnerable theology, as MCC already lives and celebrates, would have to find ways of re-thinking church and theology without those barriers.

In writing this chapter, which only serves to meditate a few points in this theological field, I found two things: a great fascination with the consequences of a celebration I enjoy in every service and a celebration that I find spiritually, emotionally, and intellectually refreshing, good, and holy. To live in a church of radical Christmas seems to be the best place in this time of the history of theological development. And I really enjoy being there.

The other thing I found is the fear and the struggle of Mary. To live and even think some of the necessary conclusions of being an open and vulnerable church frightens me. If MCC or I personally would consequently follow some of the thoughts in this chapter, MCC and I personally would have to give up a lot of security and certainty. It would mean to leave the Temple of my theology and live a faithful life of radical Christmas. This is both an exciting and a very scary thought.

NOTES

1. This chapter cannot and does not want to give a full systematic theology of Rites and Sacraments for MCC. It cannot, because this chapter only reflects my personal viewpoint. And it does not want to because such a determined systematic theology would be contradictory to the radical vulnerability and availability MCC celebrates with its open communion. And it also cannot, because I will show that some of the consequences of radical thinking are very much in contrast to traditional thinking.

2. MCC does not follow a common liturgy. Every church decides independently how they organize their service. This is a conscious liturgical decision that allows a wide variety of different styles of worship among different local congregations. In many cases a local congregation offers different styles at different services.

The following is a nonrepresentative list of different invitations to the open communion that are currently in use in MCC. There is no commonly agreed wording for the invitation to the open communion. Some churches use a standard wording whereas others use a more free *ad lib* style. There is also no real agreement on how open the open communion really is. Often the formulation reminds the congregation of some forms of exclusion such as membership, certain beliefs, confirmation, or baptism, and declares that those exclusions do not apply here:

"It's my privilege to remind you that the communion we celebrate here at MCC of N.N. is, as it is in MCCs around the world, an open communion. This means you don't need to be a member of this or any church to come forward and receive these gifts, nor do you need to believe any particular thing about what happens as we celebrate sacrament together. Whoever you are, wherever you've been, wherever you find yourself at this moment on your spiritual journey, you are welcome at this table." "Therefore, all are welcome to share this meal: you don't need to be a member of this, or of any, church, you don't need to have been confirmed or have been to confession, or even have been baptised. All we ask is that you are looking for God in your life."

There seems to be a disagreement, though, about the question of baptism as condition for the invitation to the open communion. Other MCC congregations express the open communion in even more radical way. With this they also avoid specific wordings that might be offensive to individuals.

"Absolutely everyone without exception is welcome."

Some MCCs use a more anthropological invitation that acknowledges that different people are on different stages of relationship with God and other people, the church cannot judge this relationship with God. Ultimately the responsibility of feeling invited lies with the individual who is present.

"We are stewards, not guardians, of God's table, so we welcome you wherever you're at in your journey with God."

"If you hear or feel the invitation, you are welcome."

Another way of invitation is to remind the congregation of the biblical situation in which the original meal with Jesus took place:

The meal we now share remembers the Last Meal that Jesus shared with his friends on the night before He died. At that meal Jesus shared with Peter, who would deny knowing Him, with Judas who would betray Him, and with all the male disciples—most of whom would shortly desert Him, yet He still shared the meal with them.

Whatever we have done wrong cannot be as bad as what those disciples did wrong. Jesus longs to share this meal with us now; He is our host.

Another very important aspect of an open communion is a logistical one.

"So that everyone can share in this meal we use alcohol-free wine and gluten-free bread."

To celebrate a truly open communion it has to be totally accessible for all those who want to participate. This includes wheelchair accessibility as well as accessibility for the blind or the hard of hearing and for those suffering from addictions or allergies. For some this logistical accessibility is even more important than a theological one. Nonverbal communication can be most exclusive.

I want to thank to all my colleagues from many MCC congregations around the world who contributed their wordings and insights to this list.

3. The only liturgical rule is formulated in the MCC bylaws which state, "Each local church body shall hold services of public worship every week. Other worship services may be held as determined by the Pastor with the approval of the local church administrative body. In regard to the worship services of local church bodies, the Sacrament of Holy Communion shall be offered at weekly worship, as well as at other worship services at the discretion of the Pastor. Holy Baptism may be administered at any appropriate service of the local church body or at any other time, at the Pastor's discretion." Article VII, Bylaws of the Universal Fellowship of Metropolitan Community Churches, as revised at General Conference XXIV, Acapulco, Mexico, Effective June 29, 2010.

4. "HOLY COMMUNION is the partaking of blessed bread and fruit of the vine in accordance with the words of Jesus, our Sovereign: This is my body … this is my blood. (Matt 26:26–28). All who believe, confess, and repent and seek God's love through Christ, after examining their consciences, may freely participate in the communal meal, signifying their desire to be received into community with Jesus Christ, to be saved by Jesus Christ's sacrifice, to participate in Jesus Christ's resurrection, and to commit their lives anew to the service of Jesus Christ." Article IIIB, Bylaws of the Universal Fellowship of Metropolitan Community Churches, as revised at General Conference XXIV, Acapulco, Mexico, Effective June 29, 2010.

5. Lk 2.16.

6. Matt 2.1.

7. Even in the middle of the night, Jn 3.1.

8. Matt 8.5.

9. Lk 18.15.

10. Phil 2.5ff.

11. Jn 2.1–11.

12. Matt 12.46–50.

13. Jn 19.25.

14. Compare, for example, the Catechism of the Catholic Church # 773 "[The Church's] structure is totally ordered to the holiness of Christ's members. And holiness is measured according to the 'great mystery' in which the Bride responds with the gift of love to the gift of the Bridegroom." Mary goes before us all in the holiness that is the Church's mystery as "the Bride without spot or wrinkle." This is why the "Marian" dimension of the Church precedes the "Petrine."

Or # 967 "By her complete adherence to the Father's will, to his Son's redemptive work, and to every prompting of the Holy Spirit, the Virgin Mary is the Church's model of faith and charity. Thus, she is a 'preeminent and … wholly unique member of the Church'; indeed, she is the 'exemplary realization' (typus) of the Church." Catholic Church, *Catechism of the Catholic Church*, 2nd ed. (Vatican: Libreria Editrice Vaticana, 2000).

9

Beyond the Open Table: Queering Holy Communion

Rachelle Brown

In the later part of the 20th century, Metropolitan Community Churches (MCC) offered a bridge between LGBT persons and Christianity by offering Communion to all regardless of membership, confessional affiliation, or official profession of Christianity.[1] Liturgical and theological openness at the moment of Communion, explored in other forms of American religion, continues to expand across the globe.[2] Each week, a variety of persons participate in open communion within MCC or in other worshipping communities. Openness in participation at the Communion table is a small, yet extremely significant portion of the larger Christian sacramental history. Due to this tangible reality, one can rightly ask: Does the open table as practiced within MCC worship automatically equal a queer Communion? The answer is both yes and no. Yes, because various persons and identities converge at the open table, transgressing boundaries in ways unparalleled in modern Christian practice. The answer is also no, for the reason that when LGBT and queer persons participate, the rite or practice does not become queer by association. Consider this question: If predominately heterosexual persons practice an open communion that includes LGBT persons, is the practice queer theologically because LGBT persons are present? Once again, the answer is no because a person's orientation or gender does not mean that person is living in a way that is queer.

These questions illuminate the need for a queer critique and theological exploration of Communion. As with any regular practice, and especially because Communion is a central Christian rite, a closer critique reveals boundaries and assumptions previously ignored due to the practice of an open table. Descriptions of an open or closed communion, common in the past few decades, maintain a cycle of dualism inherent to traditional theological thought. The outcome at best is an open communion that answers a revolutionary call to acceptance through celebration, but remains less than queer theologically. Whether intentional, or not, arguments asserting a particular practice is queer based on participants avoid a deeper critique of theological implications of practices. Open communion for the sake of inclusion results in a correlation of doing good deeds, meant to do no harm, a somewhat veiled ethic of reciprocity rather than a clearly stated queer theology.[3]

This project moves beyond the open table as a deconstruction of Christian tradition through queer theory to begin a queer theology of Communion. Application of queer theory to theology is necessary to overcome doctrinal certainty, whether formally stated or implicit in practices. Queer theologian Laurel Schneider and feminist Carolyn Roncolato explain the importance of the new work, "theologians who have become frustrated with the binary limitations of orthodox boundaries use queer theory to think differently about the bases of doctrinal elaboration in concepts of creation, of spirit, of God, incarnation, and church."[4]

A queer theology of Communion focuses on the roles of power, all persons, and preparation, to transform the open communion feast into a living queer Communion. As a ritual, the danger of boundaries arises with repetition. Uncovering the radical love of Jesus offers an unconventional starting point inherent to queerness. Patrick S. Cheng, in *Radical Love*, asserts radical love demonstrated by Jesus defies human expectations and "so extreme that is dissolves our existing boundaries."[5] God disrupts categories of humanity in the person of Jesus, crossing boundaries through a touch or a word previously considered impossible or impenetrable.

The discourse for queer Communion begins with radical and boundary dissolving love. The focus turns away from modes of presentation most typical of Communion theology correlating meaning to bread and drink. A queer Communion of radical and boundary dissolving love begins with a critique of persons and power prior to the presentation with the intention to honestly expose decisions, whether intentional or not, as to what is prepared, how, why, and with what attached meanings.

This chapter is a creative approach to begin a queer theology of Communion that seasons and mingles flavors typically associated with food and body theology. The critique analyzes power dynamics related to persons and preparation to expose a unique mixture of boundary crossing.

A queer Communion beyond the open table employs an allegory that through the imagination of the queer kitchen includes the tools and techniques of queer theory to describe a recipe, ingredients, mixture, and variations to form a queer Communion. The purpose is to enter a queer kitchen and utilize tools and techniques that defy expectations and previous experience. Recipes expose previous boundaries to introduce ingredients that offer various textures. The blending of ingredients, as multiple contextual layers as textures, evoke senses, which encourage touch and lead to communal responses. The recipe formulated in the queer kitchen points toward intentionality and communal abundance with an emphasis on mixture and variation. Initially, the allegory may focus on food. Yet, this is not the primary intention. In order to accomplish the theoretical and theological goals, theology *as* food is queered and applied. The methodology delves deeper into the process, placing the persons and preparation before the presentation. Imagining Communion beyond the open table introduces another horizon of expansive application transforming Communion into a queer boundary dissolving radical love.

Conversation partners for this exploration of queer Communion include foundations of early queer theological articulation, whether intentional or not, which began to dissolve boundaries of the sacred and profane. Gathering around the table to offer their own articulations leading to the allegory and queering include Carter Heyward, Robert E. Shore-Goss, Lisa Isherwood, Gerard Loughlin, Elizabeth Stuart, Marcella Althaus-Reid, Angel F. Méndez Montoya, Patrick S. Cheng, and many others without titles or publications, who live their queer theology when gathering at tables for multifaceted meals of celebration. Each voice and experience forms the recipe that follows, engages various participants in preparation, within a kitchen as an open the space for the creation of queer Communion.

THE QUEER KITCHEN

The queer kitchen where this recipe is formed is an open floor plan, visible from living, dining, and areas of reclining. The design of the kitchen includes open shelving without labels. The layout compels participants to explore the cabinets visually and with touch, inviting all to handle the tools. In this kitchen is a shelf of books and folders documenting experiments in formulating physical and spiritual provisions over the past four decades. This shelf represents the continued development of recipes and explorations of a queer Communion. Initiators of theological change and deeper discourse continue to engage a new generation of participants through the arrival of new recipes that are prepared in the kitchen.

Each person entering the queer kitchen gazes deeper into spiritual practices and the underlying theological assertions to expose, intrude, and interrupt assertions related to open communion. Queer theory is a vital tool of this kitchen. The kitchen resides within intersections of class, race, gender, sexuality, and ability to challenge and disrupt categorical essentialism. Queer theory provides tools and a queering of theology provides the techniques to intentionally push and even defy boundaries of theological discourse to expose intersections and edges previously avoided.

The kitchen of queer theology presents a disintegration of private and public space. Similar to a kitchen made available for a full visibility as in a television program, the queer kitchen is open for all to experience, yet in this kitchen anyone can enter and touch. The public nature of a perceived private space crosses a boundary and invites with the intention to remain authentic to the performance and consumption of Communion in public spaces.

As described thus far, the queer kitchen is a public location for participation in boundary crossing and experimentation in queer theology. In this kitchen, openness moves beyond categorical labels of persons and identities. Openness represents a challenge to dualistic categories, including open or closed, into a space of mutual and relational sharing. The kitchen displays various recipes formulated over the years and creates opportunity for exploration of new combinations. Since recipes are what typically lead to meals, it is important to explore the meaning of a recipe in the quest to create a queer theology of Communion.

THE RECIPE

A recipe for queer Communion applies, reconfigures, and inserts ingredients in an effort to mingle and dissolve barriers of taste and touch. In this recipe, ingredients seem familiar, yet there are variations, new techniques, and differences in quantities. Consider the practice of Communion globally. Multiple recipes exist for the same dish with differing descriptions and ingredients. What makes one recipe more appealing over another? The key to the recipe for queer Communion is an intention to evoke desire, engage in a sensual experience, and offer a meal to satisfy an appetite with abundance and overflowing in decadent hospitality.

Recipes are written with titles to create appeal. The concept of a title challenges queer theoretical categories because the naming, or a title, may create boundaries. In the hope to name, the purpose of a recipe title is to provide representation without imposing meaning as a label or artificial category. The naming of recipes points toward representation of an ingredient or purpose. In this sense, recipes become a signifier of tools and techniques meant to encourage the reader to look further, review, and explore ingredients and variations.

Queer Communion, expanding beyond the open table, is a recipe with theological roots of transformation offered in a communal abundance in order to give and receive nourishment. Specific theological components include a theology of alimentation, abundance, and decadent hospitality.

Intentionality

The adaptation of a recipe for queer Communion begins with intentionality: a theology of alimentation, meaning the giving or receiving of nourishment. Communion beyond the open table ensures giving and receiving of nourishment to all in multiple ways. Catholic theologian, Angel F. Méndez Montoya developed a theology of alimentation, which envisions theology *as* food in such a way to "imply transformation" and "interdependence between human communities."[6] For Montoya, theology *as* food is a mixture, even an overlapping, of ingredients, "such as the body and the senses, materiality and the Spirit, culture and the construction of meaning, and a divine-human blending of desires." Through his definition, a particular portion is emphasized: theology *as* food, which seeks to "preserve traditions and experimentation and creativity."[7] The rich theology of alimentation, applied in a queer way, offers transformation of the Communion table through mixture to intentionally dissolve boundaries and offer radical love.

Initially, Montoya describes the history and making of *mole* (or Mexican *molli*) as a method to illustrate the dynamic of recipe formation and sharing of meals. One particular function of a recipe, such as *mole*, includes the care for the creation of the meal, yet integrates the importance of communal sharing. Montoya makes a bold theological statement when he moves away from food as representative toward the preparation and participants. Out of the careful formulation of a recipe, theology *as* food is new creative space that is bodily and sacred, ready for desire and satisfaction through preparation and sharing. Montoya's theological intention for nourishment, "implies being in the care of the cosmos, the earth, family, loved ones, and . . . in divine care."[8] In this new space where preparation and participants mix and overlap emerges an application of queer theology.

A theology of alimentation adapted in a queer kitchen builds upon the concept of theology *as* food. As a recipe for queer Communion, theology *as* food points to a different starting point for the entire concept of Communion. Typically, the focus of Communion is on the ritual during the act of presenting and delivering the elements of bread and drink. In this recipe for queer Communion, the preparation gives and receives nourishment. Emphasis on the word "as" in to the recipe for queer Communion delves deeper than a theology *of* food. Theology *as* food points to the sharing and participatory features that nourish and create an "interdependent network of edible signs—that participates in God's nurturing sharing."[9] The entire purpose of the recipe for a queer Communion shifts from a final product and presentation, to the creation of an experience of communal sharing. The act of communal sharing appeals to our bodily satisfaction and completes a communal experience of God's sharing among and within one another.

A queering of theology as food within a queer kitchen, writes a recipe beyond the open table, creating a space of preparation intended to embody abundance and decadent hospitality. The recipe, in the frame of theology as food, expands the meaning of Communion beyond the elements or actual items presented, into the interdependence of the participants through preparation and public consumption. The first portion of the recipe, communal intentionality through preparation and participation, in place the next feature is the communal role of abundance toward decadent hospitality.

Communal Abundance

How can queer Communion formulate a recipe that embodies abundance and decadent hospitality? Often the best demonstrations lie within experiences. Deep within my own cultural tradition is a love of food and spices. My father's less-than-traditional Creole style of cooking, infused with a rural Cajun influence from my mother, resulted in a distinct set of recipes. Some staple dishes such as Jambalaya, étouffée, and others were created and remain written to serve at least 50 people. Sometimes the preparation, mixing, and cooking occurred at a family function beginning in the kitchen, but usually the entire process occurred outside the volunteer fire department or an event with the local veteran's organization.

My father cooked in a large pot over an open flame, preparing the roux, adding ingredients one by one. Each step of the blending flavors was done methodically. He carefully stirred the ingredients with a long-handled wooden spoon, cut and crafted for the exact purpose of creating the meal within the particular pot. Measurement of ingredients typically relied upon the weight of the spice in the palm of his hand. The vegetables were carefully added in ratio to meat and sausages soaked in various broths and herbs. Television cooking shows are only beginning to capture ethos created by the cook who customizes their utensils in the workshop, then continually adjusts the recipe to the type of pot and quantity without a conversion chart or measuring cups with neat lines. From the texture of the handcrafted wooden spoon to the rough outside of the pot, the smell of onions, peppers, and celery freshly chopped by hand, each element of the recipe including the tools, provide a variety of textures. Types of spices vary with individual tastes, though red pepper and Tabasco pepper sauce ensure the final taste and texture of the dish.

This example from a particular cultural context demonstrates the public nature of preparation in abundance. The adaptation of tools and ingredients demonstrates an ethic of decadent hospitality that evokes participation in multiple ways. The recipe customized for the moment in space and time, unrepeatable to the exact details, honors particularity of participants, tastes, and textures. Finally, the recipe represents an occasion, a gathering that becomes a celebration in the consumption of what was created communally.

Granted, Communion in the Christian context is not about a dish or a series of spices. In order to apply these features to a recipe for queer Communion, how can the simplicity of bread and juice begin to integrate the complexity of the recipes for 50, involving meats, vegetables, and spices? This is an important boundary to cross: the symbol or the sign. While the texture of traditional tangible elements associated with Communion resist direct correlation, once the boundary from the tangible into the symbolic is crossed, the one preparing for queer Communion focuses on a recipe with communal purpose. The effort is less about the cook than the intent of abundance and decadent hospitality of the recipe.

The recipe for queer Communion is written with a longing for nourishment, transformation, and even experimentation in order to connect with God, self, and others. Hesitancy to create and employ such a recipe for the Communion table is a result of restrictive interpretations of not only the table, but also the intent, reducing a call to abundance with sampling, and a degradation of the value of the participants through inhospitality. The recipe that includes the tools and techniques for a queer Communion is engaged by and with others, not in private, with only a few asked to touch or blend. Rather, the recipe is a guide, stirred with tools formed by those in the community, held within an open container, adapted to the environment of participants and context, measured with hands, created in public, and modified as needed to demonstrate abundance and decadent hospitality.

INGREDIENTS AND MIXTURE

Descriptions of a recipe lead to a key component: the ingredients. Food enthusiasts focus on ingredients and the layering of various tastes and textures. Ingredients when placed near, against, or on top of one another induce descriptions such as robust, full-bodied, savory, sweet, salty, and aromatic, among others. Ingredients work together as layers of particularity, provide complexity, and power. In this particular recipe, ingredients represent participants and contextual complexity laden with power. As described thus far, theology as food relies on overlapping of ingredients. Participants and contextual complexity represent an overlapping in flavors of difference with power to challenge dualistic categories and move in-between previously understood descriptions.

When formulating a recipe, instructions guide the blending of ingredients. Specific techniques combine but more importantly also transform ingredients during an interaction. Recognition of power within each ingredient and the potential power for transformation guides those in the queer kitchen to closely evaluate quantity to ensure a mixture enhances communal appeal and participation. The person as a key ingredient appears bodily as a member of the whole. The person is also remembered in multiple overlapping contextual layers. Queer challenges ways in which visible bodies are described and categorized in the most basic states such as race, gender, orientation, class, ability, and so forth. Essentialist categories appear as ingredients yet do not stand alone. Each body represents multiple contextual layers out of which power emanates, intersects, and challenges boundaries.

The power of ingredients as persons, embodied and complex, carries an ability to challenge the stability or dominance of another differing ingredient. Ingredients within one person can overlap boundaries of gender, race, sexuality, and class simultaneously. Imagine the potential overlapping and blending that occurs when multiple persons are forming a queer community. Layers of power emanating through combining of ingredients during intentional touching and mingling requires attention to detail. Mixing ingredients without attention to power may neutralize one or more ingredient, due to the potency of a particular ingredient.

The importance of queer theology as radical love that dissolves boundaries comes with an ethic of intentional overlapping that does not disintegrate, overwhelm, or destroy another ingredient. Thus, the dissolution of boundaries between ingredients offers complexity in layers without erasure of an ingredient.

The justice-making ethic of ingredients blended without erasure of another begins with acknowledgment of bodies. The next important feature of persons as ingredients includes awareness of contextual complexity. Ingredients originally included providing nourishment and transformation appear as open, decadent, and hospitable. Yet when examined through a lens of queer critique disappears in a layer of context and class.

The use of bread in more traditional Communion tables reflects the sustenance of early Christian life. Bread, prepared daily, provided a basic ingredient for living. The labor to create, or purchase bread, represented an ability to survive. Without nourishment, hunger thrives and persons are vulnerable. Feminist theologian Paula M. Cooey quotes the poetry of Argentinean Alicia Partnoy on the deeply spiritual and relational attributes of bread,

> Bread is . . . a means of communicating, a way of telling the person next to me: "I am here. I care for you. I want to share the only possession I have." Sometimes it is easy to convey the message . . . Sometimes it is more difficult; but when hunger hits, the brain becomes sharper.[10]

In a Communion table, often the relational aspect of sharing the only possession we can present disappears in the midst of context and class. Bread is rarely scarce in modern American society. What ingredient represents scarcity more clearly in a queer Communion than the critique of context and class? Moving beyond the open table includes assessing basic ingredients that restrict and even poison. In the most basic way, many persons now realize if the juice is alcohol, some are excluded, and in the same fashion, if all of the bread contains gluten, others are prohibited from participation. Granted, the queer Communion does not necessitate the exclusive use of juice and bread. A plain review of two basic Communion ingredients illuminates the potential of marginalization exposing greater complexity. Bread, as a symbol, tangibly presented, is about self-emptying, even when the supply is challenged. How often do the ingredients of a queer Communion represent self-emptying? The sharing of power between persons is a far more sustaining bread and drink dissolving boundaries in radical love.

The ingredients of participants aware of power and representing over-lapping contexts in a justice-making ethic blend together and finally move closer to a queer Communion. Yet the mixing of communal giving and receiving is incomplete without a closer critique of difference. Concerns of power and identity continue, like lumps of batter, within the mixing process. A technique to address difference within identity includes the work of queer theologians who describe Jesus as the first master of mixture related to bodies, questioning power, confronting and being confronted by context and class. One area recently tested is the purity of Jesus as a human sent to represent humanity. Theologian J. Kameron Carter forms a Christological argument, while initially employed to address the construction of racial identity, also applies to the queering of Communion. The crux of the argument is as follows: Jesus represents a mixture demonstrated through his ministry and divine identity which broke down divisions between Gentile and Jew. The very identity of Jesus, sent to all people was mixed, "mullatic" in representation without erasure of one part for the sake of the other.[11] How does this apply to a queer Communion? The ingredients, racially and within the context of geography and class, embodied by the Christ provide a precedent of mixing beyond proper boundaries. The mullatic Christ, present to and for multiple groups at any given time, dissolves boundaries, as a liquid bonds multiple ingredients without erasure. Difference remains within the mixture to enhance and flavor employing Christ as the example of mixture's validity.

With ingredients applied, mixed, and presented, this stage of the recipe continues to push against formulaic prescriptions. Bodies intersecting particularity of both visible and invisible boundaries participate in justice-making sharing of self. The queer kitchen is a place for exposure and experimentation keenly aware of performance. A recipe is incomplete without opportunity for variation. The substitution of ingredients and techniques for mixing incorporate the importance of variation and continued dissolution of boundaries.

CONFRONTING VARIATION

Variation of established methods and familiar ingredients become a challenge even for the queer theologian. Living into a queer Communion beyond the open table includes another push into unfamiliar spaces of performance directly related to the presentation of the Communion table and participants. Formulation and acceptance of variation is a new queer theological location. Variation has three particular loci: the presentation, the meal, and the participants.

Proper presentation continues to challenge the Communion table. If certain words are out of order, or even omitted, is the Communion incomplete? What if motions such as breaking of the bread and lifting of a cup are not performed, are the elements impaired? Decades ago, primary questions related to sexuality and gender emerged challenging validity of same-gender sexuality due to technical assertions of proper sexual method. Similarly, these questions of proper ritual behavior apply. Is Christ not present at the table because of improper speech or motion? If so, how can we uphold the sacredness of queer bodies participating? These questions deliberately push boundaries of symbol and meaning to expose the need for deep theological evaluation. The theological terrain is variation. If the performance, words or motions, is varied during the presentation of Communion, is it acceptable behavior? Acceptance of variation is a new queer theological location. Variation has two particular loci: the meal and the participants.

Secondly, variation shifts the focus from elements to centralize Christ in the giving and receiving of the meal. Participants engage in the actions of giving and receiving in communion with Christ and one another. Participants receive in order to consume and be filled. The person experiencing the giving is not Christ, yet remains empowered to give as Christ gave. The power of the meal resides outside of symbolic words or motions of presentation. The communal construction of meal qualifies the meal through participation rather than the specific elements of the meal. Accepting variation began with the experience of early Christians and continues into the lives of queer persons gathered. Early Christian controversies included acceptability of uncircumcised gentiles with improper appetites and practices. Debates related to expectations of gentiles following Christ with Jewish followers of the same Christ parallel challenges of queerness and variation. Peter's inability to accept the gentile appetite led to his vision to rise up and eat because what "God has made clean, you must not call profane" (Acts 10:1–35). As the vision ended, Peter was called to home of a Roman centurion Cornelius. Due to his new learning, he was able to participate and even explain to Cornelius, "God has shown me that I should not call anyone profane or unclean." The power of this message is how the vision began with food and directly correlated to persons. The queer Communion is about persons, variation in bodies, appetites, and presentation, giving and receiving. Variation at the table is the call to proclaim the value of all persons as no longer profane or unclean before the table of God. Words and motions symbolize, yet do not constitute the intersection of the divine and the human.

The final point in the importance of variation includes the distinction of participants. This point sharpens through the lens of social respectability within the Christian community. Recent acceptance of marriage equality in various states in the United States begins a new form of social respectability related to same-gender coupling and families. The transgression of acceptable behavior in family formation continues as a discourse on class and the new socially acceptable gay and lesbian. Relationships and family formation is where bodies intersect and carry potential to transgress boundaries of gender, race, sexuality, and class. Janet R. Jakobsen describes family formations as kinship and a location for sexual regulation.[12] Jakobsen argues social norms seek to regulate sexuality thus kinship formed in queer families defy borders and consequently multiple forms of respectability. Yet, with marriage equality, respectability increases through social validation of kinship. Respectability is a powerful temptation. Gays, lesbians, and some transgender folks experience social validation, even normalization, through marriage and children. Similar to middle-class symbols of houses, cars, and designer clothing, the new respectability empowers creating a new social norm and a different form of class. The new class illuminates others who chose to not remain monogamous, bisexual persons who may marry and form other sexual relationships, those who choose to remain single, or others who define sexual pleasure or fidelity differently. Sexual variation outside of marital kinship forms a social location without clear definition. When participating, especially in the receiving, kinship formations appear in variety. The challenge of respectability arises as queerness in body which includes relational variation. Similar to the altering of words and motions of the presentation, queer relational variation also challenges boundaries of senses and pleasure.

NOTES

1. In this chapter, the use of the word Communion refers to the rite during worship in an MCC worship service, which intends to directly refer to the same rite also named Holy Communion, Eucharist, or the Lord's Supper.

2. Early gatherings of early 19th-century American, typically frontier congregations, initiated an open communion. Many of these congregations led to the formation of the Disciples of Christ. In early American religious practices through present time, what may be considered an open communion also present limitations of Christian profession in order to participate. These limitations are overcome in open communion as practiced within MCC.

3. Some American Christian denominations identifying as open, affirming, or reconciling, who adopt some form of an open table are still unable to resolve theological challenges that LGBT persons and queerness presents to Christianity.

4. Laurel C. Schneider and Carolyn Roncolato, "Queer Theologies," *Religion Compass* 6, no. 1 (2012): 1–13.

5. Patrick S. Cheng, *Radical Love: An Introduction to Queer Theology* (New York: Seabury Books, 2011), 19.

6. Angel F. Méndez Montoya, *The Theology of Food: Eating and the Eucharist* (West Sussex, UK: Wiley-Blackwell, 2009), 3.

7. Ibid., 3–4.

8. Ibid., 4.

9. Ibid., 3.

10. Paula M. Cooey, *Religious Imagination and the Body: A Feminist Analysis* (Oxford: Oxford University Press, 1994), 18.

11. J. Kameron Carter, *Race, a Theological Account* (New York: Oxford University Press, 2008), 192.

12. Janet R. Jakobsen, "Why Sexual Regulation? Family Values and Social Movements," in *God Forbid: Religion and Sex in American Public Life*, ed. Katheleen M. Sands (Oxford: Oxford University Press, 2000), 104–23.

10

Innovations in Queer Theology: Embodying MCC's Open Communion through Theatre of the Oppressed

Kerri Mesner

INTRODUCTION

My own understanding of Metropolitan Community Churches' (MCC's) open communion has evolved as an integral aspect of my own ministerial journey. The open table is central to my understanding of queer Christianity—from my first experiences as a non-Christian newly out lesbian in my 20s unexpectedly finding myself moved to tears by MCC's communion liturgy, to a long journey of study and training for the ordained ministry, to pastoral ministry itself, to my current work in artistic-theological-scholarly activism. While my theological beliefs have shifted and changed over the years, this conviction—that MCC's open table is central to our shared faith—has endured, and indeed, I sense a growing conviction that to truly embody our open commensality requires of us a radical return to our shared activist roots. I would suggest that despite

A version of this chapter originally appeared as an article: Kerri Mesner, "Innovations in Sexual-Theological Activism: Queer Theology Meets Theatre of the Oppressed," *Theology & Sexuality: The Journal of the Institute for the Study of Christianity & Sexuality* 16, no. 3 (2010): 285–303.

significant gains in lesbian, gay, bisexual, transgender, and queer (here-after queer) human rights, religiously motivated homophobia, bipho-bia, and transphobia ensure that LGBT people may well be what queer theorist Michael Cobb terms the "last safe group to hate."[1] This chapter aims to introduce an emerging area of ministry (explored in my master's thesis[2]), utilizing arts-based theological inquiry to address issues of reli-giously rooted antiqueer violence as one living expression of MCC's open communion.

SETTING THE CONTEXT

The convergence of queer[3] theory with emergent queer theological thought has led to groundbreaking theologizing not just for lesbian, gay, bisexual, transgender, and queer but for the broader range of academic theological thought as well. Over the past 40 years, queer theologies have moved from simple apologetics (e.g., the movement towards affirmation or inclusion of lesbian, gay, bisexual, transgender, and queer people within ecclesial systems), to forging new theological ground through a uniquely queer lens—for example, in the theological exploration of the profound intersections between sexuality, gender transgression, and global economic systems. Queer theology involves the deep recognition that "theology is a sexual ideology performed in a sacralising pattern: it is a sexual divin-ised orthodoxy (right sexual dogma) and orthopraxy (right sexual behav-iour)."[4] Furthermore, queer theology challenges thinkers both within and outside the theological academy to recognize the need for the "coming out of other discomforts and areas of tensions such as economics and racial structures of suppression of subjectivities, because heterosexual matrices not only provide us with the master narratives for bedtime, but economic epistemologies and social patterns of organisation."[5] Through this queer-ing of multiple intersectional issues, as well as its epistemological rooting in the body's knowledge, queer theologies offer a prophetic challenge to the academy and the church.[6]

However, despite this irruption of new thought, a noticeable gap has emerged between queer theological thought and lived praxis. The his-torical rootedness of queer theologies within the contextual knowledge of the body makes this gap all the more troubling and pronounced. Queer theologies, uniquely positioned to challenge the historical academic and ecclesial mind–body split, run the risk of disconnecting from the embod-ied realities of the communities for whom it aims to speak. Put plainly, what does it mean if we are doing queer theology only from the head up?

This chapter suggests that Theatre of the Oppressed (TO) offers a unique bridge between queer theological thought and queer theological praxis. TO, created by Brazilian director, activist, and educator Augusto Boal, is a rich and varied set of theatrical methodologies designed not only to break down the separation between an actor and audience, but also to bridge the gap between art and activism. This work aims, then, to bring into conversation two key thinkers: Augusto Boal, the originator of the TO school of thought and methodologies, and Marcella Althaus-Reid, a preeminent queer and global theologian. Both Boal and Althaus-Reid shared a prophetic approach to their work that not only values but also prioritizes the marginal voice. Their shared roots in Latin American political contexts and Freirean pedagogies make them uniquely suited to engage in this conversation between theology and praxis. At the same time, each brought an important piece to this theological puzzle to complement the other: Boal, the critical engagement of oppressive realities through theatrical praxis, and Althaus-Reid, the critical analysis of religio-ecclesial oppressions through theological reflection.

STRUGGLING IN THE MARGINS . . . LURED BY THE CENTER . . . THE CHALLENGE FACING QUEER THEOLOGY

Postmodern and poststructural theories have brought with them an increasing wave of what writer and director Ali Blackwell refers to as "post-queer" theories, where labels are irrelevant, and "fundamentally [post queer society] is about good manners and an open mind."[7] Increasingly in academia, post-queer discourse manifests as a trend towards post-identity politics and a desexualization of queer theory. Queer theorist David Halperin suggests that "there is something odd, suspiciously odd, about the rapidity with which queer theory—whose claim to radical politics derived from its anti-assimilationist posture, from its shocking embrace of the abnormal and the marginal—has been embraced by, canonized by, and absorbed into our (largely heterosexual) institutions of knowledge."[8] Current headlines in fact contradict this only theoretically apparent lessening of the need for radical queer activism. When one looks at recent disconnected media stories over the past year, a troubling political relationship emerges.

We can start by recollecting statements made by U.S. President Barack Obama's inaugural pastor, mega-church Pastor Rick Warren, during an election that also included the Californian "Proposition 8" repeal of the state's legalization of same-sex marriages. Warren's statement to his thousands of congregants was unequivocal: "Let me say this really clearly: We support Proposition 8. If you believe what the Bible says about marriage, you need to support Proposition 8."[9] It is not a huge leap from this kind of politics dressed in biblical legitimation to Pastor Rick Warren's antiqueer outreach work in Uganda. Unsurprisingly, queer communities called on Warren to denounce the bill that recently emerged in the Ugandan parliament. The bill "would imprison anyone who knows of the existence of a gay or lesbian and fails to inform the police within 24 hours. It requires the death penalty for 'aggravated homosexuality'—defined as any sexual act between gays or lesbians in which one person has the HIV virus."[10] It is also not surprising that links have been inferred between Warren and antiqueer minister Scott Lively, who has also done prolific antiqueer church work in Uganda. Lively's own antiqueer rhetoric is clear. In writing, for example, about his belief in a global gay agenda, he states that "Matthew Shepard is the Horst Wessel of the modern 'gay' movement," and equates the mythologizing of Wessel in the rise of Nazism to the gay movement's "mythologizing" of Matthew Shepherd.[11] Warren eventually denounced the Ugandan bill and denied connections to Lively, and Lively himself also denounced the Ugandan bill, saying it was too extreme.[12] Despite both ministers' eventual backpedalling, however, the political damage had already been inflicted, both locally and abroad. These escalating statements are all linked by an implicit assumption—their acceptability because of their religious roots. This kind of antiqueer rhetoric—in campaign speeches, virulent online publications, and national legislation—points to the ongoing need for queer political activism that confronts religiously justified bigotry directly.

The social location for this kind of queer activism, however, has long been a point of struggle within queer religious and secular communities. Historical and contemporary queer liberatory movements wrestle with the tension between utilizing a credible voice that can be heard by the mainstream and maintaining a prophetic stance that is willing to challenge those self-same centrist structures. This lure of the mainstream, often motivated by a legitimate desire for effective political agency and legal protections, has led to a troubling normalization of queer theological and political thought. Queer theologies, with their particular critical analysis of multiple oppressions, as well as their unique appreciation of the particularity of embodied contributions to theological discourse, run the risk—when mainstreamed—of disconnecting from the social justice praxes in which they were originally rooted. The increasing normalization and mainstreaming of many queer religious activist movements, while perhaps initially politically expedient, run the risk of losing their critical edge which had been formed in that unique nexus of the sexual, the political, and the spiritual. Only by moving to the sexual, theological, and political margins can a queer theological voice and praxis remain true to its potential for socio-political transformation and the creation of queer life worlds.

In short, a queer theology in the 21st century encompasses a fully sexual and embodied approach as well as a keen awareness of the complex interplay between theology and globalization. Marcella Althaus-Reid offered a prophetic voice that began to address this gap through the deliberate "indecenting" of sexualized orthodoxy, theology, cultural normalization, and global economics.[13] Looking through the lens of Althaus-Reid's "indecent theology," we turn now to an overview of some of her work to help us to better articulate a queer theological voice from which a social-justice praxis can emerge.

INDECENTING ORTHODOXY

The political terrorism of her homeland, Argentina, informed Althaus-Reid's unique approach to queer theology with its emphatic emphasis on the sexual and economic natures of theology. In what is likely her best known work, *Indecent Theology*, Althaus-Reid critiqued mainstream theology as "a sexual ideology performed in a sacralising pattern."[14] Traditional theology, she argued, is focused primarily on "a sexual divinised orthodoxy (right sexual dogma) and orthopraxy (right sexual behaviour)."[15] Althaus-Reid aimed to expose, for example, the heterosexist patterns of thought in systematic theology, as well as the sexual hierarchies embedded within traditional ecclesial practices. Her location as a feminist theologian was evidenced in her challenging the supposed sacrality and neutrality of heterosexuality. She took this analysis further than most feminist theologians, however, in calling for an indecent theology that "works here as a coming-out process which consists of simply doubting traditions of sexual presuppositions, a process that being public can have transformative political implications."[16] While her liberationist roots in Argentina and in her own direct work with Paulo Freire clearly informed her theology, an intentional disruption of liberationist approaches also emerged in her vehement challenge to liberation theology's historical dismissal of sexual and gender issues.[17] She critiqued, for example, liberation theologian Gustavo Gutierrez's perpetuation of a false dichotomy between gender and political liberation, refusing in her own work to sacrifice the former for the latter.[18] Althaus-Reid not only challenged traditional, western Christian orthodoxy, but the emerging orthodoxy within Latin American liberationist traditions as well.

INDECENTING THEOLOGY

From this deliberate shaking of the foundations, Althaus-Reid aimed to explicitly indecent theology and ecclesia (i.e., the institutional church), through a subversive queering of specific elements of classical elements of Christian theology and practice. Althaus-Reid challenged what she refers to as "T-Theology"—that is, "theology as ideology," as "a totalitarian construction of what is considered 'The One and Only Theology' which does not admit discussion or challenges from different perspectives, especially in the area of sexual identity and its close relationship with political and racial issues."[19] She deliberately employed queer sexual hermeneutics within her theology, calling for a "critical bisexuality as a pre-requisite for being Christian . . ." and, furthermore, for "a critical transgender, lesbian, gay, heterosexual-outside-the-closet, that is, full queer presence, as a requirement for doing theology."[20] These are not simply rhetorical semantics, however. For Althaus-Reid, the call was for nothing less than a full queering of God, Christ, and Holy Spirit.

She proposed, for example, a Christology of a Bi/Christ, challenging the reader to move outside the boundaries of heterosexist and binary definitions of Christ.[21] Contemporary queer theologians took up this challenge. Robert E. Shore-Goss, for example, suggests expanding this to a model of a Bi/Transvestite Christ, further incorporating the emerging complex fluidities of queer identities within queer theologies.[22] Shore-Goss points to bisexuality as a key disruptor of heteronormative, binary Christologies, further suggesting that transgender experiences might offer a critical additional expansion of our Christologies. Building on his belief that transgression is essential to queer hermeneutics, Shore-Goss also explores the promiscuity of Christ, redefining our understanding of a divinely rooted promiscuity in the process.[23] Minister and theologian Martin Quero brings another challenging voice to the conversation with the suggestion of a trannie[24] God who embodies the fluid reality of gender transitions. Quero takes inclusive God-talk a step further with the insertion of a transgender hermeneutics, by questioning whether it is "possible for God to be *GodtoGoddess or GoddesstoGod*? How about a God that is in *transition* but never becoming one or the other?"[25] Goss's and Quero's expansive, transgressive models of God continue to develop the indecent trajectory begun by Althaus-Reid.

Likewise, Althaus-Reid explored a more queerly relational understanding of God, through the "transcoding exercise of intimacy and the liturgical exchanges of desire happening amongst people."[26] She articulated a mutuality within the human–divine relationship, believing that human emotional and sexual lives inform God's identity too.[27] Drawing on her Freirean background, Althaus-Reid suggested a move away from the grammatical structures of theology to a queer, lived observation of God's polyamorous nature within the Trinity. In so doing, she asked, "Could a Freirean conscientization[28] process be a crucial factor in the process of the kenosis of God?"[29] She aimed to kenotically dislocate, or empty out western logic, suggesting that the coming out of God might in and of itself be a form of holy kenosis, a leave-taking from God's own closet.[30] Through mutual relationality, then, the queer theologian discovers a God who is willing to kenotically come out into new ways of divine being.

Althaus-Reid's process of queering also included biblical hermeneutics that were "hesitant, tentative, deeply contextual while sexually suspicious of any notion of stability."[31] Through a biblical hermeneutics that incorporates a Freirean contextuality, the queer theologian discovers a dynamically fluid reading of Scripture. This transgressively queer reading of the Bible reveals an indecent Trinitarian model that informs theology's foundations. By employing indecent models of God, Christ, and biblical hermeneutics, then, we find not only queer theological possibilities but also very intentional resistances to theological normalization.

INDECENTING CULTURAL NORMALIZATION

Althaus-Reid's transgressive approach resisted the cultural institutionalization of the decent as normal. Through this refusal of normalization, queer theologies resist "current practices of historical formation that make us forget the love which is different."[32] Here, we get to know Althaus-Reid's queer God of the margins, the God of that "love which is different," and her reminder of the keen difference between a God that *visits* the margins and a God that deliberately *resides* in the margins.[33] As she frankly put it, "It is a theology from the margins which wants to remain at the margins . . . [This] does not mean that a theology from the margins should strive for equality. Terrible is the fate of theologies from the margin when they want to be accepted by the centre!"[34]

Whether in her explorations of the theological connections between Christianity and the Marquis de Sade,[35] her deconstruction of traditional Mariology, or her exploration of a Christianity that fully embraces the theological gifts inherent in sexual sadomasochism, Althaus-Reid strategi-cally placed herself at the hermeneutical and theological margins.[36] These margins were—and are for queer people today—margins of sexual nor-mativity. In explicitly choosing this sexual–theological edge, the queer theologian simultaneously reclaims socio-political agency in the theolo-gian's own queer world-making.

One hears echoes of this power of the margins in constructive theo-logian Sallie McFague's notion of "wild space," the space where one does not fit into hegemonic strictures, and as a result, where "our 'failures' to fit the hegemonic image are our opportunities to criticize and revise it."[37] Theologian Anita Fast also echoes this in her call for a "hermeneutic of foolishness," and in her reminder that "by making the 'fool', the 'queer', the transgressive one a part of the mainstream social order, the trans-formative potential of those who reside on the margins is relinquished." When this happens, Fast reminds us, "liberal apologists can accurately an-nounce that homosexuality is NOT a threat to society."[38] Like Fast, I am afraid of losing this political wild space, since it promises a queerly pro-phetic voice and praxis in contemporary Christianity.

This complex pull toward the center is perhaps best exemplified by the debates within queer communities about same-sex marriage. Conserva-tive gay theorist Andrew Sullivan, one of the earliest proponents of same-sex marriage, sees the institution of marriage as a cultural legitimator of queer relationships, and believes that members of the next generation "see themselves as people first and gay second."[39] Despite his persuasive analy-sis of the constitutional and socio-cultural advantages conferred by mar-riage, the troubling lure of normalization is evidenced in his belief that only marriage will give queer love dignity, equality, and a future.[40] I am concerned that Sullivan is advocating an acceptance of the strictures of political normalization as opposed to creating new forms of life and the new articulations of justice they need to flourish.

Queer theorist Michael Warner warns against the dangers of idealiz-ing same-sex marriage, noting that marriage as an institution selectively legitimizes discrimination both within and beyond queer communities. The inherent focus on coupling created by both heterosexual and ho-mosexual marriage results, Warner argues, in a lack of recognition of the many other relational and sexual configurations that are contained within the range of human experiences. He also challenges the widespread as-sumption that most queer people *want* queer marriage as a significant priority, and suggests that this particular issue represents, again, a co-optation of the queer movement by mainstream and often class-based interests.[41] This argument forms part of his broader analysis of the "politics of shame" that reduces "the gay movement to a desexualized identity politics."[42] I share Warner's concern regarding the prioritization of same-sex marriage as a preeminent activist issue within MCC as well as within broader queer communities. It's a challenging issue—both personally and politically—on the one hand, as a clergyperson I've been honored, many times, to witness the power of public celebrations of queer relationships. Liturgically and pastorally, I sense tremendous value in our religious reclamation of these public rites celebrating the many manifestations of our love. Politically, however, while I understand the strategic value of the focus on the legalization of same-sex marriages, I wonder how much of this collective drive is unconsciously fuelled by a desire for mainstream validation and acceptance.

Such a pull both toward and away from the cultural center is a complex dialectic that continues to challenge the queer community at its very core. Queer theorist Janet Jakobsen explores the complex relationship between queerness and resistance. She queries, "Can we articulate the complications of embodiment so as to actualize new possibilities for bodies and pleasures, or will such complications continue to work against us?"[43] The interplay between sexuality and politics in the mainstream and the margins grows even more complex when viewed through the lens of globalized economics.

INDECENTING GLOBALIZED ECONOMICS

Theological analyses of the undeniably interwoven forces of globalization and capitalism with issues of sex and the body were integral to Althaus-Reid's work, differentiating her from most other queer theologians. As she stated, "indecent theology sees an immediate link between structures of international oppression and heterosexual thinking in terms of hierarchical thought, ideological inflexibility and suppression of diversity. Queer theologies interrogate much more than sexuality: sexual epistemologies are seen as the foundation of current political and economic systems that have generated the external debt and trade agreements which produce hunger and oppression."[44] Quite simply, systems of heterosexist theology and systems of globalized debt inform and reinforce one another.

The concrete ramifications of this sexualized economic order were disturbingly present in Althaus-Reid's description of "lunchtime crucifixions." In these performative acts reminiscent of street theater, Argentineans voluntarily tied themselves to crosses in a public park to protest the crucifying violence of external debts.[45] Intriguingly, Althaus-Reid connects these public demonstrations to Boal's TO, a connection which will be explored more deeply later in this chapter.[46]

Debt-based Christianity, Althaus-Reid argued, was integral to the theology of substitutionary redemption, wherein theological and economic debt function to cancel grace, rather than (as is usually stated within Christian dogma), the reverse.[47] She offered the model of the Latin American *Ayni* economy, one based on a communal reciprocity system, rooted in generosity, as a theological and economic alternative.[48] Her global economic analysis offered a critical piece to the theological puzzle of North American theologies as well, especially given the latter's tendency to ignore the often symbiotic relationship among theology, sexuality, and economics. She explored how "a Bi/Christ gives us food for transformation, breaking down monopolistic economic and affective relationships." She asked, "Which other category, apart from a bisexual one, can contradict this economic, sexual and theological monotony?"[49]

One hears echoes of this enforced sexual–political monotony in queer and transnational theorist Jasbir Puar's analysis of American "homonationalism," the phenomenon of a sexual exceptionalism that evidences in the emergence of a national homonormativity that corresponds with American exceptionalism.[50] Puar argues that American patriotism becomes politically intertwined with queer narratives, dictating what it means to be an exceptional American homosexual. Puar now takes our analysis further afield, exploring intersections of American racism, homophobia, and Islamophobia. Nonetheless, one can hear what might be a North American parallel to Althaus-Reid's critique, particularly in Puar's critique of a "privatized, depoliticized gay culture anchored in domesticity and consumption."[51] Her analysis of homonational spending as a means of American inclusion through the pathway of consumption[52] connects to other thinkers on global commodification—specifically, Janet Jakobsen and Ann Pellegrini.

Jakobsen, for example, troubles the economic underpinnings of Christian family values, a discourse which "articulates a particularly potent secular-Christianity precisely by providing this type of connection between the (value-free) market and a discourse of values employed in the service of nation-building."[53] She notes the propensity for family to be integrated into both national and transnational economic systems.[54] Queer theorist Ann Pellegrini echoes this concern in her belief that the moral privatization of families actually functions to support capitalism. She argues that the insecurity invoked in families by capitalism itself resulted in the scapegoating of many queer people.[55] Jakobsen and Pellegrini explain that "homosexuals become the repository, the degraded and devalued holding place, for these buried remainders, those disavowed aspects of the self that must be, at all costs, charged to the account of the other."[56] They challenge the notion of tolerance as a sufficient end, suggesting "that although American commonsense valorizes tolerance as a response to violence and social division, in practice tolerance works to affirm existing social hierarchies by establishing an us—them relationship between a dominant center and those on the margins."[57] I would further argue that religious tolerance is particularly insidious in its violent impact on queer lives. Leaving aside more obvious examples such as religiously motivated hate crimes, religious tolerance can result in queer people either denying their embodied lives or their Christian faith, or both; either way, the end result is a form of spiritual violence.

Queer theorist Michael Cobb takes the exploration of religious intolerance a step further in his analysis of the dangers of religiously motivated antiqueer rhetoric. In *God Hates Fags: The Rhetorics of Religious Violence,* Cobb examines the prevalence of antiqueer hatred as a mainstream phenomenon.[58] He notes that the religious hyperbole of figures such as antiqueer minister Fred Phelps (whose placards are quoted in the book's title) are not as atypical as might be assumed, but are in fact rooted in a rhetoric that is connected to more mainstream Christian and political movements.[59] Intriguingly, he unpacks the use of broad biblical rhetoric (as compared to specific belief systems or theological statements), as a tool to broadcast broad authoritative antiqueer statements that are less likely to be challenged because of that apparent authority.[60] He also explores the distinct link between conservative Christian rhetoric and American nationalistic discourse.[61] Cobb argues that both America and the religious right need queer "enemies inside and outside its borders," as exemplified by a journalists' coining of the "Married Gay Terrorists" threat.[62] While tongue-in-cheek, the "married gay terrorist" statement in fact offers a pithy summary of the socio-political and theological projections evoked by many conservative voices. Cobb, Pellegrini, Puar, and Jakobsen all point to different aspects of this subtly violent trend in antiqueer rhetoric and its shaping of cultural politics, and as such, offer an additional political nuance to Althaus-Reid's work on the sexual theology of globalization.

INDECENT CONCLUSIONS

Queer theology is more than a simple integration of the sexual and the spiritual. It requires us to engage in "indecenting" as a verb—that is, to actively transgress theological, political, and cultural structures. It involves a deliberate choice to move to the margins of Christian decency, making explicit the interwoven nature of theology, sexuality, politics, and globalization. Althaus-Reid reminded us that "claiming our right to limbo means to claim our right to queer holy lives and innocence and by doing that we end up destabilising many powers and principalities by simply refusing to acknowledge their authority in our lives . . . As such, queer saints are a menace and a subversive force by the sheer act of living in integrity and defiance."[63]

Indeed, as Althaus-Reid suggested, a queer theology needs to radically object to the forces of theological violence, whether in the subtle guises of tolerance or mainstream normativity, or in the more obviously violent rhetoric of a national bill calling for the death penalty for the crime of being queer. A determinedly queer theological stance therefore needs to remain deliberately marginal and provocative. By raising the ceiling of decency on sexually scripted orthodoxies, theologies, trends toward normalization, and global economics, Marcella Althaus-Reid offered such a voice.[64] As we weave other theological and theoretical voices into this conversation, a distinctly queer theological trajectory begins to emerge, one that requires a deep integration of the sexual, the political, the theological, and the economic. This makes of theology, as Althaus-Reid puts it, "something worth the effort."[65]

If we are indeed aiming to wrestle with a fully sexual–political theology, however, a theoretical model is not enough; somehow, this theological *thought* must be translated into theological *praxis*. We turn, then, to the theatrical strategies of Augusto Boal as a praxis-oriented response to begin to bridge this gap.

QUEER THEOLOGY'S PARTNER IN PRAXIS: FOUNDATIONS OF TO

How do we bridge the gap between queer theological thought and theologically rooted queer praxis? Theater offers one such bridge. However, we look here not to traditional theater as we understand it, the primary goal of which is to stimulate empathetic audience responses to a problematic situation without any ensuing action.[66] Rather, we seek theater that carries the potential to bridge the gap between reflection and action, theater that serves as what theater activist Daniel O'Donnell identifies as a form of "social acupuncture," which uses theater to explore, articulate, and provoke different aspects of the social body. O'Donnell explains further:

> In the social body, an excess of power or opportunity held by one group—white people, for example—is contingent on a deficiency in other parts of the social body . . . Classism, racism and sexism can all be read this way . . . social acupuncture offers the opportunity to directly engage with social flows, applying the same principles as real acupuncture, only the terrain is the social body instead of the physical body . . . [this] will usually generate discomfort, the social equivalent of confusion, a necessary part of any learning process.[67]

Theatre of the Oppressed refers to a broad set of theater methodologies created by Augusto Boal, a Brazilian actor, playwright, director, and activist. Developed by Boal from the early 1970s until his death in 2009, *Theatre of the Oppressed,* drew its title from the inspiration of Paulo Freire's *Pedagogy of the Oppressed.* Boal, like Freire, sought to find explicit ways to activate subjective awareness and capacity for change in the journey toward *conscientization.* Like Freire, Boal developed his theories and methodologies within the context of Brazilian political dictatorship; both Freire and Boal were also eventually exiled for their revolutionary work. These shared historical and philosophical roots emerge clearly within Boal's theatrical methodologies.

In TO, the audience is challenged to explore all the possibilities within a given oppressive situation, and to actively engage in the theatrical process to attempt to overcome that oppression.[68] This process is not simply limited to verbal or intellectual analysis—action is required as response. Boal shared Freire's belief that without radical transformation education has not taken place. As Boal wrote in his groundbreaking book *Theater of the Oppressed,* the focus is on the action itself:

> the spectator delegates no power to the character (or actor) either to act or to think in his place; on the contrary, he himself assumes the protagonic role, changes the dramatic action, tries out solutions, discusses plans for change-in short, trains himself for real action. In this case, perhaps the theatre is not revolutionary in itself, but it is surely a rehearsal for the revolution. The liberated spectator, as a whole person, launches into action. No matter that the action is fiction; what matters is that it is action![69]

Like Freire, Boal challenged coercive models of education, suggesting that educators should start not with alienating techniques, but with strategies arising from the bodies and lived experiences of the participants themselves.[70] The deliberate use of images was central to Boal's work. In his *Image Theatre* techniques, participants explore and unpack the many layers of analysis and meaning within a particular nonverbal image. Boal chose to deliberately subvert our traditional reliance on verbal expression, challenging actors instead to find nonverbal means of communication and expression. Paralleling Freire, *intervention* is also critical: Through onstage interventions, *spectactors* (Boal's term replacing traditionally passive audience spectators) are challenged to actively test out potential responses to oppressive situations rather than simply watching passively as professional actors intervene on their behalf. In *Theatre of the Oppressed*, the *Joker* plays the critical role of facilitator, problematizer, and intermediary between the actors and the *spectactors*, challenging both groups to create a community of critical reflection and action. (Within this chapter, *Joker/ing* refers to that role, as well as to an active verb-ie: "to Joker.")

While Boal initially developed TO to address systemic oppression within the context of political dictatorships in Brazil and other parts of Latin America, he discovered, particularly during his subsequent exiles in other countries, that its relevance extended to other cultures and contexts. As his work traversed into Western Europe and North America, he also developed additional methodologies that explored internalized oppressions at personal levels, and, over the years, increasingly sophisticated combinations of the various techniques that bridged both individuals and systems, both the personal, and the political. Boal's *arsenal*[71] of techniques includes *Forum Theater*[72] (where a short play is presented and audience members have opportunities to intervene on stage to try to combat the oppression presented), *Image Theater*[73] (a series of exercises utilizing frozen and then activated images to explore the layers of meanings within a particular area of oppression) and *Rainbow of Desires*[74] (a complex series of strategies designed to make explicit the internalized oppressions experienced at individual and collective levels). More recently, Boal also developed *Legislative Theater*, whereby TO methods are used to explore and effect political change in local governments; he used these methods successfully to effect legislative change during his tenure as a Councilman in Brazil.[75] Boal's work has been contextualized in a variety of cultures, communities, and issue foci. TO has spread around the world and its applications are diverse, flexible, and innovative, reflecting the practitioners and communities where those applications are rooted.

JOKERING AS QUEER MINISTRY: QUEER THEOLOGY MEETS TO

In drawing together the theological–theatrical conversations between Althaus-Reid and Boal, a new thread of thought and praxis begins to emerge: *Jokering* as queer ministry. As we interweave the theological and artistic roots of this ministry with its applied practice in a variety of contexts,[76] we can begin to articulate the notion of *Jokering* as a queer ministry that is rooted in bodily, theological, artistic, ethical, and prophetic awarenesses.

Jokering as Queer Ministry Is Embodied

Jokering as queer ministry recognizes that theology begins in the body. Not only do we challenge the historic dualistic split between theology and praxis—*Jokering* as queer ministry believes that a fully integrated bodily awareness can revive much-needed authenticity and integrity in theologies and ecclesiologies. Embodied awareness begins with the *Joker's* own awareness of queer theology as an "I theology";[77] the *Joker* brings *the Joker's* own embodied experiences to the work of ministry and in so doing, encourages other participants to do the same. Participants bring their own bodily truths to the work, and are challenged to engage in "a disclosure of experiences which have been traditionally silenced in theology."[78] Such disclosures include not only the essential life-giving process of coming out into queer identities, but moreover, coming out into places of practice and belief that have been historically excluded from mainstream *and* queer theologies. Such disclosures constitute a prophetic re-envisioning of processes of coming out—in the sharing of previously silenced truths; new justice-building can begin.

Jokering as queer ministry challenges the church and the theological academy "to start engaging with unease and discomfort."[79] Through the deliberately provocative use of embodied theatrical strategies, the historic ecclesial and academic mind–body split is exposed and challenged. Whether through the use of *Image Theatre* or *Forum Theatre* within the body of a sermon, through the invitation to congregants to move out of their pews and into a theatrical conversation, or through the actual content of the theatrical work that addresses issues of the physical, the sexual, and the erotic as they relate to our lives in the church, the goal is, quite simply, to bring the *body* back into the *church.* Such a goal brings with it productive discomfort and a lack of familiar ecclesial or theological ground. O'Donnell's reflections on the theatrical process apply equally well to *Jokering* within theological or ecclesial contexts:

> The social awkwardness and tension it [social acupuncture] generates can feel stupid, the projects seeming to constantly teeter on the brink of embarrassment and failure. As any system experiences a shift into higher complexity, there will be a time when it feels like there has been a drop in understanding, dexterity or control.[80]

Jokering as queer ministry, through its passionate embrace of the body itself, equally embraces this discomfort as a sign that transformation may well be at work.

Jokering as Queer Ministry Is Rooted in Queer Theological and Theoretical Analyses

Jokering as a distinctively queer ministry aims to move queer theological discourse and activism beyond issues of ecclesial inclusion or scriptural apologetics. It is a ministry rooted in queer theory's challenges to mainstream—and sometimes queer communities'—normalization, as well as queer theology's exposure of the hidden sexual structures of the church. Althaus-Reid's "method of *indecenting*" is applied to bridge the gap of sexual honesty that she exposes in Feminist Liberation Theology[81]—and, I would argue, to bridge a similar gap in many other branches of ostensibly progressive theologies. Such sexual honesty includes the telling of our sexual stories, as well as an explicitly sexual reading of the Bible.[82] Sexual honesty requires us to expose the truth that "theology is a sexual ideology performed in a sacralising pattern: it is a sexual divinised orthodoxy (right sexual dogma) and orthopraxy (right sexual behaviour)."[83] Sexual honesty requires us to bring our full queerly sexual–erotic–spiritual selves into our lives in the church, knowing that the church will be richer for it.

Jokering as queer ministry continually examines the interplay between systems of sexual, religious, and economic disparity, injustice, and violence, recognizing that they cannot be viewed as compartmentalized issues. This is a ministry that recognizes that our spiritual and economic lives are at stake in this work—that as Althaus-Reid declares, "an Indecent Theology using deviancy as a methodological source, would have a better chance of challenging the accepted which is at the root of the powers which control and dehumanise people's lives. Indecent proposals in economics could decolonise our spiritual souls, which are also economic souls."[84] Such a spiritual decolonization is perhaps the queerest—and most urgently lifesaving—act of all.

Jokering as queer ministry applies a queer hermeneutic to Freire's *conscientization* cycle of action—reflection—action, requiring the theologian or practitioner to continually queer the processes of self-reflection, activist praxis, and ensuing self-reflection. This is a ministry that values theological fluidity and instability—affirming, as Althaus-Reid did, that it is "a sense of discontinuity which is most valuable."[85] As a result, queer theology will likely have a distinctly different face a few years from now, as will queer theology's ministerial applications.

Jokering as Queer Ministry Is Artistically and Spiritually Grounded

Jokering as queer ministry is firmly rooted in the artistic disciplines framed within Boal's *Theatre of the Oppressed* methodologies. Grounded in a realization that participatory theater is in and of itself an artistic discipline, this ministry recognizes, as Boal explained, "the first word of the theatrical body is the human body."[86] Giving voice and expression to the human embodied experience is a central goal in this artistic discipline. It involves, as Boal noted:

> developing in everyone, professional actor and non-actor alike, what everyone already has: theatre within. We all are theatre, even if we don't make theatre . . . skilled professional actors should use the work to go deeper into their possibilities, because theatre is their profession; non-actors should go as far as they choose or feel able to go, because theatre is their vocation.[87]

While an artistic discipline, *Jokering* is also an accessible discipline. Furthermore, it is an integral part of the vocational journey of every person. TO's artistic discipline is not simply art for its own sake. It is art with the direct goal of what Boal termed "dynamisation"; Boal believed that "we should exit from the theatre galvanised with our desire and our decision to bring about change on that which is unfair and oppressive."[88] Art as justice-making lies at the heart of the disciplines of TO and their applications to queer ministry.

Such a dynamic artistic discipline must be equally grounded in spiritual disciplines. The *Joker* as queer minister recognizes that the art of spiritual praxes must form an integral foundation to personal and ministerial approaches. In the work of queer justice-making, the *Joker* heeds theologian Ched Myers' warning that "we mourn before we organize . . .

[that we] can't simply conscientize ourselves and others out of our dysfunctional social systems."[89] The *Joker* engages in spiritual practices that enable both rigorous self-reflection and deep spiritual connection, valuing the foundational wisdom that these practices provide in *Jokering* ministry. The *Joker* as queer minister also recognizes the value of mystery in the work, knowing, as Salverson argued, that "we may possibly have no recourse but to fall back on faith, however we understand it, because this is surely the territory of the unnameable moment, the illusive place we can only reach through play."[90] *Jokering* as queer ministry is a dynamically artistic and spiritually rooted endeavor, with the boundaries between art and spirit being distinctively permeable.

Jokering as Queer Ministry Is Ethically Reflective

Jokering as queer ministry acknowledges the critical importance of ethical reflection and accountability. The *Joker* recognizes both the tremendous power and influence of the *Jokering* role, as well as the potential this role carries to do great damage. The *Joker* as queer minister works to strike the delicate balance between productive social discomfort and socially responsible boundaries of care. The anti-oppressive analysis of personal perspective and privilege is a key tool in this accountability; the *Joker* has an ethical responsibility to be aware of subjective biases, vulnerabilities, and unresolved issues prior to asking participants to work with the same in their own lives.

The *Joker's* ethical reflection must also include an analysis of personal motivations within the role as minister. The *Joker* must have a courageous willingness to examine individual subjectivity as it informs and interplays with the role as facilitator. This may include revealing what Salverson calls the "mask of solidarity"—the dangerously charitable perspective when "identification with the other, however unconsciously, becomes a substitute for our own identity—solidarity is about equal partnership."[91] In order to enable an ethically rooted praxis, the *Joker* as queer minister retains a clear and boundaried self-awareness, even while immersed in the work of spiritual and social transformation.

Jokering as Queer Ministry Is Prophetic

Finally, and most importantly, *Jokering* as queer ministry engages in prophetic justice-making in the church, the academy, and the arts. While personal growth and transformation will undoubtedly result from participation in the work, personal development is not the primary goal.

Rather, a prophetic analysis, exposure, and transformation of systemic sexual, religious, and economic injustice remains the paramount focus. The *Joker* strives to raise what Althaus-Reid termed the religious "ceiling of decency,"[92] to challenge communities to engage in what Boal called "creative heresies"[93] in the potent work of social change. The *Joker* as *difficultator*[94] strives to maintain a queerly prophetic voice in theological and theatrical discourse.

The *Joker* as queer minister holds in tension the profundity and the simplicity of Micah's call to justice: "and what does God require of you but to do justice, and to love kindness, and to walk humbly with your God?"[95] Micah's call captures much of the work of the queer *Joker* as minister. Humility born of ethical self-reflection and spiritual discipline informs a passionately relational loving-kindness—one that is unafraid of *all* aspects of God's love. Groundedness and embodied relationality in turn fuel the prophetic flame of justice that lies at the heart of this work.

CONCLUSIONS

Freire and Boal both recognized that the dialogical nature of their processes often generated more questions than it answered. Queer theologies, in turn, recognize such uncertainties as theological gifts. This newly evolving ministry interweaves these two disciplines, and as such, requires that instability and change be fully embraced. Althaus-Reid's exploration of the instability of a Bi/Christology offers wisdom relevant to this point:

> Bi/Christology walks like a nomad in lands of opposition and exclusive identities, and does not pitch its tent for ever [sic] in the same place. If we consider that in the Gospel of John 1:14, the Verb is said to have "dwelt among us" as in *a tabernacle* (a tent) or "put his tent amongst us," the image conveys Christ' high mobility and lack of fixed spaces or definitive frontiers. Tents are easily dismantled overnight and do not become ruins or monuments; they are rather folded and stored or reused for another purpose when old. Tents change shape in strong winds, and their adaptability rather than their stubbornness is one of their greatest assets. The beauty of this God/tent symbolic is that it can help us to discover Christ in our processes of growth, the eventual transformation through unstable categories to be, more than anything else, a Christ of surprises.[96]

In conclusion, this chapter has aimed to outline the scope and possibilities for a new ministry model. This prophetic ministry recognizes, simultaneously, the profound value of a queer embrace of the changeability and instability of its theological roots and its praxis-oriented applications. In the spirit of Althaus-Reid, Boal, and this particular queer minister, this model is offered as a beginning question to open up and challenge ministry and theologizing for queer and mainstream communities. May the Christ of surprises continue to open life-giving possibilities through this work in, prophetically speaking, an increasingly queer world!

NOTES

1. Michael Cobb, *God Hates Fags: The Rhetorics of Religious Violence* (New York: New York University Press, 2006), 3.

2. Kerri Mesner. "Jokering as Queer Ministry: Queer Theology Meets Theatre of the Oppressed" (master's thesis, Vancouver School of Theology, 2010).

3. There continues to be broad and constantly evolving debate around the definitional parameters of language surrounding sexuality and gender identity. For the purposes of this thesis, queer will be utilized as a term that traverses lesbian, gay, bisexual, transgender, and intersex identities, as well as the many other sexual, gender, and relational configurations that do not conform to traditional heteronormative patterns.

4. Marcella Althaus-Reid, *Indecent Theology: Theological Perversions in Sex, Gender and Politics* (New York: Routledge, 2002), 87.

5. Ibid., 83.

6. While Althaus-Reid's work is the primary theological focus of this thesis, additional examples of preeminent queer theologians include Lisa Isherwood, Robert E. Shore-Goss, Marvin Ellison, Virginia Ramey Mollenkott, Carter Heyward, Mona West, and Mark D. Jordan, among many others.

7. Ali Blackwell, "Post Queer Theory," http://www.aliblackwell.com/post-queer-theory (accessed December 2009).

8. David M. Halperin, "The Normalization of Queer Theory," *Journal of Homosexuality* 45, no. 2–4 (2003): 341.

9. Amy Sullivan, "Is Rick Warren Scared of George Stephanopoulos?" *Time*, April 13, 2009, http://swampland.blogs.time.com/2009/04/13/is-rick-warren-scared-of-george-stephanopoulos/?iid=sphere-inline-bottom (accessed December 2009).

10. Geoffrey York, "Uganda's Anti-Gay Bill Causes Commonwealth Uproar," *The Globe and Mail World*, November 25, http://www.theglobeandmail.com/news/world/ugandas-anti-gay-bill-causes-commonwealth-uproar/article1376503/ (accessed December 2009).

11. Scott Lively, *Redeeming the Rainbow* (Springfield, MA: Veritas Aeterna Press, 2009), 159.

12. Howard Chua-Eoan, "Rick Warren Denounces Uganda's Anti-Gay Bill," *Time*, December 10, 2009, http://www.time.com/time/world/article/0,8599,1946921,00.html?xid=rss-topstories (accessed December 2009).

13. Marcella Althaus-Reid, *Indecent Theology: Theological Perversions in Sex, Gender and Politics* (New York: Routledge, 2002).

14. Ibid., 87.

15. Ibid.

16. Ibid., 69.

17. Ibid., 5. See also: Althaus-Reid, "'Let Them Talk . . . !' Doing Liberation Theology from Latin American Closets," in *Liberation Theology and Sexuality*, ed. Marcella Althaus-Reid (Burlington, VT: Ashgate, 2006), 5–18.

18. Althaus-Reid, *Indecent Theology*, 133–34.

19. Ibid., 172.

20. Marcella Althaus-Reid, *The Queer God* (New York: Routledge, 2003), 108–9.

21. Althaus-Reid, *Indecent Theology*, 117.

22. Robert E. Goss, "Marcella Althaus-Reid's 'Obscenity no. 1: Bi/Christ': Expanding Christ's Wardrobe of Dresses," *Feminist Theology: The Journal of the Britain & Ireland School of Feminist Theology* 11, no. 2 (2003): 161–62.

23. Robert E. Goss, "Queer Theologies as Transgressive Metaphors: New Paradigms for Hybrid Sexual Theologies," *Theology & Sexuality*, no. 10 (March 1999): 47. See also: Robert E. Goss, "Proleptic Sexual Love: God's Promiscuity Reflected in Christian Polyamory," Theology & Sexuality: The Journal of the Institute for the Study 11, no. 1 (2004): 62.

24. "Trannie," a word often used within some transgender communities, is utilized here as a shortened (and deliberately provocative) form of the word "transgender."

25. Martin Hugo Cordova Quero, "This Body Trans/Forming Me: Indecencies in Transgender/Intersex Bodies, Body Fascism and the Doctrine of the Incarnation," in *Controversies in Body Theology*, ed. Marcella Althaus-Reid and Lisa Isherwood (London: SCM Press, 2008), 117.

26. Althaus-Reid, *The Queer God*, 40.

27. Ibid., 53.

28. Conscientization refers to the Freirean process of developing an emerging consciousness of one's own lived situation, as well as the ability to actively intervene in that historical reality.

29. Althaus-Reid, *The Queer God*, 56.

30. Marcella Althaus-Reid, "Graffiti on the Walls of the Cathedral of Buenos Aires: Doing Theology, Love and Politics at the Margins," in *Religion and Political Thought*, ed. Michael Hoelzl and Graham Ward (New York: Continuum, 2006), 249. See also, *The Queer God*, 38.

31. Althaus-Reid, *The Queer God*, 79.

32. Ibid., 50, 114.

33. Marcella Althaus-Reid, "The Divine Exodus of God: Involuntarily Marginalized, Taking an Option for the Margins, or Truly Marginal?" in *God: Experience and Mystery*, ed. Werner Jeanrond et al. (London: SCM Press, 2001), 33.

34. Marcella Althaus-Reid, "Introduction: Queering Theology," in *The Sexual Theologian*, ed. Lisa Isherwood and Marcella Althaus-Reid (London: T & T Clark, 2004), 3.

35. Althaus-Reid, *The Queer God*, 85–93.

36. Althaus-Reid, *Indecent Theology*, 146–55.

37. Sallie McFague, *Life Abundant: Rethinking Theology and Economy for a Planet in Peril* (Minneapolis: Augsburg Fortress, 2001), 48–49.

38. Anita Fast, *Called to Be Queer: Towards a Theological (re)Vision for the People of God* (Vancouver: Vancouver School of Theology, 1999), 44.

39. Andrew Sullivan, "My Big Fat Straight Wedding," *The Atlantic Online*, September 2008, http://www.theatlantic.com/doc/200809/gay-marriage (accessed December 2009).

40. Andrew Sullivan, "Why the M Word Matters to Me," *Time*, February 8, 2004, http://www.time.com/magazine/article/0,9171,588877,00.html (accessed December 2009).

41. Michael Warner, *The Trouble with Normal: Sex, Politics, and the Ethics of Queer Life* (Cambridge, MA: Harvard University Press, 1999), 81–148.

42. Warner, *The Trouble with Normal*, 13, 24.

43. Janet R. Jakobsen, "Queer Is? Queer Does? Normativity and the Problem of Resistance," *GLQ: A Journal of Lesbian & Gay Studies* 4, no. 4 (1998): 530.

44. Marcella Althaus-Reid, "The Bi/girl Writings: From Feminist Theology to Queer Theologies," in *Post-Christian Feminisms: A Critical Approach*, ed. Lisa Isherwood and Kathleen McPhillips (Burlington, VT: Ashgate, 2008), 107.

45. Marcella Althaus-Reid, "Lunchtime Crucifixions: Theological Reflections on Economic Violence and Redemption," in *Weep Not for Your Children: Essays on Religion and Violence*, ed. Lisa Isherwood and Rosemary Radford Ruether (Oakville: Equinox, 2008), 66.

46. Ibid.

47. Ibid., 69, 74.

48. Ibid., 72.

49. Althaus-Reid, *Indecent Theology*, 119.

50. Jasbir Puar, *Terrorist Assemblages: Homonationalism in Queer Times* (Durham, NC: Duke University, 2007), 2.

51. Puar, *Terrorist Assemblages*, 38.

52. Ibid., 61, 63.

53. Janet R. Jakobsen, "Can Homosexuals End Western Civilization as We Know It? Family Values in a Global Economy," in *Queer Globalizations: Citizenship and the Afterlife of Colonialism*, ed. Arnaldo Cruz-Malave and Marvin F. Manalansan IV (New York: New York University Press, 2002), 57.

54. Ibid., 56.

55. Ann Pellegrini, "Consuming Lifestyle: Commodity Capitalism and Transformation in Gay Identity," in *Queer Globalizations: Citizenship and the Afterlife of Colonialism*, ed. Arnaldo Cruz-Malave and Martin F. Manalansan (New York: New York University Press, 2002), 137.

56. Ann Pellegrini and Janet R. Jakobsen, "Melancholy Hope and Other Psychic Remainders," *Studies in Gender & Sexuality* 6, no. 4 (2005): 430.

57. Ibid., 434.

58. Michael Cobb, *God Hates Fags: The Rhetorics of Religious Violence* (New York: New York University Press, 2006), 3, 6.

59. Ibid., 3.

60. Ibid., 6.

61. Ibid., 6, 14.

62. Ibid., 31.

63. Althaus-Reid, *The Queer God*, 166.

64. Althaus-Reid, *Indecent Theology*, 167.

65. Ibid., 148.

66. Augusto Boal, *Theatre of the Oppressed* (New York: Theatre Communications Group, 1985); See also Daniel O'Donnell, *Social Acupuncture: A Guide to Suicide, Performance and Utopia* (Toronto: Coach House Books, 2006).

67. O'Donnell, *Social Acupuncture: A Guide to Suicide, Performance and Utopia*, 47, 49–50.

68. Augusto Boal, *Games for Actors and Non-Actors*, 2nd ed. (New York: Routledge, 2002), 262.

69. Boal, *Theatre of the Oppressed*, 122.

70. Ibid., 127.

71. Boal uses the term *arsenal* to refer to his own wide range of theatrical strategies, perhaps as a response to the politically violent context within which they originally were formulated.

72. Boal, *Theatre of the Oppressed*, 126.

73. Boal, *Games for Actors and Non-Actors*.

74. Augusto Boal, *Rainbow of Desire: The Boal Method of Theatre and Therapy* (New York: Routledge).

75. Augusto Boal, *Legislative Theatre: Using Performance to Make Politics* (New York: Routledge).

76. This work has been utilized in a variety of contexts internationally, including congregational workshops, sermons, conferences, and theological gatherings.

77. Marcella Althaus-Reid and Lisa Isherwood, "Thinking Theology and Queer Theory," *Feminist Theology: The Journal of the Britain & Ireland School of Feminist Theology* 15, no. 3 (2007): 308.

78. Ibid.

79. Daniel O'Donnell, *Social Acupuncture: A Guide to Suicide, Performance and Utopia* (Toronto: Coach House Books, 2006), 23.

80. Ibid., 50.

81. Marcella Althaus-Reid, *Indecent Theology: Theological Perversions in Sex, Gender and Politics* (New York: Routledge, 2002), 7.

82. Ibid., 130.

83. Ibid., 87.

84. Ibid., 194.

85. Ibid., 4.

86. Augusto Boal, *Theatre of the Oppressed* (New York: Theatre Communications Group, 1985), 125.

87. Boal, *Games for Actors and Non-Actors*, 17.

88. Ibid., 25.

89. Mady Schutzman, "Brechtian Shamanism: The Political Therapy of Augusto Boal," in *Playing Boal: Theatre, Therapy, Activism*, ed. Mady Schutzman and Jan Cohen-Cruz (New York: Routledge, 1994), 169.

90. Julie Salverson, "The Mask of Solidarity," in *Playing Boal: Theatre, Therapy, Activism*, ed. Mady Schutzman and Jan Cohen-Cruz (New York: Routledge, 1994), 169.

91. Ibid., 168.

92. Althaus-Reid, *Indecent Theology*, 167.

93. Boal, *Games for Actors and Non-Actors*, 9.

94. Boal coined the word "difficultator" in his training workshops to distinguish the difference between traditional facilitators and the provocatively challenging role of the *Joker*.

95. Mi 6:8 (New Revised Standard Version: inclusification added).

96. Althaus-Reid, *Indecent Theology*, 119–20.

11

Communion: Playing with Redemption

Nic Arnzen with the Cast and Friends of *Corpus Christi*

As a Catholic boy growing up in Iowa, each week I dreaded Sunday mornings when my mother bellowed from her room that it was time to get to church. My parents would drag us to mass where I literally counted the minutes until it was finished. On the mornings where I wasn't recruited to step in for a missing Altar Boy I found myself scouring the pew and church for something, ANYTHING interesting. I'd play a game with the bible where I tried to see how many times I could read the same line the priest was reading before he got through it. I'd imagine a Poseidon Adventure scenario where the church was upside down and wondered how

---

Note from Robert E. Shore-Goss: Thomas Bohache speaks of the event of Pentecost that the Christ Spirit cannot be contained: He writes, "The queer Christ animates his/her followers to speak to others in their own languages: this tells me that there are many diverse ways to tell the Christ story and to share the Christ Spirit." Nic Arnzen and I met to discuss performing *Corpus Christi*. I used the play in *Queering Christ*, but we both wanted to queer the play further with a cast of women and men, instead of 13 men that the play was originally cast. Queer Christ, for a number of the contributors, is an empowered Christology that comprehends queer people finding and reflecting the Christ in their own experience. Many of the cast were alienated from church or temple because of religious homophobia. But the first night before the performance at MCC in the Valley, I found the cast hands joined and in prayer. This tradition has continued with every performance. The cast found their spirituality in Terrence McNally's play, and it became a missionary effort to tell the story of the queer Christ against the backdrop of religious homophobia and bullying of LGBT youth. The play went to the Scotland Fringe Festival, the Dublin Gay Festival, and Off-Broadway for two weeks. But the spirituality of the play and community drove them to create a documentary: *Playing with Redemption*.

we would get out, who would choose to find their way out with me, and who would survive. Although it certainly wasn't on my mind at the time, that film had a highly religious undertone. The leader of the group of survivors was a priest who had lost his trust in religion but was full of passion and love for Jesus and for his fellow human beings. He was flawed and judgmental but ultimately he believed that to find your way to the light you must save yourself. There was no Jesus coming to rescue you but if you look for him he will guide you. I wouldn't put that together until revisiting the film in my college years.

The only part of the service that consistently interrupted my escapist imaginings was Communion. There was something about the act of rising from our seats together in an orderly manner and all of us taking part in the same ritual. I guess it made me feel safe to be bound to these other people, that I wasn't alone in the world. Of course like my perception of *The Poseidon Adventure* this would change as I got older. By the time I was in my teens my warm feelings about religion began to sour. The idea that Jesus was reserved for those who were found worthy enough to receive him was such a contradictory notion to me and felt elitist. Of course my catholic schooling was full of contradictions.

Jesus loved everyone, except. . .
     We should always help the needy—but apparently gossiping about the single mother or poor family after service was another way of helping?

Children should be raised to be gentle and loving—but if you didn't play aggressively in sports and crush the opposing team you were benched and knocked down the social ladder.

For me, like so many others, the structure of religion didn't match the actions of the clergy, teachers, and adults who were supposed to keep me on the right path. I became confused, angry, and judgmental, a perfect Catholic! But that was not for me because beyond all else I had the secret of being gay and it was abundantly clear there was no way I was going to heaven. Why would I want to continue a relationship that was going nowhere unless I lied to myself and to them? I wanted to be a good Christian, I wanted to walk down the aisle and receive communion and I wanted to feel part of a community. My walking away from the church did not come as some big event or dramatic revelation. It was a slow sulk away with my head hung low. I was embarrassed for who I was, and ashamed that I had failed but mostly I was sad. I was sad that I let my parents down, that I learned so many wonderful things about being good but no matter how hard I tried I could not rid myself of the flaw that would damn me to hell. I was devastated that I would no longer be allowed to walk down that aisle as a welcomed member of the parish. No more helping as an Altar Boy, no more Communion and of course never, never would they let me walk down a Catholic Church aisle to marry the person I loved. My relationship with the church was over because I loved it but it would not love me as I was, as God made me. I left feeling that I was no longer a part of this community and sincerely believed I would never find true love. I would miss Communion.

In my 30s I began to grow up all over again. I had spent my 20s embracing the sinful life I was dealt. The church was no longer part of my life so why should I follow the rules and commandments that were drummed into my head? I had a few relationships that were meaningful but mostly I drifted from one to the other eventually causing them each to self-destruct and finding comfort in the arms of the next one. I was in an ugly cycle reliving the experience I had with the Catholic Church. I would jump in completely and faithfully but always find a way to destroy what was usually working so that this time I would not be the one pushed out. I was out of control and by the time I moved to Los Angeles in my late 20s I was at my worst. I was happy; don't get me wrong, the city of angels is certainly not the ideal place to get yourself back on track or find yourself but it's a fun place to be lost!

I spent my 30s struggling to figure out who I was and why I was so destructive in my relationships. I was lucky enough to find a patient partner and start a family. We chose to try worshiping together within the MCC and I felt myself coming back. The combination of a strong partner, the weight of fatherhood and the reconnecting with my spiritual side began to put me back on track. What I really came to realize was that of course I had never really been lost. I just needed to embrace the journey I was on, something I was still working on, something I AM still working on. It was around this time that the play *Corpus Christi* came into my life. The playwright, Terrence McNally, imagines Jesus as a gay man growing up in 1950s' Texas. I was fascinated by the logistics of staging it but the truth was my fixation on how to move 13 actors around a simple set and tell such a grand story was really just a distraction from the real journey the play was about to take me on. The play itself faced distraction as well. When it opened Off-Broadway in 1998 there were threatening calls and letters sent to the theater, bomb threats and hundreds of people protesting nightly as it opened. It became a spectacle that easily drown out the gentle loving message of the play. It became about the sensation of the concept of a gay Jesus and had nothing to do with this play, which was more of a gift to Christianity than the blasphemy they claimed it to be.

Terrence McNally had grown up in conservative Texas as a gay boy. He was undoubtedly teased, bullied, and made to feel like he was not worthy of God's love let alone anyone else's. Instead of turning his hurt into anger he wrote a play that was incredibly respectful to the source material, the Bible. He showed those who chose to put him down, both in his childhood and during the play's opening days that it is better to love than to hate. It was an amazing lesson that he had no intention of teaching, he was simply doing what he felt was right in his heart. As too many of us become bitter and jaded, I was fascinated and in awe of Mr. McNally's ability to look beyond the cruel words and actions directed at him and respond with compassion and a desire for understanding.

Rev. Bob Shore-Goss, our spiritual leader at MCC North Hollywood was eager to bring the excitement and energy of live performances back to his church. He asked if I would direct a play there and I quickly said yes and suggested *Corpus Christi*. He responded immediately and passionately. Not only was it a play he knew, but it seemed to be one he was eager to see staged there as well. So we began the production process in the spring of 2006 and the play was scheduled for nine performances at the church early that summer. None of us had any idea how far beyond the church this production would go or what an intricate part of our lives it would become. In our first run-through before opening I caught a glimmer of what we were creating. Goss popped in to see how things were going and I suspect to see what he had gotten himself and the church into. He happened to catch the scene in the play where Joshua, the Jesus character, performs the miracle of the fishes. I was paying attention to the specifics of the scene and the pace and such, but near the middle of it I turned to Bob who was wiping tears from his eyes. His beautiful and heartfelt reaction had me look back at the action with a less analytical mind, and I was able to relax and let go of my concerns as a director and recognize the magic that was transpiring in front of me. It was a turning point for me in my experience with this play and as a director. He reminded me it was important to let the emotion come over me and to recognize when the play is becoming more than a performance and is actually connecting with an audience. That is exactly what was happening and the play went on to tour the world for five years (and counting). We played in hot spots such as Ireland and Texas where they take their religion quite seriously and despite the tumultuous history the play had, we faced little to no resistance on our amazing journey. It was as close to being a missionary as I ever imagined I would be. This troupe was taking the kind and powerful words of scripture to audiences around the world. Ironically they were doing it through a Gay Jesus play. Although the protests were relatively nonexistent the production was certainly being noticed; the tour inspired a documentary titled *Corpus Christi: Playing with Redemption*. The film chronicles the journey of the play but became much more about where gay men and women belong at the table of spirituality (and they DO belong), and why they would want to come back to religions that so often pushed them away and made them feel unworthy. The film witnesses how the cast amazingly transformed from random actors to a family spreading the word of the Lord around the world. They embraced their roles on and off the stage and found themselves seeking redemption of all kind and often finding it before they even began to look. Their commitment to the play easily transitioned to their willingness to open up in interviews for the documentary. They told their stories with a beautiful trust and abandoned all pretense or fear of being judged. What was created for the film was a gorgeous portrait of a family that embraced the journey of self-discovery they continued on together.

I clearly learned that in my lonely walk away from the church I was actually not alone. There were so many other broken people walking around in search of healing. More importantly, they too were willing to look at their spiritual side and reexamine their beliefs. One of them was Brandon. I cast Brandon as Joshua, the reluctant Jesus character. I recognized that like Joshua, Brandon was a dear gentle soul. His good looks and confidence made it hard to see he was as damaged and lost as I was. Until we were deep into performances I had not fully realized this. Until he was healing he was unable to truly express his need to be healed.

October 26, 2006

Faith follows you around like a swirling dust storm. It is easy to get swept in it.

It is even easier to cough it away in an uproarious asthma attack.

Tonight I learned more about "Faith"—faith in the universe, faith in the world, faith in the community, faith in the Self.

The scene when Bart exclaims his outrage and sense of despair at wanting to help and heal others but not feeling like he can, and my response: "you are a man who has lost faith," touched me like never before—hitting my heart and almost swallowing the words. When I get choked on words, I know my truth is being tested.

What is faith?

I, too, struggle with this simple truth—faith in knowing I am supported, knowing I am loved, knowing I have the financial means to live,
all of this can be brought to surface at one time or another.

Lately I have missed faith. I lost it somewhere along that dusty trail. I think
I was holding on too tight to it. Clutching it like a baby blanket that is torn
to shreds but you just can't let go of. Maybe I was afraid of it. Maybe it wasn't
really me having faith but thinking I had more faith than others. Maybe
it was my ego who had faith. Whatever it was, somewhere as I was walking along, skipping along my merry little way down the sweet little stream
of consciousness, I turned around and it disappeared. I remember feeling a
sense of loss. This emptiness pervading my soul; fear crept in like that nasty
little black crawling mess in Spiderman. I had ideas, thoughts, questions that
were usually answered and for some reason now couldn't be. Where did you
go little blanket of faith? Why did you leave me? I was good wasn't I? What
did I do for you to desert me? Was I mean to you? I didn't mean to be, but if
I was why didn't you tell me? Will you ever come back again?

Thoughts entered me, swelling my soul like a crashing thunderous
wave of grief and somewhere I stood still, silently in the eye of the storm,
waiting.

I was alone.

I was afraid.

But there I stood.

Waiting.

Nothing appeared. Nothing happened. Nothing changed.

But there I stood.

Waiting . . . for . . . ?

And then I realized something.

Even in the grief in the tiredness in the question in the fear

I still stood. Silently waiting.

That waiting, that looking around, that simple observation

WAS the faith.

lost and found again.

It was that glimmer of sunshine, that little sliver of light peeking
through the miniscule scratch in the proverbial steel surface that allowed
me to continue waiting.

Because it is in the waiting that the knowing appears. It is in the silence
that the answer is revealed. It is sitting in the eye of the storm and allowing the chaos to swirl all around you, watching it all go by piece by piece
moment by moment

And, yet, you still stand.

That is faith.

It seems like faith is tested when you get caught up in that swirl, which
can be so easy to do today.

To do to do to do to do

Faith is living in the question. It is knowing that the question IS the answer itself.

Actually it seems, then, faith is never lost. It is as much a part of you as your skin. It IS you. It is just the swirl that sucks us away.

When I said those words last night it was like hearing them again for the first time. "You are a man who has lost faith." And I think Joshua, too, hears them again for the first time. Bart's reply, "What kind of world do you live in?! We've ALL lost faith."

And, thus, the work begins.

It is not our job to find faith if we think it is lost. Faith is never lost. It is always there. It is our work to FEEL faith. To be so in touch with our feelings in each moment and allowing our feelings to guide us along our path—THAT is the essence of faith. The heart knows. Listening to it is faith. With Faith, all things are truly possible.

Again, I bring it back to the experience of the play. I am starting to really feel now that this play, as I've said before is not a thing outside of me anymore. This play IS me. Realizing this profundity is quite remarkable. It is a creation of love that has made this possible.

I can forget this simple truth so easily in the day-to-day moments—keeping myself locked into the lack rather than the abundance even if it is not readily visible in the moment. It is Faith that makes it so.

The play, after almost a year of shows, continues to surprise and amaze me. It continues to open the doors for experiences such as the one we shared last night, it continues to teach me a deep sense of honor, humbleness and love, it continues to create an abundance of wisdom and truth for us and the audience—what a blessing.

—Brandon

I was surrounded by actors who seemed to have a need for this play. Each performance felt like a new awakening and it was breathtaking. I watched them get stronger. I watched them resist and discover and break down. In theater you become accustomed to moving on, the play is done and it's time to get started on the next project with your next team. This was different. The play took hold of us and we took hold of each other. Something mysterious and beautiful was happening. It was beyond explanation except to say we became a family. That's a word often used in the theater community and it certainly holds true even in the shortest of runs. You are out there with these people and you must trust them. You learn to love them through that trust. The *Corpus Christi* family went far beyond this normal display of trust. They were opening up to each other like I have never seen, both on stage and off stage. There were nights during the performance where I saw them look into each other's eyes and become someone else. Actually it was more like they were becoming their true selves. They were fully exposed and every time they fell other actors were there to catch them. It was most beautiful in the final moments of the play as they shared in the grief of the loss of their savior but found hope and warmth in the solace that they had with each other.[1]

As incredible and joyous as this period was I must admit it was at times difficult for me. I was drawn to the play for my own reasons including a need to heal and here I was essentially leading a group of loving souls into an exploration of spirituality. It was often thrilling and occasionally maddening but what really surprised me was how lonely it began to feel. I felt myself becoming short tempered and snapping at the actors, allowing them to see I was irritated and frazzled, something I had wished I could keep to myself. Of course I am human, but I wanted them to feel safe on this journey and in the first year or two I spent a lot of time beating myself up and distancing myself from the cast in some ways. I watched them laugh and bond while I tried to keep the production moving forward and doing multiple jobs as we had no real crew to speak of. I felt isolated and envious of their bonds and happiness. It was an ugly thing to be feeling but I just wanted to be more a part of the group and not so much the leader. I missed the learning from each other and evolving like they were. I missed Communion.

As varied as their backgrounds were the actors were discovering how alike they were as well. Their stories were wildly original and unique but at the heart of all of them was the need to be loved. Many of them were searching for redemption or even forgiveness. In some cases forgiveness from their family, friends, or themselves but in most cases they were searching for a way to forgive those who turned their backs on them. The churches and people that told them they were not worthy and sending them down a lonely road away from what they were taught to hold dear and love. Like me, so many of them were still walking away with their heads hung low and refusing to look back.

Paul, one of my actors and a dear friend, truly embodied the essence of this spiral of shame and anger and refusal to look back. By the time the play came into his life he had seemingly worked through many of his demons but he discovered with us that this journey is never at an end. There are always new obstacles and opportunities before us.

I grew up in a small town in South Texas. My father was the President of a black Christian college and a Baptist minister. My mother was a Christian school teacher. We went to church every Sunday and our family would come together after dinner and read from the Bible. I came from a very loving family but I experienced an undercurrent of fear because of my secret. I was attracted to boys and felt immense shame about it. It was difficult for me to talk to anyone about it and this secret would eat at me. As much as I wanted to connect with others from my Texas high school, I guarded myself so no one would know my secret. If I told anyone at school, I would be teased and harassed. If I told my parents, I would be warned about burning in hell for all of eternity. All I really wanted was to love and have friends. If I could change my attraction to boys I would. So I would spend most of my days avoiding others and not wanting to be noticed.

Our Southern Baptist Church, where I was baptized, was a temple for a judgmental God. I was taught one sin would keep me out of heaven and to be ready because the Rapture could happen anytime. Their version of God was stern and harsh. He loved you if you were following his way, but if you weren't, you would spend and eternity in hell. The congregation spoke in tongues at every service. Tongues were a foreign language of gibberish but we were told it was a language that God could understand. You just started speaking gibberish and letting it flow out of you. I find it ironic that they were so happy that you could speak a language that could make no sense, yet if I spoke the real truth of me being gay, it would not be received well at all. So I spoke in tongues to try to fit in. To belong. And yet it seemed strange and untruthful to me. Nothing made sense. Why do I have to speak this gibberish to God that would bring him happiness, yet if I shared from my heart what I was really feeling, I would be damned to hell. How ironic being afraid of living an eternity in hell when what I was experiencing in that moment was hell, a place of fear, hiding and judgment.

Football and sports were a big deal in my high school. The high school football team was a big turn on for me, but I felt like I needed to avoid them because I was already being called faggot in school. I was too much in denial to acknowledge I was attracted to boys. Being called faggot and sissy was so hard for me and that bullying pushed me further away from everyone and into a closet of isolation. I decided to attend my high school drama club, an eclectic group of misfits that I started to befriend. Instead of being bullied, we came together to laugh and tell stories through plays. They started to become my theatre family. A place I fit it and belonged. Although I still couldn't share my secret of being gay, I felt like I was in a group of kids who embraced the theatre and wanted to have fun without being judged. It became my home away from home and I started to develop the courage to express myself through plays. I could lose myself in different characters. In one way I was afraid to be noticed, yet doing plays forced me to put myself out there as an artist and make friends. Being a part of the drama club was my saving grace in high school. Amidst the harassment and being bullied, I connected with my theatre family and that brought me comfort and a place I fit in.

Yet this secret of being gay was eating me up inside. I needed to talk to someone because the guilt I was feeling was pure hell. I wasn't ready to talk to my parents about it, so I went to a minister from a different church to discuss these gay feelings. He then acknowledged that I didn't receive enough love from my father when I was growing up and that I was seeking it from boys now as I was becoming an adult. It was true that my father was more interested in his work with the Christian college than being with me. And my loving and caring mother easily expressed her love to me. Maybe I was seeking more masculine love and affection that I didn't get from my father. But the pastor reminded me that these homosexual feelings were a sin and that I would go to hell for them.

"But all I really want to do is love someone." I explained. "I don't want to hurt anyone. It just so happens that I'm attracted to boys. Why is that a sin?" The pastor looked at me thoughtfully and clearly, "God created man and woman to be together to procreate and make children. This is what God intended."

And yet, something just didn't register with me. I believed that love was the answer. But it was challenging to believe it when there was so much fear and judgment being pushed down my throat.

The fear that is placed upon you about living an eternity of hell is a lot to digest for a 17 year old boy. When I finally spoke to my mother about it, she revealed to me about how she had feelings for a girl in college. But she acknowledged that these feelings were sinful and she didn't act upon them because it would be a sin and Jesus would not approve. I asked her, who do I pray to? Do I pray to God or Jesus? She explained that I could pray to both. I decided to go straight to God. Jesus was a holy man but I would cut out the middle man and go right to the source. During our family Bible readings at night, my Mother started quoting many scriptures of how homosexuality was a sin. It became too much for me. I told her that if she continued down this road that I would leave and I would never come back. It moved into a Don't Ask, Don't Tell situation. Such a horrible secret to hold in and not talk about. Don't ask, don't tell doesn't really heal the situation it just leaves a void of not being able to talk and share. Because of the inability to talk about things it leaves the person feeling ashamed and isolated.

So I moved to Chicago when I was 21 to truly live my life as a gay man. Knowing I would go to hell when I died, I decided it was more important for me to live my life in truth and acceptance than living in fear. It was so freeing to finally be out and proud in Chicago. Even though I was afraid of burning in hell, I prayed that God would understand.

I eventually moved to Los Angeles to continue my work as an actor and enjoy the West Coast sunshine instead of the harsh mid west winter cold. Los Angeles seemed a very spiritual place. It was the city of angels after all. I trusted my path and began to believe more in a loving and compassionate God. Someone who would love and support me as I am. Such a different belief than the judgmental God I was taught growing up.

So in 2006, Nic Arnzen approached me about being a part of Corpus Christi, the play about a gay Jesus. Knowing how blasphemous this subject was, I was intrigued. As an artist, I was interested in doing work that challenged people and allowed them to question what they believed. So I jumped aboard. I really didn't have a relationship with Jesus in my life. I still just prayed to God and considered Jesus a holy man who did God's work. But there was something happening with this production that moved me deeply. A group of artists coming together to bring a bridge between Jesus and homosexuality. It just felt this was the place I needed to be. I was first cast as John and my role consisted of baptizing each actor and giving them their role for the play. I was baptized when I was 13 because I felt it was an obligation. You were expected to be baptized. But in Corpus Christi, I was the one doing the baptizing and it was my role to recognize the divinity in each one. What a profound thing to learn, to recognize the divinity in all. Instead of looking at their faults or judging them, I saw their divinity. I saw the light in each one of them. This brought me so much love and joy. It touched my heart.

The bond I felt with this theatre family was filled with joy and laughter. The joy of telling a story of love, compassion and forgiveness with a family of artists who accepted me as I was. This was Heaven to me. I stopped caring about the afterlife and embraced this moment right now. I could choose to live in fear and hell, or see the divinity in everyone and embrace heaven in this moment. The line that God tells Joshua when he is a baby, "All men are divine" really hit home with me. To embrace that divinity within myself and see it in everyone. Recognizing the divinity in the process and struggle. Being aware that my parents wouldn't approve of me being a part of a gay Jesus play, yet also seeing the divinity of their love for me and wanting me to be happy. I still don't talk about being gay a lot with them, but it's no secret. We've moved beyond Don't Ask Don't Tell to just being considerate of their feelings and not forcing it upon them. I'm just true to myself and their acceptance to me being gay will come at their own time. My mother is still afraid that I won't be in Heaven with her in the afterlife. But I just tell her to not worry about that. Trust the love and support she gave us when she raised us, and let's embrace Heaven in this moment right now. Recognizing that everyone may not understand or agree with me and my lifestyle, but it is my journey. We all have spiritual paths we walk. And it is not my place to judge or force people to believe how

I believe. I just need to stay true to myself and trust the process. I'm exactly where I need to be here and now.

I am grateful to Corpus Christi for teaching me many lessons.

Connecting me to the divinity in all beings.

Reminding me of the love and joy a theatre family can have.

Bringing me a deeper connection to Jesus and how he lived his life.

Living with an open heart, on stage and off.

—Paul

The play and its message was transforming people. This cast was transforming the play. The playwright expressed that to me many times but I wasn't fully realizing it. Now I see what he meant. As Rev. Bob Goss noted, *Corpus Christi* had become our religion. The play had moved far beyond the church we began in and so had I. Goss described us as a missionary troupe, spreading the inclusive love taught by MCC and by Jesus. I think it was hard for me to see us this way since it still felt like a gift to me not from me. The play had become my way of connecting and healing. I felt no guilt or shame on Sunday mornings any more. I didn't HAVE to attend a service, I could choose to completely of my own will. The best part was the synchronicity of all the elements that had come into my life.

My partner was steadfast in his beliefs but had no bottom line of attending church. He was as casual as I was—that made me feel safe.

The church we were attending had been very clear of their doors still being open to us but had no demands or warnings for us on our lack of attendance—that made me feel welcomed.

The play was touring the world and seemed an endless supply of enlightenment and energy—that made me feel strong.

Then there was the cast. The cast and crew were my family; they were a perfect source of inspiration and acceptance—that made me feel loved.

What I didn't expect and turned out to be the greatest gift of all was the audience we were privileged to interact with along the way. Every location provided new stories and new healing. As they healed we healed, a beautiful and divine cycle. One of the many locations the show played was the gorgeous Grace Cathedral in San Francisco. Here Brandon reflects on our time there.

Grace.

To me, this weekend at Grace Cathedral truly was an experience of Grace. Again we celebrated pride weekend and again the energy of the city buzzed around us with such intense electricity that I would find myself exhausted and awake all at once—a strange feeling if you've ever felt such a sensation. Beautiful. Grace.

Performing the shows, we were greeted with the most beautiful hearts imaginable—something magical exists in this city—an underlying magnetism of love and light and pure positive power that seeps through the city streets, clanging in the trolley bells into the worthy veins of open souls. And one's heartbeat pulses. If this city were a poster, I would simply draw one big red heart with the words "Be Open" written in bold letters underneath—you can feel it the minute you start to climb the hills and cross the bridge—a part of me did leave my heart in San Francisco and those famous words in the singular verse never rang more true in my soul. Beautiful. Grace.

The people here are truly the most unique cast of characters—and they are so willing to share. One beautiful man came up to me after the show and said "Before I came here I thought I was dying of AIDS, now that I am leaving here I know I am living with it and will live a happy life of many years with it. I feel healed." I started crying. Although numerous occasions along this path have offered me some incredible stories, this took it for me. I don't take credit for it though. I am simply a vessel. And, as an actor, it is my job to believe the words myself onstage so therefore stepping into that truth I merely share what I am learning to know for myself. I know what he meant. It's not that "I healed him," it's that the words healed him. He got it.

"As I believe so shall I be . . ."

He heard it and he got it. Beautiful. Grace.

Another man came up to me perfectly clear minded and level headed, offered his hand to shake mine and said "My name is (Tom) and I just want to say . . .," and as if a sudden realization of his own just occurred to him, he burst into a weeping puddle of shimmering tears. Beautiful. Grace. I held his hand. He held mine. His eyes closed. I closed mine. And I felt what one might call "the infinite connection," another might call "an emotional heart tug," and another might simply call "feeling moved." I call it "love," the truest, deepest, most pure love that exists. A connection to a stranger who is actually a part of me out there in the world wanting simply to be the best person I can be, and it went so deep my heart shuttered. It was the connection we seek to share with all of humanity in that moment. And it was so deep and infinite and expansive and whole that I felt in the one singular moment, I was standing in the middle of the matrix of life looking at all the directions and laughing my ass off at the absurdity of it all. Beautiful. Grace.

Interestingly I found myself in the second show losing my voice. I was talking and then I was raspy. I would try and clear it a few times when I could, and be conscious of the grounding breath and connection to voice—and yet it stood in the wings quietly wisping away. For a moment I was shook—wondering what exactly caused this and noting where it was in the script it began to further analyze it later (for curious seekers, it started in the Philip scene where I say "As you believe so shall you be" for the first time . . . I noted the significance of wondering how deeply I believe that myself, and had a good laugh at it, but also, see story above . . .) then I went directly to the place of "Well let's work with this now" . . . how to speak when you are a speaking leader and followers want to listen to your every word. A challenge? Not at all. The simpler the voice, the more direct the language. The less I could yell, the more I had to really emphasize the points across and I found a new direction for Joshua to "get through" to those crazy minds that like to get in the way of the heart, which is the ultimate leader. New words were heard, new thoughts were formed and I could feel a new pulse in the air. A true lesson in being. Not being thrown off, but simply being, allowing and accepting. Then, beautiful Nic at some point in the play had run off stage to grab some water from the dressing room to quench my thirsty voice. I was on the mount, and followers were "flocking" to me—"Love thy neighbor as thyself" I exclaim, and a Sparkletts water bottle was handed to me in the middle of the flock. Without a second thought, I grabbed it, heartily drank the delicious nectar and said "thank you" to my friend who knew me so well he could sense every little need I desired. Judas. Of course it was Judas who brought me the water. And of course it was he that healed my voice as the play continued. Art imitates life imitates art as our profound Mr. Wilde has once said (paraphrased of course). And as we continued, our community on stage deepened—because I knew I was supported and I knew I was cared for and I knew we were all coming together in a deeper sense of grace than ever before. Simply because a water bottle ended up in my hands out of nowhere.

As we all together released tears of joy and pain frustration and light—there was a spider web connecting us all in this pattern of undeniable love. It was stunning. It was magic. I found myself in a completely new state of being. I feel the pulse of each person on stage with me and as we walk together those final steps after clicking back on the light, our own pulse becomes one. We are connected. We are family. We are one.

I don't like to leave the show and immediately meet audience. I take my time. To be with me. Partly there is a personal release of my own that comes forth, partly there is an embarrassment of coming "back to Earth" and standing in my humble shoes and partly I simply don't feel the desire to hear if I did or did not do a "good job" as an actor. It is not what I am up there to be a part of. However in this space there wasn't all that much of a choice—I could hide in the kitchen a bit, but it wasn't easy, especially because people saw where I walked to and waited. So there I was naked for the world to see, un-composed and completely open. And you know what

I found? The most beautiful sense of community I had ever felt. People were hugging each other, wiping their own tears away, sharing personal stories with each other, laughing, hugging, loving—everyone. Not just one. Everyone. As one. I wondered how they all knew each other and then I realized most likely they didn't. They knew each other because they were open enough to go on the journey and finally recognize each other. And so, right there in front of my eyes, a community was formed. Beautiful. Grace. I was honored to witness that, humbled to be a part of it, and enamored at the words that we spoke and the journey we've taken so far to get us here.

And I suddenly stood back, opened myself, walked into the crowd and sat down hearing the stories, wiping the tears away and smiling so deep my heart grew a few inches wider. And as I sat there with everyone, I felt the grandest sense of grace in my earthly existence. Do you know what grace means? I looked it up to be sure, but I was even more delighted in its' meaning when I read "the influence or spirit of God operating in humans to regenerate or strengthen them."

Truth beyond reason lies in the stunning combination of those words. And I am lifted higher than I ever have before.

—Brandon

It was the audience, it always was. This was where we would learn the true lesson of the play. It is by our communion with others that we find ourselves. Not just with those we surround ourselves with most often but the strangers, the ones who come into our lives briefly and then are gone and easily forgotten. That is where we find the grace and the divine within ourselves. When we open to them and they open to us in return we feel connected to more than just a play or our friends we feel connected to the world and realize we will never be alone. That is where Jesus still lives and why the play can culminate in a crucifixion but end with hope. We learned to listen to these strangers and quickly found they were not strangers at all. They felt like part of us and we were part of them. In some cases they even began to travel with us. Such is the case of our glorious friend Steve Susoyev.

In Spite of Myself

Corpus Christi came into my life in spite of my best efforts: Two friends had been seduced, as far as I could tell, by a poster featuring a loincloth-clad stud in crucifixion pose. Expecting beefcake Jesus in heels, I declined to join them for what they called "A play about gay Jesus." But my friends had purchased three tickets as a birthday treat for me. They insisted, and I half-heartedly looked forward to a mildly entertaining evening.

Once at the theater, upon seeing that Corpus Christi was the work of Terrence McNally, I allowed my expectations to rise a bit. The creator of Master Class was capable of profundity. And even in the comedies I had seen, The Full Monty and The Ritz, he had created fully human characters.

While we found empty seats, the cast and crew laughed and hugged onstage. I could see from their gentle teasing that this would not be the campy twaddle I had earlier expected. Sincerity and commitment shone through in their banter.

Moments into the play, the performers' extraordinary professionalism further surprised me (this was pay-what-you-feel-like-paying theater—predictably heartfelt, but often amateurish). As the story developed, I found myself laughing, then weeping. Jesus, Mary and Joseph, and the disciples, were being depicted with human frailties and complexities. Even God, portrayed by a black woman, was emotionally accessible, alternatively sad and gleeful.

Within minutes I had become absorbed in a play that I knew I would recommend to friends, and perhaps even see again if I had the chance.

About forty minutes into the play, a fire broke out in my soul. Philip, the hustler, accosts the young prophet Joshua. Philip is an angry gay man who uses his sexuality to intimidate and hurt other people. But he is honest enough to tell a prospective customer that he is HIV-positive. While Joshua's followers shun Philip, and warn Joshua to stay away, Joshua sees the beautiful human spirit within this injured man, desperate to break free.

I've wanted to think that I am like Joshua—the enlightened being who looks upon all people with loving acceptance. But in truth, I have at times behaved more like Philip—wielding my sexuality as a weapon, alienating my brothers and sisters. Philip's scene caught me short and affirmed the path I want to travel. I can no longer turn away from angry, dangerous people without realizing that their humanity is hiding somewhere inside their destructive behavior. And I can no longer breeze through relationships with my morally threadbare, 1970's-style "I do my thing and you do your thing, we are not in this world to live up to each other's expectations" attitude. Corpus Christi helped me to embrace the knowledge that I am in this world to touch other people's hearts, and to allow my own heart to be touched.

In the five years since the performance that brought Corpus Christi into my life, I have used that same photo of the shirtless Brandon on the cover of several editions of the souvenir program—something I designed to help the troupe with fundraising efforts. I no longer see the photo as a tool of seduction, but as an expression of vulnerability. And each time I see the play, I'm reminded that I have the opportunity to choose how I will treat each person I encounter.

—Steve

That is it right there! We have the opportunity to choose how we will treat each person we encounter. We choose! What an amazing lesson. How do we forget that?

Steve had a strong feeling of being incarnated into the play through the character of Philip. That is where our greatest lessons are, in the commonalities we find in others. His vulnerable reaction to the play cemented in me the importance of what we were doing. Goss was right; missionary was a fine word to use. We left our family, jobs and lives behind for weeks at a time to perform this play for thousands around the world for no pay but it was never about what we left behind, it was about what we brought back with us. We returned from every trip with a feeling of connection, a sense of being a part of something bigger than we could imagine or describe and an incredible feeling of communion.

Like Steve, so many of us saw ourselves in the play. We found ourselves speaking the words and truly living them. Even after hundreds of performances the words seemed to continue to grow inside us, and we all felt changes and shifts to who we were and who we were becoming. There was so much pain and anger from our past brought up while we were on the stage and it was always welcomed because with each other we felt the security of a family that would catch us and support us. For another cast member, Suzanne, the play seemed to offer answers and affirmation that she had been seeking after a childhood filled with gender confusion. We forget we can choose what person we want to be. We get set in our ways through the words of others or our abuse of ourselves. We decide early on who we are and that is how it will always be. Yet all around us people seem to be going through amazing changes and evolutions and we think, why not me? Suzanne was breaking away from the confines of who she was supposed to be and the shell she was pushed into by herself and others.

Gay, Lesbian, Queer, Gender Fuck, Gender Bend, Transsexual, Transvestite, Transgender. These are some words that I have considered in using to describe my identity. How do I identify? I can't describe myself in these ways. It's claustrophobic. I am Suzanne. I am Me. I am Love. I AM. I just AM.

My existence happens to challenge social "norms." "Norm" is not the right word either because "normal" would mean that I am not that, and I frankly disagree. I AM. And so is everybody else. However, any chance that I have to stretch my or another's definition of my identity, I take it. It all started with a haircut.

Long hair never suited me. While growing up I usually threw on a baseball cap. I don't wear makeup. I don't wear feminine clothes. Dresses give me a panic attack. I think the only reason I have any feminine gestures in my physical vocabulary is due to spending a lot of time with effeminate gay men. I play sports, not just for fun, but because I love to compete. I am masculine on the inside. I never understood why I did not mature into a very male body. It has felt very wrong, a betrayal, to my inner understanding of who I am by society's definition of gender. As I have matured and grown spiritually, I have come to understand that society's definitions of many important things, especially love, are pretty screwed.

I cut my hair short at first, and then I made it into a faux hawk. I did this with the excuse of Corpus Christi, but I did know deep inside that it would feel so much more comfortable for me. Strangers were uncomfortable around me. Especially when I walked into the women's restroom there could be some awkward moments. As I walked out, a woman walking in would start to double back because she thought she had walked into the wrong restroom, then give me a strange look. Walking into stores and restaurants I get called "sir." This happened once in Victoria's Secret. I pretended I was buying undergarments for my girlfriend. The cashier sure looked confused when she read "Suzanne" on my credit card.

As a teacher, I've been asked by 5–7 year olds, "Are you a boy or a girl?" I have experimented with various ways of answering. "I'm a clown!" Or "I'm a performer. And when you're acting you can be anyone you want to be. Same in regular life too." Or "I'm a girl, but I dress like a boy. Boys can wear what they want and girls can wear what they want, right?" Or "Does it matter? We're all friends no matter if we're boys or girls. What matters is that we're nice to each other."

One morning when I was student teaching I saw some kindergarteners struggling to carry their lunch boxes down the stairs. I stopped and I asked if they needed help. I felt the stare, and the dreaded question came quick: "Are you a boy or a girl?" I had to meditate on how to answer because usually the answer comes from an instinct geared for the moment, but with small children I was afraid to trust my instincts. Before I could say anything, the 5-year-old, blind-sided me: "Or are you both?" He went on, "You're both huh? So is a boy in our class. I'm just a boy, and so is him." He pointed to his lunch box buddy. "But there's another boy in our class who is both." He said it so nonchalantly. I replied, "Yeah, I'm both." He nodded yes and continued walking to his classroom. He was being taught and was learning that there are simply other options in the world of gender. I thought, so it IS possible to teach this. Our society has been teaching our children to divide and segregate by gender. This moment for me was a culmination of a long journey trying to figure out how to explain gender to young children. It gave me hope. It gave me a light at the end of the tunnel.

The tunnel; I wonder if there's just one big long one or smaller ones that have breaks between them so you can breathe. Or maybe it is one big long one and we get closer to the end and those lights we see, as we get closer, just get really bright from time to time. That way we are reminded that the end is there, it's just mostly dark. Maybe there's a small elfish or angelic creature at the end of each of our tunnels blowing up fireworks each time we have a spectacular or insignificant revelation. The firecrackers are brighter and bigger when the revelation has a deeper meaning. That 40 seconds I spent with two 5-year-olds was like watching fireworks on New Year's Eve over the Space Needle.

I'm guilty of having reluctant revelations, and at those times the firework lights aren't so spectacular. I'm referring to the lessons I need to learn, but resist learning them because they trigger a little bit too much of my shit. Dublin, Ireland was the place, long before I met the evolved 5-year-olds. Our two lonely protestors stood in front of our theatre. My dear lovely friend Steve was bending over, knees deep, legs wide, head forward, yelling something at the protestors. Dare I walk into that? I don't know what compelled me to grab a camera. I did know these two people were a lot like my classmates at the conservative college I had attended. They really believed that what they were doing was right because it was for their God of their understanding, and I knew there was no changing their minds. All I wanted to do was gain a deeper understanding of who they were and why they were there. I really didn't want to lose my shit at them because I had 4 years of ammunition.

Steve stopped yelling and walked away, and I approached and asked the pair if I could interview them on video. They surprised me by consenting, and as we talked I felt we were all carefully choosing our words. I knew to not get angry or to raise my voice. I had learned that this just pushes people away from having any kind of dialogue. I had to keep them talking. These two had just been yelled at, so they were most likely feeling defensive. So I just started asking questions. I do remember feeling nervous and shaky. I didn't know what these people were going to say to me, but I knew I had to talk to them openly and lovingly. I had moments in the interview that were small victories, like when the lady said that they hadn't read the play. I knew the only way to discount them was to let them reveal and admit their own closed-mindedness.

After the other cast members and I watched the interview, we talked about whether I should have invited the protesters into the show to watch it for free. I wish I had in some ways, but I thought to myself, if that were meant to happen, I would have said it. I had just got that gut feeling while I was speaking with them that they were dead set on protesting and then leaving. They had felt called to do that. And they had a long drive back to County Cork. I tried to really listen to them and to not give away too much of myself while speaking with them. I didn't want to be attacked. I did my best to love my fellow humans by having a simple dialogue.

I did really say a prayer for them to travel back safely though. And in those generous minutes they gave me on camera, I could really see their fears, courage, and their love for God.

Love. That's what this play and this life are all about it. Nothing else really matters in the entire universe. Let's be real. Love is what everyone wants. We just are reluctant to give it, especially when it comes to loving ourselves. I never liked myself growing up because I didn't fit in the right body. Now, I can say I love myself because bodies, faces, and hair create our shell that is home to our beautiful divine selves. I don't have to be any way for anybody. What's important is what's on the inside. It's like when Joshua says, "You can come no closer to me than my body. Everything important is hidden from you. Everything else you will never touch."

—Suzanne

In our desperation to connect with others we forget that we still maintain a solitude within us. In that solitude we have a spirit that no one can touch. There are those that may try to break it but the truth is it is always protected if we just remember it is there. It is the place we can go when the clamor of the world is too much. When things seem like they are out of our control or just overwhelming. I call it our solitude but it is not a lonely place. I believe that it is connected to but not controlled by others. When we are there we are seemingly alone but it's in that place that we find the peace and comfort of communion. It is truly a place where we become one with everything around us and within us. Look, I was never EVER this spiritual. I never sought to be and I was certainly never taught to be. My memory of those dreaded Sunday morning sermons was more about fear and warnings than about becoming one. I longed for it though. I was thrilled when that moment came where we all began to rise and line up for communion. We were moving! We were communing and I loved it. It wasn't because we were finally doing something it was because we were doing it together. Whether you find others in the rituals or in the quiet moments you take for yourself it is the communion that brings us together and makes us feel safe and loved.

Now the communion of our *Corpus Christi* family will be shared with even thousands more as we embark on the next phase of our journey: The "I AM Love" Campaign. As an extension of the play and film, this international movement's mission is to disempower religious bullying and homophobia, in all ages and walks of Life, by first learning to Love the Self. We look forward to sharing this unique experience across the globe combining screenings of the film, performances of the play, and community involvement addressing issues of spirituality in the gay community, bullying, and equality. As happened with the teachings of Jesus, this experience has become much bigger than us; although we are certainly catalysts for the movement, we are simply along for the ride it now wants to take us on. That, to me, is the ultimate communion with Spirit.[2]

NOTES

1. James Langteaux writes about the impact on himself in experiencing the play plus his heterosexual married friend Ian who held that Jesus can change you "straight": At the crucifixion of Jesus, "my friend Ian jumped out of his seat and ran to the foot of the stage, (Oh my God Ian . . . what are you doing,) With reckless abandon and utter humility, Ian leapt up on the stage and fell on his face where he wept loudly and kissed the actor's bare feet." James Alexand Langteaux, *Gay Conversations with God: Straight Talk on Fanatics, Fags, and the God Who Loves US All* (Scotland, UK, Findhorn Press, 2012), 136–37.

2. The cast of *Corpus Christi* has joined Soul Force and its style of taking the message love against religious homophobia across the United States. They are taking the play and the documentary across the United States as ministry outreach of MCC in the Valley and joining Soul Force to tell the story of the Queer Christ to overcome religious homophobia and LGBT Christophobia. The cast began its journey at the Castro Theater on April 29, 2012. The theater received 10,000 emails, asking the Castro Theater not to show the documentary. The documentary uses the medium of Corpus Christi, but the documentary is about the discovery of the story of Christ, love, changed lives and healing, and spirituality.

12

Bodhisattva Christianity: A Case of Multiple Religious Belonging

Robert E. Shore-Goss

Be compassionate as your Abba is compassionate to you.

—Luke 6:36

A Bodhisattva should not learn many doctrines. If a Bodhisattva thoroughly upholds and thoroughly understands one doctrine, all the qualities of a Buddha are in the palm of his (her) hand. What is the one doctrine? Great compassion.

—Dharmasamgiti Sutra

The open invitation at table in MCC worship has an embedded inclusivist pluralist theology of grace. As a queer post-denominational church, open commensality at the table has functioned as an umbrella theology of grace for the inclusion of LGBT Christians exiled from their own denominations. It has been both unifying Christian diversities and attractive to those Christians who want to follow in the footsteps of Jesus, God's Christ, and his practice of indiscriminate invitations to table fellowship. The open commensality of MCC's table invitation attracted me as a queer Catholic priest to join and participate in this adventurous movement for radical inclusive love because I could maintain my Catholic spirituality and my evolution as a queer Buddhist Christian. I will propose that a radical inclusivist pluralism is embedded in the MCC table practices that all are welcome to God's table includes hospitable welcoming not only LGBT Christians from all denominations, but also heterosexual

Christians attracted to the mission of radical inclusion. It also includes the welcoming of non-Christians into the gracious symbolics of table fellowship, recognizing that God's grace and loving actions are also outside the MCC church and even outside of Christianity.

Few MCC members, outside Los Angeles, remember that in 1972, MCC LA under the leadership of Rev. Founder Troy Perry helped found the first Jewish LGBT synagogue and extended hospitality to a newly founded congregation in its church—Beth Chayim Chadashim— A House of New Life. It is now a prospering synagogue in Los Angeles with a mission: "Founded in 1972 as the world's first lesbian and gay synagogue, today BCC is an inclusive and green community of progressive lesbian, gay, bisexual, transgender and heterosexual Jews, and our families and friends."[1] Troy Perry's and MCC's open invitation at table theology directly influence the mission of BCC, and the history of the two communities continue to be intertwined in a creative collegiality and intimate friendship.

The open commensality practices of MCC at table provide a theology of grace that allows theological space and extend table hospitality to those peoples of faith with multiple religious belonging or hyphenated or hybrid religious identities. My exploration will include a narrative of personal and grace-filled encounters with Buddhism from an initial Christian exclusivist model of engaging non-Christian religions to a fulfillment model and finally to an inclusivist pluralist model of multiple religious belonging as a Buddhist Christian and practicing a Bodhisattva Christianity. The journey has been a grace-filled adventure of discovery how my Christian practice of open grace has led me to appreciate how the wisdom of the Christ is given to serve other religious traditions. Buddhism, in this case, has been a grace of discovering anew the depth of Christ's compassionate love and revelation of God's unconditional love for us. Both traditions do not have to compete with each other, for they complete one another in personal discovery of God's grace.

CHRISTIAN MODELS OF ENGAGEMENT WITH NON-CHRISTIAN RELIGIONS

Pre-Vatican II Catholicism maintained exclusivist model of religious truth that there was "no salvation outside the church" (*nullus salvus extra ecclesiam*). As a youth, I met wonderful Protestants and thought that the doctrinal limitation on salvation did not make sense with my experience of God's grace in Christ. The Protestant doctrine that there is no salvation outside of Christ also was unsatisfactory with the billions of non-Christians in the world. This notion became problematized as I came to know Jewish students in high school and later years. How can I maintain the truth and uniqueness of Jesus as God's Christ with the reality and truth claims of non-Christian people of faith? Did God intend other religions as means toward salvation? How can Christians relate to faithful and loving non-Christians? Attempts at conversion appeared to me as aggression and lack of respect for non-Christians and their religions. These were significant questions with which I as a young Catholic college student struggled as I centered my spirituality on Jesus and remained as a Christ-centered disciple for the rest of my life. I engaged and encountered non-Christians with love but searched for a theological framework to process my encounters with non-Christians in a growing religiously pluralist and postmodern American culture. Ultimately, my exploration and engagement of another religious tradition—Buddhism—was initially framed in a Christian theology of grace, stretching the notions of grace to non-Christian religious experience. I continue to encounter God's grace and action outside of Christianity.

In college, I studied the works of John Dunne and read his book: *The Way of All the Earth*.[2] There Dunne presents a "passing over," a phenomenological hermeneutics of compassion for Christians to engage other religions.[3]

> Passing over is a shifting of standpoint, a going over to the standpoint of another culture, another way of life, another religion. It is followed by an equal and opposite process we might call "coming back," coming back with new insight into one's own culture, one's own life, one's own religion.[4]

For Dunne, it was a figure like Gandhi, "a man who passes over by sympathetic understanding from his own religion to other religions and come back again with new insight to his own. Passing over and coming back, it seems is the spiritual adventure of our time."[5] Dunne's notion of passing over into the stories of religious figures such as the Buddha, Muhammad, and Gandhi and returning to one's life and religion meant that if you engaged religious figures and their insights, you would come back transformed—changed by the engagement. Lawrence Cunningham noted about Dunne's notion of passing over:

> One cannot "pass over" . . . in Dunne's sense of the term unless one has a deep experiential center that serves as an anchored reference point.

Otherwise, "passing over" loses the sense in which Dunne intends for it and become a kind of dabbling in religious experience(s), a kind of spiritual tourism.[6]

His hermeneutics of compassionate passing and return is a clever means of introducing the Buddhist notion of "no-self," that ourselves are not self-enclosed but open to expansive, compassionate explorations in passing over into the lives of religious figures and religions, enriched by new insights and understandings. Only later did I realize that Dunne was presenting a basic hermeneutics of the Buddhist notion of the bodhisattva.

Dunne's notion of "passing over" became a comfortable theological framework of grace for engaging other religious traditions with integrity to my own Christian tradition. I was anchored in the contemplative traditions of Ignatius of Loyola but open to the meditative practices of other religious traditions. Later, in theological studies, I became acquainted with the theological writings of Raimon Panikkar, a Roman Catholic priest, whose father was a Hindu and whose mother was Catholic. In his engaging multiple religious traditions within his family and culture in India, he describes his journey of passing over: "I 'left' as a Christian, 'found myself' a Hindu, and 'returned' as a Buddhist, without having ceased as a Christian."[7] He mirrored the traditional Asian phenomena of several millennia of multiple religious participation—a more recent development emerging in the religious landscape of western societies.

Interrogating the universal significance of the Christ event and attempting to correlate that significance from experiences of grace in encounters with non-Christians and a loving God moved me from my childhood Catholic replacement model of a theology of non-Christian religions to a fulfillment model to my current pluralist-dialogue model as I write this chapter.[8] Many mainline Protestant and Catholic theologians operate today with a range between modified, inclusivist fulfillment and pluralist-dialogue models, recognizing the positive values that other religions have for Christians. They comprehend interreligious dialogue as an important Christian practice and service to establish mutual religious understanding, friendships, and cooperation in service of Jesus' vision of the reign of God.[9]

TWO EXPERIENCES TO CONTEXTUALIZE THIS EXPLORATION

Several years ago I led a diversity panel for an MCC Regional Conference in St. Louis. I presented the topic of religious pluralism. At the time, I fell in a position between an inclusivist and pluralist perspective on Christian approaches to non-Christian religions. My MCC audience, geographically from mostly southern MCC Churches, was generally exclusivist: There is "no salvation outside of Christ." I took a presentation strategy of fulfillment theology adopted from Mona West for Southern Evangelical Christians. She has used such an approach with MCC folks of trying to endow value to other traditions by helping folks to comprehend other religions as analogical to the Hebrew scriptures. That is, the Buddhist scriptures are the "Old Testament" for Buddhists, and so on. Years before, I had superseded such a fulfillment theological approach when I struggled with Karl Rahner's "Anonymous Christians," which recognized the existence of implicit Christianity or God's grace within non-Christian religions.[10] It was a stepping stone to comprehend other religions as having salvific significance or grace embedded within themselves. But MCC lacks the missiological experience of Roman Catholic inculturation and interreligious encounters with other religions traditions in Asia and Africa, but the increased religious diversity of U.S. culture has compelled theological reflections within many MCC communicates on how do I love and encounter my non-Christian neighbor.

Needless to say, my talk was not well received. In fact, MCC clergy and laity resorted to quoting such verses as "No other name . . ." and "I am the way, the truth and the life. . . ." It was a theological and a pedagogical disaster or as Buddhists might say a failure in "skill in means." Many MCC Christians find themselves in a replacement model of engaging other religious traditions, as a denomination, it has an underdeveloped missiological experience in non-American cultures and has not theologically wrestled sufficiently with the growing diversity of American religious context.

When I spent several months teaching in Thailand, I had the opportunity to visit a number of Thai Buddhist Watts. At one monastic complex, I had the chance to meet and talk with the abbot. As he discovered that I was a Christian clergy and professor teaching Buddhist studies, we had a chance to share conversations about meditation and prayer, compassion and love, and interreligious dialogue. At one point, he looked me in the eyes and said, "At the level of love, there are no differences between Buddhists and Christians. We share a profound experience of truth at the level of love." I understood that what he meant by love in his Theravadan Buddhist perspective was loving-kindness and compassion. And I agreed with him, easily understanding we were speaking what Christians have understood as the language of grace. As I pushed our conversation further, I said that "I was not there to convert Buddhists to Christians but to convert Buddhists to be the best Buddhists that they could be and likewise, to convert Christians to be the best Christians that they could be." My hope was that when Buddhists and Christians engaged one another, they could pass over into one another's traditions, and come back spiritually richer from such a gracious journey. The abbot and I were talking the language of grace, and our encounter was a profound moment of grace in my life. What flashed in my mind was Hans Kung's prophetic statement: "No peace among the nations without peace among the religions. No peace among the religions without dialogue among the religions."[11]

So I write this section of this anthology because of the depth of my gracious religious encounters and in particular with Buddhism that I have had over the years, both outside and inside the context of MCC. I ground my experience in openness to other religions from the multiple prayerful and loving encounters that I have had over the years with non-Christian practitioners of many faiths and the attempt to reconcile my position as an MCC clergy with the invitation of open commensality at the MCC Communion table. Theologian Edward Schillebeeckx summarizes my theological position well when he writes:

> The revelation of God in Jesus, as the Christian Gospel preaches this to us, in no way means that God absolutizes a historical particularity. . . . We learn from the revelation of God in Jesus that no individual particularity can be said to be absolute, and that therefore through the relativity present in Jesus anyone can encounter God even outside of Jesus, especially in our worldly history and in the many religions which have arisen in it. The risen Jesus of Nazareth also continues to point to God beyond himself. One could say: God points via Jesus in Christ in the Spirit to himself as creator and redeemer, as a God of men and women, of all men and women. God is absolute, but no religion is absolute.[12]

Through many encounters with non-Christians, I have widened my theological position to comprehend that Jesus as unique, universal savior does not exclude the possibility of non-Christians being saved. By placing God's incarnation as a Trinitarian event, Christians can reclaim a Logos Christology of the early Christian writers and allow for a Spirit Christology operative in other religious traditions.[13] The Holy Spirit, united with the Logos, is also distinct from the Logos and operates salvifically beyond the Logos and blows where the Spirit blows. This means that the Holy Spirit is gracefully operative in other religions, and these religions are paths to salvation through the Spirit. Exclusivist Christians arrogantly limit God's grace of the Incarnation and the Spirit when they narrow down the paths to salvation. God solely establishes paths of salvation, not humans. If this is the case, I look to discern the Spirit's presence in other faith traditions and find elements of grace and truth from my own Christian perspective.

Each Sunday, I proclaim, that "You neither need to be a MCC member, nor even a Christian, all are welcome to God's table . . ." My worship practice as Senior Pastor has led me to welcome Buddhists, Druids, Jews, Muslims, Hindus, Wiccans, and others at the communion table at MCC in the Valley. Non-Christian religions, for myself and many others, are ways of salvation insofar as they contain truth and grace, and they are part of God's providence whether Christians may admit it or not. Christians need to let go of their supersessionist theological arrogance and learn humility to comprehend divine providence for the existence of other religious traditions.

THE PASSING OVER INTO BUDDHISM

My journey started as a Catholic called to service as a Jesuit priest, found myself within Mahayana/Vajrayana Buddhism, came out as a queer clergy, and returned as a Bodhisattva MCC Christian clergy. To unpack the theological and narrative context of the previous sentence is too long for the focus of this chapter.[14] I will highlight several autobiographical experiences that formed the matrix of my theological journey to become a queer Bodhisattva Christian clergy. I have covered previously my queer passages from Roman Catholic priest to MCC clergy.[15] My accommodation of Christian theology to queer identities has a parallel to my appropriating a Buddhist identity to my Christian practice. The focus will be on the Buddhist–Christian encounters, but coming out as queer has shaped the context of my passing over into Buddhism and my return to Christianity. My marginalization from institutional Christianity as a gay man and an outsider deeply impacted my journey and made me sensitive to non-Christians and Buddhists as outsiders of Christianity.

I spent the summer of 1973 in India, working at a Jesuit mission station at Bhaktiyapur (Bihar, India), with the Missionaries of Charity in the House of the Dying Destitute in Calcutta, and a leper colony at Shantinagar. The experience shattered my parochial worldview—experiencing poverty and disease on an unimaginable scale, witnessing firsthand Jesuit missionary adaptation to Indian religious culture, participating in a culture where Catholic Christianity was a very small minority, and witnessing incredible piety and faith of Hindus, Buddhists, and remarkable Jesuits writing and studying Hinduism. I met a Jesuit sadhu, who had set up an ashram to engage Hindus,[16] and met Belgian Jesuit scholar Jacques Dupuis at St. Xavier's College in Calcutta.[17] He spoke after dinner about how early Christian apologists such as Clement of Alexandria had developed a *Logos* theology of other religious traditions. The Logos (Divine Word) has been active spreading seeds (*spermatikos*) in the world, including Hindu and Buddhist religious cultures. Christian truths, albeit partial, were embedded in Hindu and Buddhist religions, and that his task was to engage Hindus to assist them in understanding that the seeds of truth and love (*Logos spermatikos*) within their own religion are contained in the revelation of Jesus God's Christ. Dupuis was heavily influenced by the grace theologies of Henri de Lubac, Jean Danielou, Karl Rahner, and Hans Urs von Balthasar. These incipient Catholic theologies of world religions came to birth in the decade prior to Vatican II and received prominent attention during Vatican II.[18]

I made a Zen Retreat at the Trappist Monastery, St. Joseph's Abby in Worcester, Massachusetts. It was led by Joshu Sasaki Roshi from the Rinzai School of Zen Buddhist. The Trappists had been involved in an exchange of mediation practice since Thomas Merton in the 1960s. I was accustomed to Ignatian contemplative practices and enjoyed meditation. In first interview, Sasaki Roshi gave me a koan, a mind puzzle to meditate upon. He took his walking stick and hit the floor, saying, "God hears that sound, you hear the sound, how do you experience God." I had already completed my first year of theological practice and a Jesuit intercultural experience in India.[19] I threw myself into the task of solving the Zen mind puzzle and had recently completed Martin Buber's book—*I-Thou*. I comprehended that God's relationship to human beings and myself was an I–thou relationship, a subjective relation, rather than I–it or objective knowledge. So I went back to the Roshi in the afternoon session and told him, "That was God was in the sound." The Roshi laughed and said, "No!"

I left and tried to solve the mind puzzle. As an alpha male accustomed to solving problems, I immersed myself into the problem. It was like a Rubik's cube, maybe a different angle of perspective would lead to the solution. As I turned over the Zen puzzle in mind, I tried to conceptualize a solution to the problem. But each time I returned to Sasaki Roshi, he said "No, too much thinking!" in more agitated tones. I became more flustered, and by the end of the weekend, I went into his interview room— contritely, flustered, and muttered, "I don't know." He smiled and made the Catholic sign of the cross, "How do you experience God in the sign of the cross? Same answer."[20] The Zen retreat was an unsettling experience, for I was confused and bewildered. Sasaki Roshi used an important and very familiar ritual practice of making the sign of the cross into a koan for myself. The search for an answer was to be found in the engagement of Christian and Buddhist spiritualities.

I left the retreat house, emotionally frustrated and shaken. Of course, I felt that there was a solution, so I crossed over from Jesuit Weston School of Theology and audited a two-semester course in Buddhism at Harvard taught by Dr. Masatoshi Nagatomi to find an answer to the koan. While I was sitting in on the course on Buddhism, my interest shifted from doctoral studies in theology to a Christian theology of religions and comparative religion—with a specialty Buddhism. Richard Drummond's *Gautama the Buddha: An Essay in Religious Understanding* provided a positive theological interpretation of the Buddha. He argues that the Dharma functions in Buddhism as a gracious presence and power assisting practitioners to achieve the goal of nirvana and concludes that it is comparable to the Holy Spirit.[21] Drummond concluded, "the Buddha was indeed in contact with aspects of the Reality that Jesus termed the kingdom of God, even though I also wish to affirm, on the basis of Christian faith, that unique and fuller aspects of the same kingdom were manifested through the person and work of Jesus the Christ."[22] For Drummond, the Buddha's description of nirvana represented a way of speaking of the kingdom of God. For the mid-1970s, Drummond's work was remarkably bold in its theological correlation between the Buddhist Dharma–Nirvana complex with Spirit and God and his attempt at interreligious understanding. It initiated a movement from the model of preparation or fulfillment to engage in interreligious theology.

Throughout graduate studies at Harvard University and work at the Center for World Religions, I immersed myself in studying, engaging in interreligious dialogue with Buddhists and other non-Christians, and participated in the ritual celebrations of non-Christians. Interreligious dialogue and shared ritual participation in major festivals of other religions transformed me to increased realization of how important the world religions are to Christianity and its future development. I studied Buddhist texts, doctrines, philosophy, meditation practices, and rituals. The more I studied, the more I found points of convergence with Catholic Christianity.

One of the memorable events at Harvard was meeting the Dalai Lama on his first trip to the United States. He came to Harvard University to speak, and he wanted to meet the four students who were studying Classical Tibetan. In the private audience with Dalai Lama, I was profoundly moved at the depth of his spirituality and his humanity. He spoke about compassion for all sentient beings as the universal responsibility of humanity. I just finished a paper on the Bodhisattva spiritual practices, Mahayana missionary inculturation, and Jesuit missionary inculturation practices. The Bodhisattva spirituality and meditative practices parallel the Jesuit spiritual meditative practices of finding God in the world. My encounter with the Dalai Lama changed the course of my studies; I specialized in Tibetan Buddhism. I realized how much the Dalai Lama as a living bodhisattva modeled a vision of spiritual values in a multireligious society and world. But on the level of religious identity, I took a major step in multiple religious belonging by taking the bodhisattva vow privately in prayer. Later, I took the vow before a Tibetan lama and started the practice of Bodhisattva Christianity. I had reached a critical point in my learning, engaging, and experiencing Mahayana Buddhism while returning to my Christian practice and deepened by the experience. Living in a multiple religious space did not lessen my Christ-centered spirituality; it widened my spiritual practice, committing myself to a complex path filled with ongoing dialogue, dual religious tensions that provided a creative matrix for my spiritual path as Buddhist Christian.

BODHISATTVA CHRISTIANITY

I was attracted to the Mahayana Buddhist notions of no-self, emptiness, and compassion. The negative aspect of the no-self doctrine of Buddhism denies that there is anything substantial or unchanging that we can describe as the self. From the perspective of dependent origination or what Thich Nhat Hanh calls "interbeing," the self is not the center of existence but a composite network of interrelationships. This enables Mahayana metaphysics to develop a thorough understanding of the self, the world, and other beings. We are all interconnected. Thus, as humans destroy the rain forests, we are impacted. We as beings are impacted by the sufferings and joys of human beings, and this enables us to develop a compassionate solidarity with the world and other beings (human and nonhuman) to alleviate suffering. To understand Buddhism required not only studying and reading Buddhist scriptures and spirituality texts, but also entering into conversations, rituals, and meditative practices.[23]

Dunne's passing over into the life of the Buddha and Buddhism is not merely an intellectual exercise entering into a different perspective, it is what Frank Whaling describes in the following passage:

> To know the religion of another is more than being cognizant of the facts of the other's religious tradition. It involves getting inside the skin of the other; it involves walking in the other's shoes, it involves seeing the world in same sense as the other sees it, it involves asking the other's questions, it involves getting inside the other sense of "being a Hindu, Muslim, Jew, Buddhist, or whatever."[24]

Whaling's description of knowing by "getting inside of the skin" of another religion was easy from my training at Ignatian contemplation, of entering a gospel scene from Jesus' life to comprehend and imaginatively taste the narrative envisioning. It was a hermeneutics of passing over, a hermeneutics of compassionate and imaginative re-experiencing of the gospel with myself inserted into the narrative.

Many Christians have participated in the Buddhist–Christian dialogue since Thomas Merton and in other cultures earlier than Merton.[25] Buddhist philosophy of emptiness has opened new insights for Christians into notions of Trinity and the kenosis of Christ.[26] Buddhists and Christians have worked on environmental issues, the peace movement, and human rights. Buddhists have, in turn, written books about Jesus and Christianity.[27] Christians have written on the Buddha and Buddhism, incorporating Buddhist insights into their practice of their Christian spirituality.[28] The Buddhist ideal of compassion is the positive side of the caring for and about the lives of all human beings, the implementation of the notion of no-self. Ego-centeredness impacts the way people act, think, and live. For Mahayana Buddhists, compassion is based on a metaphysics of codependent origination or what Thich Nhat Hanh refers to as "interbeing." The Bodhisattva vow incarnates grace; it is a kenosis of self-centeredness:

> By the virtue collected through all that I have done, may the pain of every living creature be completely cleaned away. May I be the doctor and the medicine and may I be a nurse for all sick beings in the world until everyone is healed. May a rain of food and drink descend to clear away the pain of thirst and hunger, and during the aeon of famine may I myself change into food and drink. May I be a protector for those without one, and a guide to all travelers on the way; may I be a bridge, a boat and a ship for those who wish to cross (the water).[29]

Dunne describes the process of passing over into another life or religion as passing over into the standpoint of God:

> To pass over to the standpoint of God, a man would have to go beyond caring simply about his own life or about the lives of a small circle of family and friends to caring about the lives of all beings human and non-human. The ideal of the Bodhisattva is the ideal of the human being who would do this, who would wait for all others to enter Nirvana before entering himself, who would wait "until the grass is enlightened."[30]

Asian Christians, living in a Buddhist context, express the meaning of Jesus in Buddhist terminology.[31] Frequently, in Mahayana cultures, it is the image of the bodhisattva whose spiritual freedom and radical openness that compassionately connects him or her to suffering beings and attempts to alleviate suffering becomes the most descriptive metaphor for Jesus the Christ. The process of incorporating Jesus as bodhisattva enriches and expands the Christological search for understanding God's Christ.

There was a tectonic shift in my theological practice from a doctrinally Christian practice to a hybrid Buddhist Christian practice that stressed a spiritual practice of faith, love, peacemaking, and compassion. Christianity in its early centuries had stressed practice over doctrine before the institutional periods of creeds. My engagement with Buddhism shifted Christian practice and a relationship to Christ and God as primary, doctrine as secondary. It was a clear reversal from my earlier practice as a Jesuit priest where doctrine was primary and practice flowed from that perspective. Buddhism helped me to remember that following Christ was primarily a practice. And it prepared me for MCC with its post-denominational perspective originating from many Christian denominations and the attempt to create unity through practice rather than through doctrinal conformity.

A second significant consequence was that I found that Buddhism provided a complementary tradition, and often corrective perspective, to a violent and doctrinally restrictive Christianity. Christianity has a toxic history of violence, conquest and war, persecution of various groups (women, Jews, sexual minorities, gender variant, indigenous peoples, and non-Christian peoples of faith), colonialism, and triumphal arrogance.[32] Buddhism has a long history of nonviolence, peacemaking, compassionate care, and ecological metaphysics. My passing over into Buddhist meditation practices and incorporation of the bodhisattva ideal has helped me to bring insights of peacemaking, equanimity, patience, and compassion to my practice as a Christian. My earlier involvement in protest movements against the Vietnam War had opened me to the writings of John Yoder, Dorothy Day, James Douglas, and Dan Berrigan opened me to the Buddhist writings of Thich Nhat Hanh, the Dalai Lama, and Aung San Suu Kyi, and Sulak Sivaraksa.[33] I met all the Buddhists mentioned in the previous sentence, except for Aung San Suu Kyi, but I had Suu Kyi's husband, Michael Aris, for Tibetan studies at Harvard and read parts of her manuscript in advance. Buddhist writings on peace, universal responsibility of compassion have assisted me and others to rediscover and reappropriate a nontoxic Christian practice, committed to peacemaking, love, and compassionate care.

Not only do Buddhist past and present authors impact my life, they actively shape prayer, meditation, my responsibilities as a worship leader, and preaching. For example, I have introduced Tibetan Buddhist meditation practice of *tonglen*, breathing in suffering and breathing out compassion into centering prayer in our worship or the dedication of receiving Communion, not for ourselves, but to dedicate the grace of Communion for those suffering, victims of war and oppression, and for the exploited and ravaged earth. Here Buddhist meditation practices, incorporated into Christian worship instill a sense of interbeing, Buddhist language of compassionate grace and connection with all living beings and their sufferings. These simple practices have enriched the spirituality of our worship, compassionately connecting us to the suffering in the world.

Joseph O'Leary, a Christian scholar engaging for decades Buddhism in Japan, speaks of Buddhism as having a role in healing and correcting Christianity:

> One way in which Buddhism may fall within the divine plan is as a pharmacopeia of antidotes for the sickness of religion . . . . Buddhism tempers the elements of fixation, irrationality, emotivity, and violence in Christian thinking and presents a peaceful, reasonable, wholesome mode of being present religiously to the contemporary world. In an age when religious fundamentalism and sectarian strife are more virulent than ever, the healing critique of Buddhism has perhaps a more central role to play than the classical dogma of Christianity, at the least forefront of history, whatever the ultimate shape of the "divine plan of salvation."[34]

My decades of experience and study of Buddhism has reinforced my intuition that Buddhism contains profound elements of grace and truth that Christians share and that it is a way of salvation in God's plan. They are related to each other and have a promising history of engagement of their differences on the level of monasticism, ecological issues, social justice, and liberation of peoples, human rights, peace, and many others. Not only has Buddhism been complemented by Christianity, but Christianity has also been complemented by Buddhism. While I may find convergences within the two religions, I recognize equally the differences that separate the two. Professor Wilfred Cantwell Smith continuously stressed that the differences between religions were equally important as points of convergence. I have recognized this from the beginning of my passing over into Buddhism when I shared with folks that the Christ is on my right shoulder and the Buddha on the left and that both the Buddha and the Christ engage in an ongoing, creative conversation within myself. The differences form a continuous process of creative dialogue within myself and offer me some unique perspectives in reading scripture. The differences provide the two and the two religious differences provide a creative matrix for mutual interpretation.

From a Buddhist perspective, my reading of the gospels has opened up to new enriched interpretations. For example, Jesus' "taking up the cross' sayings" can be interpreted from the Buddhist notion of no-self—leaving ego-centeredness for other centeredness. I have replaced various violent redemptive or atonement models to embrace a compassionate, nonviolent, redemptive model. John Keenan wrote two books, *The Meaning of Christ: A Mahayana Theology* and *The Gospel of Mark: A Mahayana Reading*.[35] These appropriations of Buddhist perspectives give a different contextual reading of Christian tradition and scriptures that open Christians to the multivalent mystery of Christ in word and tradition.

Theologian Paul Knitter writes how Dunne's notion of passing over into Buddhism saved and renewed his life as a Buddhist Christian. He asks in his conclusion whether it is promiscuity or hybridity in becoming a Buddhist Christian. Knitter understands promiscuity from its meaning to "mix-up," and he continues to discuss a Christian identity that mixes it up with Buddhism:

> We have an identity, but that identity in its origins and in its ongoing life comes to be and flourish only through mixing it up with others. Hybrids are stronger, live longer, and have more fun than purebreds.[36]

Hybrid forms of Christian identity will only strengthen the mission of Christ and Christian practice in the future. Knitter reiterates, if theologian Karl "Rahner was right that the Christians of the future will be mystics, they will also have to be interreligious mystics."[37] Christians passing over into other religions will develop the tools for spiritual development from their engagements and develop Christian identities with multiple religious belonging.

OPEN TABLE AND INTERRELIGIOUS DIALOGUE AND MULTIPLE RELIGIOUS BELONGING

MCC's practice of open commensality each Sunday celebrates God's unbrokered love and unconditional grace freely offered. Most churches place some fence around the wild grace of open commensality, and my observation is that MCC often places a fence around the table when it comes to non-Christians. I want to end with a saying of Jesus taken from the historical context of his table practices: "I tell you, many will come from east and west and will eat with Abraham and Isaac and Jacob in the reign of heaven" (Mt 8:11). Here Jesus envisions an eschatological commensality that many people from east and west will come to sit and eat together. Such eschatological imagination is embedded in the command of the Eucharistic celebration, "Do this in memory of me."

The open commensality of Jesus' eschatological imagination is symbolized by people coming from all the ends of the earth—from all other religions and their eating together at the Lord's table. And the very people who had been considered by contemporary exclusivist Churches least worthy of God's grace such as queer Christians and non-Christians suddenly come to prominence in the Messiah's reign of God. I would argue that the core theological principle of the open invitation at the communion table requires MCC to participate in interreligious dialogue and opens its table to non-Christian participants and allows for multiple religious belonging as working of Christ's Spirit today in our world. The open table without policing allows a more accurate symbolic representation of God's unconditional economy of grace.

Multiple religious belonging, participating in the spiritual practices of other religions, has been prevalent in many Asian countries for millennia. In the past four decades, many families in the United States have already experienced multiple religious participants.[38] Joseph O'Leary writes about one of the early 20th-century Buddhist scholars Winston King and his wife Jocelyn:

My models of "double belonging" are the late Winston and Jocelyn King. They meditated together every morning, he as a Buddhist Christian, she as

a Christian Buddhist. Here was a marriage of traditions that left all theological caviling far behind, demonstrating that there is no fundamental
contradiction between the gospel and the Buddha's path.[39]

The growth of religious pluralism in the United States has changed the religious environment, enabling cross-religious friendships and fostering interreligious engagements producing multiple religious belonging. And on
many campuses, students are not making the traditional commitments
to Christianity because of its dogmatism and moralism, but they are embracing fragments of spiritual practices from a number of world spiritualities. Here Catherine Cornille's comment is an apt description, ". . . it
seems that idea of belonging to more than one religion can be tolerated
only when the idea of religion has accepted the complementarity of religions."[40] Many Christians involved in the Buddhist–Christian dialogue
or specialists in Buddhism studies have been impacted by their engagement beyond academic studies. Among those Christians that self-identify
as Buddhist Christians are Roger Corless, Sallie King, Paul Knitter, and
more recently Ross Thompson.[41]

Multiple religious belonging means not only interfaith dialogue but
also engaging other religious communities in an open and neighborly
loving spirit, working in collaboration on social issues and justice, and
in religious experiences of prayer and contemplation. Now I do not want
to leave the impression that I am the only one with multiple religious
belonging in my own MCC congregation. There are Jewish Christians,
Vedanta Christians, Wiccan Christians, Buddhist Christians, and other
forms of multiple religious belongings. This is to say that these Christians
have a full commitment to Christianity but also that they extend their belonging to other religions through attending other services, incorporating
the symbols and ritual-meditative practices, and even members of other
communities into the life of our church.

The paradigm I envision comes from an open spiritual practice that
MCC in the Valley provides each month. We walk an earth-centered,
ecological labyrinth that two Druid leaders designed and painted for
our community. On the first Thursday of the month, the labyrinth is
available to everyone, and often times both Christians, Christians with
multiple religious belongings, Druids, and other folks with different spiritualities meditatively walk the labyrinth—each of us weaving our stories
and lives together, with great love for one another and for the Earth. We
walk under the guidance of the Spirit in the greatest spiritual adventure
of passing over into each others' lives and into God's life. Here we practice

open commensality that Jesus eschatologically imagined and passed on to his disciples. Such a vision of an interfaith Christian practice may scare those hanging onto a Christian church that builds walls between religious communities.

NOTES

1. Check out Beth Chayim Chadashim, http://www.bcc-la.org/.

2. I actually read a series of Dunne's books. John S. Dunne, *The City of the Gods: A Study in Myth and Mortality* (New York: MacMillan, 1965); *A Search for God in Time and Memory* (New York: MacMillan, 1969); *The Way of All the Earth: Experiments in Truth and Religion* (New York: Macmillan, 1972).

3. Dunne, *The Way of all the Earth*, 53–55.

4. Ibid., ix.

5. Ibid.

6. Lawrence Cunningham, "Crossing Over in the Late Writings of Thomas Merton," in *Toward an Integrated Humanity: Thomas Merton's Journal*, ed. M. Basil Pennington (Kalamazoo, MI: Cistercian Publications, 1987), 194.

7. Paul F. Knitter, *Introducing Theologies of Religions* (Maryknoll, NY: Orbis Books, 2008), 126.

8. Paul Knitter divides Christian responses to other religions into four general models: (1) The Replacement Model ("Only one true religion"), (2) The Fulfillment Model ("The one fulfills the many"), (3) The Mutuality Model (Many true religions called to dialogue), and (4) The Acceptance Model (Many true religions, so be it.) Knitter, *Introducing Theologies of Religions*. I locate my inclusivist or pluralist model within a synthesis of models three and four.

9. For a good articulation of interreligious dialogue, see James L. Fredericks, *Buddhists and Christians: Through Comparative Theology to Solidarity* (Maryknoll, NY: Orbis Books, 2004), 103–4.

10. Karl Rahner, "Christianity and Non-Christian Religions, in *Theological Investigations*, vol. 5 (London: Darton, Longman, and Todd, 1966), 115–35; "Anonymous Christians," in *Theological Investigations*, vol. 6 (London: Darton, Longman, and Todd, 1969), 390–98. For good discussion of Rahner, see Knitter, *Introducing Theologies of Religions*, 68–74. For Rahner's notion of grace, see Leo O'Donovan, ed., *A World of Grace* (Washington, DC: Georgetown University Press, 1995).

11. Hans Kung, *Global Responsibility: In Search of a New World Ethic* (New York: Continuum, 1993), 105.

12. Edward Schillebeeckx, *Church: The Human Story of God* (London: SCM Press, 1990), 165–66.

13. Many exclusivist Christians fail to remember early Christian authors who wrote about the cosmic Christ, God's Logos, who spread seeds of truth and grace in other religions. For a good summary, see Jacques Dupuis, *Towards a Christian Theology of Religious Pluralism* (Maryknoll, NY: Orbis Books, 2006), 53–83.

14. The question of Christian identity is a complex issue. When I look back at the formative factors of my Christian identity, there is the factor of denomination, class, maleness, Jesuits, gay man and the feeling of an outsider, Buddhism, and other religious traditions. Only years later did I realize how much outsider status impacted my appreciation of Buddhists and non-Christians as outsiders, my doctoral dissertation on the mad saint movement and *Life of Milarepa* in Tibet, and my passion for queer theologies.

15. Robert E. Goss, *Queering Christ: Beyond Jesus ACTED UP* (Cleveland: The Pilgrim Press, 2002), 3–35.

16. See "The Jesuit Swamis in India," http://www.time.com/time/magazine/article/0,9171,945244,00.html.

17. Jacques Dupuis gave me a volume produced by Jesuits in India: *Religious Hinduism*. It was lost with a box of books when I moved to California. It was a sympathetic reading of Hinduisms by Jesuits. In my opinion, Dupuis' works are some of the best of Jesuit Catholic scholarship on theologies of interfaith dialogue and the Christian interpretation of non-Christian theologies. Dupuis, *Christianity and the Religions: From Confrontation to Dialogue* (Maryknoll, NY: Orbis Books, 2001); *Toward a Christian Theology of Religious Pluralism* (Maryknoll, NY: Orbis Books, 2006).

18. Dupuis, *Toward a Christian Theology of Religious Pluralism*, 130–57.

19. I read Kyozan Joshu Sasaki's book over and over. *Buddha is the Center of Gravity* (San Cristobel, NM, Lama Books, 1974). This is a marvelously profound spiritual book that impacted my theology of the cross.

20. Only years later within a winding path of studies and experiences, did I come to the realization of the koan. Sasaki Roshi was attempting to move me from the lens of concept and word to an insight of an unmediated presence—God. My answer is private and part of my own spiritual practice.

21. Richard Drummond, *Gautama the Buddha: An Essay in Religious Understanding* (Grand Rapids, MI: Wm. B. Eerdmans Publishing Company, 1974), 137, 188.

22. Ibid., 194.

23. Buddhists and Christians have been sharing joint meditation practices and instructions since Thomas Merton. For one example, see Susan Walker, ed., *Speaking of Silence: Christians and Buddhiss on the Contemplative Way* (New York: Paulist Press, 1987).

24. Frank Whaling, *Christian Theology and World Religions: A Global Approach* (London: Marshall Pickering, 1986), 130–31.

25. See Whalen Lai and Michael von Bruck, *Christianity and Buddhism: A Multicultural History of Their Dialogue* (Maryknoll, NY: Orbis Books, 2001).

26. John B. Cobb and Christopher Ives, eds., *The Emptying God: A Buddhist-Jewish-Christian Conversation* (Maryknoll, NY: Orbis Books, 1991). Masao Abe and Steven Heine, eds., *Buddhism and Interfaith Dialogue* (Honolulu: University of Hawai'i Press, 1995).

27. Thich Nhat Hanh, *Living Buddha, Living Christ* (New York: Riverhead Books, 1995); The Dalai Lama, *The Good Heart: A Buddhist Perspective on the Teachings of Jesus* (Boston: Wisdom Publications, 1996); Kenneth S. Leong, *The Zen Teachings of Jesus* (New York, Crossroad Publishing, 1995).

28. I read Thomas Merton as a teenager and was exposed to his dialogue with Buddhism. Thomas Merton, *Mystics and Zen Masters* (New York: Farrar, Straus and Giroux, 1967); *Zen and the Birds of Appetite* (New York: New Directions, 1968). See Donald W. Mitchell, *Spirituality and Emptiness: The Dynamics of Spiritual Life in Buddhism and Christianity* (New York: Paulist Press, 1991).

29. From Shantideva's Bodhi-caryavatara: Peter Harvey, *An Introduction to Buddhist Ethics* (Cambridge: Cambridge University Press, 2000), 124.

30. Dunne, *The Way of All the Earth*, 52.

31. Brinkman explores Asian Christians concerns whether Jesus must always in remain Judeo–Greek categories such as Lord, Son of Man, and others. His point is that Asian Christians are continuing the Christological process of describing Jesus in cultural religious categories by appropriating the metaphor of bodhisattva for Jesus. Martien Brinkman, *The Non-Western Jesus: Jesus as Bodhisattva, Avatar, Guru, Prophet, Ancestor or Healer?* (London: Equinox, 2007), 79–100.

32. For non-Christians perceive Christianity's violence and colonial past, see Paul J. Griffiths, *Christianity through Non-Christian Eyes* (Maryknoll, NY: Orbis Books, 1990). There are countless examples of Christian violence towards women, peoples of color, and, of course, queer folks.

33. Some Christian pacificist authors that I read in college: James Douglas, *The Nonviolent Cross: A Theology of Revolution and Peace* (New York: MacMillan, 1969). John Howard Yoder, *The Politics of Jesus* (Grand Rapids, MI: Wm. B. Eerdmans Publishing Company, 1972). Daniel Berrigan, *The Dark Night of Resistance* (Garden City, NY: Doubleday, 1972). Dorothy Day and the Berrigan (Daniel and Phillip) went to prison for their antiwar convictions, and they were my heroes in college. For Buddhist writings, Thich Nhat Hanh, *Being Peace* (Berkeley, CA: Parallax Press, 1996); Donald W. Chappel, ed., *Buddhist Peacework: Creating Cultures of Peace* (Boston: Wisdom Publications, 1989). Dalai Lama, *Ethics for a New Millennium* (New York: Riverhead Trade, 2001); Aung San Suu Kyi, *Freedom from Fear* (New York: Penguin Books, 1991); Kenneth Kraft, ed., *Inner Peace, World Peace: Essays on Buddhism and Nonviolence* (Albany, NY: SUNY, 1992).

34. Joseph O'Leary, "Toward a Buddhist Interpretation of Christian Truth," in *Many Mansions? Multiple Religious Belonging and Christian Identity*, ed. Catherine Cornille (Eugene, OR: Wipf & Stock, 2010), 41–42.

35. John P. Keenan, *The Meaning of Christ: A Mahayana Theology* (Maryknoll, NY: Orbis Books, 1989); *The Gospel of Mark.*

36. Paul F. Knitter, *Without Buddha I Could Not Be a Christian* (New York: Oneworld Publications, 2009), 215.

37. Ibid., 217.

38. John H. Berthrong, *The Divine Deli* (Maryknoll, NY: Orbis Books, 1999), 24–69.

39. O'Leary, "Toward a Buddhist Interpretation of Christian Truth," 29.

40. Catherine Cornille, "Introduction: The Dynamic of Multiple Religious Belonging," in *Many Mansions?*, 2.

41. Roger Corless, "A Form of Buddhist Christian Coinherent Meditation," *Buddhist-Christian Studies* 14 (1994): 139–44; Sallie King, "Religion as Practice: A Zen Quaker Internal Dialogue," *Buddhist Christian Studies* 14 (1994): 157–62; Knitter, *Without the Buddha I Could Not Be a Christian*; and more recent a good exploration of being a Christian in a Buddhist way: Ross Thompson, *Buddhist Christianity: A Passionate Openness* (Washington, DC, O-Books, 2010).

13

Unzipping Church:
Is There Room for Everyone?

Thomas Bohache

Parking the car. Hoping it will be safe. I go up to the front door, dark of course. I look around. No one is there to see me . . . I hope. What am I doing here? I ask myself that every time I come here. A locker is cheaper, so that's what I get. I get buzzed in. I find my locker. I get undressed. Anticipation pounds in my ears. I drape the towel around me, although it doesn't fit particularly well. Should've lost more weight before venturing out. I hear a sound. I turn toward the door, and he's there. The most beautiful man I have ever seen. Our eyes meet. He smiles. So do I. "Will you be here long?" "As long as it takes." "Maybe I'll see you later?" Yeah, right. Like HE would want ME.

So I walk down the hall, trying to forget how much I want him. I pass rooms with open doors. I look in; they look back. Do I want to go in? Do I dare? I see so much beauty and feel so much pain. There's a door that everyone seems to be focused on. I look over their shoulders. It's him. So desirable. So beautiful. Yet so alone. No one will approach him. What are they afraid of?

I walk toward the orgy room. There are so many there, in various stages of ecstasy. I walk out. It's too intense. I stroll down another corridor, and there he is—the one everybody wants. But what's he doing? He's blowing a guy who's even fatter than me—rolls of flab encasing his cock so it's not even visible. And yet this Adonis is on it, gobbling it, enjoying it, taking the fat man to heaven. Is this happening?

I retreat, walk down another corridor. The selling point of this particular establishment is that it's like a maze. You never see the same person twice. That's the way it's supposed to be. Then why do I keep seeing this guy? I turn the corner. He's getting peed on by somebody. I go the other way. He's getting fucked by a guy with one leg. I take the stairs to the roof, to get some air. He's there with a bunch of guys I've seen here for years who never seem to score. And he's doing every single one of them. What gives?

I make my way back to my locker. Start to get dressed. But then I feel a hand on my back. "What's your hurry? Where you goin'?" I stumble as I try to get into my pants. Not used to such a direct approach. And of course it's him. "I told you I'd see you later. Weren't you going to wait for me?" "I didn't know you meant it. You were pretty busy." "There's enough of me to go around!" He smiles. His eyes light up. They take me in. They love me. I've never felt this wanted before. Maybe I'll stay for a while. . . .

* * *

Does God have a sexual orientation? Sometimes I think so, but most of the time I don't. After all, isn't sexual orientation a social construct? How do we know who we are? Do we choose? Are we chosen? Is it predestined? Perhaps God meets us in our circumstances and becomes who we need God to be? If that's the case, then I guess that was God who cornered me in the locker room at the baths. That was God who was sucking and fucking and making out with the ones nobody else would touch. Isn't that the truth of the gospel?

* * *

The problem with most Christian churches is that they would be scandalized by a story like the one above, never embracing anything overtly erotic or countenancing our sexual peccadilloes. You must not sully the sanctuary with semen-laden thoughts or wet panties! You must not be conscious of your various body parts or allow yourself to become aroused if you are within the House of God. The Body of Christ is, after all, a eunuch! But you know what? In the basement of the church—beneath all the holiness and the hypocrisy and the wistful longings—God lies on a cheap pallet (maybe a sling?) waiting to be filled by our need. We are so accustomed to leaving our desires at the door that we don't realize God is inside, empty, bereft, with no one to fill Him to overflowing with Love or to quench Her longing with Joy.

God waits like an unwanted person in a sex club—holding out Hope that someone might take a chance; yearning for someone to stop walking by, to cross the threshold, to start something that might take God over the edge into oblivion. Have you ever felt this way? Have you ever dared to let yourself feel this way? Have you ever fallen forward into a future that was not prohibited by the past?

* * *

It is a commonplace of our postmodern world that theology is autobiography. Contextual theologies from women, people of color, the poor, and sexual minorities have exposed the untruth of a previous commonplace that one could be theologically objective or approach texts such as the Bible as a disinterested observer. All of us bring our own presuppositions to the study of the Divine and Her interactions with Creation; likewise, we bring our histories—particularly our sexual histories—with us as we approach a God who meets us in our circumstances, even when we would seek to keep those circumstances private or a secret. This God blows the doors off of our closets, infiltrates our decent lives, and makes us take a closer look at who we really are, not whom we want the world to see.

As a middle-aged, well-educated, white gay man who has somewhat reluctantly begun to call myself "queer," I have come to realize how easy it is to hide behind delusions of normality, how easy it is to pass in a world that in some ways seems more accepting of difference than when I was growing up in the 1960s and coming to sexual maturity in the 1970s. But then current events intrude into this fantasy and force me to acknowledge that things have not really changed all that much. What has changed is that I have found for myself a comfortable niche where I can pontificate about sexuality and spirituality from a place of entitlement and privilege.

I have been a pastor in the Metropolitan Community Churches (MCC) for almost 25 years. I have been a biblical scholar and theologian for much of that time, always seeking to educate myself further so that I might in turn educate my congregations. In my living room or my pastor's study or in a university library I explore worlds I have not personally experienced. I read about oppressions that go beyond those I have endured. I learn about the struggles of heroes, sheroes, and queeroes of the faith who have walked the walk, not just talked the talk. In my sermons and writing I have remained pretty mainstream (dare I say "malestream"?), even though some over the years have seen me as too liberal, too political, or too heretical.

But I have come to a point in my life where I realize that there is no safe place in decency. Pat Robertson and Benedict XVI do not care that I have not been a flamboyant queer or that I live a pretty boring middle-class lifestyle. To them, my choice of affectional partner and what I do or think of doing with various body parts renders me indecent. To the majority of Americans I am undeserving of common courtesies or the institution of marriage; when people like me endeavor to speak the truth of our daily lives as others do so freely, we are castigated for making public what should be kept private. Since the heteronormative logic of our world labels as indecent or depraved what we see as normal, what's the point of trying to fit in? After all, what does it mean to be normal, and who gets to decide? Who keeps score as to whether you have played by the rules, and which or whose rules are we even talking about?

One of my favorite stories in the Bible is contained in the Book of Esther. Esther is a young Jewish girl living in the Persian Empire who wins a beauty contest and becomes queen. No one (including the king) knows she is Jewish, however. All is well until one of the king's ministers decides to persecute the Jews. Esther's kinsman Mordecai sends a message to her asking for help from her position of privilege. She is at first disinclined to help, noting that she is only one wife among many and must wait her turn for intimacy with the king. Mordecai confronts her fear and trepidation—her unwillingness to show her truth to the world—by pointing out that her place in the royal household will not protect her if her Jewish identity becomes known. "Perhaps you have come to royal prominence for such a time as this," he suggests to her. Esther's mind is changed by his words (she repents—*metanoia*!), and she comes out as a Jew to her husband the king, saving her people in the process. This is a story with a nice tidy happy ending, but it imparts an important truth: We are never safe, even when we think we are, even when we have carefully erected an edifice to seal us off from real people with real problems.[1]

What this means for me at this time of my life is that there is no refuge in decency. As long as queer people remain colonized by heteronormativity and the church is seen as the province of those who are right with God (which frequently translates to those who are "on the right"), none of us will be safe. Like Esther, I need to come out and become disreputable, indecent, non-accomodationist, non-assimilated, queer. While the MCC as a denomination has been on the forefront of inclusion of sexual minorities in Christianity,[2] and while I believe that it is still for me the best place to pursue a Christian life, I nevertheless believe that MCC needs to go further than it has gone. There is still work to be done.

Indeed, I believe in some ways MCC has gone backwards in seeking to show the dominant society that we are just like everybody else and in striving for marriage equality above all else, often at the expense of other important issues.[3] The truth as I see it is that queer people (including those who identify as gay, lesbian, bisexual, transgender, intersex, questioning, asexual, and supportively straight[4]) will NEVER be just like everybody else by virtue of the fact that we (like African Americans) have a legacy of discrimination in our genetic memory and through our sexual activities, affectional preferences, and/or bodily integrity challenge the dominant heterosexist, heteropatriarchal, heteronormative mind-set that (in)forms American structures, systems, laws, customs, and everyday moralities. It is within this context that I would like to propose what I call a disreputable ecclesiology.

* * *

The late queer postcolonial theologian Marcella Althaus-Reid rocked the theological and academic world when she described an "indecent theology," that is, a theology that prescinded from the experience of those not considered "decent" by church and/or society.[5] She boldly stated that theology should come from sexual storytelling of everyday people, rather than the grand narratives of old white straight men in the academy.[6] Moreover, she challenged both liberation theology and feminist theology for losing touch with their constituent base by selling out to the dominant forms of (heterosexual) theology, which she called "T-theology" (for totalitarian or tradition-based theology).[7]

A disreputable ecclesiology must start from this notion of indecent theology, for a church of decent people keeps its doors barred against those who might upset the status quo or insist that the church do the gospel.[8] Indeed, I have often thought that a decent church of the 21st century would probably turn away Jesus himself, inasmuch as he would—for starters—need to get a haircut, trim his toenails, and wash his feet, not to mention use some deodorant and probably even "man-groom"! Furthermore, Jesus would probably be asked to leave contemporary Christian churches because of those who make up his entourage—whores, drunkards, cast-offs from society who might engage in behavior considered inappropriate by the decent. They might laugh at the wrong times, clap their hands, or speak too loudly; they might even flaunt their differing sexualities. It seems to me that the doorkeepers of decency are like the U.S. Supreme Court justice who said he couldn't define pornography but would know it if he saw it: Their subjective opinions about behavior (including such items as manners, breeding, and social comportment) become the nebulous criteria that leave many on the wrong side of the church doors. And these are churches that, if asked, would pride themselves on being welcoming of newcomers, not recognizing that the newcomers who are welcomed must have already passed an unwritten test of decency and propriety. The ones who don't are simply frozen out.

Who are the disreputable in this scenario? They are the blacks who don't act like white people, the Latin@s who don't confine themselves to English when speaking, the gays and lesbians who might act effeminate or mannish (according to whose standards?), the transgendered or intersexed who do not fit one gender or another as clearly as the majority might like and—deeper still—want to use restrooms they shouldn't (according to whose dictum?). They are those who do not pursue a heterosexual binary or a monogamous style of relating. They are those who might have a different view of God or Christ or sin or church. They are any people who make the majority feel uncomfortable and lead them to question their privilege and the definitions behind which they hide.

I have become aware of this on many occasions during my ministry in MCC, but two particularly obnoxious examples immediately come to mind. The first occurred a number of years ago when a local association of churches—at the urging of two member congregations—had decided to review the propriety of MCC's membership in their organization on the grounds that we were not a Christian church because—among other things—our website pointed out that we ministered to gays and lesbians without expecting them to repent and that we did not regard Christianity as the exclusive path to salvation. What surprised me the most during the course of this debate was when a clergy colleague of mine, who had always been extremely supportive of MCC and prided himself on the fact that his church was a welcoming church, announced that, whatever the other churches' feelings about MCC or our ministry, we could all certainly agree that "we have all sinned and fallen short of the glory of God." It was at this point that I realized that the churches around me were probably more tolerating than welcoming and that they were oh-so-magnanimously allowing us into their presence because they were letting sinners into the fold. I did not and do not want to be part of a community that regards who I am as a sin that needs to be overlooked or "given up to God." Certainly I do not claim that I am not a sinner, but my particular sins do not include being gay.

The other incident took place just a couple of years ago when I attended a continuing education event at a prestigious seminary. During the break, a professor at the seminary asked me what church I was from, to which I replied the MCC and began to explain who we were. "Oh no," she interrupted me with a big smile, "I've heard of your church. But I would imagine that the Unitarians would be more appropriate conversation partners for you." I was speechless at this statement, not because I have anything against Unitarians, but because it was clear to me that beneath her words was the implication that I did not belong in dialogue with other Christians. Why? Who was she to say that I was less able to follow Christ than Presbyterians, Methodists, Episcopalians, or Baptists? Did her heterosexuality or her traditionalist orthodoxy somehow make her an automatic doorkeeper for Christianity? Maybe I should have offered her a "W-W-J-D" bracelet, but somehow despite her academic and ecclesiastical pedigree I don't think she would have gotten it.

A disreputable ecclesiology does not countenance incidents such as these. A disreputable ecclesiology does not think of ways to keep people out but is instead always trying to figure out how to bring more people of as many different varieties inside. A disreputable ecclesiology does not insist that certain people only deserve the crumbs that fall from the masters' tables. A disreputable ecclesiology does not have checklists for membership but instead simply says, "Welcome. You are loved." A disreputable ecclesiology is not repelled by what the world judges indecent but is drawn to it and utilizes it as a hermeneutical key for understanding the promiscuous love of God.

During its more than four decades of ministry MCC has been a vocal proponent of inclusivity. We were among the first denominations to ordain women and practicing homosexuals, to minister to those suffering with HIV/AIDS, and to empower non-gendered language in worship and hymnody. Over the years MCC has widened its ministry beyond the gay and lesbian communities and has reached out to the transgendered, the intersexed, and the supportively straight. Some congregations have been inviting of leatherfolk, the polyamorous, those attracted to S/M/B/D, the differently sexual, and the nonsexual, while certain MCC clergy have blessed relationships that included more than two people.[9] We have pursued bar, bathhouse, prison, and internet ministry. Theologically, we have justified this radical inclusivity by comparing it to the Reign of God as envisioned and announced by Jesus himself—a place where, according to him, the disreputable will enter before the proper and the downtrodden will precede the elite.

But we must go further! Instead of apologizing for our sexuality, we must begin to flaunt it even more! Instead of being ashamed of our sexual acts and assuring decent Christians that we are just like them because we favor "long-term, committed relationships" or "faithful, monogamous partnerships" that look just like marriages,[10] perhaps we need to queer the scenario, upset the apple cart of the status quo, talk about our deviances, and explore the ways in which our sexual stories might tell God's story. As some in MCC are fond of saying, "If you can't fix it, feature it!" For example, what might it mean to explore the theological ramifications of gloryholes? I am from a generation of gay men that, for whatever reason, was either forced or chose to conduct much of our intimate behavior in the shadows, in the streets, in alleys or doorways, or in subterranean parking lots. Was it personal shame or the specter of the closet or the impossibility of openness or the tyranny of heteropatriarchal laws and mores that led us to the parks and the baths and the sex clubs? Or was it the exuberance of sexual feelings that did not want to be confined to one room of the house but desired to roam free of constraints? (And at the same time sounding an awful lot like God's erotic love!) A disreputable ecclesiology is not afraid to talk about these types of experiences; it does not force them to be confessed in hushed tones but rejoices in the possibilities for spiritual growth to be found in them.

Marcella Althaus-Reid through her indecent theology pointed us in this direction and now, in Christic fashion, has gone on ahead of us to prepare a place for all of those whom T-theology and imperialist Christology would deny a place at the table. She believed that the future of all theology lay in queer theology, arguing that we must fetishize the theological discussion.

> A queer liberation theology (or "indecent theology") needs to look for other love locations . . . we need to turn to another route, a perverted turn in the road. This is the point when queer thinking is required. . . . The point is that by queering body theology we may be led to discover the traces of a queer God and through that the traces of Other covenants, lost pacts and revelations of God in an underground history of love. . . . In theology, and especially in the configuration of a queer body theology, fetishism is the praxis of transfiguration of reality in the sense that it reflects something: it is the reflection of spiritual Otherness.[11]

I quote her at length because she saw so clearly how, in the words of Audre Lorde, the master's tools would never dismantle the master's house.[12] We must indeed look in other love locations to find the piece of God that has been excluded with the Others who are not here but could be if we asked them.

This is where inclusivity can become problematic. Latin American liberation theologian Frederico Pieper Pires, from Brazil, has pointed out that the problem with inclusion is that it welcomes people only to a point. Ironically, there is usually a norm that people still need to adhere to if they are to be included: We are including them in *something*; they want to be included in *something*.

> All systems create criteria to distinguish truth from untruth. . . . [E]very system produces its own truth and policies of truth in order to control existing differences and indicate the transgressors. . . . Inclusion, then, presupposes an absolute identity as the organizing centre of all differences. Everything moves towards an absolute identity. . . . Differences have to be overcome. . . . Multiplicity is, then, reduced (again) to the One . . .[13]

Oftentimes churches—including MCC—state in their publicity and evangelistic materials that they welcome diversity and differences, but once people are brought in by this message, the congregation (wittingly or not) begins to erode those differences that they were trying to attract in the first place, somewhat like lovers who, after they have come together and formed a relationship, try to change the exact things about the beloved that they were initially drawn to. Truly inclusive churches (disreputable ones?) must be on guard against molding newcomers to standards that dissolve their individuality and uniqueness as children of God.

In order for true inclusivity to work—and this is where a disreputable ecclesiology as I have begun to describe it becomes important—all bodies must be seen as important. Toni Morrison vividly illustrates this in her novel *Beloved*, when former slave Baby Suggs, Holy, is preaching to other former slaves in her makeshift church in The Clearing.[14] She points out to these human creations of God, who had formerly been the chattel of other human creations of God and yet had somehow made their way to freedom, that they must love their flesh: "'Here,' she said, 'in this place, we flesh; flesh that weeps, laughs; flesh that dances on bare feet in grass. Love it. Love it hard.'" Nobody else is going to do it for them: "Yonder, they do not love your flesh. They despise it. . . . *You* got to love it, *you*! . . . This is flesh I'm talking about here. Flesh that needs to be loved." Moreover, every part of that flesh is important—not only the heart and the mind (the decent, respectable parts?), but also the liver and the neck and even or especially the private parts.[15] (Recall the statement of St. Paul in 1 Cor. 12:23 that the parts of the body which are the least respectable are the ones we treat with greater dignity.)

Thus, in the disreputable ecclesiology I am proposing, church members must be encouraged to value all *their* members—the feet and armpits that sweat and smell, the genitals that make us feel good and help us to make others feel good, the hands that we use to caress ourselves and others, the mouths which thirst and with which we praise God, ingest food, and lick and suck and kiss our beloved. And once people appreciate their own members, they can then turn and encounter and embrace and encourage the members of other members. In the Christological controversies of the early church, Gregory of Nazianzus pointed out that "what has not been assumed cannot be redeemed." In the same way, in our churches today what we do not acknowledge and treasure, we cannot welcome and include in any truly meaningful or theological way.

But for the bodies of sexual minorities to be counted and countenanced—in order for us to be heard into speech—we must talk about our sex. Unlike other minorities (women, people of color, the differently abled), one cannot immediately see our status of Other by looking at us, for the markers of our minority status lie within. Our Otherness is written on our body but must be translated by our minds, hearts, and spirits. It is deep within that we carry the scars of our Othering. Since one of the ways in which we have been Othered is through the charge that it is our sexual selves that constitute us as sinners, that by virtue of the ways in which we express our eroticism and our intimacy we sin, I would like to suggest that we SIN REALLY BIG. Heteronormative paradigms will always see us as sinners, whether they will own up to it or not. (Note such doublespeak as "I support gay rights, but marriage is between one man and one woman," endorsed even, until recently, by the president of the United States.) So why not be the best sinners we know how to be? Why not express our sexuality in such a remarkable and authentic way that it is the quintessence of sin in the eyes of the majority? That would be truly disreputable!

Lest the reader think I am being facetious, I call to our consciousness the first major essay of feminist theology, by Valerie Saiving, who pointed out that sin was usually defined according to the experience of (white, heterosexual) males.[16] For them, the greatest sin against God was pride, the making more of oneself than one ought. Nevertheless, as Saiving showed so brilliantly, for women pride is the opposite of sin; it is unpride which was for generations their sin. For many women, on Saiving's view, pride would be a virtue and not a sin, for what women needed was confidence in their authentic selves, not denigration; thus, the true sin was to not practice pride and to disparage the brilliant creation of God that women represented.

In her last book, the late radical feminist theologian and philosopher Mary Daly concurred. She noted that, because today's world is still in the grip of patriarchy, women need to overcome the disconnect within them so as to heal the fragmentation that patriarchy continues to inject into the planet.[17] As Daly reminded her readers over and over again in her body of work, this disconnect, which women apprehend from their daily lives in a world ruled according to men's desires and rules, teaches them that their very nature is a sin against the male norm. Efforts to empower woman's full personhood sin against the structures and systems set up to serve men. The sins of womankind are presided over by a male God, who has been created in the image of men and served by the Church, which Daly terms a "phallocracy."[18]

In the same way, queer Christians must SIN BIG! We must flaunt the abominations God created us to be, for our authentic personhood involves manifesting what T-theology calls sin. Indeed, for queers true sin would be to *not* practice our sexuality, for by such a sin of omission we would be denying our personhood—a blaspheming of the Holy Spirit, which Jesus called the unforgiveable sin (Mk 3:29). Oftentimes queer Christians are reluctant to show who we really are and to be vocal about our sexual stories for fear decent people will not like us anymore.[19] But, you know what? If that's all it takes, then they don't really like us anyway. If they wanted the best for us, if they saw us as true children of God on an equal par with themselves, they would not withhold basic human rights. They would not insist that we conform to standards of so-called decency not of our making. They would not suggest that our unions are less than theirs or that we pose a threat to their children.

In joining women and others who have been Othered by the dominant culture, queer people who decide to sin big by being disreputable are turning away from T-theology and turning toward that with which we have been gifted by our loving, amazing God. When we feel and claim what our bodies in all their sexual, gender, and emotional complexity are telling us, we are giving birth to God, who has been birthed and rebirthed in bodies since time immemorial. Moreover, we are exposing the lie that any one person or group can make decisions about other people that result in their being labeled sinners and dismissed from a human-based (heterosexual) economy of salvation founded on supposed decency.[20] Thus, Samoan theologian Tavita Maliko, in discussing the way gender and sexuality among indigenous Samoans have been categorized by European scholars, asserts, "The church defines people according to its theology of sin. Whatever you do, if you don't use your penis the way you are supposed to, then you are a homosexual. Whatever that means!"[21] In explaining that there are more than two genders recognized in Samoa and that these genders do not neatly align themselves according to western binary notions of sexual orientation, Maliko insists that one should not judge another according to standards that have been artificially created from another culture's data and prejudices. To do so is to perpetuate the worst sort of colonialism. Postcolonial theology has therefore demanded an undoing of this First World (Christian) dominance and has called for self-naming and personal theologizing by the colonized themselves,[22] much the way feminist theologians a generation ago encouraged women to engage in a process of self-naming resulting from consciousness raising.[23]

Indeed, one of the most controversial ways in which women raised their consciousness during the Women's Movement of the 1960s and 1970s was by passing around a speculum or mirror during group meetings, so that each woman could examine in detail—perhaps for the first time—her own vagina. By looking at and talking about what the overarching patriarchal culture told them they should not look at or talk about, thus reclaiming their vaginas from the pornographic male gaze, women were empowered not only to love their bodies as they were but also to employ a metaphorical speculum to other parts of their lives which had been heretofore unexamined.[24] In the same way, I believe that disreputable churches might offer the same sort of forum for self-examination to those in today's world who have had their sexual stories muted and their sexual assertiveness taken away by notions of decency and propriety. I have often as a pastor wondered why congregation members are able to talk in whispers in the corner or at a party about their intimate lives but feel ashamed to share the same sorts of matters out in the open at church. Do we really think that God does not know what we do with our bodies? Are we naïve enough to think that we can divorce our sexual selves from the rest of our lives? At times like these, God reminds us, "Before I formed you in the womb I knew you" (Jer 1:4); and Jesus chimes in to point out that there is "nothing hidden that will not be revealed" (Lk 8:17).

"But what are you really getting at?" the reader might ask at this point. "Are you saying that churches should become a forum for sex talk where anything goes?"[25] My answer to this important concern is of course not. We must always, in all of our church discussions, be sensitive to the feelings and sensibilities of others. We must always look for ethical ways in which to discuss matters of behavior, as I have noted elsewhere in this anthology. However, at the same time we must guard against unnecessary prudishness which comes from deep-seated sex negativity and erotophobia and continually monitor whether we are slavishly pandering to the heteronormative status quo. Each community will approach this differently, based upon its context, history, and demographics. Issues such as when and where discussions of eroticism should take place, as well as how to include the input of parents of young people, should be kept in mind whenever a faith community embarks on the journey to disreputability. But we avoid the invitation to disreputability at our peril, for we can see this disreputability among the earliest followers of Jesus, who were castigated as sinners by the dominant society. As New Testament scholar Greg Carey reminds us, in the ministry of Jesus (and among his contemporary followers) what is at stake is the difference between deviance and legitimacy.[26] And if the earliest Christians took the risk of sinning big according to their culture's estimation, then we can do no less.

One way in which a church community can encourage itself to sin big is to begin discussing the notion of sin altogether, something that many queers, including those in MCC, have been reluctant to do. When we articulate what sin really is—and how queer folks' sin may not look the same as that of nonqueers—we will be in a better position to welcome those whose existence we might not have even acknowledged at a previous time in our lives. The recent work of queer theologian and MCC minister Patrick Cheng is foundational in this regard, for he has proposed "a Christological model of sin and grace" by introducing various models of Christ for LGBT people, with each model including a sin against that model and a type of grace that flows from that model.[27] For example, the Erotic Christ is "the very embodiment of God's deepest desire for us." The Erotic Christ models the appropriateness of physical touch as he empowers the human eroticism that derives from the Godhead Itself. To sin against this Erotic Christ is to concentrate solely on one's own self-gratification at the expense of the grace of reciprocity and mutuality with one's erotic partner.[28] Cheng's other Christic models are equally productive of a theology of wholeness sorely needed in queer communities; the Erotic Christ, however, is perhaps the most helpful for my purposes here because this Christ presides at the sacrament of our transformation from keepers of unexamined decency to practitioners of full-blown (!) disreputability.

In a disreputable church made up of disreputable people who are indecent by virtue of who they are, how they believe, and why they live as they do, mutuality and reciprocity as the grace of the Queer Christ and the fruits of a Queer Spirit are essential, as is the recognition that sins of self-centeredness and self-focused thinking or behavior do not help the church progress or prosper. The Greek word for "church" is *ek-klēsia*—an entity "called out" to be or do something. The word "community" is from the Latin word *com-munire* meaning "to build together." A church community, then, is a gathering of people "called out to build together"—what? Perhaps the Reign of God that Jesus mentions so much in the gospels? An early Christian teacher instructed his followers that they were "a chosen race, a royal priesthood, a holy nation, a people who are God's own possession," whom God has "*called out* of darkness" into the amazing light, reminding them, "Once you weren't a people, but not you are God's people" (1 Pet 1:9–10).[29] Those whom society would cast aside and whose very personhood many governments and churches do not recognize come to realize in a disreputable church that they are indeed home, that God has called them together for such a time as this and chosen them to be God's very own.

In speaking of Jesus' announcement of the Reign of God in Mark 1:15, biblical scholar Melinda Quivik writes, "Anyone who introduces a whole new way of thinking is bound to a difficult task."[30] Her words could also apply to the building of a disreputable church founded on the dangerous precept that everyone is welcome not only in God's Reign but also in God's Church—two entities that do not always have the same constituents. It is a difficult task to vision beyond decency, respectability, and appropriateness. The graced and gracious mutuality that is required as an organizing principle is what moral theologian Thomas Breidenthal has termed "radical availability,"[31] noting that in discussions of sexuality, spirituality, and salvation one must constantly ask the question, "Who is my neighbor, and what does that have to do with me?"

> To say that I am radically available is to say that anyone can become my neighbor: anyone can get under my skin. The word *neighbor*, after all, simply means someone who is *nigh* to me, close to me. . . . Nearness is experience of the other as neighbor . . . [, one who is] neither reducible to being an extension of myself nor able to be dismissed because he or she is different from me . . . [H]owever much we may prefer to think of ourselves as essentially separate from and independent of one another, . . . the truth is that we are always already available to every other human being, and cannot prevent even a momentary encounter with a stranger from touching us to our very core.[32]

Whenever we encounter another person, we do so with our physical bodies, and this physical nearness engages our sexuality—our ability to relate to another. Breidenthal asserts that every human being is made in the image of God, and for him that image is our capacity to love. We love our neighbors through our bodies, and, in reaching out to another, our action is "always an answer to God," who calls us to relationship with those who are "nigh."[33] This nearness to others sanctifies us—makes us holy, like God. The process of sanctification that traditional theology tells us is the work of the Christian Church is, then, actually a drawing near to others and a recognizing of our radical availability to one another—the grace of reciprocity.[34] To cut oneself off from this is, as Cheng reminds us, sin—a relational brokenness between us and God, tangibly manifested in the rupture between us and one another.

Thus, anyone can be our neighbor. Everyone is, in fact, already our neighbor, whether or not they look, act, talk, or think like us. When we reach across divides of respectability or decency to join ourselves to a neighbor, we are indeed creating the Reign of God which Jesus, in older translations, said had "drawn nigh"! Indeed, Breidenthal sums up his argument Christologically with the emphatic statement, "The whole point of the Incarnation is that the Word of God has become our neighbor,"[35] or, as the literal translation of the Greek would have it, "has pitched its tent among us" (Jn 1:14).

It was as a body that the Word of God—Jesus, God's Christ—pitched that tent. It was as a body that he welcomed a disparate, often motley group of followers. In the words of ethicist James Nelson, we experience the Gospel ("good news") in our bodies or not at all![36] It is in our bodies that we meet the world and interact with our neighbors in radical availability and grace-full mutuality: our black, white, red, yellow, brown bodies; our male, female, transgender, intersex bodies; our gay, lesbian, bisexual, straight bodies; our young, middle-aged, old bodies; our fat, thin bodies; our beautifully smooth, beautifully wrinkled bodies; our fully abled, differently abled, disabled bodies; our pierced, tattooed bodies; our laughing, crying, bleeding, shitting, fucking bodies. The body is the vehicle through which we apprehend and live the message of church. Ministry is about meeting the world, and we meet the world in our own bodies, one body at a time. We must never downgrade these bodies or apologize for them or what we do with them or pretend that they are any different than they are. As Toni Morrison reminds us, we need to love these bodies, love them hard: "For this is the prize."[37]

* * *

So what would it take to make the church disreputable? I would like to suggest that the answer lies in the title to this chapter: We must unzip church! Think about what happens when we unzip our clothing: We are not restrained. We can breathe. Our junk falls out! When we unzip, we no longer cover over those parts of the body some deem less worthy of respect. We show our unmentionables. We shatter the illusion of what might be kept hidden within. What is revealed might in turn contradict the image we present by our zipped-up appearance. Unzipping forces us to take an honest look at ourselves, and it allows others to see us as we really are.

Much has been made in the queer communities of coming out of the closet (i.e., telling the truth about one's sexual self). Nevertheless, it is possible to be out of the closet and still zipped up to protect what others might label indecent, unacceptable, or just plain nasty. Moreover, keeping ourselves respectably zipped up allows us to conform to the heteronormative logic that controls our culture. It allows us to pretend that we are just like everybody else. I remember my father, years after I had come out to him, watching coverage of the Los Angeles Pride Parade on television and turning to me to say, "You aren't like that, are you?" At that point in my journey, I was keeping myself pretty zipped up, so rather than engage him I pretended not to know what he was getting at and said of course not. Talk about blaspheming the Holy Spirit! I may have been ready to tell him I was gay, but was not yet ready to tell him how queer I was!

It is fear that keeps us zipped up, and fear that keeps us from unzipping church. For once you unzip and your junk falls out, you can't pretend anymore. You can no longer claim to be something you're not. You can't aspire to decency when your indecency and disreputability is there for all to see. But unzipping brings with it a sense of freedom and a feeling of ultimate relief—sort of like wearing pants that are a size too small in order to make yourself appear thinner than you are. When you unzip and let it all hang out, you feel so much better.

Pioneering gay priest, psychotherapist, and theologian John McNeill, who is now a proud member of MCC has discussed the necessity of queer Christians overcoming our fears. For McNeill, fear not only stands between us and our personal authenticity but also between us and our sisters and brothers:

> The fear that we should seek to be liberated from is that kind of paranoid fear that impoverishes our conscience and cripples our response to those around us, numbing us to their needs because of anxiety about our own needs, blinding us in such a way that we fail to recognize those around us as our brothers and sisters.[38]

As long as we are in the grip of this fear, we will be unable to envision, create, and see to fruition a church where everyone is welcome, included, and equal. McNeill points to the coming of the Christ as the moment when the world was challenged to give up its fear; in the infancy narratives the birth of Jesus is accompanied by the repeated admonition, "Do not be afraid" (Matt 2:20; Lk 1:14, 1:30, 2:10).[39] If Jesus' birth signaled that one could live without fear, how much more his announcement of the Reign of God showed people tangibly through his words[40] and deeds that they could come out of fear into God's love and grace. It is this Reign of God that a disreputable church enacts day by day.

How? New Testament scholars have pointed out that one of the hallmarks of Jesus' ministry was what they call his "open commensality,"[41] that is, his policy of eating with many different types of people. MCC pastor and queer theologian Robert E. Shore-Goss has asserted that this policy of open commensality is at the heart of the message and ministry of MCC: "The practice of open commensality enables a queer church to invite the sexual stories of disparate queers into a matrix of dis/grace."[42] I concur and would go so far as to say that it must be the cornerstone of any church that claims to be inclusive or demonstrative of the type of radical, unconditional love that Jesus embodied. For it is in this "matrix of dis/grace" that the Church of Jesus Christ becomes disreputable.

Sociologists suggest that meals reflect society in microcosm. We can tell a lot about people by whom they eat with.[43] Open communion is paradigmatic of the Body of Christ which includes all people. And just as Jesus Christ, through his *physical body*, enacted the meal that was to become the Christian Church's primary sacrament of grace that incorporates us into the Body of Christ (the Church), we receive that Communion (common/union) into our *physical bodies*; or, as I suggest in my Prayer of Consecration on Sundays in MCC, just as the physical elements of bread and fruit of the vine become part of our physical bodies, so too the Christ Spirit contained in it becomes a part of our spirits, Christing us and making us one. In the Eucharist the bread is *opened* to us (not broken!)[44] as God is *opened* to us and we enter in: One might say we are invited to *penetrate* God in the Eucharistic celebration. But to do so we have to unzip.

I find it incomprehensible that any church would dare to invoke the communion of saints in its communion liturgy and then deny physical communion to anyone. But as Roman Catholic womanist theologian M. Shawn Copeland reminds us, "Even as the table includes, it excludes."[45] I recall my two most recent experiences in the Roman Catholic Church of my upbringing—my nephew's wedding and my father's funeral. I had intended to receive Communion with my family, for I still consider myself in some ways a Catholic; but then the celebrant noted that if you were not a baptized Catholic "in a confessed state of grace" you were welcome to come forward and receive not Communion but a blessing. That changed my mind (made me repent?) instantly: Would Jesus have offered a blessing but no food? I doubt it. When my older sister (a fellow refugee from Catholicism) whispered to me, "Are you going up?" I replied, "No way. If I can't have their communion, I don't want their blessing." I am sure there are many who have felt as I did, who have felt pushed away by the very churches that they have supported with their presence, their participation, their loyalty, and their money. At those times, Jesus says, "Come on! Let's go eat somewhere else!"

How often we take for granted our inclusion in that Communion meal—until it is taken away from us. I wandered for six years with no church home before I was invited to an MCC, and on that first day over 30 years ago, I can still remember hearing the invitation to open communion, spoken by a lesbian woman to a church full of disreputable queers. Even then, however, I still had to turn to the person next to me and say, "This is my first time here. May I take communion?" She looked at me and said with a smile, "Of course you can! You are home!" But is everyone at home, even in an MCC congregation? Or do we still place restrictions on the table? Are cross-dressers able to come forward without hearing tittering from the pews? Are those who flag red or yellow or brown able to come forward and be embraced the same as others, without question or judgment? Are lovers in a three-way relationship able to stand at the altar just as they are, or do they have to pretend that they are just friends taking Communion together? Can a daddy bring his boy to Communion on a leash without the pastor being brought before the board of directors? Can a straight couple with their children step forward without being asked by the usher if they are sure they are in the right place? I wonder. Some MCC pastors still disinvite people to open communion by requiring in their invitation that the person be a baptized Christian who has confessed their sins!

Is MCC a disreputable church? Not yet, but it could be if we would unzip it and let our junk come out. We have the choice whether to live out our sexual stories every day of the week, wherever we are, or to go back into the closet of respectability that requires we be fit and suitable according to a heteronormative logic of decency. I live in the hope that those who have known restriction and discrimination will not feel compelled to practice it themselves. I live in the hope that we will embrace our disreputability in Shore-Goss's matrix of dis/grace, within the tension that lies between Cheng's sin of self-focus and grace of mutuality. I live in the hope that we will not only queer the table but the entire Body of Christ. Only then will there *really* be room for everyone.

NOTES

1. I am reminded of the professor in Philip Roth's novel *The Human Stain* (New York: Vintage Books, 2000), who was dismissed from his position for use of a racially charged epithet and branded a racist, when in actuality he himself was a light-skinned African American passing as white.

2. See Troy D. Perry with Thomas L. P. Swicegood, *Don't Be Afraid Anymore: The Story of Reverend Troy Perry and the Metropolitan Community Churches* (New York: St. Martin's Press, 1990).

3. I must acknowledge that my husband and I did, after much soul searching, get legally married in Massachusetts in 2005. We recognize that the institution itself is heteropatriarchal in structure but hope that, by our modeling of a different sort of marriage partnership, we might queer the institution and give others food for thought.

4. I am aware, with my colleague Susannah Cornwall, that not all of those who self-identify in this way wish to be included under the umbrella category queer. See Susannah Cornwall, *Sex and Uncertainty in the Body of Christ: Intersex Conditions and Christian Theology* (London: Equinox, 2010), 205–6. Rather than use it in this way, I agree with Patrick S. Cheng that perhaps a more productive use of the term is as a signifier for the notion of transgressiveness and a shattering of boundaries and binaries. See Patrick S. Cheng, *Radical Love: An Introduction to Queer Theology* (New York: Seabury Press, 2011), 5–8.

5. Marcella Althaus-Reid, *Indecent Theology: Theological Perversions in Sex, Gender and Politics* (London: Routledge, 2000).

6. Ibid., 130–31.

7. Marcella Althaus-Reid, *The Queer God* (London: Routledge, 2003), passim but see esp. her definition at 172, note 4.

8. "Decency, like money and like religion, is a currency of power." Kathleen M. Sands, "Civil Unions, Colonialism and the Struggle for Sexual Decency in Hawaii," in *Dancing Theology in Fetish Boots: Essays in Honour of Marcella Althaus-Reid*, ed. Lisa Isherwood and Mark D. Jordan (London: SCM Press, 2010), 59.

9. For a wonderful example of this sort of "dis/grace-full" church in MCC, see Robert E. Shore-Goss, "Dis/Grace-full Incarnation and the Dis/Grace-full Church: Marcella Althaus-Reid's Vision of Radical Inclusivity," in *Dancing Theology in Fetish Boots*, 10–16.

10. This is what some apologetic gay theologians stress in their work; see, for example, Eugene F. Rogers, Jr., "Sanctification, Homosexuality, and God's Triune Life," in *Theology and Sexuality: Classic and Contemporary Readings*, ed. Eugene F. Rogers, Jr. (Malden, MA: Blackwell Publishing, 2002), 227–28.

11. Marcella Althaus-Reid, "Feetishism: The Scent of a Latin American Body Theology," in *Toward a Theology of Eros: Transfiguring Passion at the Limits of Discipline*, ed. Virginia Burrus and Catherine Keller (New York: Fordham University Press, 2006), 146–49.

12. Audre Lorde, "The Master's Tools Will Never Dismantle the Master's House," in *Sister Outsider: Essays and Speeches*, ed. Audre Lorde (Trumansburg, NY: The Crossing Press, 1984), 110–13.

13. Frederico Pieper Pires, "Liberation Theology, Modernity and Sexual Difference," in *Liberation Theology and Sexuality*, 2nd ed., ed. Marcella Althaus-Reid (London: SCM Press, 2009), 114–15, 117, 119.

14. Toni Morrison, *Beloved* (New York: Alfred A. Knopf, 1987), 87–89.

15. For an excellent discussion of this scene, see Joy R. Bostic, " 'Flesh That Dances': A Theology of Sexuality and the Spirit in Toni Morrison's *Beloved*," in *The Embrace of Eros: Bodies, Desires, and Sexuality in Christianity*, ed. Margaret D. Kamitsuka (Minneapolis: Fortress Press, 2010), 277–96.

16. Valerie Saiving, "The Human Situation: A Feminine View" (1960), *Womanspirit Rising: A Feminist Reader in Religion*, ed. Carol P. Christ and Judith Plaskow (San Francisco: Harper & Row, 1979), 25–42.

17. Mary Daly, *Amazon Grace: Re-Calling the Courage to Sin Big* (New York: Palgrave Macmillan, 206), 2.

18. Mary Daly, *Beyond God the Father: Toward a Philosophy of Women's Liberation, with an Original Reintroduction by the Author* (Boston: Beacon Press, 1985), passim but esp. 1, 19, 69, 71.

19. Another frequently made argument for not talking explicitly about sexuality is that we will confirm what the majority thinks about us rather than encouraging them to see us as just like them. African Americans have found themselves in a similar predicament vis-à-vis sexuality, for the white majority has held up the stereotype of the hypersexual black person, which has made some black people reluctant to discuss sexual matters at all, for fear of confirming the stereotype. See Kelly Brown Douglas, "Black and Blues: God-Talk/Body-Talk for the Black Church," in *Sexuality and the Sacred: Sources for Theological Reflection*, 2nd ed., ed. Marvin M. Ellison and Kelly Brown Douglas (Louisville, KY: Westminster John Knox Press, 2010), 54–57.

20. Althaus-Reid, *Indecent Theology*, 76.

21. Philip Culbertson and Tavita Maliko, " 'A G-String Is Not Samoan': Exploring a Transgressive Third-Gender Pasifika Theology," in *Homosexualities*, ed. Marcella Althaus-Reid, Regina Ammicht Quinn, Erik Borgman and Norbert Reck (London: SCM Press, 2008), 62.

22. See, for example, Musa W. Dube, *Postcolonial Feminist Interpretation of the Bible* (St. Louis, MO: Chalice Press, 2000); Kwok Pui-lan, *Postcolonial Imagination and Feminist Theology* (Louisville, KY: Westminster John Knox Press, 2005).

23. See, for example, Nelle Morton, *The Journey Is Home* (Boston: Beacon Press, 1985).

24. For the culmination of this liberating mind-set, see Eve Ensler, *The Vagina Monologues* (New York: Villard, 2007).

25. A similar question is addressed by Alison R. Webster in her book *Found Wanting: Women, Christianity and Sexuality* (London: Cassell, 1995), 32.

26. Greg Carey, *Sinners: Jesus and His Earliest Followers* (Waco, TX: Baylor University Press, 2009), 126.

27. Patrick S. Cheng, "Rethinking Sin and Grace for LGBT People Today," in *Sexuality and the Sacred*, 105–18. This argument is expanded in his book *From Sin to Amazing Grace: Discovering the Queer Christ* (New York: Seabury Books, 2012).

28. Cheng, "Rethinking Sin and Grace," 108–10.

29. This translation is from the Common English Bible, www.commonenglishbible.com, 2011 (emphasis added).

30. Melinda Quivik, "Third Sunday After the Epiphany," in *Preaching God's Transforming Justice: A Lectionary Commentary, Year B*, ed. Ronald J. Allen, Dale P. Andrews, and Dawn Ottoni-Wilhelm (Louisville, KY: Westminster John Knox Press, 2011), 77.

31. Thomas Breidenthal, "Sanctifying Nearness," in *Theology and Sexuality*, 344.

32. Ibid., 344–45.

33. Ibid., 347.

34. Ibid., 352.

35. Ibid., 351.

36. James B. Nelson, *Between Two Gardens: Reflections on Sexuality and Religious Experience* (New York: Pilgrim Press, 1983), 17–18.

37. Morrison, *Beloved*, 89.

38. John J. McNeill, *Taking a Chance on God: Liberating Theology for Gays, Lesbians, and Their Lovers, Families, and Friends* (Boston: Beacon Press, 1988), 47.

39. Ibid., 47–48.

40. The gospels record Jesus himself telling people not to be afraid (e.g., Matt. 10:26, 14:27, 17:8; Lk 12:32; Jn 14:27). See McNeill, *Taking a Chance*, 48–50.

41. John Dominic Crossan, *The Historical Jesus: The Life of a Mediterranean Jewish Peasant* (New York: HarperCollins, 1991), 341–44. See also Marcus J. Borg, *Jesus: A New Vision* (San Francisco: Harper & Row, 1987), 131–33; and Thomas Bohache, *Christology from the Margins* (London: SCM Press, 2008), 247–48.

42. Shore-Goss, "Dis/Grace-full Incarnation and the Dis/Grace-full Church," 11.

43. "Few human activities so reveal the truth about our social lives as our dining company. . . . Meals reflect basic social realities. Social scientists would say that societies *encode* their values in their dining practices." Carey, *Sinners*, 18.

44. This phrasing is a hallmark of the consecration liturgy of MCC's Rev. Elder Darlene Garner.

45. M. Shawn Copeland, *Enfleshing Freedom: Body, Race, and Being* (Minneapolis: Fortress Press, 2010), 61.

Part III

OPENING THE TABLE PASTORALLY

Mona West

Over the years Queer theology has dealt with approaches to scripture and models for God and the church. What we find in the essays in this section is an expanding understanding of the ways in which queering Christianity weds theory to practice. Jesus' radical table fellowship was not only a subversion of the purity laws of his day—but it also changed people's lives.

Joe Shore-Goss in his chapter, *Pastoral Care of Transgendered Youth* and Joan Saniuk in her chapter, *Putting on Wedding Drag* queer pastoral care by claiming that activism is core to our work as caregivers in LGBTQ community. Being present in this caring way means that we understand the unique stresses of being queer in a heteronormative culture and that we create safe places for people's stories to be heard and valued. For Joe this has meant educating himself on the issues facing the transgender youth he works with in the Harm Reduction Program of the Trans Youth project of Children's Hospital in Los Angeles, California. As a pastoral caregiver in this context, he is aware of the many layers of identity that transgender youth must navigate in the midst of adolescence: race, class, sexual identity, gender identity, and stages of transgender emergence. Their journey to wholeness also includes several paths to harm reduction which culminate in assessing their spiritual needs as well as medical needs. It is Joe's understanding of the transgender journey of his clients, not his certification as a chaplain, that is the locus of his authority.

Joan Saniuk uses a trauma model to claim that Metropolitan Community Churche's (MCC) congregations can be powerful places of healing for LGBTQ people, who have experienced spiritual violence. She also notes how the spiritual abuse that individual members bring to a congregation can have an impact on the congregation's overall health and functioning. Citing previous studies on trauma survivors, Saniuk outlines three things necessary for overcoming spiritual trauma: a place of safety, remembering and mourning the trauma, and reconnecting to life. She claims that MCC congregations still have work to do in the grief stage of the trauma model and does her own version of queering pastoral care and liturgy by offering a model of a queer Tenebrae service that weaves the stories of queer folks with the story of Jesus in an effort to remember, mourn, and move through the grief of the trauma to a place of healing.

We are invited and challenged to remember the life-saving relevance of MCC's history and message in the essays by Neil Thomas and Lea Brown. In his essay on *Marriage Equality* Thomas notes that the very first Holy Union was performed in MCC in 1969 less than a year after its founding and in 1970 MCC filed the first lawsuit to have gay marriage legally recognized against the state of California. These two events in MCC launched three decades of debates and struggle for marriage equality. Neil, as Senior Pastor of the founding MCC church and President of California for Faith Equality, calls the LGBT community to work on both legal and religious fronts in our efforts to live into a theology of radical inclusion for marriage equality that springs from a queer communion table.

Lea Brown fears that at least in North America MCC seems to have forgotten or stopped believing in our message that our spiritual power is grounded in the truth of our sexual experience. In her essay, *Coming to the Table in Leather,* Lea shares her own story of full inclusion in MCC as a clergy person, who celebrates communion openly as a leather person and as someone who practices sadomasochism and Domination-submission. The mutual consent and pleasure she experiences in the communities with which she plays have profoundly impacted the way she understands and connects to the divine source in all of life. As she navigates the ebb and flow of her own erotic power in the time and space constraints of a scene she is also empowered to let her Eros move without interruption in her day-to-day life.

Pastoral practices spill over into spiritual formation in the essays by Mona West (*Queer Lectio Divina*) and Joe Shore-Goss (*Spiritual Companioning*). West invites queer people of faith to trust scripture with their spiritual formation. Just as Lea Brown emphasizes the importance of embodied spirituality, Mona West emphasizes that reading and trusting the Bible with our spiritual formation involves bringing the listening that we are to the text. As queer people imagine themselves as characters in the text (the second movement of *lectio divina*), they make the text itself queer. Spiritual formation itself is queered or subverted from a hetero-normative assumption that gay people would be changed or healed from their homosexuality as part of their spiritual development to a model of spiritual development that celebrates the whole selves LGBT people bring to their encounter with scripture.

Shore-Goss attempts to subvert the language of spiritual direction by calling this ancient practice "spiritual companioning." He points out that it is not a clinical act but an art and a gift. He explores the dimensions of spiritual companioning for LGBT people and along with Mona West identifies coming out as a primary lens through which spiritual formation happens for queer people of faith. He expands his thoughts on spiritual companioning to include journeying with people of other faith traditions claiming that what is most important is "loving the traveler through authentic presence, concern and care."

Jim Mitulski ends our anthology and this section with a thought-provoking essay on "gay hymnody." He claims, "When churches say they don't want us in their pews—here we are in their hymnbooks." Just as Lea Brown lifted up the power of people of all kinds of sexual identities singing together in church, Mitulski demonstrates that hymnody has been used in the work of liberation by LGBT hymn writers and our allies. His cross-disciplinary approach identifies the stories, texts, and tunes of hymns that have been written to celebrate inclusiveness, speak to HIV/AIDS, and commemorate Holy Unions. Then there are those hymns such as "America the Beautiful" with no particular gay theme but have been written by Katherine Lee Bates who had a female lover. His closing admonition is fitting for this volume: "As you sing 'This is my story, this is my song,' (from Fanny Crosby's hymn "Blessed Assurance") put yourself in the place of gay and lesbian people who have found liberation and salvation in believing that these words apply to them too."

14

Pastoral Care of Transgendered Youth

Joseph Shore-Goss

Since the first meeting of Metropolitan Community Church (MCC) in Rev. Troy Perry's living room, two unique things arose. The first was that the Eucharistic celebration would happen every week, and the second was that the invitation to come to the table would be open to all. At MCC all around the globe we affirm you do not need to be a member of this church or any church this is God's table and that it is without boundaries or restrictions.

With that thought in mind we know that lesbian and gay, straight or bisexual, and transgender come to the table. Yet we are called to more than that for if you sit at table with a person every week, week in and week out than that person is not a stranger but family. As a family, we are called to care for each other beyond the table to walk with each other in our good times and bad, and especially to be there through our coming into ourselves. This is why I am so adamant about pastoral care for transgender youth, the youngest and at times the frailest of the LGBTQIA community. Hence, when I saw an opportunity to serve the transgender youth project of Children's Hospital, I jumped at it. I entered into this relationship knowing that I am serving from a margin to another margin.

While working at Children's Hospital Los Angeles I had the opportunity to work with the Transgender Harm Reduction Program. This is a program that exists as part of the Division of Adolescent Medicine. This program provides education, medical, psychosocial, and social support to young people who believe they may be transgender.

As an openly gay clergy and chaplain, I felt called to serve this community. I have firsthand experience of living with and working with the transgender community. There is a great need for positive interaction with the transgender community, and I saw this as one way in which I could bring in pastoral care.

I served as a chaplain to a drop-in group as part of the harm reduction program. In doing so, I had discovered that my knowledge was lacking. In the attempt to expand my own knowledge base I found there was very little material addressing this particular sector of the transgender community and there is nothing written on pastoral care. The sector I am addressing is the sector I served at the hospital, which comprised youth, aged 13 to 24 who, due to many varieties of circumstances, are at risk.

These young people are at risk for HIV infection, at risk of dropping out of high school, at risk for criminal activity, and at risk of being left behind in our urban settings. We, as MCC, are called to work with these young people and find some patterns in care that may assist others who are called to pastorally care for this population as well.

Before entering into any ministry, and especially a ministry with youth, you must know yourself and know where you come from and the choices you have made and the reasons behind them. As an older person entering into care of the younger, you are greeted with suspicion, questions, and challenges to who you are. You best be prepared to give those answers and answer honestly. For example, I choose to come out at a young age.

I had a choice; I could have stayed in the closet and lived a quiet normal life, perhaps marry a nice girl, pretend to be straight having children, and then come out much later in life or not at all. However, I chose to come out and thus, instantly lost my status of middle-class white kid. Chris Glaser believes that, "coming out of the closet as a sexual minority also requires breaking free of confining expectations that previously governed and possibly inspired our lives."[1] Suddenly I was a different person; I had made an ontological change in my life.

This change meant I could be either accepted or rejected. I choose to be an open person living as an out, proud, and loud gay man. I believe that, "coming out is a sacrament that may be shared with one other person, a community, a congregation, a denomination, or the world."[2] I chose to share it with the world. This has caused great heartache and great blessing, and all of these choices and situations stand at the core me.

God calls us to be our true self, and that the true self must be honored and shared. It is my experience and belief that "those who do not welcome another's coming out receive it unworthily, without discerning either the sacred gift or their sacred kinship with the person offering her or him-self."[3] In other words to those that I do come out, if they reject me, they are not worthy of me as whole person or not ready to receive the sacrament of coming out that I have invited them to participate in.

It is this strong conviction that shapes me and my ministry. It is in this sacredness of the self and sacrament that I enter in to intentionally serve the community around me. I belong to the LGBTQI (lesbian, gay, bi, transgender, queer, intersex) community, and therefore, must serve that community. I serve in the margins as a marginalized person myself.

I am serving and bringing pastoral care to the margin of the LGBTQI community, which is the most passionately discriminated against. The transgender community is not my community, however, it is part of my community and thus I am called to serve. I did not enter into service as a privileged white man coming to save the community either. Upon entering into this group on the first day I introduced myself:

Hi I am Joe. I am a Chaplain from Children's Hospital and I would like to participate in your group here very much. Let me start by saying I am not transgender. I am an openly Gay man. I have friends who are transgender. I have done drag before and I know the difference between being a drag queen and being a transgender person. I am here to be an added facet to your care.

As a pastoral caregiver, I approached this group aware of my own self. I am a middle-aged white gay male living with AIDS. I was born in a middle-class Catholic family in the Midwest. My only experience with transgender people up until now has been of middle-class or upper-class privileged white men who could afford the surgery or who chose not to have the surgery and live as women without it.

My spiritual belief system, developed from my life experience, also informs my approach. For instance, I know that God created day and night, and yet, I also know that God created all the shades and colors that lay in between. In some Native American traditions, "Sexuality and gender roles were seen on a continuum represented by a circle rather than limited by linear stages or rigid categories."[4] Sexuality and gender are fluid and can develop as one grows into knowledge of oneself. Sexuality, for me, very much lies within all the shades and colors that lie between the day and the night.

The Rev. Dr. Justin Tanis, a transgender FTM (female to male) has said it well, "Scriptures tell us that God was intimately and actively involved in our creation; Psalm 139 says that before we were formed in other mother's wombs, God knew us. God set the stars in orbit and evolution in motion and we are a part of that same creative process."[5] Along with Rev. Dr. Tanis, the transgender person is created to be a cocreator with God in the ongoing process of creation, the creation of oneself into being fully human and fully alive.

Many times in our daily lives as we try to discover who we are and what we need to be, we struggle with the concept of the God who calls us to be ourselves. "We often find that we are more concerned with being 'right' and appearing to have it all together than being faithful to God's holy calling to live our lives with as much integrity as we can muster."[6] Unfortunately, with the constraints of society, culture, faith, and family we tend to shy away from these true callings.

For the transgender person it is often even more of a challenge. Virginia Ramey Mollenkott has found that:

> As gender variant people we have also been and continue to be the unwilling, undeserving targets of a pervasive lack of social and spiritual integrity. That is why we must do all we can to move the gender-variant persons out of the category of "victim" into that of "survivor" and even "thriver."[7]

Society must cease its targeting and seeking out, or in some cases, ignoring the transgender person. The transgender person has an inevitable right to live life as a recognized and valued member of society. It is the call of the clergy to walk beside the transgender person and empower him or her as he or she claims his or her right to stand in society free, open, and proud.

It is through knowing myself, my community, and the people I serve that I am allowed to enter into this relationship honestly and openly. In the *Dictionary of Pastoral Care* in the section on "Philosophy of Self," it boldly states; "It is also essential in all personal relations to be deeply sensitive to the genuine inner existence of the one another."[8] This can be true on a community level, because it is essential to be really sensitive to the inner existence of the transgender community. This inner existence leads to the exploration of the definition and what it means to be transgender.

TRANSGENDERED CONTEXT

Before discussing what it means to work with a transgender youth group or how this particular group functions, we must first explore some general concepts. First, what does one mean when one speaks of transgender? Some think of Rocky Horror picture show immediately. Others may think of the hooker they just saw murdered on some television show that turned out to be a man in woman's clothes. A more recent concept is the middle-aged man, who discovers that he is truly a woman inside, disappears for months, only to return to his family as a woman and creates all sorts of social turmoil.

These altered images are extreme and very, very stereotyped Hollywood productions. The fact is we all live in one or the other state of transgender. A short but precise definition is: "transgender" is an umbrella term to include those who contravene the commonly accepted definitions of gender, all or part of the time, often shortened to "Trans."[9] In other words, it goes from the cross-dressing female who likes to dress as a man on Friday night for sexual pleasure to the person who chooses to live completely as the opposite sex they were born with and to the person who was born intersexed and allowed to make the choice of who they are later in life. It is interesting to note here that these are the definitions established by and used by the LGBTQI community:

> The term Transgender from within the community, according to Leslie Feinberg, has at least two colloquial meanings. It has been used as an umbrella term to include everyone who challenges the boundaries of sex and gender. It has also been used to draw a distinction between those who reassign the sex they were labeled with at birth, and those of us whose gender expression is considered inappropriate for our sex.[10]

This would cover anyone from a man who likes to wear a dress, to a drag queen, to a person who has had sexual reassignment surgery.

When conducting a survey for her book, Leslie Feinberg asked people to identify themselves:

> Those polled named: transsexuals, transgenders, transvestites, transgenderists, bi-genders, drag queens, drag kings, cross-dressers, masculine women, feminine men, intersexuals, androgynies, cross-genders, shape-shifters, passing women, passing men, gender-benders, gender-blenders, bearded woman, and women body builders who have crossed the line of what is considered socially acceptable for a female body.[11]

With such a wide range of possible self-identifying terms and such a broad spectrum of self-expression, I will propose that no definition is wrong, that all of the above and many more than we can imagine fall under the category of transgender. It is an expression that manifests from the interior and is expressed on the exterior. It may be expressed every day and then it becomes a way of living, and/or, perhaps, surviving in this world.

It is important to know that no matter what one calls themselves in this rainbow of possibilities; one still exists at a margin. This margin has the tendency to be recognized as an extreme part of society that people do not understand, nor do they care to confront. "Gender is expressed differently in diverse nationalities, cultures, regions and classes."[12] The fact that it is marginalized to the dark corners of society must come to an end.

Sometimes, when one speaks of a transgender person, images of the American Indian belief in the Two Spirited person arise. The concept of the Two Spirited did not exist among all the tribes. The tribes it did survive in describe it as Spirit.

> Spirit gives to each of us Visions of who we are, which must be manifest in the material world to the best of our ability. Transgender people, combining elements of male and female, are interstice of the material and the spiritual worlds and thus able to act as mediators for the benefit of the communities.[13]

The transperson is to be honored and respected not only as a mediator between the world of men and women but also of the physical and the spiritual.

A little more than 30 years ago "the American Psychological Association (APA) removed Gay, Lesbian, and Bisexual from the list of mental illness."[14] Originally, the diagnosis stated this as an illness coming from a blending of religion and medicine, but as medical knowledge and researched increased, so did the realization that being gay was not a disease. "Unfortunately, transgender people were not included when the APA made its changes, and 'Gender identity Disorder' is still listed in the *Diagnostic and Statistical Manual* (DSM-IV), which is the handbook used most often in diagnosing mental disorders."[15] Hopefully with continued research and more medical support this too will go the way of the gay and lesbian diagnosis.

Dr. Randi Ettner, who specializes in gender issues, believes that there is a biological basis for some transgender people. She believes "that gender dysphoria may have a biological basis . . . the body develops in opposition to the brain, and the person may be born with a feminized brain in a male body, (or a masculinized brain in a female body)."[16] The body and the brain do not match.

Whether it is physical or mental, a drag queen, or a transmale, does not matter to me, for as a spiritual caregiver I am called to work with and walk with all of God's people. Yet to be working with adults who can fight their own battles and stand up for themselves as opposed to be working with young people who are still trying to map their way can make a world of difference. What does it mean to be a transgender youth in the world? What goes through the minds of the young people as they discover who they are and/or who they might become?

The first thing one hears on a television show or in the movies when a mother has just given birth is the cry of a new born child and the question: is it a boy or a girl? There is a great answer to that one going around: "We don't know; it hasn't told us yet."[17] If only every doctor and parent lived in this ambiguity for, then the self-loathing and/or stigmata of any sexual identity or gender role would not be placed upon any child.

There are social expectations placed upon us from the moment of birth. From the minute we are born our parents start to place their dreams and society's hopes upon us. Sexual orientations and high school rituals have been laid out in film after film and family upon family. However, this is not true for the LGBTQI youth. "Self-identification of sexual orientation likely takes longer for LGBTQI youth to resolve because of social stigma."[18] The fear of being different affects the lives of this population.

Young people of minorities, whether they are of racial or newly migrant, face an additional challenge. Whereas in a white middle-class school in a large city it may be viewed as acceptable or even trendy to be gay: "The minority youth face additional challenges. They must try to develop a strong LGBTQI identity and a strong ethnic identity in environments marred by homophobia and racism."[19] This may be a stronger oppression as it comes within family, culture, and church settings.

In the United States, society is just beginning to accept the lesbian and gay person as part of the society. The United States tends to be more tolerant than some other societies that tend to be more conservative. In the United States, "society is far from affirmative of lesbian and gay sexual orientations, it is relatively more tolerant than some ethnic/racial cultures in dealing with sexual minorities. Minority youth who strongly embrace traditional ethnic cultures that reject homosexuality may have difficulties developing a positive lesbian or gay identity."[20] This is only compounded when one adds transgender, as this group tends to be outcast from within the GLB community let alone outside in ethnically influenced cultures.

TRANSGENDER YOUTH

Transgender youth find that they are excluded more drastically than the average GLB youth. "Transgender youth may find even less acceptance in the world than lesbian, gay, and bisexual teenagers. Severely gender-atyp-ical adolescent boys, for instance, have been observed to experience an abnormal amount of depression and social conflict resulting from peer rejection, isolation, and ridicule of their feminine behavior."[21] The trans-gender young person is at a higher risk for exclusion and depression when inclusion and feeling good about oneself is most critical.

In a study conducted in New York City, "youth indicated that they were on the average, 10.4 years old (range 6 to 15) when they first became aware that their gender identity or gender expression did not correspond to their biological sex."[22] As this realization came about so did the under-standing that that other people perceived this as well. It is interesting that of the youth studied one quarter reported "that they knew of relatives who also were transgender."[23] However, the study never stated if these were role models or of any help in their identity development.

In looking back over their lives the young transgender person can see signs or clues that they might be different from an early age. "As one youth (M to F) said, 'I used to play baseball and hangout with the boys, but I always felt like a girl.'"[24] Although the young person went through the motions and put on an exterior front, the inner voice was already stat-ing something is different.

Another youth relayed a story of longing, "I knew that I was biologi-cally a girl, but ever since I was little, I always wanted to be a man so bad. Other people said I want to be a lawyer, a doctor, and I said I want to be a man."[25] This type of innocent statement by a child whose longing is openly stated can lead to a series of negative reactions.

These reactions can vary from a simple questioning of what their gender identity is because they may appear rather androgynous to actual physical harm from family members. One youth relays the story, "When my mother, who is a PhD, found out what I was (i.e., transgender), she used to hurt me with things. She hit me on the head with an iron once, and I have five sta-ples. Finally, she disowned me."[26] This story is terrible in as far as the physi-cal abuse but, worse yet, it finally resulted in a young person being homeless.

Homeless youth face another series of problems. If they try to go to a young people's shelter the staff is often unaware of or not prepared to deal with a transgender person. When contacting shelters on their policy con-sidering transgender youth Vivian K. Namaste found that most claimed to be free from oppression. She was told that people are "'asked to keep their prejudices to themselves,' and that, 'discrimination is not tolerated here.'"[27] Yet when pressed these institutions had no particular policy re-garding transgender youth.

Often what happens in youth shelters is further abuse. The shelter only has a binary system of housing. They only have a men's side and a women's side there is no place for a third gender person to stay. One staff member even admitted that "youth with gender issues might not feel that this is a safe place for them . . . [with regard to] how the other men would act."[28] Most shelters are not prepared nor have any experience in dealing with gender issues.

Once a youth finds a shelter that might allow them in they are then subject to subtle if not blatant abuses. "Staff demand strict adherence to their idea of masculinity and/or femininity . . . 'No makeup, no nothing . . . try to dress as masculine as you can.'"[29] In other words once a youth leaves home they are often subject to the same abuses out in the world.

Should a young transgender person find safety at home, or learn to survive the home environment, the next place they have to face is the school environment. The young transgender person's fear and insecurity is often compounded by the school they attend. Teachers and administration may never have encountered a transgender person until one comes out at their institution. "'Our society hasn't even begun to deal with transgender issues,' Says Michael Ferrera, clinical director of group homes for the Los-Angeles-based Gay and Lesbian Adolescent Social Services."[30] There are only a handful of schools even dealing with this issue in the United States.

The experiences of transgender youth in the school system become almost universal as one hears story after story:

Joe Saladimini, a teacher in the Out Adolescents Staying in Schools (OASIS) program in Los Angeles, gave us a similar account of teachers humiliating a seventh grader who later identified as Transgender. "One called her a faggot and told her she wouldn't have any problems if she only acted like a boy. The teacher would embarrass her in front of all of the kids and call her sissy," he reported adding that at least one other teacher in the students school was "very helpful."[31]

When a student is in school they depend upon their faculty and administration to protect them. It is unspoken and school is assumed to be a safe place. When a student hears these epitaphs and attacks from fellow students it is one thing; when they hear taunts from trusted adults it just adds one more level of despair. Blossom R., who grew up in a rural part of the country relays just such a story to Human Rights Watch:

I stopped talking in fifth grade. Just quit participating. I sat alone at lunch. I had absolutely no friends. My grades were bad and I was told my conduct was unacceptable. I felt completely ostracized. I heard the word "fag" every single day. Kids used it as a weapon, but I didn't care.[32]

The youth in a study in New York spoke of verbal and physical assaults by classmates and sometimes faculty. "The kids would say, 'That's just the faggot of the school.' I was the towns faggot and they would taunt me."[33] Kids can be cruel to other children but this often goes beyond that. "When I was in gym with another feminine boy and I had my pen in my mouth, there was this teacher; and he asked me if I wanted something else in my mouth."[34] This gives a young person the feeling that no place is safe. Often the young transgender person learns what one must do just to survive and get through it.

These types of experiences for the transgender youth can start at any point in the school career. L. Mauer relays her own story of being a "Tom-Boy" and a straight A student until fifth grade. First her teacher thought she was in the wrong class for she assumed her to be a boy. Then the teacher started clandestinely lowering her grades and basing it upon poor penmanship. Feeling this can't be right, L. Mauer tries an experiment.

> This was crazy! But I had to see if it was true. I swallowed my pride—and a few tears—and in a flower-print polyester jumper and peter pan—collared blouse, both borrowed from my mother's closet (at barely eleven years old, I was already her height and size, I hoped to go on to become a professional basketball player someday . . . but that's another story), I reported for penmanship tutoring.[35]

As L. Mauer tells her story as she added more feminine clothing, her responsibilities and grades went up congruently. She explains how she had to subdue her natural self to please an abusive teacher who understood that the lines between boys and girls was well established and roles must be played in order to succeed in this world. In the end "Mrs. Kay apparently satisfied that my gender reeducation had been completed awarded me an A in penmanship."[36] The gender variant youth of L. Mauer's childhood learned a hard lesson that no child needs to learn. To conform to traditional gender roles is the only way to succeed in life.

For the young transgender person, there seems to be a layer of vulnerability that is constant; "the absence or lack of safe environments, lack of access to health services, few resources for their mental health concerns, and a lack of continuity of care giving by their families and communities."[37] With so much missing in the young person life, they live in a constant fear. One youth stated it best; "I have no comfort or safety zones, and that puts me at risk for suicide."[38] The hatred and violence seems to escalate more as the youth is looked upon as possible sexual prey or worse yet merely an object to be used.

The stories I have heard from the Transgender Harm Reduction Program at Children's Hospital Los Angeles are not much different. The participants are young people from a very different social status than my own. Most are underprivileged youth who upon disclosing their sexuality and gender identities were kicked out of their homes or were already in the foster care system. Some have been victims of violence in school and/or on the street. "When People cross those dividing lines or obliterate them entirely, a great deal of fear and hatred can be unleashed upon them."[39] In some cases these youth have been victims of rape and in other cases some have chosen to fight back. Therefore, some have parole officers; some choose to live "the life" (Hooking), while others are working to get their degrees and are trying to find main stream jobs.

The young people in the group are mostly Latino or African American ranging from age 12 to 24, technically though most I have seen are from the ages 18 to 23. Most of the people identify as male-to-female transgender yet there have been one or two female-to-male transgender that have participated from time to time. Most of these young people have a history of sexual abuse, drug abuse, and have practiced survival sex at one time or another. Survival sex is a sexual act carried out for money, food, or shelter. It is a sexual act used strictly for trade as opposed for pleasure or for love.

These young people are struggling with their own sexual identity in the midst of adolescence. They are dealing with judgments placed upon them by their family, social context, and religious institutions. They have come with questions about their belief systems or what they have heard from their own pastors.

Trina[40] came seeking understanding. She was pulled aside by the pastor of her church, and told that she "had one week to start dressing as a boy or get out." Here is a young person, who all her life went to church. Her family and neighbors all participate in this community. She is now told by the authority figure, the leader, that she must live a lie or get out.

Another young person relays the story of an angry father. Shay tells how he entered the gangs seeking safety after his father beat him and raped him while screaming, "I'll show you how to be a woman, bitch!" When he tried to tell someone at school, no one would listen. Shay has stated that he no longer can trust anybody; that they will just use or hurt him. He feels he is better off alone, just taking care of himself.

One of the reasons that this topic is so important is that the research seems minimal. "The research on gay and lesbian persons is slim; the research on transgender persons is almost non-existent."[41] Although there are many personal stories, the empirical research is hard to find. It is often through the personal stories that theories and practical models of care have come about.

Through the stories that have been collected and reviewed, four themes seem to emerge: "(1) a long history of tension between the person's biological sex and his or her preferred gender, (2) an awareness and experience of being different as a child, (3) a current internal struggle to reconcile the conflict between psychosexual identity and biological sex, (4) the need for continued coping with the negative social responses to the disclosure of these feelings."[42] All of these experiences have often culminated in substance abuse or attempts at suicide.

The tension that exists in a transgender young person comes about externally and internally. "They realize that nondisclosure of their gender and sexual identities hide their self hood and uniqueness; however, the negative reactions they receive on disclosure will often have severe negative effect on their self-esteem."[43] This creates an inner tension as well as an exterior tension. This often can lead to youth acting out in school or home situations. One way this manifests itself is in suicide attempts.

Suicide among the LGBT community is higher than the average. "Lesbian, gay, bisexual, transgender and questioning youth are up to four times more likely to attempt suicide than their heterosexual peers (Massachusetts 2006 Youth Risk Survey)."[44] For the youth who come from families that reject them the risk is even greater. "Lesbian, gay, bisexual, transgender and questioning youth who come from a rejecting family are up to nine times more likely to attempt suicide than their heterosexual peers (2007 San Francisco State University Chavez Center Institute)."[45] Because of this suicide rate there is a need for extreme diligence on the part of the caregiver.

The warning signs to watch for are a tendency toward isolation and social withdrawal and increase in substance abuse. The young person may express self-hatred and feelings of hopelessness. One may start to display a lack of interest in their everyday activities and start to give away their valued possessions to friends. If one has been depressed for a long period of time they may seem to come out of it as they have a clear plan in their mind.[46]

The social aspects that manifest in a young transgender person may be conflicts at home. These abuses that occur can affect the feelings of non-worth or feed the concept of internalizing the hatred. One youth described their experience; "throughout my whole life, I was abused physically and mentally by relatives in my family. I have marks on my body. I have things I remember happened to me."[47] This type of experience often leads the youth to leave their homes and strike out on their own to face life on the streets.

Part of the life on the street is the substance abuse problem. The substance abuse problem in the transgender community is not limited to strictly recreational drugs but socially enhancing drugs; by this I mean hormone abuse. "Many, who have used hormones to develop desired female or male secondary sex characteristics, have obtained these hormones on the street, fearing negative reactions from health care providers."[48] This leads to misused amounts of hormones and/or shared needles. The misuse of hormones can lead to health problems down the road such as heart diseases. The use of shared needles can lead to infections, hepatitis, and/or exposure to HIV.

MODELS OF COMING OUT

From the stories and experiences reflected it can be easy to assume that the transgender person leads a very hard life full of risk, hatred, and abuse. Yet it is essential that the world becomes aware of the needs of a transgender person and all that they could possibly go through in order to provide the best and safest care.

> Transgender people often live in a confusing and painful internal world where their perceived sense of self is at dissonance with the societal norms surrounding them. They have learned to hide not only from others but also from themselves. This process of developing an authentic self for transgender people means they must move through an experience of emergence— of realizing, discovering, identifying, or naming their gender identities.[49]

The experience Arlene Lev describes above is the experience of coming out. The experience of coming out is highly individual for each person and yet there are some commonalities one can look for and perhaps even help with, as we walk with a transgender person as spiritual caregivers. Coming out is a term that is often applied to the gay and lesbian experience of acknowledging publicly who they are. "Coming out is a useful concept only within a society that defines and prescribes a normative direction for sexual desire, i.e., people could not come out as gay unless everyone is assumed to be straight."[50] The assumption is the problem here.

In the same way society assumes that everyone can identify with the gender their bodies are presenting. This is not the case with the transgender person and thus there is a process of coming into one's identified gender. To help understand what a transgender person goes through in their own "coming out process," Arlene Lev believes it is helpful to understand the process of coming out gay and/or lesbian.

A person who decides to come out must move through several stages. There have been numerous studies that have set up their own models. "The models describe the process of internalizing a positive self-image of an identity that is socially stigmatized."[51] Although the researchers have assigned different names and one, more or less, stage they all agree that there are stages one must move through during the coming out process. One does not move through these stages in any particular order nor does one stay in a certain stage for any particular amount of time.

Lesbian and Gay Identity Formation[52]

Cass (1979)	Coleman (1982)	Sophie (1985/86)	Hanley-Hacken-bruck (1988)	Troiden (1993)
Identity inclusion	Pre-coming out	First awareness	Prohibition	Sensitization
Identity comparison	Coming out	Testing and exploration	Ambivalence/ practicing or compulsion/ exploration	Identity confusion
Identity tolerance	exploration	Identity acceptance	Consolidation/ integration	Identity assumption
Identity acceptance	First relationship	Identity integration		Commitment
Identity pride	Integration			
Identity Synthesis				

These models of coming out, it should be noted, are particular to a western culture and that "all human identities are impacted by the construction of particular cultural and social location."[53] It is also important to note that these models do not fully address the experiences of the bisexual community.

The reason for displaying these models is to give a slight understanding to the coming out process for gays and lesbians as well as to show that "there are some similarities in coming out homosexual or bisexual and emerging transgender and transsexual people."[54] The first of these is coming to terms with the fact that one is outside the social norm and have been taught to despise that part of the self.

Not all transgender people choose to transition from male to female or female to male; all do "move through a psychological, sociological, and perhaps a spiritual process of coming to terms with their variant gender identity."[55] It is said that to transition is "a rite of passage akin to traditional tribal rituals that formalized the movement from one stage or status to another."[56] This process includes claiming the term as transgender for oneself then experiencing oneself as the gender one wants to live in and then finally, for some, transitioning.

Arlene Lev identifies six stages of development for transgender emergence. Emergence is influenced by many things such as; "The place of residence and the values of society and culture a person is born into (e.g., urban versus rural, North American versus Middle Eastern)."[57] Other influences are class, race, and religion, anything that affects the world in which one lives and/or the world that one perceives influences the way a person will move through the stages of emergence.

The first stage is awareness which often occurs from an early age. "One mother described being in a supermarket with her three-year-old son, when someone stopped them and said, 'What a sweet little girl.' When she tried to correct the person her son said. "No, Mama, you know I am really a girl."[58] Stories like this one, stories in this chapter, and hundreds of more untold stories exist. The transgender person knows there is something different inside them.

The second stage is seeking information or reaching out. In this stage the transgender person has named what they are. I am transgender. "This stage involves not just to oneself, but coming out to other people."[59] This is when the person starts to seek out support groups or places where other transgender people may gather. This is not coming out to family and friends but like-minded supportive people.

The third stage is disclosure to significant others. This is the stage when one starts to open up to loved ones and close friends. For the young transgender person this is often when the trouble really starts in their lives for in disclosing they have opened themselves up to disappointment, and perhaps, even danger. The family and friends have to go through their own stages of acceptance and often times they are not in the same place as the transgender person.

The fourth stage is exploring identity and transition. In this stage "transgender people begin to explore the meaning of their transgenderism and search for a label or identity that best explains who they are."[60] This is a label for oneself not a label that is used to explain who they are to others. This includes the development of the transgender personality, be it Lovely or Mike, there is a lot that goes into choosing one's name. This stage involves investigating possibilities of how far one may choose to go in their own transgender body, be it full operation, implants, or just dressing and living a certain way.

The fifth stage is exploring transition and possible body modification. This is the stage where the final decisions are made. One decides just how many surgeries one needs to be one's true gender identified self. This involves deciding whether to use hormones or not, deciding on implants, and whether to have full transitional surgery.

There was once a time when a transgender person had to choose between full operation or not. This is no longer the case; some transgender people "take pride in being between genders. They enjoy switching back and forth."[61] Some transgender people see finance as a roadblock and choose to compromise who they are called to be. Some may want to preserve certain aspects of their physicality for a slew of reasons. As there are colors of the rainbow so are the different levels at which one can live as transgender.

The final stage is integration and pride. In this stage, the transgender person is no longer struggling with his or her identity. They have incorporated who they are into their daily lives and successfully live as they have chosen. Again this stage is unique for each and every person. "Some may choose to live 'stealthily' and others choose to be more 'out' about their history or current transgender status."[62] The point being is that the life of the transgender person is the life they have chosen and are now fully comfortable living the way they choose.

The final part I want to address in the research deals particularly with the transgender youth. In spite of the stories, the hindsight and the probability of one who believes them to be transgender, the medical professional is very hesitant to address the transgender youth. "The chance of making the wrong diagnosis and the consequent risk of postoperative regret,"[63] makes one hesitant to work with young adults.

The problem comes in when one places a gender-variant youth on hold till adulthood they get a feeling of stuck by the system. This can create another set of issues or compound the ones that already exist. As has been pointed out in this paper; "youth dealing with sexual and gender identity struggles have higher suicidality, homelessness, depression, acting out, and substance abuse issues."[64] This can be avoided through proper education of both the health profession and the families of the young person.

The family and the education system can be educated to support the youth in their road to gender identity. There is a story of Maxine who was on a transgender trajectory in her development. "When it was recommended that Maxine began living full-time as a female, her family, school officials, and a handful of clinical experts breathed a near audible sigh of relief."[65] Although the officials were not quite sure where to begin, Maxine took her life in her hands and led the way by modifying her hair, clothes, and nails and informing everyone she knew of the proper pronouns to use when around her.

Medically speaking there is a medication now that can stop puberty in its tracks. These are called LHRH (luteinizing hormone-releasing hormone) agonists. "Treatment with LHRH agonists buys time . . . [and] can be used when there are clear signs of sexual maturation to delay pubertal development until an age that a balanced and responsible decision can be made."[66] Should a person change their mind, they decide they are not gender variant, the medication can be stopped. Puberty resumes and even catches up quite fast.

TRANSGENDER HARM REDUCTION

So what is recommended to help reduce the risks that transgender youth face? First, transgender expression must be accepted and treated as normal. This can only be done through education and will take time. Second, we who provide care must take on the responsibilities of being advocates. Third, resources must be made available to young people to provide them with proper care and attention that is needed to create healthy transitions. Finally, programs should be created to assist the families and communities in creating safe environments for young people to come out as transgender. There needs to be in place a way to help youth create a plan, much like an individual education plan, but in this case it would be an individual transition plan so that we can take the steps to logically and thoughtfully help the young person achieve their own unique identity. Wouldn't that be helpful to all young people?

While working with the Transgender Harm Reduction Drop-in Group at Children's Hospital Los Angeles, I was presented with George Fitchett's *Assessing Spiritual Needs*. I thought it would be interesting to bring forth the points of the 7 by 7 model of assessing spiritual needs and discuss what they look like within this particular community.

The first dimension in this model is that of the medical dimension. The concern here is to see if there is something medical happening that has impact on the spiritual functioning of the person. What we are looking to see is if "what is happening in the person's life at this level is having an impact on his or her spiritual well being"[67] Fitchett has stated that he believes that this aspect is obvious and that stands true for this group. This group is formed around the aspect that these youth are considering the possibility that they are transgender and they are exploring what that means in their daily lives and what it may hold for their future.

They are learning what it means to express themselves as the person they are called to be from the inside, which may not necessarily be the appearance on the outside. So here are young people who believe they may be the opposite sex than what they present to the world and thus choose to present as the sex they are called to be. This all happens even before they start on a medical treatment of any kind.

These revelations and processes of becoming who they are lead to the next three holistic dimensions: the psychological, psychosocial, and the family systems dimensions. Most of these young people are going through some sort of psychiatric care. It is a requirement for the transition to occur.

Yet their lives are disrupted on a much deeper level. Because of the cultures through which many come they have been rejected or kicked out of their homes by their families. They have had to create and find ways of surviving in the world. Through this many have ended up in the parole system and that is how they have found their way to the program.

Others have ended up in GLASS housing; Gay and Lesbian Adolescent Social Services (GLASS) is a private, nonprofit 501(c)(3) social service agency dedicated to providing a wide range of social and health care services to children and youth who are in foster care, on probation, or who are homeless. We provide these services in safe, loving, supportive, nonjudgmental living environments, while providing full access to all of the educational and vocational opportunities to which these youth are entitled.[68]

These are not the privileged youth with understanding parents who are willing to do whatever it takes to make their son or daughter get the medical care they need. These are kids, for the most part, who are scraping by on their own wits and street smarts.

From the fact that many of these kids come from the streets one must consider other medical aspects, such as HIV education and risk factors. Have they now, or are they considering street work as a viable way of earning an income? If so, their HIV status and how they live and/or work with their understanding must be taken into consideration. Also have they tried getting hormone treatments in other ways?

Often times before these young people make it into our clinics they have been running with a crowd already. They may have had opportunity to get hormones on the street and may have taken opportunity to do so. This brings needle sharing and all the problems of that to the foreground.

This is just the first dimension of the 7 by 7 model and yet already just by bringing in the medical I have also brought into it psychosocial considerations as well as psychological considerations which are riding right alongside family systems. All who participate in this program are required to have a social worker or case manager, physician, and a psychological work up as well as continued psychological group and one-on-one counseling.

Family systems . . . I wanted to look at family systems here in a brief overview as well. It is interesting to consider the many different family systems I can name in this group as it exists today. From supportive to exclusion, from abusive to loving, they all exist in this small group just as they exist throughout the world.

We have one young lady (again note that when I refer to the sex of a person I am referring to the sex they are presenting), who comes to the meetings with her mother and her sister. They drive in all the way from Riverside, 52 miles one way. Her mother is mostly Spanish-speaking while the siblings both speak English fluently. This appears to be a family struggling with being supportive. The older sister (not the one in the program) seems to be the one of major support for her younger sister while mother seems a bit wide-eyed and outright dismayed by what she has seen. A lot of time was spent in comforting mother and making her feel as welcome as possible.

Another young man speaks of being a rape survivor, living in foster care, having gang affiliations which he is trying to break and being on parole. His experience of family is one of distrust, fear, anger, and abandonment. He relayed to me the story of an alcoholic father who raped him as a young girl so he turned to the gang as a means of survival. Now he is in foster care doing what he needs to do to get an education, stay out of trouble, and live his life.

The next level in the 7 by 7 model speaks of ethnic and cultural dimensions. "Our racial and ethnic backgrounds have a strong influence on our behavior."[69] This plays out strongly in the diversity of experiences and backgrounds of our youth. The majority of our clientele are either of

African American or Latino descent. Yet it is not that cultural dynamic I want to address today. What does need to be addressed is the house or ball culture. This is the culture made famous in the 1990s' documentary of "Paris is Burning."

Houses become alternative kinship networks that selected a Mother and Father as their leaders (parents can be of any gender) and children as their general membership body. The houses are a literal recreation of homes, in the sense that these groups become real-life families for individuals that might have been exiled from their birth homes. However, contrary to popular belief, many house kids are still deeply connected to their biological families but still seek the unique protection, care, and love the street houses provided.

> In attempt to make sense of this growing array of gender performance, ball kids adopted a complicated language system that accounted for the different types of identities they noticed in the community: "Butch Queens" was a term used to describe any biologically born male that presented himself off as male, "Butch Queens Up in Drag" on the other hand came to signify gay men who dressed in drag specifically for the balls, but still lived his everyday life as a man. "Femme Queens" were pre-operative male to female transsexuals, often known for their alluring beauty and uncanny "realness." "Butches" was a term used to describe either aggressive lesbian women or female-to-male transsexuals. The term "woman" was only reserved for either heterosexual, biologically born women or feminine lesbians that did not identify with the "Butch" title. Finally "trade" was meant to describe men whose sexuality might have been in question even if their masculinity was not. This language system for describing gender in the house-ball scene exists to this day.[70]

By this description we have families of choice that are serving through an ethnically generated medium. Just as gender lines are getting blurred so are systemic lines of culture, ethnicity, and family.

The final level on the holistic side Fitchett's 7 by 7 model addresses the societal issue. He says, "it is a way of checking to see if any of the person's distress is being caused by or compounded by dysfunctioning and oppressive social and cultural systems."[71] Anyone who lives with anything that can be categorized as outside the norm or as marginalized, I would venture to say can answer this with a definitive yes!

The fact that most of society does not accept this or understand this as a normal part of society compounds the experience of these youths discovering and claiming who they are. To be transgender is to be on the margin of the marginalized. There are very few societies where this is looked upon as a normal or accepted part of everyday life, even in the LGBT community they are often looked upon as outcasts.

The next part of Fitchett's 7 by 7 model is the spiritual dimension. This he divides up into several units itself. The first aspect addressed is belief and meaning. As within any group at the Children's Hospital, drop-in group youth have a variety of beliefs from "God made me this way" to "I am a freak" to "I do not believe in God." All I can do is be present with them and listen to their stories. The stories, as I have demonstrated are wide and varied and each and everyone is unique. One young lady has stated that she believes she is made this way and it is natural and yet to be gay is unnatural. Another person has stated that she has found a wonderful community that is supportive of her at Unity Church.

Fitchett believes that "attending to what people say about what gives their lives meaning, however, is not always the best way to find out how they handle religious meaning."[72] No one has to consider what is giving importance in their lives by observing their actions. Take interest in their lives. Learn where they have gone, what they are doing, and who they are doing it with. This will also help to create a stronger sense of familiarity and allow me to slowly achieve more access into their lives and their needs.

The next aspect focuses on vocation and consequences. This is an interesting aspect in this group for these are mostly adolescents still in high school finding their way in the world. Some are turning 18 and realizing they are facing the world and are not quite ready yet. We have seen issues of foster care when the person turns 18 it is "okay we are done you have to move out." We also work with finding viable ways to get the proper education so that these youths can become whoever they choose and help them to see there are many choices before them not just the old standards of working the streets.

The third aspect of experience and emotion, for this group, would translate as experiencing life as the gender they feel they are, the emotions of being accepted by their peers and, for some, their family. It becomes about actually deciding who and how they will be in society and what comes with that experience and all the emotions of just being a teenager compounded upon that.

Some of these experiences may be directly related to religion and faith. An example is the previously mentioned member of the group who relayed the story that her pastor gave her one week to stop dressing as herself and start acting like a boy or get out. Imagine all the emotional ties to that on so many levels, and it is more than simply choosing to leave one's own church. It is also an issue of self-worth. A Pastor, who is the representative of God's authority, has just told you that, as you are now, you are worthless in his sight and are therefore worthless in God's sight.

Fitchett has stated that he is still looking for the best way to make this aspect precise and he goes on to suggest words like "grateful, serene, joyful, stoic, timid, worthless, angry, guilty, and exhausted."[73] I believe a few of those words apply to the story above as well as other stories that have been related during our drop in group and throughout this chapter.

The next aspect is that of courage and growth. Here I say there is nothing but courage expressed with these young people. To stand up in the face of all that is considered normal and say I am different and I have a right to be and need to express that difference is amazing. To be willing to do the work that is required both physically and emotionally to walk in this society as a transgender person is just amazing to me.

The next aspect is that of rituals and practices. This refers to "any rituals or practices that give expression to a person's sense of meaning and purpose in life."[74] For the transgender person, this may be painting the face before one goes out. This may be the ritual of getting dressed before going to a ball perhaps. The ritual of learning what it means to express who you are from the inside so that it can manifest on the outside. This also incorporates learning how to protect oneself, where it is safe to be who one is and when it may not be, the discussion of proper disclosure techniques and if one should disclose or not and when.

In some churches, such as MCC, one may see a naming ritual. That is an actual ceremony to commemorate the day when the name on the driver's license matches that of the person we see. To be recognized legally as the gender that one has been manifesting is a huge event in a transgender person's life.

The next aspect is that of community. Here is where things overlap. We have the transgender community which moves in between the straight and the gay world. They may start in the gay world where they find more acceptance and later, post op, may be found in the straight world and can go on living a normal life. Yet because surgeries and things are so expensive most people in the transgender community spend time straddling both worlds not really identifying with one or the other. This is what makes groups like this one at Children's Hospital so important. It helps to nurture that sense of community.

The final aspect of the 7 by 7 model focuses on authority and guidance. This is where, for me; as a spiritual caregiver, I must examine myself. Am I given authority to work with this group? I can safely say that basically I do. I have relayed who I am, what I know, and my understanding of the transgender community. To which the reply came "Oh you get us, you're okay." That is my license, whether I am considered valuable as a chaplain or not as long as I have a sense of understanding, I am welcome. What impact my role as a spiritual caregiver has may never be seen by me.

Fitchett also mentions part of this aspect as considering whether or not the person has autonomy or their own authority to get by in life. I would be brave enough to say that since they are coming to this group, they are on their way. One of the greatest challenges to any of us is finding the resources that will help us grow into the adults we hope we will, I mean, have become. Imagine how much more work these young people have already done just to find their way here to Children's Hospital and to find a support program that truly cares.

COMPASSIONATE CARE FOR TRANSGENDER YOUTH

The transgender youth have a long and hard road ahead and as a spiritual caregiver it is our call to help make that road run a little smoother. We are here to comfort, walk with, and be a witness to their process. We stand as witnesses to the good days and the bad days. We stand as people of authority pronouncing that God, the God of our understanding, loves you and is with you.

We can be roadblocks to those who would dare to challenge the person's right to be who they are called to be. We can be mediators in the families who desperately want to love and understand their child. We can bring a gift of education, compassion, forgiveness, and wholeness to that which was misconceived to be broken. We can help the world to comprehend and love justly and rightly the gift that is the transgender person. As a pastoral caregiver that is the call we must choose to answer.

NOTES

1. Chris Glaser, *Coming Out As Sacrament* (Louisville, KY: Westminster John Knox Press, 1998) 73.

2. Ibid., 9.

3. Ibid., 10.

4. Mary A. Fukuyama, and Todd D. Sevig, *Integrating Spirituality into Multicultural Counseling*, Multicultural Aspects of Counseling Series (Thousand Oaks, CA: Sage Publications, 1999), 127.

5. Justin Tanis, *Trans-Gendered: Theology, Ministry, and Communities of Faith* (Cleveland: Pilgrim Press, 2003), 182.

6. Virginia Ramey Mollenkott and Vanessa Sheridan, *Transgender Journeys* (Cleveland: Pilgrim Press, 2003), 30.

7. Ibid., 30.

8. *Dictionary of Pastoral Care and Counseling*, ed. Rodney J. Hunter, expanded ed. (Nashville: Abingdon Press, 2005), 1126.

9. David Kundtz and Bernard Schlager, *Ministry Among God's Queer Folk: LGBT Pastoral Care*, The Center for Lesbian and Gay Studies in Religion and Ministry (Cleveland: Pilgrim Press, 2007), 13.

10. Leslie Feinberg, *Transgender Warriors: Making History* (Boston: Beacon Press, 1996), xi.

11. Ibid., xi.

12. Ibid., 115.

13. Leslie Feinberg, *Trans Liberation: Beyond Pink or Blue* (Boston: Beacon Press, 1998), 64.

14. Kundtz and Schlager, *Ministry Among God's Queer Folk*, 96.

15. Ibid., 96.

16. Randi Ettner, *Confessions of a Gender Defender: A Psychologist's Reflectionson Life Among The Transgendered* (Evanston, IL.: Chicago Spectrum Press, 1996), 25.

17. Kate Bornstein, *Gender Outlaw: On Men, Women, and the Rest of Us* (New York: Vintage Books, 1995), 46.

18. Patricia E. Stevens and Sarah Morgan, "Health of Lesbian, Gay, Bisexual, and Transgender Youth," *Journal of Pediatric Health Care* 15, no. 1 (2001): 25.

19. Ibid., 25.

20. Ibid., 25.

21. Ibid., 26.

22. Arnold H. Grossman and Anthony R. D'Augelli, "Transgender Youth: Invisible and Vulnerable," *Journal of Homosexuality* 51, no. 1 (2006): 121.

23. Ibid.

24. Ibid.

25. Ibid.

26. Ibid., 125.

27. Viviane K. Namaste, *Invisible Lives: The Erasure of Transsexual and Transgendered People* (Chicago: University of Chicago Press, 2000), 174.

28. Ibid., 175.

29. Ibid., 176.

30. *Hatred in the Hallways: Violence and Discrimination Against Lesbian, Gay, Bisexual, and Transgender Students in U.S. Schools* (New York: Human Rights Watch, 2001), 60.

31. Ibid., 61.

32. Ibid., 62.

33. Grossman and D'Augelli, "Transgender Youth," 123.

34. Ibid.

35. Joan Nestle, Clare Howell, and Riki Wilchens, eds., *GenderQueer: Voices From Beyond The Sexual Binary* (Los Angeles: Alyson Books, 2002), 198.

36. Ibid., 201.

37. Grossman and D'Augelli, "Transgender Youth," 123.

38. Ibid., 123.

39. Tanis, *Trans-Gendered*, 10.

40. I should note I always use the gender to which the person identifies, other than that all identifying information is omitted.

41. Grossman and D'Augelli, "Transgender Youth," 114.

42. Ibid.

43. Ibid., 124.

44. "Suicidal Signs," 2007, The Trevor Project, http://www.thetrevorproject.org/info.aspx (accessed March 14, 2009).

45. Ibid.

46. Ibid.

47. Grossman and D'Augelli, "Transgender Youth," 124.

48. Ibid., 114.

49. Arlene Istar Lev, *Transgender Emergence: Therapeutic Guidelines for Working With Gender-Variant People and Their Families* (New York: The Haworth Clinical Practice Press, 2004), 229.

50. Ibid., 230.

51. Ibid.

52. Ibid.

53. Ibid.

54. Ibid., 232.

55. Ibid., 233.

56. Ibid., 232.

57. Ibid., 234.

58. Ibid., 235.

59. Ibid., 241.

60. Ibid., 254.

61. Ibid., 260.

62. Ibid.

63. Ibid., 341.

64. Ibid., 343.

65. Ibid., 348.

66. Ibid., 349.

67. George Fitchett, *Assessing Spiritual Needs: A Guide for Caregivers*, Guides to Pastoral Care Series (Minneapolis: Augsburg Fortress, 1993), 43.

68. Gay and Lesbian Adolescent Social Services, "GLASSLA.ORG," 2008, http://www.glassla.org (accessed January 3, 2007).

69. Fitchett, *Assessing Spiritual Needs*, 44.

70. Frank Leon Robert, "History of House Ball Culture," February 13, 2007, http://brooklynboyblues.blogspot.com/2007/02/history-of-house-ball-culture.html (accessed February 1, 2009).

71. Fitchett, *Assessing Spiritual Needs*, 44.

72. Ibid., 45.

73. Ibid., 48.

74. Ibid., 48.

15

Putting on Wedding Drag: Pastoral Care for Healing and Wholeness in the Queer Congregation

Joan M. Saniuk

PRELUDE: THE OPEN TABLE; OR, JESUS THROWS A POLISH WEDDING

> [The king] told his servants, "We have a wedding banquet all prepared but no guests. The ones I invited weren't up to it. Go out into the busiest intersections in town and invite anyone you find to the banquet."
> —Matthew 22.8–9 (The Message)

I have always imagined that the wedding banquet of Jesus' parable in Matthew 22.1–14 was like the Polish weddings of my childhood. A wedding in our family meant an afternoon and evening of partying, with a full buffet dinner, music, drinking, and dancing. The whole family is included; you wouldn't think of leaving the children or the older folks at home. Beer flows freely, as do stronger spirits. A cash bar was unthinkable at a Polish wedding!

Yes, a wedding celebration reinforces heterosexual norms. But when I think of a Polish wedding, what I remember most has nothing to do with pairing off males and females. I remember the joy of feeling at home with a very large number of people. Just for this day, everything is free; everyone has a good time; everyone is welcomed as family. The kin-dom of heaven, as I hear Jesus describe it, is like one big eternal Polish wedding. What's not to like about that?

There is one catch, though. You have to come in the right party clothes—or, to put it another way, you have to put on wedding drag. Why would you not? In Jesus' story, however, one guest inexplicably does not dress for the occasion and by doing so, insults the host.[1] Yes, the table is open; however, it is also expected that each guest will reciprocate the host's generosity by putting on an appropriately festive and generous attitude. The most important thing, you see, is that no matter how many guests come in, the table remains open to all comers. A thoughtful guest, then, will share in creating a party atmosphere.

Just as a wedding cannot be festive without every guest's participation, the Communion table and the doors of our churches remain open because of our congregations' commitment to welcome all who come. Metropolitan Community Churches (MCC) came to exist as a necessary refuge for people who have been hurt by religion. We have continued this ministry for more than 40 years, committed to demonstrating the Good News by showing radical hospitality. However, as those of us who have served congregations know well, our individual journeys of recovering faith and joy can be long and complicated. To use the image of Jesus' Polish wedding, some of us may not put on the wedding drag and that in turn affects the experience of the other guests.

Our pastoral experience has also taught us that a church that is made up of people who have been spiritually abused risks becoming a place in which hurt and angry people continue to hurt each other. If such a congregation is small, especially if it operates under a congregational polity, it will not be able to thrive under those conditions. I believe it is essential to our mission, then, that our leaders and congregations pay attention to the processes involved in healing from antiqueer hostility.[2]

In this chapter, I make the case that we must intentionally promote healing from the shame and traumatic stress of homophobia, transphobia, and other layers of oppression that we experience. I begin by reflecting briefly on the theology that underlies our practice of the open table. I next examine the psychological impact of an antiqueer dominant culture on queer individuals. I compare the behaviors and emotions that tend to result with those of a church that is recovering from trauma, and with the behaviors and emotions of a congregation that is thriving. In doing so, I problematize the spiritual and psychic hurts that queer folk sustain. I describe processes of recovering from these hurts and identify existing queered religious resources that can help in healing from spiritual violence. Finally, I propose queered pastoral and worship practices that I believe can help us in all the stages of healing, with particular attention to the most uncomfortable parts of our healing journeys.

A NOTE ON THEOLOGICAL METHOD

A useful queer theology begins by affirming the goodness of our lives and by acknowledging the truths of our lives as queer people, whether as individuals or in community. With this information in mind, we examine the Good News of Christ, who welcomes all to an open table, and reflect on the guidance that it gives for our situation. In the spirit of liberation theology, I assume that the Holy One is at work in our lives as a liberating influence as we, in turn, seek to offer a welcoming and joyful experience to others. In the spirit of queer theology, I understand that God or Goddess rejoices in the diversity of our varied, queerly embodied selves. It must then follow that if the Christ is the one in whom God or Goddess became and continues to be one of us, then Christ encompasses all of that same diversity.

The liberation theologians of the 1970s stressed the importance of orthopraxis or doing truth in addition to orthodoxy or teaching truth.[3] I love the way that MCC's theologies of Eucharist follow from our orthopraxis of the open table. Three theological implications of the open table are worth noting. First, the open table says that God's or Goddess's love is for everyone and that the church may not place barriers between people and the divine love that they seek. Second, in declining to engage questions of transubstantiation, consubstantiation, or memorial meal, it acknowledges that none of us completely understands the mystery of Holy Communion. Third, perhaps most importantly, the history of our Communion practices implies a theology of church that defines MCC by its mission.

This last point is worth examining more closely. The practice of Holy Communion MCC-style fundamentally arose out of pastoral need rather than theology. Because some of the first MCC'ers came from Eucharist-centered churches, it was important to offer Communion every week. Because some original members (including the founder) were accustomed to services that included an altar call, Communion came to include the laying on of hands. Because MCC sought to be a house of worship for people who had been thrown out of other houses, it was important that Communion be open to all. The practice of the open communion table can set an example for the rest of our worship activities: The intention and purpose of worship is to facilitate the worshiper's encounter with the Holy One *in whatever way the participant needs and understands it.*

Because MCC historically comes from the North American free-church Christian tradition, we have no common prayer book, but rather are united by our mission. MCC has already taken advantage of this freedom to construct the sacrament of Holy Communion in a way that responds to the needs of the people. I argue in the following that we can, and ought to, tailor the very structure of worship experiences to respond to our common pastoral needs. In focusing on the practices and theology of MCC, I do not mean to dismiss the abundant resources of other faith communities.

A NOTE ON QUEERING CHURCH AND THEOLOGY

I use the word queer, first of all, as an umbrella term for those of us whose gender performance, sexual orientation, or attitude toward the above differs from dominant social norms. I recognize that this usage masks significant differences in our experiences; however, I am most concerned with the common threads of our experiences. I ask the forbearance of the reader for whom queer carries echoes of past abuses.

To queer theologies is, in part, to cast visions of an unrealized eschaton. Queer theologies such as Marcella Althaus-Reid's "indecenting," Robert Goss's "expanding Christ's wardrobe of dresses," and Patrick S. Cheng's queered systematic theology parody and unmask, if not demolish, boundaries that are socially, economically, and religiously imposed around sexual orientation, sexual variety, and gender identity.[4] It is freeing to envision a world that is not constrained, for example, by the gender binary; in the four decades of our movement, MCC'ers have celebrated the spiritual and psychic liberation that flows from our queered gender performance. However, we live in an already or not-yet-queered world. It is countercultural to live in a way that defies gender classification. Even the most vanilla of us are boundary-crossers in a world system that is very much invested in gender and sexual norms. Living in this cultural border zone is not always easy on the psyche; the attendant stresses constitute a continuing pastoral care concern.

My purpose is to extend the implications of queer theology to the realm of pastoral care. I explore practical applications that can encourage us as we live into the not-yet kin-dom of the Holy One in which there is neither male nor female, insider or outsider, dispossessed or privileged, or even reason to think in those categories. In addition to discussing pastoral care responses, I make a case for queering church by breaking down a different type of boundary that between pastoral care and worship. Incorporating pastoral care concerns into our liturgies and celebrations reflects the truth that our healing and growth occur in community.

The practical applications are drawn from the insights of congregational studies, as well as those of psychology and queer spirituality. I begin by sketching the situation in which we live.

IN NO MOOD FOR PARTYING: ALL OF US, WHETHER OR NOT WE WANT TO ADMIT IT, HAVE BEEN WOUNDED

I Tried to Write A Letter
Lined yellow paper,
   flying off my desk
      one sheet after another,
          scribblings, crossouts,
CAPITALS SCREAMING!!!!!
Pages, crumpled and tossed,
   in the end, mute.

No words to say
   How deeply I was hurt.
Even after all these years.[5]

We are a richly diverse queer people. The common thread of our experiences is that we face some degree of oppression because of who we are and/or whom or how we love. Many if not most of us came to MCC after having been shunned or condemned in other spiritual communities. Some of us have experienced physical violence, some have lost jobs or families, and all of us live in a climate where antiqueer hostility is sometimes evident in public statements. In the United States, antiqueer attitudes are often exploited, even encouraged, for political gain. Whether we experience acute violence, or quotidian oppression, this ill treatment affects our body-selves.[6]

Every MCC pastor can spot a first-time churchgoer who is in the process of coming out. Descriptions of a first-time MCC visitor will not be found in the plethora of books on church development, but many leaders have ourselves been this visitor. He is the one who enters church after the service has started, sits in the back row, and leaves without speaking to anyone. Or, she is the one who sits near the front, knows all the hymns, and sings with unusual fervor. She may be the newcomer who will not leave a name or contact information, but stays in the sanctuary after the service, silently praying or weeping. This person is the reason we exist. Our continuing mission, perhaps even our primary mission, is to give refuge and healing to other queer people who are deeply hurt. We owe it to these seekers, and to ourselves, to reflect deeply on what seekers need— and, truth be told, what all of us still need in some way.

In *Coming Out Through Fire*, clergywoman and therapist Leanne McCall Tigert describes recurring themes in the reactions of her clients and other queer people in her life—as well as her own experiences—in the face of antiqueer hostility. She describes her observations in this way:

> [M]any gay/lesbian/bisexual/transgender persons experience symptoms and traits of survivors of trauma, especially sexual and/or physical trauma, whether or not they have even been physically or sexually abused. . . . [Each] of us is traumatized by some degree by the external and internalized homophobia and heterosexism in which we live, grow, and come to know ourselves socially, spiritually, and sexually.[7]

Following this observation, Tigert applies the theory of recovery from psychological trauma or traumatic stress as she describes how gay, lesbian, bi, and/or transgender individuals negotiate the coming-out process. Citing Judith Herman's definition of "psychological trauma" as an experience in which "the victim is rendered helpless by overwhelming force,"[8] Tigert argues that to the extent that we spend our daily lives dealing with threats or oppression against which we are helpless, each of us experiences some measure of trauma. No matter how safe we may feel in church, perhaps even in daily life, and no matter how long ago we may have come out into our current sense of ourselves, we are nevertheless hurt. These hurts affect each of us individually and, as I discuss later, collectively.

Consider some of the common relational and behavioral qualities of people who have survived trauma. B. A. Van der Kolk and his collaborators noted that survivors of trauma frequently exhibit "impairment of basic trust; lack of a sense of responsibility; negative effects on identity; impact on play and relationships with others; excessive interpersonal sensitivity; victimizing others; revictimization; increased attachment (to abusers) in the face of danger."[9] For purposes of later comparison, I summarize these behaviors as manifestations of three general emotional states: defensiveness, rage, and violation (with attendant shame).

Two comments are in order. First, I do not mean to pathologize the adjustments that we make in coming out, transitioning, or otherwise altering our accustomed gender and sexual performance, nor the natural responses that we have in the face of bullying, ostracism, violence, or harassment. Each human being has experienced hurt, just as each has experienced joy. Some of us encounter hostility, even violence, in living out as we choose; some fortunate people never encounter significant harassment. My intention is simply to make the psychological processes explicit, especially as guidance to the pastoral-care worker who responds to another's distress.

Second, I do not want to minimize the validity of rage and mistrust. Holy rage is at the heart of queer activism; each person's survival requires some healthy boundaries when trusting others. Rage and mistrust become problematic only when they are unexamined and misdirected.

Antiqueer hostility affects the corporate body as well as individuals, perhaps to an extent we do not realize or have forgotten. As we move from observations of individuals to observations of groups, consider what congregational dynamics theory tells us about trauma and vibrancy.

THE LIFE OF THE PARTY: COMMUNAL STRENGTH REQUIRES INDIVIDUAL WHOLENESS

Like Nic, at Night (Part One)

At five o'clock, every Sunday,
 we unlock the closet doors,
take out the linens and candles
 and set the communion table;
we bring out the rainbow flags
 and raise them, inside of the entrance.

We sometimes have better attendance
 in those months when it's dark before six;
it's a safe place for those who don't want
 their identities out in the open—
for those men who, like Nicodemus,
 prefer taking risks in the dark.
It's not just a church: in a way,
 it's our own sort of private 'hush harbour'. . .

While each of us copes with antiqueer oppression in our own way and on our own timing, we do so in community. This means that we share each other's joys as well as each other's burdens. When some of these spiritual burdens are borne on a daily basis, do they become invisible? If so, we need to make them visible again, to understand how they affect us in community.

The congregational studies literature abounds with models of what makes a church healthy or vibrant. Some characteristics associated with congregational health describe outward manifestations of ministry: small groups, good worship, empowerment of members that matches ministries with gifts and passions, and the like. However, other important qualities are less tangible or measurable; these have to do with the character of interpersonal relationships in the group.[10]

In an earlier work, I surveyed three models of church health, of which one was developed in an MCC context.[11] Not surprisingly, I found some common themes: a capacity to manage conflict, a generous and inviting mood, loving relationships, leadership that empowers each member to develop their gifts. The emotional climate in the congregation flows from the emotional states of its individual members, whether or not those members have designated leadership roles. The crucial emotional elements of congregations that are thriving and life-giving, to group them loosely, are trust, love, and generosity. Because trust, love, and generosity tend to be contagious, they promote spiritual healing to those who wish to receive it.

The trust, love, and generosity of an individual or a community can also be abused. We might not find it easy to define a nonvibrant or dysfunctional church but can probably say, in the famous words of Justice Stewart, "I know it when I see it." Some common patterns of dysfunction have been chronicled; for example, Hopkins and Laaser's volume *Restoring the Soul of a Church* (1995) discusses what pastors can expect on entering a church whose previous pastor was removed for unethical behavior.[12] Such afterpastors find a remarkably predictable environment of disease resulting from their predecessor's betrayal of trust, and feelings of (especially sexual) shame on the part of congregants. When a congregation has been hurt by abusive behavior or keeping sick secrets, congregants predictably act out their anger and distrust against the next pastor. A more superficial analysis might simply label these congregations as pastor-eating churches,[13] but a more careful view reveals trust issues that can be identified so that the congregation can heal and move on.

Chilton Knudsen describes such congregations' "tenacious patterns of organizational chaos" in her 1995 essay. Typical defensive behaviors include: 'Persistent confusion about responsibility . . . Focusing on the trivial and routine . . . Sabotaging or undermining persons in the exercise of their tasks . . .'"[14] Rage can also be discharged through blaming, faultfinding, selection of anger targets, deep depression, and dependency. These organizational behaviors of an after church stem from the same emotions of trauma survival: defensiveness, rage, and violation (with attendant shame).

This analysis from congregational studies, added to observations about the effect of trauma on queer people, suggests a predicament for queer congregations. On one hand, the predictable after-effects of trauma include defensiveness, rage, violation, and shame. These same feelings, and the organizational behaviors that follow from them, also abound in dysfunctional congregations. On the other hand, the qualities that are desired in growing and vibrant congregations include feelings of trust, love, and confidence—the exact opposites of the former.

Heterocolonial models of church growth will not help us here.[15] We can study and imitate the mega churches until we are blue in the face, but it will avail us nothing if we do not intentionally care for the stresses, or outright traumas, that we experience through living queerly. If we want to build churches where healing occurs, we need to help each other restore the trust, confidence, and generosity that can be shattered by the experience of antiqueer violence. We need to queer our pastoral care, and by extension both our activism and our worship. This queering must include transformative, healing activities.

RESTORING THE PARTY MOOD: PREDICTABLE PROCESSES OF OVERCOMING TRAUMA AND TRAUMATIC STRESS

> I remember your stories, but not
>   your faces. I remember your faces, but not
>   your names. I remember your funerals, but not
>   the tears.
> I stood on the beach
> At Santa Barbara Pride, finding I'd forgotten
>   who still lived,
>   who had died.

Recovery from trauma can be described as a journey involving three phases: getting into a place of safety, remembering and mourning the trauma, and reconnecting to life.[16] Eric Rofes and Mona West have previously used this model to describe the processes of recovering from the trauma of AIDS.[17] Like any model of psychological and spiritual growth, progress through these phases is more spiral than linear, and need not take place in a predictable time frame. Herman's three-phase model describes the grand sweep of the recovery process; while there are more details to consider, the following overview will suffice for this chapter.

When we have been attacked, our first need is safety. A safe space is a place where a trauma survivor can relax and be free from further attacks. It includes connections with people who understand and do not judge the trauma survivor's experience. Establishing safety also involves limiting contact with people or situations that cause further hurt.[18] If only for this reason, MCC congregations offer an important resource for queer folks who have been spiritually traumatized. Our churches are places where we can expect to be free from sermons and prayers that condemn us, and where we can expect to be free from physical violence.

After safety, the logical next phase is mourning and remembrance. Once we feel safe, we can process our memories and fears from past abuse. Remembrance often includes the repeated telling of our personal narratives, talking them out in the presence of others until the memories lose their power to hurt us.[19] If done well, remembrance and mourning require expression of the emotions of grief, loss, and anger, and ultimately a confrontation with internalized shame. For some, the first visit to an MCC is a chance to not only experience safety, but also to begin mourning, as suggested previously in the descriptions of a newcomer. In the safety of people who do not judge, perhaps in the privacy of a back pew, a visitor can cry as well as pray.

The third phase of recovery, reconnecting to life, includes learning (or relearning) to fight, reconciling with oneself, and reconciling with others. Many of these tasks are familiar to MCC congregations. We model fighting for one's rights; in fact, activism for justice is a tacit part of every MCC clergyperson's job description. Most, if not all of us, decenter sin and shame in our preachings, teachings, and prayers, in favor of a celebration of our original goodness in the sight of God or Goddess. To the extent that we model and teach opposing our adversaries, but still seeing them as God's or Goddess's beloved, we show each other how to reconcile, when possible, with those who have hurt us. Perhaps most importantly, we celebrate queer lives—at the various pride festivals at which queer communities gather openly, or in the day-to-day celebration of our loves and families.

Queering pastoral care, if we are to do it well, requires that pastors understand the stresses that queer folk commonly experience, and know the antidotes to traumatic stress or outright trauma. All of these stages of recovering or maintaining wholeness are important and need to be on the radar screen of every pastoral-care worker. Those of us who are not trained as therapists know that we need to make referrals to people who are, especially when severe trauma is involved; understanding the territory will help us to make the appropriate referrals.

Activism is also part of pastoral care. For MCC clergy, being visibly present in queer activism gives a witness to people who may never attend church. Our visibility also confronts the public discourse that claims that Christian faith condemns queer folk. Our public presence encourages others and contributes to their wholeness.

Finally, our pastoral care concerns must inform our corporate worship. The one place where congregants most frequently interact with each other is in the weekly worship service and coffee hour. What people experience on Sunday can affect their self-esteem, their self-confidence, and their attitude toward the coming week—for better, or for worse. If a worshipper expects the coming week to be difficult, it is all the more important that the church time be encouraging and affirming.

The historically black church in the United States, I think, understands this. For all of their challenges and, too often, spiritual violence regarding queer folk, African American churches have historically provided a safe space where being of African descent is normal, if not normative. In my admittedly limited experience in black churches, I have felt a climate of affirmation that I think white folks do not expect from church. People who are already privileged do not need affirmation; but for the most part, those of us who are queer can always use a little reassurance. MCC's self-image resembles what Hart M. and Anne Kusener Nelsen have termed an 'Ethnic Community-Prophetic' model of the historically black church. This church understands itself to be "a base for building a sense of ethnic identity and a community of interest among its members," but also turns its vision outward as a prophetic voice to "a corrupt white Christian nation."[20] Our experience in church has the power to sustain us and—this is where putting on the wedding drag comes in—if we conduct our time together in a way that supports recovering from trauma and helps us avoid being re-traumatized, it increases the odds that the congregation will be a good place for other people. When we also look outside ourselves to work for justice, we become builders of the already or not-yet divine realm of Jesus' teaching.

Christians believe that in Jesus, God or Goddess became one of us. What would our worship look like if queer Christians really explored the possibilities this implies?

PUTTING ON WEDDING (OR FUNERAL) DRAG: QUEERING OUR PASTORAL-CARE REPERTOIRE

Purple Heart

They never gave you a Purple Heart
    for wounds sustained in action
    in the service of Love, and Jesus:
heart ripped open, raw and bleeding,
a million cuts, the sudden ambush,
traumatic mind injuries,
        the lost companions,
      the ones you could not save

They never gave you the medal,
    the thanks of a grateful nation,
    that you earned ten times over.
They should have.

Let us consider some things that our congregations already do well and sketch some new possibilities.

In the past 40-some years, MCC and others have articulated new interpretations of the Bible; we have described strategies for healing from abusive uses of biblical texts.[21] We have developed queer-centered spiritual resources that, taken together, reflect all possible strands of the Christian tradition. We have developed queer theologies, demonstrated by the diverse chapters in this book. We have no use for worship services or preaching that re-traumatize congregants or leave them feeling beat-up, hopelessly sinful, damned, or inferior, or that legitimize the social and political arrangements that marginalize us. We delegitimize religious messages that have hurt us, through claiming our original goodness and proclaiming the Holy One's love. When we do these things, we facilitate the re-scripting that is essential to safety.

From necessity, we have become experts in reengaging life by working for justice. We have originated pride parades and HIV/AIDS vigils; we have been *de facto* community centers; we have lent the collar to public demonstrations. We have reworked and refined ways to assure ourselves, and other queer folks, that we are safe at the church and safe in the presence of the Divine. We have reengaged our world with a vengeance.

Still, something important is missing.

I believe we have done less to facilitate entry into that uncomfortable place between safety and reengagement. Aside from some valuable work around HIV/AIDS and the U.S. National Transgender Day of

Remembrance (TDOR), we have done more to celebrate and agitate than to facilitate grief and mourning of what we have lost in coming out, in separation from families and churches of origin, or through violence and discrimination. We neglect this grief at our peril.

Avoiding grief is understandable. Nobody, especially a leader, wishes to look weak. We don't want to embody negative energy; we want to project confidence and pride. Most of all, we are usually afraid to revisit our hurts and our pains. Nobody wants to feel the hurt again. Unfortunately, however, healing requires that each of us must eventually remember and mourn what we have lost. At some time and place where it is safe for us, we need to *feel* the hurt.

In *Weaving Heaven and Earth*, Wendy Farley reminds us that when our desire for the Holy One, and for each other, becomes wounded, this wounding may lead us to greater compassion and empathy for others. On the other hand, if we are stuck in our hurts, Eros cannot flow.[22] We become like the guest who refuses to put on wedding drag and spoils the party for the rest of the guests. If we are to maintain our power to experience other people as beloved human beings—in other words, our erotic power—we must yield to the whole human experience, including grieving for our losses and disappointments. We might even do this . . . in church.

QUEERING OUR LITURGICAL WARDROBE: REMEMBER THAT JESUS WAS ONE OF US WHO KNEW HE WAS LOVED, KNEW VIOLENCE, AND ROSE AGAIN

> . . . Maria, Myra, Amanda, Sandy, Chanel, Toni and Roy
>   no longer dance and laugh in our midst.
> Victoria, Gypsy, Justo, Ashley, Stacey and yet unknown
>   their music and joy now but only memory.
>
> Rachel cries loudly again, 'Where are my daughters and son?'
>   **She refuses to be comforted for her children.**
> First they are fired, refused housing and health;
>   now they lie buried by murderous hands.
>
> Rachel cries for your children
>   When you are not here. . .
>
> —*Johnston, 2010*[23]

Religion is perhaps most powerful when dealing with death and with hope. Although everyone remembers and mourns in their own way, the

seasons of the Christian year offer obvious opportunities to evoke mourning, and renewal, especially through the sacred tale of death and rebirth
that forms Holy Week and Easter. As we recall the events leading to Jesus'
death and resurrection, we can be mindful to open our hearts to sadness
as well as to celebration.

I sketch one possibility here, a re-imagining of the *Tenebrae* ("shadows") service. This service consists of alternating songs, prayers, and Bible
readings that describe Jesus' suffering and death. Multiple candles are lit
at the beginning of the service; one candle is snuffed after each reading,
until the church is left in near-darkness at the end. The service is designed
to evoke horror and grief at the torture that Jesus endured, and traditionally invites meditation on the notion that we are restored to the love of
the Holy One only by Christ's agony. A queered remembrance, however,
would instead invite participants to identify our communities' own abuse
with the violence that Jesus endured.[24] This kind of prayer could become
an occasion to grieve our own hurts while claiming Jesus' solidarity and
alliance with us. It recognizes, in the words of Robert Goss, that "Jesus the
Christ is 'queer-bashed.'"[25]

Consider the parallels between queer lives and Jesus' sense of differ-
entness, living in danger, rejection, and relentless challenge of religious
authority. An abusive man kills his toddler son because he fears the child
is gay; Jesus was in danger even in infancy (Matt. 2.13–23). A male-to-
female transgender teenager wins the right to wear skirts to school; at a
young age, Jesus takes a different path from other children and youth
(Lk 2.41–51). Queer communities of faith in Eastern Europe, like Jesus,
have challenged the religious authorities of the dominant culture (Mk
2.3–12). In response, the religious leaders condemned Jesus as a fraud
at best, and evil at worst, just as religious leaders in Malaysia condemn
a queer pastor and congregation. Church members who attempt to pray
away "the demon of homosexuality" surround a young gay man; Jesus
was likewise accused of being demon-possessed (Mk 3.22). The Markan
Jesus' family sought to make their son and brother "normal" again (Mk
3.20–21, 31–35); the parents of a modern-day lesbian force her into abusive pseudo-psychiatric treatment. Not to be deterred, Jesus continued
to gather a family of choice (Lk 8.1–3; Jn 11.1–5), in the same way that
people affected by AIDS have formed circles of care. Religious leaders said
that Jesus could not be holy because Jesus associated with disreputable
people (Mk 2.15–17; Lk 7.36–50); some contemporary Christians consider *all* queer people to be disreputable. Gay men in Egypt and Iran have
been executed simply for being gay; the elites of Jesus' country found him

so threatening that they plotted his arrest and murder (Mk 3.6). A lesbian government employee sues the United States to gain access to health care and pension benefits for her wife and her child; when at last Jesus was captured and executed, he made sure that his loved ones would be taken care of (Jn 19.26–27).[26]

NOTES

1. For this interpretation, see, for example, Bruce J. Malina and Richard L. Rohrbaugh, *Social-Science Commentary on the Synoptic Gospels*, 2nd ed. (Minneapolis: Fortress, 2003), 111.

2. I use the term "antiqueer hostility" rather than "homophobia" and "transphobia" in part following Gregory M. Herek's comments on the use of the term "phobia" and in part as an umbrella term to include the stigmas associated with gender identity as well as sexual orientation. See Gregory M. Herek, "Beyond 'Homophobia': Thinking about Sexual Prejudice and Stigma in the Twenty-First Century", *Sexuality Research & Social Policy: Journal of the National Sexuality Research Center* 1, no. 2 (2004): 6–24.

3. Gustavo Gutiérrez, *A Theology of Liberation: History, Politics and Salvation* (Maryknoll, NY: Orbis Books, 1971), 8.

4. Marcella Althaus-Reid, *Indecent Theology: Theological Perversions in Sex, Gender and Politics* (London: Routledge, 2002); Robert E. Goss, *Queering Christ: Beyond Jesus Acted Up* (Cleveland: Pilgrim Press, 2002); Patrick S. Cheng, *Radical Love: An Introduction to Queer Theology* (New York: Seabury Books, 2011).

5. Poems not otherwise credited are my own compositions.

6. Leanne McCall Tigert, *Coming Out through Fire: Surviving the Trauma of Homophobia* (Cleveland: United Church Press, 1999), 20.

7. Ibid., 20.

8. Judith Lewis Herman, *Trauma and Recovery* (New York: Basic Books, 1992), 33.

9. Bessel A. Van Der Kolk, Alexander C. McFarlane, and Lars Weisæth, eds., *Traumatic Stress: The Effects of Overwhelming Experience on Mind, Body, and Society* (New York: Guilford Press, 1996). Cited in Tigert, *Coming out through Fire*, 30.

10. See, for example, Peter L Steinke., *Healthy Congregations: A Systems Approach*, 2nd ed. (Herndon, VA: Alban Institute, 2006); Christian A. Schwarz, *Natural Church Development: A Guide to Eight Essential Qualities of Healthy Churches* (St. Charles, IL: Churchsmart Resources, 1996); Richard Warren, *The Purpose Driven Church: Growth without Compromising Your Message & Mission* (Grand Rapids, MI: Zondervan Pub, 1995).

11. Peter L. Steinke, "Promoting Healthy Congregations," *Alban Weekly* no. 116 (2006); Nancy J. Horvath-Zurn, "The Eight Essentials of a Healthy Church" (2005), www.mccchurch .org; Schwarz (1996) cited in Joan M. Saniuk, *Come to the Water: The Queer Congregation as Healing Community* (Cambridge, MA: Episcopal Divinity School, 2008).

12. Nancy Myer Hopkins and Mark R. Laaser, eds., *Restoring the Soul of a Church: Healing Congregations Wounded by Clergy Sexual Misconduct* (Collegeville, MN: Liturgical Press, 1995).

13. Chilton Knudsen, "Understanding Congregational Dynamics," in *Restoring the Soul of a Church*, 85.

14. Ibid., 83–4.

15. I am indebted to Thomas Bohache for the term "heterocolonial."

16. Herman, *Trauma and Recovery*; cited in Tigert, *Coming Through Fire*, 81–87.

17. Eric E. Rofes., *Reviving the Tribe: Regenerating Gay Men's Sexuality and Culture in the Ongoing Epidemic*, Haworth Gay & Lesbian Studies (New York: Haworth Press, 1996); Mona West, "The Gift of Voice, the Gift of Tears: A Queer Reading of Lamentations in the Context of AIDS," in *Queer Commentary and the Hebrew Bible*, ed. Ken Stone (Cleveland: Pilgrim Press, 2001), 140–51.

18. Tigert, *Coming Through Fire*, 83–4.

19. Ibid., 86.

20. Nelsen M. Hart and Anne Kusener Nelsen, *Black Church in the Sixties* (Lexington: University Press of Kentucky, 1975), cited in C. Eric Lincoln and Lawrence H. Mamiya, *The Black Church in the African-American Experience* (Durham, NC: Duke University Press, 1990), 10–11.

21. For an example of the latter, see Rembert S. Truluck, *Steps to Recovery from Bible Abuse* (Gaithersburg, MD: Chi Rho Press, 2001).

22. Wendy Farley, *The Wounding and Healing of Desire: Weaving Heaven and Earth* (Louisville, KY: Westminster John Knox Press, 2005), 21.

23. Brianna Johnston, *TDOR Lament Prayer* (Hartford, CT, 2010). This excerpt reprinted by permission of the author.

24. I am grateful to Thomas Emmett III for his suggestions about this service.

25. Robert Goss, *Jesus ACTED UP: A Gay and Lesbian Manifesto* (San Francisco: HarperSanFrancisco, 1993), 85.

26. Thanks to David Ingram, Robert M. Leahy, Sharilyn Steketee, and David Twiddy for their valuable suggestions.

16

An Inclusive Table: Same-Sex Marriage

Neil Thomas

Entreat me not to leave you or to return from following you; wherever you go I will go, and wherever you lodge I will lodge; your people shall be my people, and your God my God; where you die I will die, and there will I be buried. May the Lord do so to me and more also if even death parts me from you.

—Ruth 1:16–17

Same-sex marriage or marriage equality has become both a theological and social issue in this new millennium. Across the world, its impact is finding itself firmly planted in both the political and secular spheres as well as the LGBTQ civil rights movement. This has not always been the case. In the United States the move toward marriage equality has been resisted, specifically among the LGBTQ equality organizations and became clearly evidenced in the actions of much of the leadership that have organized the several March on Washington events. The content of these events have often laid out their agenda for LGBTQ civil rights in the United States and the resistance to any mention of marriage equality as a potential issue is well understood.

Of course the resistance to a move toward marriage equality in the United States, and elsewhere in the world, specifically among the early LGBTQ leaders, has its roots in at least two arenas. The first would be a sense of our own internalized homophobia; the unrealized internal messages that have been absorbed by our interactions with the general populous that we are not worthy of equality, and, therefore, we do not move forward to combat, what is often referred to as the final frontier of equality, marriage, and the second is our fear of the religious community and spirituality.

Marriage, especially in the United States, with its history of less than 350 years, has evolved to embrace Christianity, if not as its country's religion (the United States still holds on to the separation of church and state), it has become the dominant religion and much of its social, civil, and secular life is governed by the influence of the predominant Christian influences.

Until recently, the predominant Christian theology has held to a traditional stand that homosexuality is incompatible with Christian belief. It has cited six dubious scriptures from the Hebrew and Christian Bibles to support their stand. In recent years most mainline Christian denominations have reevaluated these same scriptures and have come to a new understanding both of them and of the LGBTQ community.[1] Many theologians and Protestant denominations have wrestled with this theology of radical inclusion and, to date, have asserted that the clobber passages that have been traditionally used to exclude LGBTQ peoples from both religious and secular equality are misused and have nothing to do with homosexuality and the care and love of same-gender peoples that we know today. They have concluded that it is time for the church to reevaluate its position and interpretations and, specifically in the United States, to allow practicing homosexuals full equality, at all levels of leadership, including ordained ministry.

In 2011 the Presbyterian Church (USA) voted to ordain openly gay and lesbian people to the role of Clergy, and they joined nearly every other mainline Christian denomination (with the exception of the United Methodist Church) in moving toward full inclusion of LGBTQ people in their leadership. In the same way that we came to understand that scripture could not be used to oppress women, support slavery, and inter-racial marriage, biblical theology has evolved to understand that scripture does not condemn same-gender loving relationships.[2]

On October 6, 1968, a gathering of 12 women and men, including those who self-identified as lesbians, gays, bisexuals, transgendered, and heterosexuals, gathered in a front living room of a home in Huntington Park CA. The home belonged to the Reverend Troy Perry, and their purpose, to provide a safe space for those who had been rejected by the church to worship freely and openly. This gathering sparked a revolution, a movement that would transform the Christian (and other faith communities) forever.

Today, Metropolitan Community Churches (MCC) reach across the world. New countries and communities enquire about how they can begin or affiliate with this church whose simple message is that God loves everyone, including homosexuals and that LGBTQ are made in the image of God and deserve equal religious and civil rights. Many fundamentalist, evangelical, and mainline Christian denominations still exclude LGBTQ Christians' full participation in their churches. In some of these new and developing countries MCC is referred to as the "Human Rights Church."

From its first gathering, MCC has declared its stand for full inclusion at the Communion table. Communion, the sacred rite of the Christian church that Jesus instituted the night before his death, is something that most Christian communities offer. Some offer this meal every Sunday, while others on special occasions when the church gathers for worship. It was a meal that came out of the Passover celebrations of the Jewish faith and, according to Scripture, became a meal of liberation and became a symbol of the final sacrifice offered by Jesus Himself to restore and establish a new relationship with God—one that was based not on law or sacrifice in the Temple, but on Spirit, where the body is the Temple of the Holy Spirit.

In many traditions today, Communion is a meal of separation, and the politics of the Communion table has remained a scandal. This meal that Jesus offered to all has become bound in rules and regulations and often times, the invitation to the table is not one of welcome, but expresses exclusion. It is often said that the Priest or Pastor or Minister spends more time telling members of the congregation who is not welcome, rather than who is!

One of the unique theological perspectives that MCC has brought to the Christian world is a return to this notion of the open table of welcome. At every MCC, each time it gathers, MCC opens the table to liberation and welcomes and invites everyone to participate. It has become a hallmark of its communities and this embodied theology permeates its way into every other aspect of its ministries, theologies, and works.

MCC began its work of radical inclusive love right there at the "Table of Welcome" and has sought to use its progressive religious voice ever since toward a radical theology of inclusion. This radical theology of inclusion has involved fighting for LGBTQ nondiscrimination and the right to marry, and in 1969, less than a year after its founding, MCC performed the first service of Holy Union.[3] This ceremony was similar to a marriage, but because legal marriage was only afforded to people of the opposite sex, the Holy Union was a religious marriage. In 1970, MCC filed its first lawsuit in the United States to legally recognize the marriages it performs. In the first-ever court case of its kind, MCC sued the State of California seeking legal recognition for same-sex marriages. We lost that fight—but as a church, we launched three decades of debate and struggle for marriage equality. This action sparked the debate for marriage equality in the United States that continues more than three decades later.

The Christian church has often made its own rules and accommodations about whom it will or will not marry under the auspices of its own understanding of marriage in a religious context. For instance, the Roman Catholic Church will not, generally, marry people who have been previously married and divorced. The Church of Jesus Christ of Latter Day Saints (Mormons) will not marry those who are not members of its own church—the same can be said for many other churches. MCC does not believe that it is morally, ethically, or theologically wrong to love someone of the same gender and for this reason there is no reason to withhold a religious marriage. Its theology of the open table has led to an inclusive view of marriage equality.

MCC's theology of inclusion, which includes marriage equality is well documented, specifically in Canada and the marriage of its founder, Rev. Troy Perry to his husband, Philip De Bleik. They were married in Canada in 2005 and won the right for their marriage to be recognized in the State of California when the California Supreme Court struck down Proposition 22 on May 15, 2008—prohibiting same-sex marriage.[4]

Rev. Dr. Brent Hawkes, the Senior Pastor of MCC of Toronto, was instrumental in the 2005 passage of the Civil Marriage Act, which legalized marriage equality in Canada. He worked for more than 30 years to ensure full equality for Canadians and presided over the world's first legal same-sex marriage. For his commitment to MCC's theology of inclusion, Hawkes received the Order of Canada, an award given to individuals for a lifetime of outstanding achievement, dedication to a community and service to a nation. Hawkes has also received the City of Toronto's Award of Merit, the Queen's Golden Jubilee Medal, the United Nations Toronto Association Global Citizen Award, and the YMCA Peace Medal.

In the United Kingdom, MCC's leadership was key in the fight for marriage equality and our churches pressed for inclusion as Great Britain began offering Civil Partnerships to lesbian and gay couples in 2005. Rev. Sharon Ferguson, Senior Pastor of MCC in North London and Executive Director of the Lesbian and Gay Christian Movement, which includes membership from most mainline Christian communities in the United Kingdom, is currently suing the British Parliament challenging bans on same-sex marriages and civil partnerships for heterosexual couples. Like many MCC leaders, she has received much hate mail for her position, specifically from Christians.

According to its Office of Communications headed for many years by Rev. James Birkitt, MCC performed more than 100,000 same gender marriages in its history. In 2008, when the State of California allowed marriage licenses to be given to same-gender couples, a law that existed for just a few short months, I personally married more than 100 couples. More than 18,000 couples were married during that time.

OPPOSITION TO SAME-SEX MARRIAGE

Why does marriage equality receive so much attention from the Christian community? The simple answer is that much of the Christian church, specifically, the more evangelical and fundamentalist Christian community, holds to the belief that marriage is a religious institution, established by God to bind together one man and one woman for the purposes of procreation and the protection of the family. They believe that both the Hebrew and Christian Bible support this belief and that they are called to defend marriage and Christian authority over it.

In the fight against Proposition 8 in California in 2008 this was evidenced in the unholy Trinity of Evangelical Christians, the Roman Catholic Church, and the Church of Jesus Christ of Latter Day Saints, who called upon their membership to pour millions of dollars into their fight to withhold civil marriage rights from lesbian and gay couples. I say unholy Trinity because these three groups have never once before aligned with one another. In fact, the Evangelical Church is well known for its anti-Roman Catholic stand, the Roman Catholic Church believes that it is the only real church and that Protestantism is not valid, and both the Evangelical church and the Roman Catholic Church have referred to the Church of Jesus Christ of Latter Day Saints (Mormons) as a sect and not a church at all.

However, they were able to overcome their differences sufficiently to fight to traditional marriage. It is suggested that the Mormon Church alone poured more than $40,000,000 into this fight and, ultimately, more than $80,000,000 was spent defending marriage. Upon the passing of Proposition 8, which took the right to marry away from same-sex couples, it was the first time that rights have been taken away from a minority in the history of the United States and wrote this into the California Constitution. The Mormon Church was left alone to take the heat, for neither the Evangelical Church nor the Roman Catholic Church came to their defense.

If the Hebrew Bible and Christian Bible are to be used to deny marriage to same-gender couples, what does it really say about marriage? A quick examination of our Bibles tells us a lot about the different kinds of relationships that were established in our evolution. While the Christian Church continues to uphold marriage as between one man and one woman as the norm, there is very little evidence that this is so. With the exception of the relationship between Rebecca and Isaac there are no monogamous relationships in the Hebrew Bible, and Jesus' values on relationships do not represent those espoused by the Evangelical Church, the National Organization for Marriage, or many of the other religious organizations that speak with biblical authority. However, we find diverse constructions of marriage and family within the Hebrew Bible. The Old Testament condones marriage between more than one man and one woman. Many of the prophets and patriarchs had multiple wives. These include Abraham, Jacob, Esau, Saul, David, and Solomon. Some interpretations also suggest that Moses had a second wife, Tharbis. King David took more wives and concubines than can often be counted, and we are often confused between his wives and concubines because ten of his concubines are also called wives in several places. We know that King David had at least five wives, Michal, Abigail, Jezreel, and Bathsheba. David's son, Solomon chose 700 wives and 300 concubines, totaling 1,000 women (1 Kgs 11:3). There is nothing comparable to contemporary traditional family values of marriage between one man to one woman. Biblical scholar Mary Ann Tolbert writes on the California Faith for Equality (CFE) website:

> Nowhere in the Bible is same gender marriage prohibited, or even mentioned, for that matter. In order to argue that the Bible prohibits civil recognition of same gender relationships, one is reduced to arguing from silence. Marriage between one man and one woman as envisioned by people today was never the ideal relationship in the Bible. Moreover, marriage is not, as some commentators, politicians, and even religious leaders, have recently contended, an "unchanging tradition of thousands of years."[5]

In the Christian Scriptures, we find marriage de-emphasized in Jesus' ministry and Paul's discussion of marriage is seen as not for the purpose of procreation but as an antidote to sexual passion. In Paul's letter to the early church at Corinth, he speaks to the married and to the unmarried. To the married he speaks to monogamy and instructs the men to carry out their marital duties. He states that this is a concession and not as a command, believing that temptation might come their way if they do not give themselves to the other. However, to the unmarried he says this: "Now to the unmarried and the widows I say: It is good to them to stay unmarried as I do. But if they cannot control themselves, they should marry, for it is better marry than to burn with passion" (1 Cor. 7:12)

In his book, *Blessing Same-sex Unions*, Mark Jordan has demonstrated that there has not been a consistent and stable notion of Christian marriage across the millennia.[6] Jordan writes,

> A collective illusion, suffered by some queer activists and by Focus on the Family among others, declares that there is or had been a single theory of Christian marriage. . . . Christian and Jewish traditions disagree about a number of fundamental issues, including the value of celibacy, the permissibility of polygyny or concubinage, and the grounds for divorce that permits remarriage.[7]

There have been instabilities in theologies of marriage, with variations due to historical and social changes of families and due to denominational differences. Jordan is correct that there is no unanimous Christian theological model of marriage. In addition, we forget that the nuclear family is a recent social development over the past century and that there have been shifting transitions in the notion of families over the millennia.[8] These all contribute to the fact that there are multiple historical and denominational variations on Christian marriage and that sociological shifts on notions of marriage and sexuality have changed over the past two centuries.

According to the National Organization for Marriage, a religious-based organization in the United States well known for its advocacy against same-sex marriage, they state that "Most Christians know from the Bible that marriage is part of God's original order."[9] They cite the Genesis 2:18 as evidence of this supposition. "And the Lord God said, it is not good that the man should be alone, I will make him a help mate." National Organization of Marriage as well as the proponents for California Prop 8 have advanced arguments on the unchanging continuity of marriage of one man and one woman over the millennia in the federal court trial, despite expert historical evidence, to the contrary, of cultural diversity in marriage and families. Both Protestant and Roman Catholic opponents of same-sex marriage will argue a complementary of the genders as the basis of marriage: "God made Adam and Eve, not Adam and Steve." It is a natural law theory of gender complementarity, concluding that because the genital parts fit together, men and women were therefore ordained for marriage and procreation.[10]

Gender complementarity interpretations, in other words, assert the patriarchal domination of men over women and the biological complementarily of the sexual organs. It ignores any models of equal partnership and the psychological complementarity of partners whether opposite sex or same sex. The late English Dominican theologian, Gareth Moore counters religious opponents of same-sex marriage as follows:

> It becomes true of each of us that it is not good for us that we should be alone, and God seeks for each of us, not the partner that pleases God, but the partner that pleases us, for it is only that he can fulfill as the needy creatures that he has made us and only thus that he can succeed in his own project of providing us with a companion.[11]

What if the person with whom we fall in love is of the same gender and completes us psychologically, spiritually, and erotically in a way that no other person does? Does this negate the fundamental human need that God calls us not to be alone and force LGBTQ folks to remain celibate? Is that theologically realistic? Or even humane?

Christian opponents go on to say that Jesus affirmed that lasting, loving marriage is basic to God's plan for us, "But from the beginning of creation God made them male and female. For this cause shall a man leave his father and mother and joined to his wife . . . So what God has joined together, let not humanity separate" (Mk 10:6–7, 9). They fail to understand the historical and social context that Jesus' intention was to protect married women who would have no way to take care of themselves if they were divorced and that marriage is God's work.[12]

Neither of these arguments of the scriptural assertion that we are not meant to be alone and that God made them male and female excludes same-gender couples from the right to marry. Indeed, it could be used to support. Gay theologian, John McNeill writes,

> On the theological level, true Christian love, even married love, can exist only between persons who see themselves somehow total and equal to each other. Christian love must be love out of fullness and not of need. It is not only the complementariness of the other sex attracts me but also the fact, while I sense that complementarity, I can at the same time sense that here is a being whole and entire in himself (or herself) and . . . worthy of standing beside me and entering my life as an equal.[13]

It is true that each person, no matter what their sexual orientation is, deserves a helpmate and when an individual chooses to leave his or her mother and father, should cleave to that partner. Secondly, as McNeill mentions above that though heterosexual marriages may have gender complementarity, but without equality of the partners, it is not Christian love.

The second story of creation found in Genesis 2: 15–24 gives us a more full and radically inclusive understanding of God's ideal for a person. God did not want a person to be intimately alone. "It is not good for man to be alone. I will make him a helper suitable for him." For Adam, it was ultimately Eve, but not before a variety of other possibilities were presented to him. God intends for all of humanity to find human intimacy and love, to find their helper as God intended for Adam. In our modern understanding, these relationships are confirmed in a tradition that has been enshrined in legal and religious terms as marriage and should be available to both opposite-sex and same-sex couples.

The National Organization for Marriage further believes that if we allow same-sex marriage we are opening the door to polygamy and who knows what next. As I have already stated, there are very few examples of monogamy in the Hebrew and Christian Bible. An examination of David's diverse relationships clearly demonstrates this, and among David's erotic relationships is Jonathan, a man for whom his love clearly surpassed that of woman.[14] While I am not advocating, necessarily for polygamy here, I am identifying a flaw in the rationale that they use and point to biblical authority to support it.

Legal marriage is the way in which we have chosen to legally support couples. Religious marriage is not legal marriage, and every religious marriage must be affirmed through the legal system. However, every legal marriage does not have to be affirmed by a religious community. If those who are so vigorously defending tradition marriage, why are they not working to ban divorce? This is something that Jesus addresses and yet, in the United States, more than 50 percent of marriages end in divorce. The Protestant churches have generally made accommodations on divorce and remarriage. Retired ethicist from Fuller Seminary, Lewis Smedes compares the former stance of Protestant churches on divorce and remarriage with the current stand on homosexuality. "Was the church's embrace of people once divorced and are now living faithfully in second marriages a precedent for embracing homosexual people who live faithfully in covenanted partnerships?"[15] Smedes laments the exclusion of Christian homosexual partners from his own Christian Reformed Church but advocates for the wideness of mercy forgotten by his church toward homosexual Christians.

However, Smedes points out the Protestant accommodation of the biblical tradition on divorce and believes that such a similar accommodation can be made for same-sex marriage within the Christian church.

It seems a compelling theory on first glance, but if marriage was indeed for procreation and based on the fact that the parts fit together, then you must also ban marriages that do not result in procreation. For instance, any women—who are past the age of child bearing—must automatically be banned from marrying because there is no opportunity to bear children. It is also true to point out that many heterosexual couples engage in anal sex as a form of birth control. Those parts fit together just as well.

It would be fair to surmise that most of the truth that lays behind the parade of religious language and religious arguments against giving the right to marry for same-gender loving couples is fear and homophobic prejudice. However, while one might be able to understand fear and prejudice, these are not valid reasons of their own to deny marriage. These same arguments were used against inter-racial marriage, against slavery, against the women's right to vote, and now against LGBTQ people. Ultimately, selective verses from the Bible—read from a perspective of fear and prejudice—form no rational argument to deny legal marriage to same-gender loving couples. Biblical scholar Dale Martin argues, "Rather than looking to scripture and tradition, we should attempt to recover and revise resources from a forgotten Christianity, vouchsafed to us in Scripture and pre-modern traditions: the long and valuable history of the Christian case against marriage."[16] Martin suggests that by engaging these traditions against marriage that we might retrain our theological imaginations to make to inclusive models and theologies for Christian marriage that would allow marriage equality. This is precisely what interfaith communities for marriage equality are actively engaged in—countering the arguments against marriage and advancing their own theologies of marriage.

In the United States, which fundamentally holds true to the separation of church and state, there is no rational reason to exclude lesbian and gay couples from the institution of marriage. This is the conclusion of Judge Vaughn Walker in his decision to strike down Prop 8 and a growing majority of Americans supporting the marriage equality.[17] However, to ignore these arguments also does an injustice to same-sex couples who want to live faithful and faith-filled lives. This has been clear in Lance Dustin's play "8 the Play," which opened on Broadway and in Los Angeles and was released on YouTube.[18]

FIGHTING FOR GRACE: MARRIAGE EQUALITY

It is from the practice of an open communion table invitation that MCC is evolving and is developing, through practical ministry, this theology of God's radical inclusivity. Marriage equality is about both the right within the Christian community to bless and sacramentalize same-gender relationships and the right to legal marriage with the same civil and legal benefits that heterosexual married couples have. It is only fair and just for same-sex couples and their families that they have the same civil and social benefits afforded to heterosexual families.

In the United States, no civil rights movement has ever progressed towards its goal(s) without bringing alongside the religious community. In the movement toward marriage equality, and ultimately full inclusion of LGBTQ people in the fabric of American culture, this has been a hard nut to crack. Religious oppression and intolerance can be seen from the very beginning of creation and more wars have been fought in the name of religion than for any other reason. In its 350-year history, American Christianities have been used to divide peoples and cultures and have, as explained earlier, been used to separate and exclude rather than unite and include.[19] The movement toward equality for women, for peoples of color, for other minority communities, and even the lesbian, gay, bisexual, transgendered, and queer community has been long and difficult. The United States was born out of more puritanical peoples who settled, fleeing Europe and its more liberal, nonreligious viewpoint. As they settled, they came to rely on God and developed a more conservative theology that, as evidenced today, is more evangelical and fundamentalist.

While, in recent times a more progressive theology is making its mark, most Americans, whether or not they believe in God, still hold to a more traditional standpoint on scripture. In a recent study it was demonstrated that more than 98 percent of Americans believe in God. Of that number 83 percent of Americans claim to belong to a religious denomination, 40 percent claim to attend services nearly weekly or more, and 58 percent claim to pray at least weekly.[20] More than 76 percent of Americans identify themselves as Christians, either Protestant or Roman Catholic.[21] From the above, we can understand that when religious people speak about any subject from a stand of "God's Word," whether right or wrong, it holds authority and power.

The LGBTQ community, in its secular movement, must confront head on this religious question if it is indeed to attain full equality and marriage equality in the United States and elsewhere in the world. We can no longer dismiss religious arguments and discourse as irrelevant or not applying to a country that, in theory, believes in the separation of church and state, but in practice has imbedded it into the very fabric of its workings.

Therefore, it is important for the LGBTQ community to grapple with the religious texts and arguments that are used to deny LGBTQ marriage equality. LGBTQ religious communities are reading the scriptures from their own queer context and advancing new creative perspectives.[22] Queer Christians read the scriptures from their own social location for social liberation and full equality to become a reality in the United States.

In Genesis 1:27, we read, "God created humankind in God's image, in the divine image, God created them, male and female. . . ." God affirms the equality of humanity, both male and female, and that all human beings—whether they are heterosexual, gay, lesbian, bisexual, transgendered, intersexed, or queer. A queer reading of this verse stresses that all are equally made in the divine image and that all people have equal access to marriage. A theology of radical inclusive love is built on the foundation of the equality of all humanity bearing the divine image. This common grace embodied in humanity requires Christians to respect and recognize others similar to themselves. It also means equal access to Christian marriage.

Gay ethicist Marvin Ellison writes about a single standard for sexuality:

> Christian ethical concern should be grounded in an open-ended commitment to actualize three interrelated components: an affirmation of the goodness of sexuality, a genuine honoring of sexual difference and respect for sexual minorities, and a willingness to attend to both the personal and political dimensions of sexual injustice and oppression.[23]

Mutual pleasure and growth in intimacy are values worth moral pursuit within a relationship, no matter what the gender of the partners. In another writing, Ellison advances his conviction that theological arguments about marriage need to move away from the preoccupations of gender and gender roles in partnerships to the quality of the relationship:

> Rather than promoting marriage per se, the church should promote only egalitarian marriages, in which the parties are each honored and protected as persons in their own right, share power and resources in a mutual give and take, and are committed over the long haul not to their own well-being, but also to the building up of the common good. In other words, the church's educational and pastoral focus should be on helping people,

regardless of gender, to figure out—and live out—a genuinely holy and blessed relationship.[24]

Regardless of gender, race, sexuality, class, or other labels that we care to place on ourselves or others, the need for a helper, as offered in the stories of Creation are a part of the human need. This shift in our own era towards radical inclusiveness signals a radical shift in understanding God and God's presence in the world. It further signals that the Christian Church is evolving in its more complex understandings of gender, gender identity, sexuality, and sex itself.

Clergy of numerous denominational affiliations are now either legally marrying or offering services of Holy Union (a religious ceremony offered by the church without legal recognition). As stated before, these services have been offered by MCC throughout its history.

Moving toward a theology of God's radical inclusion, as I call it, seems to be in line with the ministry of Jesus himself who, through his ministry demonstrates that the marginalized and oppressed of his day are the very people that he came to liberate and reconnect with a loving God, full of grace and hope.

From what we have discussed we have come to a better understanding of the roots of homophobia in the Christian church and how it impacts on our current culture and prejudice. The traditional interpretations of the Genesis passage have moved relationality and mutual equality with one another to one of patriarchal dominance of man over woman. It is a practice that has created a dominant culture and has secured the place of the man as the head of their household, the seat of authority in the home. It has supported the theory of complementarity and, along with a natural law reading of the text, has ensured that male authority is written into the religious ideologies and theologies that are the basis of American Christianities today. The notion of same-gender or same-sex relationships, and therefore marriage, threatens this dominant viewpoint and dominant culture.

Some queer critics argue that same-sex marriage or marriage equality provides a corrective to patriarchal theological construction of marriage. Perhaps the real challenges to opponents of marriage are the equality of gender roles embedded in the relationship. Same-sex relationships are ones that demonstrate a more equal partnership and threaten the very heart of Christian, patriarchal understandings of marriage. The complementarity of genders in its interpretation understands this simply from a biological basis and completely ignores the complementarity of any two persons or two persons of the same gender from a psychological standpoint.

Marriage has been seen as the exchange of property from one man (the father) to another (the bridegroom). The ring exchanged was historically the price paid, the dowry, and sealed the deal of ownership. The old English word, to wed, means to pledge a price or pay the bride's price. Marriage has been traditionally a property exchange or contract between two families.

As Ellison has pointed out, marriage has seldom exhibited a stand for justice, fairness, and equality.[25] However, for Christians, the reign of God and the ethics, values, and practice of Jesus are all about justice, mutuality, equality, and ultimately love. This is clearly demonstrated in Jesus and his teachings, life, and the expansion of the availability of God from those who were a part of the House of Israel to those outside.

WHY SAME-SEX MARRIAGE?

In my work with CFE, an organization that I cofounded with my colleagues Rabbi Denise Eger and Rev. Lindi Ramsden at a time that we were confident that we would be facing a ballot initiative in California that became known as Proposition 8, we knew that the religious voice would be one that needed to be raised if there was any hope of winning marriage equality in California.[26] While, ultimately the proposition won by a slim majority, the work that we began and continue to this day is one of great importance in the shift toward a Theology of Radical Inclusion. While the work of CFE is one from an interfaith perspective, we understand this to be a move of the Spirit to reform the various forms of Christianity and other religious movements that have become narrow, fundamentalist, legalistic, and exclusive.

This climate was prevalent in the days of Jesus. He witnessed it and confronted it. When Jesus entered the Temple before Passover, he turned the tables upside down and accused the religious of turning God's house into a den of thieves. From this point in his public ministry he set about widening the understanding of God and putting people back in touch with their inherent spirit and uniqueness as children of God.

As a pastor I have had the privilege of celebrating with more LGBTQ couples and their families than I can count. During the three-month period in California where same-sex couples were granted the legal right to marry, I officiated at more than 100 ceremonies. The joy of these couples and the families that surrounded them was nothing short of a blessing. I married couples who had been together for many years who had waited, longed for this day. One such couple was in their mid 70s. They had been together for more than 50 years. They were inter-racial and had been through the years when it was illegal for inter-racial couples to marry in the United States and saw those laws struck down. They had been through the times when homosexuality was illegal and saw those laws struck down and they lived to a day when they were able to legally marry and have the right and protections that are offered to married couples in the United States. Celebrating their love for more than 50 years they married and just a year later I celebrated the life of one of them who sadly passed. They, and the others that I married clearly demonstrated, in their love for one another, the kind of love that I look for in opposite-sex marriages that I have had the honor of performing. They demonstrated commitment, respect for one another, and the ability to celebrate both their uniqueness and their ability to allow mutual growth and understanding.

If our desire is to protect and promote marriage, as both opponents and supporters of this issue appear to be arguing, the only way to protect marriage is to support the opportunity for loving couples to find ways, ceremonially and legally to celebrate their love and to afford them the support that is needed to enter into such commitments, with all of the rights and responsibilities afforded to them by the law, and our religious institutions. This is a move toward the kind of space that Jesus intended, one that he lived for and one that he envisioned. This is a place of radical inclusion where MCC resides.

NOTES

1. William Countryman, *Dirt, Greed, and Sex in the New Testament and Their Implications for Today* (Minneapolis: Fortress Press, 2007). Robert E. Goss, "Homosexuality, The Bible the Practice of Safe-Texts," in *Queering Christ: Beyond Jesus ACTED UP* (Cleveland: The Pilgrim Press, 2002), 185–203. Daniel Helminiak, *What the Bible Really Says about Homosexuality?*, millennium ed. (New Mexico: Alamo Square Press, 2000). Ronald Long, "Introduction: Disarming Biblically Based Gay Bashing," in *The Queer Bible Commentary*, ed. Deryn Guest, Robert E. Goss, Mona West, and Thomas Bohache (London: SCM Press, 2006), 1–18.

2. Ibid.

3. In 1969, Troy Perry performed the first same-sex church wedding at MCC of Los Angeles, then located in Huntington Park, California. This was recently documented in *Time Magazine's* coverage of same-sex marriage.

4. See the video footage of Troy Perry's marriage and the case against California Prop 22: *Call Me Troy*, produced and directed by Scott Bloom, Frameline Videos, San Francisco, 2007.

5. Mary Ann Tolbert, "Christian Bible: Same-Gender Marriage, 2004." http:// cafaithforequality.org/reflect/christian-bible_same_gender_marriage-mary-ann-tolbert/.

6. Mark D. Jordan, *Blessing Same-Sex Unions: The Perils of Queer Romance and the Confusions of Christian Marriage* (Chicago: University of Chicago Press, 2005), 102–12.

7. Ibid., 100.

8. Rosemary Radford Ruether, *Christianity and the Making of the Family* (Boston: Beacon Press, 2001).

9. National Organization of Marriage. http://www.nationformarriage.org/site/c.omL 2KeN0LzH/b.3836955/k.BEC6/Home.htm.

10. Robert Goss argues from a theological argument that same-sex marriages can be meta-phorically procreative. Robert E. Goss, "Challenging Procreative Privilege by Queering Fami-lies," in *Queering Christ*, 88–110.

11. Gareth Moore, *A Question of Truth: Christianity and Homosexuality* (New York: Continuum, 2002), 142–43.

12. Theodore W. Jennings, *The Insurrection of the Crucified: The Gospel of Mark as Theo-logical Manifesto* (Chicago: Explorations Press, 2003), 155–57.

13. John J. McNeill, *Sex as God Intended* (Maple Shade, NJ: Lethe Press, 2008), 127–28.

14. Tom Horner, *Jonathan Loved David* (Philadelphia: The Westminster Press, 1978), 26–39; Theodore W. Jennings Jr., *Jacob's Wound: Homoerotic Narrative in the Literature of Ancient Israel* (New York: Continuum, 2005), 13–36.

15. Lewis B. Smedes, "Like the Wildness of the Sea," http://www.soulforce.org/article/638.

16. Dale B. Martin, "Familiar Idolatry and the Christian Case Against Marriage," in *Sex-uality and the Sacred: Sources for Theological Reflection*, ed. Marvin Ellison and Kelly Brown Douglas (Louisville, KY: Westminster John Knox Press, 2010), 433.

17. Judge Vaugh Walker's ruling on Prop 8. http://www.huffingtonpost.com/2010/08/04/prop-8-ruling-read-the-fu_n_671050.html.

18. http://mashable.com/2012/03/02/youtube-propostion-8-play/.

19. Robert D. Putnam and David E. Campbell, *American Grace: How Religion Divides and Unites Us* (New York: Simon and Schuster, 2010), ch. 1, note 5.

20. "U.S. Stands Alone in Its Embrace of Religion,"Pew Global Attitudes Project. (Re-trieved January 1, 2007) http://www.pewglobal.org/2002/12/19/among-wealthy-nations/.

21. "U.S. Stands Alone in its Embrace of Religion,"Pew Global Attitudes Project. (Re-trieved January 1, 2007) http://www.pewglobal.org/2002/12/19/among-wealthy-nations/.

22. Robert E. Goss, Thomas Bohache; Deryn Guest, and Mona West, eds., *The Queer Bible Commentary* (SCM-Canterbury Press, 2006; Robert E. Goss and Mona West, eds., *Take Back the Word: A Queer Reading of the Bible* (Cleveland: Pilgrim Press, 2000).

23. Marvin Ellison, *Same-Sex Marriage: A Christian Ethical Analysis* (Cleveland: The Pilgrim Press, 2004), 142.

24. Marvin M. Ellison, "Marriage in a New Key," in *Sexuality and the Sacred: Sources for Theological Reflection*, ed. Marvin Ellison and Kelly Brown (Louisville, KY: Westminster John Knox Press, 2010), 407.

25. Ellison, *Same-Sex Marriage*, 132–45.

26. See California Faith for Equality, http://cafaithforequality.org/.

17

Coming to the Table in Leather

Lea Brown

For the past 16 years I have served in ordained ministry within the context of Metropolitan Community Churches (MCC). During these years within MCC I have gained great respect for the breadth, depth, diversity, and transformational power of two forces that profoundly shape and impact our lives: human sexuality and spirituality. In the lives of the people in the churches I have served I have seen how sexuality and spirituality can bring great joy, pleasure, healing, energy, compassion, and personal growth when they are allowed to exist and complement one another in a unified way in our bodies and lives. I have watched gay men and lesbian women cry uncontrollably during their initial MCC worship services when they hear for the first time that they don't have to choose between their sexual orientation and their relationship with God. I have seen transgender folk come into their own power in MCC as they hear the affirming message that they, too, are created in the image of the Divine. I have seen joy on the faces of members of the leather community in worship services where the colors of the leather flag are present on the Communion table, and where congregants wearing leather are leading the service. I have felt indescribable vitality and spiritual energy swell in a church sanctuary filled with the singing of all kinds of voices: polyamorous voices, BDSM voices, bisexual and pansexual voices, lesbian and gay voices, monogamous voices, heterosexual voices, single voices, married voices, and transgender voices. I have watched lives change in very positive ways and deep spiritual wounds heal when people hear and receive the message, *in church, from the pulpit, and at the Communion table,* that what they do sexually and how they express their gender in their lives are things God wants us to love about ourselves. This message is the unique gift and the greatest strength of MCC.

It seems to me that, at least in North America, many of us who are a part of MCC have either forgotten or have stopped believing in the transformational power of the message of MCC. Although 2012 is quite different from 1968 in many ways and in some places, the gift and message of MCC are sorely missing from the lives of vast numbers of people all over the world. The spiritual power inherent in what MCC has to offer is something that, I believe, is high time we embrace with renewed awareness, gratitude, and pride. I speak for myself and my congregation when I say that I cannot afford to forget the power of MCC, neither for my own life, nor for the lives of those I serve.

I write from both the limitations and the truth of my own social location as a white, 46-year-old, poly-spiritual, able-bodied Christian lesbian from a working-class background who grew up in a fundamentalist home in North America. What I have repeatedly witnessed from within this social location and in every place I have served as an MCC pastor (California, Texas and now Florida) are the great damage and pain that are *still* being caused when we are forced to choose between our sexual desires and our spiritual selves, when saying yes to ourselves as same-gender loving and/or transgender people requires that we believe that God does not love us, or that we are not allowed to pursue a spiritual life because our sexual orientation or expression of gender are inherently sinful. I have watched people break under the strain of having to choose between MCC church family and the acceptance of their biological family, between God's love and their love for their same-gendered partner, between their calling to vocational ministry and their calling to live as a leather person, between what gives them sexual pleasure and what fills them with spiritual power. For the most part (although not exclusively) the people I have seen wounded in these ways most deeply have come from very conservative or fundamentalist Christian backgrounds; however, I have also seen the ways all of us within MCC are hurt on a daily basis because we live in a culture saturated by homo and transphobia built on conservative religious beliefs from many different traditions.

I have been steeped in the reality of this culture for as long as I can remember. For the first 23 years of my life I was a very good Southern Baptist girl. I was saved from my sins through the blood of Jesus Christ in the fundamentalist Bible Baptist church of my childhood at the age of eight. I attended worship services and played the piano regularly at a fundamentalist Baptist church throughout high school, and I graduated from Oklahoma Baptist University (a Southern Baptist college) at the age of 22 in Shawnee, Oklahoma. I was devoted to being a good student, a good daughter, and a very good Christian. At the same time, I lived in absolute terror that one day I might have to admit to myself that I was attracted to other girls, or much worse, that others would find out this terrible truth about me. I spent all of those years in desperate prayer, begging God to change me, to take away the sinful feelings, and to make me normal. Even as I lived every day with a passionate love for God and for Jesus in my heart, I also lived with the devastating belief that God hated me and that because of my feelings for other girls that I could not make go away, I was going to spend eternity in hell. Every day I felt as though I was being ripped apart and forced to choose between my spiritual longings and my growing erotic desires.

When I came out as a lesbian at the age of 23 and discovered MCC, it was as if I was given a whole new life. I could worship in church *and* talk openly about being attracted to other women! I could sing the old Christian evangelical hymn "Just As I Am" and know that I didn't have to change or hide anything from God or anyone else to be accepted and loved. Finally, after so many years of self-loathing and fear, I could love God, Jesus, women, and myself; it was all a miracle that seemed too good to be true. Although it did take many years in MCC to heal from the multiple layers of religious wounds I sustained when I was younger, the healing did gradually happen, and at all kinds of sexual and spiritual levels. Particularly when I began serving as an intern at MCC San Francisco in 1995 I began to expand my understanding of the Divine and faith traditions outside of Christianity. I also began to explore my own spirituality and sexuality in new ways in the affirming environment of MCC San Francisco and the sexually adventurous setting of the Bay Area. I allowed my spiritual practices and beliefs to be informed and enhanced by practices and belief systems other than Christianity, just as I also discovered BDSM and the leather community that nurtured and fed me in both body and soul.

Today I am a very different person than I was 23 years ago when I made the decision to come out to myself and to the rest of my world. Although at times I still struggle with the homophobic conditioning of my Christian fundamentalist past, I live my life openly, proudly, and gratefully as the Christian, Butch lesbian, leather dyke senior minister of the Metropolitan Community Church of the Palm Beaches (MCCPB) in south Florida. I have a passionately close relationship with Jesus, I pray to the Creator of many names who made me in his or her image, I worship with my voice, mind, heart, and body in MCCPB services and with my Femme lesbian lover who has shown me the heart and the soul of the Divine in ways I never thought possible. The humor and sensibility of my community makes me laugh and find joy in life every day, just as the many experiences of both external and internalized homophobia I witness in my congregation every week break my heart. Most days I am able to love myself and others with abundance, and I live a life blessed with sexual pleasure and fulfillment, spiritual adventure, commitment to creating social justice, and all the rich, complex gifts and challenges that come with being intimately involved in spiritual community. *All* of this has happened to me and within me over time through the healing power that permeated my being when my sexuality and spirituality were finally allowed to coexist in my body, soul, and life. Precisely because of this, my own personal lived experience, as well as the life experiences I have witnessed in the congregations I have served, I have come to believe that there is a *profound healing power that is created specifically when we are able to encounter the union of sexuality and spirituality within our bodies and lives.*

As long as I live, I will never forget that it was (and is) MCC that made this experience of healing power a reality for me. It has only been in MCC where I have been able to come to the Communion table, first with my new-found lesbian identity, and later on wearing my first leather armband. On my journey toward ordained ministry I was blessed with the opportunity to explore the possibility of professional relationship with other denominations, particularly American Baptist and the United Church of Christ. While I am grateful for those explorations and those denominations, what I discovered through them was that it was only in MCC where I would be empowered and invited to eventually wear my leather stole for the first time as I stood behind the Communion table, consecrating the feast of God's unconditional love for all as an ordained minister of the gospel. It has only been in MCC where I have been encouraged, again and again, to ask myself these questions first asked by bell hooks: "What forms of passion might make us whole? To what passions may we surrender with the assurance that we will expand rather than diminish the promise of our lives?"[1] It has been within MCC that I have learned how to live the answers to these questions, and how I have discovered, within the context of MCC spiritual community, the truths about SM and Ds that would make me whole.

Giving myself the permission to ask such questions was no easy task, given that my own sexual longings as a lesbian and as someone interested in SM and Ds were intensely internal taboo subjects. In her writing on the sexuality of Jesus, Kwok Pui-lan describes the early use of the word "taboo" by westerners who appropriated the word from Polynesian culture in the 18th century. She states that "the word 'taboo' . . . provided a vocabulary or a force field to talk about the risk, boundary, terror, and dread of the 'sacred' as well as longing, desire, fascination, and possible transgression."[2] I believe that it was precisely the taboo nature of my desires, with all the attached transgressive risks, boundaries, terrors, longings, and fascination that propelled me forward against all religious and spiritual odds. A number of years after coming out as a lesbian, I also could not ignore my as-yet faint intuition that my SM desires might just be sacred. I came to realize that I could not deny how alive and connected to my spiritual self that I felt in SM play, nor the feelings of wholeness and peace that permeated my being afterwards. Contrary to everything I was ever taught about sex and my own sexuality in the independent Bible Baptist (fundamentalist) church in which I was raised, these experiences enabled me to trust that one of the most significant forms of passion most healing for me was to be found in the *Eros* of SM and Ds.

Sexuality author and educator Pat Califia (who now identifies as Patrick) describes SM as "an umbrella term . . . for any mutually pleasurable sexual activity between consenting adults that involves dominant and submissive role-playing, physical restraint, or erotic (i.e., pleasurable) pain."[3] SM is the term universally used by its practitioners rather than the word *sadomasochism*, which is often used in judgmental ways by those outside of SM communities to pathologize those who practice it. Just as SM is an umbrella term encompassing many kinds of sexual activity, so too is Ds (Domination-submission) used to label many different methods of role-playing and power exchange between two or more people within the context of SM as described above.

To gain an accurate understanding of the true nature of SM and Ds, it is imperative to realize the importance of three characteristics in Califia's description: mutual, consenting, and pleasurable. SM and Ds are *mutual* in that all the parties are equally passionate about and desiring of the kinds of activities that will be shared. Mutuality is determined before the activity begins through communication and negotiation between all who will be involved; participants are usually described by the function of their role with the words top (the person in the dominant role), and bottom (the person in the submissive role). This communication and negotiation requires that each top and bottom share the details, as specifically as possible, about the types of activities they enjoy the most, those that they do not enjoy and/or that are strictly off-limits, as well as the types of activities that they may be curious about or intrigued by but have not yet experienced. Through this method of negotiation, the stage is set for the scene, generally a time-limited sexual experience that will take place within the parameters set by the communication shared beforehand.

Aside from being a very provocative and stimulating way to begin preparation for experiencing SM and Ds together, this time of communication also ensures that each person is fully *consenting* to what will take place. Above all else, consent is the one characteristic that defines SM and Ds and sets both apart from abusive, violent, or oppressive behavior. Not surprisingly, this characteristic is also usually the most difficult to comprehend for those who do not practice SM and/or Ds, or who do not approve of the actions of those who do. Liz Highleyman describes the challenge of understanding consent within SM and Ds in this way:

> The words "top" and "bottom" do not transparently describe a consensual SM interaction. It is the bottom's consent that allows the scene to go forward (even in a scene in which the bottom temporarily agrees to forego consent). The bottom controls the foundation upon which the interaction is built, while the top often controls the specific details and direction of the scene. The top's pleasure depends on the bottom's willingness to engage in the interaction. The failure to grasp this paradox underlies many of the moral arguments against erotic domination and submission.[4]

It is this kind of trust and consent that lays the foundation for the exchange of power that occurs during SM and Ds activity, and that enables participants to safely explore their spiritual, sexual, and emotional landscapes and depths within. It is especially important that trust is present between those who are engaging in play, and that all parties involved believe that each person will hold the utmost respect for what has been consented to, and what hasn't. One of the elements of this trust in SM play is known as a safe word, which is something that is available to both tops and bottoms. Many people enjoy protesting during a scene, and the words "no, no, no" might actually mean "yes, yes, yes!" For this reason those who are playing together mutually agree upon a neutral word (perhaps red or desk) that can be used to communicate that something has gone amiss in the scene and play needs to be suspended in order to correct the course of action. A sincere level of trust between top and bottom is essential; this enables each person to play secure in the knowledge that if a safe word is used; all activity will stop to allow for the listening and communication necessary in the moment.

Finally, SM and Ds are nothing if not *pleasurable* for all those engaged in a scene together. In order for SM and Ds to be their best, both the top and the bottom must be dedicated to their partner's pleasure and fulfillment, as well as to having fun together. It is no coincidence that practitioners of SM and Ds often refer to what they do and how they do it as play. Children engaged in play often enjoy using their imaginations, and just as often they have fun taking on the personas they would like to be in the moment. So, too, does the adult version of play within SM and Ds gives the participants the opportunity to use their grown-up imaginations and have a very good time acting out the roles that are unavailable to them in day-to-day life, while simultaneously enjoying the pleasurable physical and sexual sensations that go along with this kind of imaginative play.

While Audre Lorde was never a supporter of SM or Ds during her lifetime, I can't help but think about both when considering her words: "There are many kinds of power, used and unused, acknowledged or otherwise."[5] The power that flows in an SM scene that incorporates Ds according to the characteristics and parameters I have described above is one kind of power, deliberately used and intentionally acknowledged by those involved. However, as with most things in life that require self-awareness and that promote intense emotional and physical experiences, SM and Ds are complex and not easily contained within a box of rules and regulations. Playing with power—even according to the standard rules of mutual, consenting, and pleasurable—can be controversial even within SM communities when that play is patterned after real-world systems of oppression. Examples of such play would include scenes incorporating the use of Nazi imagery and themes, the domination of a person of color by a white person using racist slurs or overtones, or a scene involving forced sex between a male in the role of top with a female bottom. Of course, the difference between these play scenes and real life is that there is no fixed, impenetrable system of domination; the top and bottom may have negotiated their desire to change roles mid-scene, with the bottom becoming the top and the top now submitting to the one he or she had previously been dominating. Such scenes can provide incredibly liberating and cathartic experiences, especially for those who live with real-world oppression every day. An SM scene of this type can provide a safe and supportive container where all kinds of feelings can be revealed, seen, acknowledged, and released. These are feelings that are sometimes labeled as unacceptable or dangerous and often have no available place to be expressed. These powerful emotions may build up in the bodies and spirits of those who struggle to live under oppression every day: anger, rage, grief, fear, sadness, shame, and revenge can all be played out between the top and the bottom in this kind of SM activity that is sometimes referred to as "edge play." There is no denying that to play with this kind of power is to dance precariously along moral and psychological lines that require tremendous care by all those involved, but the giving and receiving of such care is one of the most powerful alchemical elements of SM. Healing on profound levels can occur when people are so vulnerable with one another that they reveal the deepest parts of themselves that have been labeled as shameful, sinful, perverted, or damaged. When a bottom or top reveals feelings and desires that have been repeatedly rejected or demonized, and when those feelings and desires are met with acceptance, understanding, and encouragement within the boundaries of a scene, shame can be transformed into pride, fear into self-acceptance, rage and anger into peace, and self-rejection into self-loving and wholeness.

It is the complexity inherent within SM and Ds, and the requirements of safety and great care demanded by such complexity that also promote the emphasis upon ethical behavior in SM communities. Such emphasis requires consistent self and community examination and soul-searching. As Liz Highleyman states, "The most important feature in a community's ethics is . . . how its members treat one another. Are we honest, trustworthy, and accountable? Do we interact with consent and without coercion? Do we take responsibility for our actions? Do we recognize and respect the fact that others may have desires and needs that are different from our own?"[6] In any type of community the answers to these questions will always vary, since communities are made up of human, and thus imperfect, beings. In my own lived experience within the SM community of the San Francisco Bay Area, however, I repeatedly discovered individuals profoundly committed to a high standard of ethical behavior. I have had the privilege of playing with many people over the past 17 years of my involvement in SM, and to a person I have experienced each one as deeply committed to the safety and well-being of their play partners, as trustworthy, responsible, respectful of differences, highly sensitive to the needs of others, self-aware, and both genuinely interested in and respectful of my life, truths, and desires. From all that I have seen and experienced I know that it has been their involvement in SM and the ethical standards it requires, along with their own experiences of pleasure and healing that SM often gives, that have helped them to become the kind of people they are. My SM sisters and brothers know a great deal about the healing possibilities that live within our mutual play. We know that healing can come in many forms. We know that there is physical healing that brings relief and strength to our bodies. We know that there is emotional healing that enables us to both honor our many feelings and also to choose wisely how we express and live according to our emotions. We know there is sexual healing that creates acceptance of who we are and what we desire and the ability to get our desires met with integrity. We know there is spiritual healing that empowers us to feel connected to something bigger in the world around us and that nurtures our connection to ourselves, other beings, and the life force of love and creation all around us. Most of all, we know that SM is one of the most significant forms of passion that makes us whole—that enables us to have and embody all of these different forms of healing in our lives. It has been my privilege to share and create with them these experiences of healing that give us wisdom, strength, and compassion in our daily lives that we take with us into the world.

In my own lived experience of Ds, I have found that its power that allows me to swim deeply in *Eros* and bring healing to my body and spirit begins with its primary nature as play. As children we play to have fun, not knowing at the time that we are simultaneously learning about ourselves and the world around us while making progress through the developmental stages of our childhoods. We are also not consciously aware of how much our imagination and our toys make play possible. We take both and create vivid worlds where we can be anything or anyone we want to be, and often the ways in which we use our imaginations reveal much of what may be important to us as adults. Even today at the age of 46, I remember playing church by myself in my room when I was under the age of 10, imagining myself to be leading a group of people who were seeking refuge from some unnamed danger. In my room, alone, far from the fundamentalist church of my childhood that proclaimed through its nonconsensual theology of domination that females were not allowed to do such things, I was already living into my truest self, even if I didn't know it at the time.

On adult, psychological, sexual, and conscious levels, my play partners and I have often found that the nature of play within Ds provides us with very similar benefits to those we received from our childhood experiences of play. To begin with, engaging in Ds with others is fun, and it often adds a degree of joy and pleasure in our interactions and relationship with one another that can rarely be achieved in any other way. Taken alone, this is reason enough to engage in Ds; however, it has also given us tremendous opportunities to learn about ourselves and one another while growing in other areas of our lives. Ds has required me to both examine extensively and communicate directly about my sexual desires and fantasies; because of this necessity I don't think there has been anything in my life that has taught me more about my psyche, my needs, and my *Eros* as much as Ds. Simultaneously, as I have supported my play partners in their own Ds explorations as well, it has also given me a keen appreciation and admiration for the sexual and spiritual depth that lives within us all. It has taught me how to navigate the ebb and flow of my own erotic power, not just within the time and space limitations of a scene, but out in the real world where I constantly seek to let *Eros*—my connection with God—move without interruption. It puts me in the very center, along with my play partners, of exactly what I believe Janet Walton refers to in her writing about worship and liturgy as "holy play." In quoting Diane Ackerman, Walton says that "we play because 'play carries one across fear and uncertainty toward the slippery edges of possibility, where one must use oneself fully and stretch human limits to achieve the remarkable.' Play is a vehicle for discovery and growth."[7] When Ds play within a scene enables me to have a direct and intense experience of my own *Eros*, it is then so much easier to push past my fears and uncertainties to that place of discovery and growth where I am able to both pursue and be aware of that same *Eros* in my day-to-day life.

Not coincidentally, the two primary components of childhood play, imagination and toys, are also two of the primary components of the holy sexual play of Ds that enable this adult discovery and growth. Imagination is key, enabling participants to be omnipotent or helpless and everything in between should they want to be. Toys (or tools as they are sometimes called) are extensions of their imagined personas, whether those toys be the rope that temporarily secures a captive or the cane of the stern headmistress. It is all of these ingredients taken together—imagination, toys, self-discovery, understanding of others, and fun that make Ds play the unique and magical experience that it can be. They are also some of the very ingredients that can make a Ds scene an intensely spiritual experience of healing within our bodies, hearts, and minds. This healing occurs as we give ourselves over to the communication, vulnerability, trust, self-exploration, and mutuality that are required of us, and in doing so we discover and have the opportunity to accept aspects of ourselves that are a part of our deepest and truest self. In other words, Ds give us the chance to discover, explore, and share our very soul.

Gabrielle Roth has this to say about the soul:

> The soul can only be present when the body and spirit are one; it cannot breathe, exist, or move disconnected from the body. Your parents gave

birth to your body . . . The birth of your soul is a virgin birth, one you must do on your own . . . If you want to give birth to your true self, you are going to have to dig deep down into that body of yours and let your soul howl.[8]

As Roth also says in this same passage, giving birth is not easy, and labor is hard work.[9] While it is true that Ds can be the kind of play described above, it is just as true that Ds can serve as both the experience of labor and the midwife in the process of giving birth to one's own soul. This act of giving birth, of digging deeply into our bodies in order to let our souls howl, is not a timid act. Roth found that she was able to let her soul howl through sweating and dancing intensely all the way to her liberation and healing. Engaging in Ds is also not a timid act; participation in a scene in a healthy and safe way may very well require a great deal of digging deeply into one's fears, secrets, shame, arousal, fantasies, desires, hopes, insecurities, inhibitions, strengths, needs, pasts, and present. I know of no other experience other than my own that has taught me this truth so well. When I first began to explore SM and Ds I was 29 years old. Throughout my entire life, since the time I was old enough to have sexual awareness of myself, my fantasies told the truth about who I was: a woman attracted to other women, and a woman drawn to both SM and Ds. It wasn't until I was 24 that I had my first sexual experience of any kind at all (it also happened to be my first sexual encounter with a woman), and it wasn't until I was 30 before I discovered the difference between just fantasizing about SM and Ds, and actually taking part in both. Getting to the place and time of that first scene was not easy. It had taken breaking through years of shame and fear to finally confess my interests to someone, followed by months of reading, talking with others, and trying to work up the courage to attend a women's SM group in San Francisco. This was followed by even more months of trying to bring myself to the place where I was actually ready to negotiate a scene and play with someone else. Certainly, though, it was in that negotiation and play that I discovered that I had indeed been in the process of giving birth to my truest self, and I learned what it felt like to have that self seen, acknowledged, accepted, and affirmed. It felt as though my soul truly did howl with release and profound relief at not having to keep so much hidden and bottled up inside anymore.

In that particular scene, with its combination of my submission to the power of another and the intense physical sensations that were played out on my body, my soul's howl was full of joy and delight. Now, many years and many scenes since, there have been other kinds of howls as well, sometimes full of sadness or grief, rage or tears, or sometimes just full of the catharsis needed in the moment. Each one, though, has been a re-claiming and embracing of my soul, of realizing there is no part of me that should ever be forced into a prison of shame or fear by anyone's the-ology, interpretation of the Bible, or faith tradition. It is because of my journey with SM and Ds, supported and encouraged throughout my si-multaneous ministry in MCC, that I can understand what Roth is saying when she describes her own journey as a teacher guiding others to reclaim their power through dance: "The soul wasn't lost; it had been buried deep in our bones, driven down under by centuries of traditions designed to control our natural urges towards ecstasy. We had become alienated from ourselves as sacred beings."[10] In large part because of my dance with SM and Ds that I have been able to experience openly while serving in MCC, I have been able to realize that I am a sacred being—that far from being the damaged and perverted abomination my church said I was, I am in-stead a sexual and spiritual part of creation that reflects the compassion, love, beauty, grace, passion, and power of all that is sacred, whole, and divine in our world.

I believe strongly that this ability to empower people to understand and embrace all of who they are is perhaps the greatest gift of Ds, thus making it a gift that goes hand in hand with the liberating message of the union of sex and spirit of MCC. The *Eros*, characteristics, and parameters of Ds reflect the value of the incredible power of sexual desire in all its forms. Although her article on the regulation of sex does not specifically men-tion Ds, Rebecca Alpert's description of sexual power and desire certainly seems to at least make room for its existence: "Sexual desire is irrational and unpredictable. We do not know what creates and stimulates desire within an individual. Love may be gentle and kind, but passion isn't al-ways, nor is it always wise to express or act on it. Recognizing the danger-ous dimension of sexual desire can enable people to find creative ways to work with it."[11] The structure and nature of Ds clearly recognize the dan-gerous dimensions of both human sexual need and desire. As human be-ings we are not always loving and kind; in fact, we often seem to be at the mercy of passionate emotions that have few, if any, morally acceptable or legal outlets. Whether we are attracted to Ds play or not, who among us has not had the sincere desire to inflict pain on someone because it might make us feel better? Who has never had the desire to be utterly free from responsibility for even a short period of time, longing for someone else to make all the decisions and call all the shots? How many times do our fan-tasies (that more often than not we never share with another living soul), reflect our needs and desires that are simply deemed unacceptable in our society? Ds recognizes these emotional and psychological realities of the human condition, and provides a safe and creative container in which to experience and explore all of who we are.

As someone who lived half of my life trying to suppress everything about my sexuality that my church and society told me was forbidden, I can attest to the tremendous and damaging power of suppression. The more I was forced to deny my desires, the bigger they became as I got older, and the more alienated I was from myself and God. In Mark 12, when asked about the details of the most important commandment, Jesus replies: "The most important one is this: 'Hear, O Israel, the Lord our God, the Lord is one. Love the Lord your God with all your heart and with all your soul and with all your mind and with all your strength.' The second is this: 'Love your neighbor as yourself.' There is no commandment greater than these" (Mk 12:29–31). Ds, along with hearing this passage in the context of worship and communion in MCC, helped me to realize that loving God with my whole being, and loving my neighbor as myself, were both virtually impossible as long as I continued to deny so much of who I was and what I desired. How is it possible to love God with all of your heart, soul, mind, and strength when your society and faith community demonize the sexual thoughts and feelings that are alive and kicking inside your heart, soul, and mind with such strength? How is it possible to love your neighbor as yourself when you are told repeatedly by those in power that so much of who you are is unlovable? How much more powerful than the nonconsensual, enforced denial of our desires is the relief and acceptance we can feel for ourselves and others when we finally have permission and support to reveal all of who we are without judgment or condemnation, even if only within the time and role-restricted environment of an SM scene? Ironically, it has been the practice of Ds, affirmed by my MCC spiritual community that has taught me more about the unconditional love of God than anything that I experienced in the church in which I was raised. When the parts of myself that my early experience of Christianity taught me to despise have been desired and celebrated by my top or bottom, the Divine revealed to me in human flesh, I have at long last finally experienced God as loving, accepting, and worthy of my devotion.

Of course, in the end, it is not only the characteristics and parameters of Ds that can lead us to a new and liberated love for God, ourselves, and others; but it is also the act of experiencing Ds in the company of our play partners that ultimately brings us the gift of healing and wholeness.

bell Hooks speaks of the healing black women, who are physical or sexual abuse survivors can find when they are supported by partners who accept all of who they are: "Since so many black women have experienced traumatic physical abuse, we come to sexuality wounded. Irrespective of our sexual preference, we need to be with partners who are able to hear us define boundaries and limits. We need partners who are able to give us the loving care that makes sexual healing possible."[12] The physical and sexual wounds that live inside our bodies, inflicted both by abuse and by religious regulation of sex, require being seen and tended to with the loving support of others. I don't believe that practitioners of Ds are inherently more loving than other human beings; however, I do know that the act of sharing needs and wounds born of shame and oppression make the love received feel all the more redeeming and transformative. When we experience love through the nonjudgmental respect and care given by another in Ds play, especially in a scene where we are revealing the parts of ourselves that have been labeled as sick or perverted, we experience the kind of profound acceptance and Divine affirmation that have the power to turn such damaging labels into the new names of whole and blessed. If this is not an experience of God's love, what else could it be called? As we often used to say at MCC San Francisco, "God has no hands but our hands, and no face but our face." I would add that God also has no other way to share unconditional love with us but through the ways we share that love and acceptance with one another.

In his beautiful book *Prayers of the Cosmos*, author Neil Douglas-Klotz offers his interpretation of "blessed are the merciful, for they shall obtain mercy" from the Aramaic: "Tuned to the Source are those who shine from the deepest place in their bodies. Upon them shall be the rays of universal love."[13] In spite of many religious voices attempting to compel us to believe differently, we have the ability to learn in ever-more powerful ways that we are in touch with the Source—however we name the Divine—from the deepest place *in our bodies*. The more we touch that deep place through sensuality, through beauty in the world around us, through erotic energy and connection with ourselves and others, and through all kinds of sexual practices and pleasures, the more we both understand love and expand our capacity to create it in the world around us. This universal love that comes from the union of sexuality and spirituality in our lives is the healing power that we have to offer to the world around us. It is the spiritual power grounded in the truth of our sexual experience that we can use to bless others. Our world needs this blessing now more than ever before, which is precisely why those of us who are a part of MCC must remember and renew our belief in the transformational power of our message.

I cannot even begin to say how grateful I am that, not only have I been able to experience the joy and healing that Ds and SM have brought to me, but that I have also been able to live my life as a self-professed leather dyke in MCC. I have been immeasurably blessed by the fact that at both the denominational and local congregational levels, MCC has never asked me to hide any part of who I am, sexually or spiritually. I have come to understand all of the truths about SM and Ds that I have shared in this chapter both as a layperson and as an ordained MCC minister. This kind of freedom is virtually unheard of by those called to professional Christian ministry. The fact that I was asked to make a contribution to this book on this very topic is yet another example of the unique spiritual and sexual ministry that is and always has been the mission and greatest strength of MCC.

It is my profound hope that my congregation and MCCs all over the world will continue to grow in our understanding of the power and the vital necessity of our mission. So many people are hungry for experiences of worship filled with this power; for opportunities to strive toward social justice for all people with words and actions driven by this kind of love and acceptance; for life made rich and full by spiritual community that dances with God in sexual joy and spiritual wonder. May we who are a part of MCC realize anew that we have been called to offer the feast at our Communion tables where this hunger can at last be satiated. May we renew our passion to set our tables with determination and without apology. May we proclaim our message boldly that the union of sexuality and spirituality is the birthright of us all, and it is ours to enjoy with the blessing of the Divine.

NOTES

1. bell Hooks, "Moved By Passion: Eros and Responsibility," in *Sisters of the Yam* (Cambridge, MA: South End Press, 2005), 95.

2. Pui-Lan Kwok, "Touching the Taboo: On the Sexuality of Jesus," in *Sexuality and the Sacred: Sources for Theological Education*, 2nd ed., ed. Marvin M. Ellison and Kelly Brown Douglas (Louisville: Westminster John Knox Press, 2010), 119–34

3. Pat Califia, *Sensuous Magic: A Guide for Adventurous Couples* (New York: NY: Masquerade Books, 1993), 6.

4. Liz Highleyman, "Playing with Paradox: The Ethics of Erotic Dominance and Submission," in *Bitch Goddess: The Spiritual Path of the Dominant Woman*, ed. Pat Califia and Drew Campbell (San Francisco, CA: Greenery Press, 1997), 155.

5. Audre Lorde, "Uses of the Erotic: The Erotic as Power," in *Sister Outsider: Essays and Speeches by Audre Lorde* (Freedom, CA: The Crossing Press), 53.

6. Highleyman, "Playing With Paradox," 161.

7. Diane Ackerman, *Deep Play* (New York: Random House, 1999), 38; quoted in Janet A. Walton, "Imagination and Improvisation: Holy Play," in *The Papers of the Henry Luce II Fellows in Theology*, vol. 4, ed. Matthew Zyniewicz (Atlanta: Scholars Press, 2000), 179.

8. Gabrielle Roth, "The Great Divide," in *Sweat Your Prayers: The Five Rhythms of the Soul* (New York: Jeremy Tarcher/Putnam Inc., 1998), 4.

9. Ibid.

10. Gabrielle Roth, "God, Sex & My Body," in *Sweat Your Prayers*, xxiii.

11. Rebecca T. Alpert, "Guilty Pleasures: When Sex Is Good Because It's Bad," in *Good Sex: Feminist Perspectives From the World's Religions*, ed. Patricia Beattie Jung, Mary E. Hunt and Radhika Balakrishnan (New Brunswick, NJ: Rutgers University Press, 2001), 39.

12. hooks, "Moved by Passion," 94.

13. Neil Douglas-Klotz, *Prayers of the Cosmos: Reflections on the Original Meaning of Jesus' Words* (San Francisco: HarperOne, 1993), 43.

18

Queer *Lectio Divina*

Mona West

In his book, *Lectio Divina: Renewing the Ancient Practice of Praying the Scriptures*, Father Basil Pennington suggests,

> The Word was made flesh. Jesus is the most complete expression of the Word in our creation. God is a Word. God is communication. And we therefore are essentially a listening, a listening for that Word. To the extent we truly "hear" that Word, receive that Word into our being and into our lives we participate in the Divine Being, Life, Love, Joy. Made in the image of God, we have an unlimited, and infinite potential to be like unto him.
>
> Each of us is a certain listening, a certain openness to being, to reality, to communication. Everything that has been a part of our lives since the moment of our creation has had its role in shaping the listening that we are . . . it is good for us to realize that we are a certain, definable listening. It is as though my listening has a certain physical shape to it.[1]

As I read this quote and as I ponder the importance of scripture in the lives of LGBT folk, the following questions arise: "How do LGBT people who have been told that scripture calls us an 'abomination' truly hear and receive the Word of God into our being, into our lives so that we might participate in the 'Divine Being, Life, Love, Joy?' How might LGBT people of faith enter into the kind of listening that embraces the power of scripture for spiritual formation?"

While each of us may be a unique listening for God in the words of scripture, the Bible has also been interpreted by groups of people with certain kinds of power and belief systems in ways that have resulted in the marginalization, abuse, and death of queer people. Over the years, people who have been victims of this kind of biblical abuse have developed different reading strategies not only to survive and deflect the abuse, but also to claim their own power as interpreters of the biblical text, and to reclaim the transformational power of scripture in their spiritual journeys.

Feminist biblical scholars, in particular, have developed numerous reading strategies that disarm misogynist texts, as well as highlight the role of women in scripture. Elisabeth Schüssler Fiorenza outlines nine strategies in her book *But She Said: Feminist Practices of Biblical Interpretation.*[2] I want to highlight three of those reading strategies which have been foundational for a queer biblical hermeneutic, and are instrumental, I believe, in empowering queer people of faith to engage the ancient practice of praying the scriptures known as *lectio divina.*

For feminists, a revisionist reading strategy attempts to rediscover all the information about women that still can be found in biblical writings. LGBT biblical interpreters have used this strategy to read stories such as Jonathan and David, Ruth and Naomi, and Jesus and the Beloved Disciple in an effort to rediscover all the information we can about same-sex relationships in the Bible. The feminist revisionist approach also seeks to address layers of androcentric interpretation of biblical texts, claiming that biblical texts have been patriarchalized by interpreters who have projected their androcentric cultural bias onto the texts. Likewise, LGBT scholars have claimed that the Bible has nothing to say in the current debate about homosexuality as a sexual orientation and any attempts to use scripture in the debate is the result of the homophobic bias of the interpreter. Along with feminists, we have learned Greek and Hebrew in order to correct homophobic translations and commentaries. Specifically, we have used this aspect of a revisionist strategy on a particular set of texts called "the clobber" passages and more recently "texts of terror" because of their misuse against our community.

These texts are: the story of Sodom and Gomorrah in Genesis 19; the abomination passages of Leviticus 18:22 and 20:13; the "unnatural acts" passage of Romans 1:26–28; and the vice lists of 1 Corinthians 6:9 and 1 Timothy 1:10. A revisionist approach has set these texts in their historical and cultural contexts and demonstrated that there is much ambiguity and homophobia concerning the translation and interpretation of such words as *yadah*, "to know" in Genesis 19; *mishkav zakur* "the lyings of a male" in Leviticus, *para pusin* "against nature" in Romans 1, *malakoi* "soft" in 1 Corinthians; and *arsenokoitai* "lying with males" also in 1 Corinthians.

Another feminist reading strategy that has been helpful for a queer biblical hermeneutic and LGBT people of faith is "imaginative identification."

For feminists this strategy imagines or assumes women characters in bib-lical stories where they might not be explicitly mentioned. Nancy Wilson, in her book *Our Tribe: Queer Folks, God, Jesus, and the Bible*, applies imaginative identification to biblical texts and claims that if at any given time in history and cultures there have been a percentage of people who have a same-sex orientation then it would stand to reason and imagination that some of these people are in the biblical story. She wonders if the eunuchs—sexual minorities in the biblical story—might be the spiritual ancestors of LGBT people today. How might their roles as go betweens and mediators be related to a similar priestly function of two-spirited (transgender) peoples in ancient tribal cultures? Wilson also ponders if the sisters Mary and Martha and their brother Lazarus could be Jesus' family of choice. Jesus spends time with these unmarried siblings and relates to them in much the same way LGBTQ people choose nonbiological family for themselves. And what about Lydia in the book of Acts—a seller of purple? A color, Wilson points out, long associated with lesbians.[3]

Another approach of feminist biblical interpretation that has informed queer biblical interpreters is what is known as *social location*. This approach recognizes that all of us interpret the Bible as members of particular communities—communities that are shaped by race, gender, class, and sexual orientation.

Another term for social location is "community situation approach." It involves a hermeneutic that takes the community's life experience into account. The community's needs determine the ways in which the texts of the Bible are appropriated. James Earl Massey, in his article "Reading the Bible from Particular Social Locations" in volume one of *The New Interpreter's Bible* indicates that most of the communities who employ this method have a social history of oppression and marginalization. They have had the Bible used against them by the dominant culture to justify their oppression. According to Massey, each group finds a point, or points, of reference from which to read, reclaim, and reappropriate the meaning of scripture for the community in liberating and affirming ways. He suggests that in African American communities the point of reference is often the theme of deliverance.

I suggest that in queer communities the point of reference for reading the Bible is often the theme of coming out. For example, the book of Exodus can be seen as a coming out story. In chapter one of Exodus the pharaoh gets nervous because there are so many Hebrew slaves. He seeks to "deal shrewdly with them" because they may overtake the Egyptians in the event of a war. LGBT people hear echoed in these words of the pharaoh such phrases as "don't ask don't tell," "love the sinner, hate the sin." When we come out of the closet we become too many and are perceived as a threat to national security. Throughout our history there have been those pharaohs who have tried to get rid of us through death and physical violence.

Just as the Hebrews risked coming out of slavery in Egypt into a new identity as God's people, so do LGBTQ people risk coming out of closets made by fundamentalist interpretations of scripture that claim we are an abomination into a new identity as God's beloved and blessed people. It took the Hebrew people 40 years in the wilderness to learn to live into their new identity as God's people and often they were tempted to return to what was familiar to them in Egypt. Coming out is like that for LGBTQ people.

The power of the story of the exodus for the people of Israel can be found in its continued telling and retelling. With each telling future generations are invited to participate in its freedom and liberation. Each generation is invited to make their own journey to become part of the covenant people.

It is similar with coming out stories. We often say "silence equals death." To keep our stories silent is to refuse a rite of passage for future generations who need to know they do not make the journey alone.

These three reading strategies—a revisionist approach, imaginative identification, and social location—have been instrumental in the physical and spiritual survival of lesbian, gay, bisexual, and transgender people as we have moved from a place of fearing the Bible to a place of finding our ancestors in it.

Yet all of these strategies approach the Bible as an object to be studied, interpreted, or debated. They function in the realm of reading for information. We are the ones asking questions of the text, its history, and its interpretation. I believe that in addition to reading the Bible for information, LGBT folks must read the Bible for formation—our spiritual formation.

Robert Mulholland has made a case for the importance for this way of reading scripture in his book *Shaped by the Word: The Power of Scripture in Spiritual Formation*. He claims the shift from reading the Bible for information to reading the Bible for formation is a difficult one to make because western culture is shaped by the informational mode. Our culture seeks to acquire more information in an effort to control outcomes and our environment.[4]

His characterization of the differences between informational and formational ways of reading is helpful. Informational reading seeks to gather as much material as it can in the shortest amount of time possible. Speed reading and skimming are quick ways of informational reading. Reading for formation is not concerned with quantifying the amount of material covered. Small portions are savored and pondered.

Informational reading is linear moving from one point to another while formational reading seeks to move to the depth of a text. Control and interpretation of a text is the goal of informational reading. In contrast, formational reading approaches the text in an open manner, to receive and respond rather than control. Treating the text as an object to be mastered or controlled keeps the informational reader at a distance from the text. Formational readers will enter into a relationship with the text—the reader is the object to be shaped by the text. Informational reading is critical and analytical with a "problem-solving mentality," while formational reading is humble and willing with "an openness to mystery."[5]

Mulholland does not want to do away with informational reading and demonstrates the helpful ways informational reading functions in the academic study of scripture. He does advocate for the interplay of informational and formational reading of the Bible but claims that formational reading must take priority when one approaches scripture for spiritual formation. He describes, "There is a necessary interplay between these two approaches to the scripture. But as far as the role of scripture in spiritual formation is concerned, you ultimately need to arrive at a disciplined development of the formational mode of approaching the text. Only in the formational mode, where that shift of the inner posture of our being takes place, can we become listeners. Only in that mode can we become receptive and accessible to be addressed by the living Word of God."[6]

It is my prayer that as gay, lesbian, bisexual, and transgender people begin to feel safer with the Bible we will be able to risk trusting the formative power of scripture. In our desire to grow spiritually, LGBT people are invited by the Holy Spirit to let the Word of God read us. In the act of spiritual reading, reading for formation, we bring the word of God spoken in us, the person God has uniquely created us to be—the listening that we are—to Christ, the Word of God witnessed to in scripture.

One way to practice the formational reading of scripture is *lectio divina*—sacred reading. Its origins are in desert monasticism. Pilgrims would seek out the Fathers and Mothers of the Egyptian desert of the fourth century and ask them for a Word from God. In the sixth century St. Benedict built into his Rule a regular time for monks to read and meditate on scripture. And by the 12th century a monk by the name of Guigo II outlined what we know as the four steps or degrees of *lectio* today: *lectio, meditatio, oratio,* and *contemplatio.*

This way of praying the scriptures introduces us to the power of the Word of God in scripture to speak to the most intimate depths of our hearts, to gift and challenge and change us, and to promote spiritual growth and maturity. *Lectio* can be practiced individually, communally, in an hour, in a day, and for a lifetime. It is not a method for producing mystical experience, but a prayer practice that deepens our relationship to God as the Beloved. Even though there are four steps or four degrees to *lectio divina,* it should be understood as an organic process rather than linear steps to a method.

Briefly, the four movements of *lectio divina* are:

- *Lectio,* which involves listening for a word or a phrase that presents itself upon a first hearing of a passage or verse of scripture.
- *Meditatio,* which places the hearer in the passage through imagination or intellect.
- *Oratio,* which involves paying attention to feelings that have arisen as a result of placing oneself in the passage, resulting in expressing those feelings to God.
- *Contemplatio,* which is often characterized as a simple resting in God.

I want to explore in more depth what happens when queer people of faith engage these movements of *lectio divina.*

LECTIO

In *lectio* as well as *meditatio* we see the interplay of informational and formational ways of reading the Bible. The reading strategy of social location empowers LGBT people to claim our unique identities and bring all of who we are to a listening for the word of God which dwells in the depths of our being. In this first movement of *lectio divina* we are being receptive to the One who speaks in us. We are listening for the indwelling word of God that is spoken in our unique, embodied humanity. It is a queer word. The queer word spoken in me as a lesbian might resonate differently than the queer word spoken in a transgender friend who is listening to the same passage. For example, Galatians 3:26–28 states, "In Christ Jesus you are all children of God through faith. As many of you as were baptized into Christ have clothed yourselves with Christ. There is no longer Jew or Greek, there is no longer slave or free, there is no longer male and female; for all are one in Christ Jesus." The initial place of resonance in this passage for me as a lesbian might be "I am a child of God," while the resonance for my transgender friend might be "there is no longer male and female."

MEDITATIO

The reading strategy of imaginative identification empowers LGBT people not only to find our spiritual ancestors in scripture but also to place our very selves in the text. In this second movement we are invited to deeply interiorize the initial listening of *lectio* by placing ourselves in the passage using our imagination. We are also invited, in the words of Father Pennington, "to chew" on the passage, using our intellect to ask questions of the text and its interpretation. It is here that queer folk also bring to bear the revisionist approach to reading scripture (the interplay of informational and formational) as we disarm homophobic interpretations that would hinder us from trusting scripture for our spiritual formation. Not only do we imagine or recover who might have been in the story as a queer spiritual ancestor but also once we place ourselves in the passage the text itself becomes queer.

Continuing with our Galatians example, in this movement of *lectio* a queer person of faith might ponder the larger themes of the letter to the Galatians, contextualizing the specific statement in 3:26–28. Patrick S. Cheng, in his essay on Galatians in the *Queer Bible Commentary* points out that "Freedom from the law is the central theme of Paul's letter to the Galatians. As such, it resonates powerfully with queer Christians who have been oppressed by numerous laws, both religious and secular, that have tried to restrict our sexualities and relationships." So, as a lesbian, if I resonated with the phrase "child of God" upon at a first listening, in this second movement I might deepen that listening by chewing on the notion that according to the larger message of Galatians there is no law that can keep me from being God's child. I am free to be God's child. I can imagine myself as a member of the church in Galatia, hearing this letter from Paul being read for the first time: "In Christ Jesus you are all children of God through faith." Because Paul was arguing against the law of circumcision as a requirement to be a child of God in the letter to the Galatians, my transgender friend might ponder that there is no law, especially with regard to one's genitalia, that legislates ones gender identity or status as God's child. My transgender friend might imagine if there were transgender members of the church in Galatia and how they would have heard this vision of a world beyond gender that Paul articulates in 3:26–28.

ORATIO

In this third movement of *lectio divina* we journey more deeply into our heart. The informational work we have done in the first two movements of *lectio divina* brings us to a place of inner awakening of God's unconditional love and desire for us as the Beloved. This happens by paying attention to our feelings and asking the question, "What prayer has my work with this passage evoked in me?" We then attempt to express that prayer to God, sometimes with words, sometimes with groanings too deep for words. In *oratio* we are invited to stay present to these feelings, trying to express them to the one who has made us and loves us. To engage in this kind of openness to God's love we will be invited to take an honest look at our humanity, to love ourselves, and in the process of loving ourselves we will be guided by the work of the Holy Spirit to look lovingly at those behaviors, attitudes, and ways of being in the world that make us false and keep us separated from our neighbor and creation.

When queer people of faith engage this movement of *lectio divina*, we queer or subvert, heteronormative notions of spiritual development that claim our sexual orientation or gender identity are what make us false. The continual conversion that takes place in *oratio* is not a shedding or denying that we are gay, lesbian, transgender, or bisexual, it is a deepening of our truest self, our divinity, as we embody the queer Christ to the world. Instead of leading us to deny our sexual orientation and gender expression, this movement of *lectio* leads us to embrace more fully who we are as God's queer children. It may be that the invitation of the Spirit in this movement of *lectio divina* is to begin or deepen one's own coming-out process.

When we practice *lectio divina* on a regular basis we find that not only do we encounter these movements as we work with a specific passage of scripture, but these movements also manifest in our spiritual journey. There may be times in our spiritual life that we would describe as *meditatio* when we are chewing on an issue, working something out with God. There may be other times in our spiritual life that we would describe as an *oratio* place—a time of great feeling of God's love for us. *Lectio divina* is not linear and often whether we are working with a passage of scripture or reflecting on how the Spirit is working in our lives, we experience a back and forth movement among these levels of *lectio divina*. I believe the back and forth movement between *meditatio* and *oratio* are essential in the work of the holy integration of our sexuality and our spirituality as queer people of faith.

CONTEMPLATIO

It is hard to write or speak about this movement of *lectio divina* because we move to an even deeper place within ourselves and God who is in us. It is the place of the union of the lover and the beloved. For all of the activity of the first three movements of *lectio divina,* and *contemplatio* is a simple awareness of the indwelling presence of Christ and an awareness of our participation in the love that is continually expressed in the life of the Trinity. John of the Cross describes it as a "secret, peaceful and loving inflow of God which, if not hampered, fires the soul in the spirit of love."[7]

When working with a passage of scripture, we simply rest in God, after we have expressed the prayer of our heart in *oratio.* To rest in God in this way is to hold a loving gaze, to enter an interior silence with no expectation but to be lovingly present to the one who dwells in your very depths. It is in this place that the Spirit works beyond our knowing, that "we entrust ourselves to God so that God may take us beyond ourselves."[8] This last degree of *lectio divina* is shear gift and grace. It is not a place of spiritual navel gazing, but a place where we experience a life in God that joins us to each other and compels us to love as we have been loved. It is a place of deep knowing that all are one in Christ Jesus.

On my kitchen counter at home I have a plaque that reads:

"When a woman loves a woman ancient silences reawaken"
                                        —Hilda Gutierrez Baldoquin

I believe that: When a queer loves and trusts scripture ancient silences reawaken.

NOTES

1. Basil Pennington, *Lectio Divina: Renewing the Ancient Practice of Praying the Scriptures* (New York: Crossroad, 1998), 12–13.

2. Elisabeth Schüssler Fiorenza, *But She Said: Feminist Practices of Biblical Interpretation* (Boston, Beacon Press, 1992), 20–38.

3. Nancy Wilson, *Our Tribe: Queer Folks, God, Jesus, and the Bible* (New York: HarperSanFrancisco, 1995), 120–32, 140, 157.

4. Robert Mulholland, *Shaped by the Word: The Power of Scripture in Spiritual Formation* (Nashville: Upper Room, 1986), 48.

5. Ibid., 49–57.

6. Ibid., 59.

7. *Dark Night of the Soul,* 10:6, 11:1.

8. Thelma Hall, *Too Deep for Words: Rediscovering Lectio Divina* (New York: Paulist Press, 1988).

19

Spiritual Companioning: The Art of Being Present to the Spiritual Traveler and Lighting the Path

Joseph Shore-Goss

"At this table I am proud to proclaim as it is proclaimed at Metropolitan Community Churches all over the world: You do not need be a member of this church or any church." These words are even included in the vision of our local churches. At Metropolitan Community Church (MCC) in the Valley our vision states:

> We are a House of Prayer for all people and welcome all people on their spiritual search and journeys. Our communion table belongs to God alone, and all God's children are welcome to our table. We do not place any barriers, walls, doctrines, or politics around God's invitation to table. This models our community life.Our Mission: At Metropolitan Community Church in the Valley, a Christian Church originally founded to serve the Lesbian, Gay, Bisexual, and Transgendered community, we welcome all humanity as a reflection of God. Through the example of Jesus the Christ, we know God's table is without boundaries—an inclusive spiritual and prayer-centered community of love, peace-making, and compassionate care.[1]

This vision of a house of prayer for all people and a table where all God's children are welcome also means we have a space where all God's children call for some type of pastoral care. One common area of pastoral care that is seeing resurgence in the world today is spiritual direction.

Spiritual direction calls for companioning people on their spiritual journey. Creating a welcoming and inviting space where the traveler (the one on the spiritual journey or the "Directee") is made to feel comfortable in sharing their path. The spiritual companion in turn is a witness to the journey and may help to point out moments of God's spark that have come along the way. I intentionally will be using language that is not commonly used. The relationship between a spiritual companion and/or friend and the spiritual traveler is rarely one of a director and a directee. As a spiritual companion I do not direct any one and I choose to stay away from those terms. I prefer companion and traveler or spiritual companion and spiritual traveler or one on the Spiritual path. This is my personal choice and I hope the reader is comfortable with that.

I currently hold an MDiv and MA from Claremont School of Theology. My MA was in pastoral care concentrating on chaplaincy. I have served as a chaplain at Children's Hospital Los Angeles and in a hospice setting as well. I also hold a certificate in spiritual direction from Stillpoint,[2] and I am a member of Spiritual Directors International.[3] My wide and varied experience in these three widely different roles as well as serving as a Pastor of Congregational Care has uniquely prepared me to serve as a spiritual companion.

In this chapter, we explore what spiritual companioning is and what it is not. We will look at some specific skills that the spiritual companion will need to have to accompany a traveler on their journey. Then we will finally explore some specific models of interfaith spiritual direction and exactly how one companions another who is, perhaps, on a different spiritual path than the companion is familiar with.

SPIRITUAL COMPANIONING

Spiritual companioning, again my preferred term, will be referred to, or is most commonly known as spiritual direction. Most of the experts I will quote will use that term and it is completely interchangeable with the term spiritual companion. Again this is my preference, and I will explain why.

A spiritual director neither directs nor is the directee directed. This is why I prefer companion. Margaret Guenther states; "The art of spiritual direction lies in our uncovering the obvious in our lives and in realizing that every day events are the means by which God tries to reach us."[4]

As companions we notice things along the path that a traveler may have missed, overlooked, or did not pay close enough attention too. We simply ask the spiritual traveler to stop, take moment, and perhaps, if they choose, notice and explore what God has placed along the path.

A good definition of spiritual companioning is in the book *The Art of Spiritual Direction* by W. Paul Jones who states:

> Providing companionship on someone's pilgrimage; walking together in the Spirit so as to provide support, discernment, and encounter; integrating spiritually the intersections of the person's intellectual, emotional, social, and cultural contexts.[5]

The opportunity to share in such a relationship is one of the greatest and most sacred gifts I can imagine. I am astounded by the grace that God has found a way to allow me to be such a companion to another and I hold the opportunity as such. The companioning relationship is truly a gift of God.

The art of spiritual companioning is as old as the earth itself. W. Paul Jones Points out that in the Hebrew Scriptures . . . "The bible's first story concerns spiritual direction. Adam and Eve had regular appointments to walk with God 'at the time of the evening breeze' (Gen 3.8)."[6] This day and age, we still continue to walk with God it is just that we sometimes need some help in noticing what God has left for us along the path of our journeys.

Spiritual companioning is not a clinical act. It is not a quick fix. It is a long enduring relationship where two people set out on a journey together intentionally listening for and seeking out the God moments in life. On the road to Emmaus, two disciples were joined by another traveler. These travelers ate, drank, and discussed many a thing about Jesus and his ministry but it wasn't until Christ was gone could they open their eyes and look back and see all the signs that God had been with them. "They said to one another were not our hearts burning inside us as this one talked to us on the road and explained the scriptures to us?" (Lk 24:32). There are times when our hearts are burning and we do not know why. It takes another companion to look lovingly along the path to help the traveler see what they have missed.

Again spiritual companioning is a gentle long walk and is not clinical encounter. It is not a medical procedure, nor is it meant to be a fix all session and then we are done. Again let me use Paul Jones to affirm this.

> Spiritual Direction is not psychotherapy nor is it an inexpensive substitute, although the disciplines are compatible and frequently share raw material.

Spiritual direction is not pastoral counseling, nor is it to be confused with the mutuality of deep friendships, for it is unashamedly hierarchical. Not because the director is somehow "better" or "holier" than the directee, but because, in this covenanted relationship the director has agreed to put himself aside so that his total attention can be focused on the person sitting in the other chair. What a gift to bring to another, the gift of disinterested, loving attention![7]

In the midst of the relationship of companion and traveler, there may arise a need of that which is more than the companion can offer. Many a time a traveler will be referred for pastoral counseling or even more medical counseling, along with spiritual direction, and the road may become easier for a person to travel. This does not diminish the companioning relationship at all in fact it may enhance it by leaving the psychological distress of everyday life at the counseling office allowing the traveler to focus on the spiritual.

It may be required here to actually distinguish between the different opportunities of services available and how one or the other is not companioning and what is. Therapy is for when mental or emotional pain becomes overwhelming, so overwhelming that one seems unable to cope with the stress of everyday living. Therapy may take many forms, but it usually is initiated by a crisis, and the relationship works to free a person so that they may cope with daily living.

Counseling is needed to resolve a problem, clarify an issue, or sort out a particular situation, usually for the sake of making a decision. Whatever methods are used, they usually evoke "now" feelings that clarify the implicit issues. The working assumption is that by providing firm support, the pros and cons can be identified, and the person is thus able to make a decision and follow through with it.[8]

Spiritual companioning is the art of entering into a relationship thoughtfully, prayerfully, and seeking out the Holy. Jeffery Gaines, the former director of Spiritual Directors International, describes companioning as "always happening in the context of two people walking into the sanctuary of God."[9] Spiritual companioning is about "the prayer and spiritual intimacy . . . discernment is based upon the intimate engagement of great unfixables in human life. It's about the mystery of moving through time. It's about morality. It's about Love. It's about things that can't be fixed."[10] It is a quiet and gentle walk as one holds open the presence of the Spirit so that eyes may observe, hearts may feel, and mystery and awe can be expressed fully with great understanding and compassion.

PRACTICALITIES

There is a practical aspect to being a spiritual companion. As one enters into a companioning relationship there needs to be guidelines and even agreements. My personal agreement that I use with travelers looks like this:

Covenant for Spiritual Companioning

Holy Listening describes a covenant in which two persons pledge to attend to the guidance of the Holy Spirit in one of their lives. By listening and reflecting together for a time, we seek to discern God's leading.

Spiritual companioning is rooted in trust that The Sacred is present in every aspect of life. God's Love is present in doubt & despair, joy & peace, fear & frustration, certainty & gratitude, holy guidance arises in times of love & loss, work & rest, praying & playing. Sometimes it is difficult to discern the movement of the Spirit: sometimes it is challenging to follow this call. God is the true Companion. An experienced companion can assist in hearing and heeding "the still, small voice" of God.

As a spiritual companion, I commit myself to pray for you, listen with you for The Really Real and support you in noticing, naming, savoring and responding to the movement of Love in your life. Prayer is at the heart of our relationship. I encourage you to practice regular prayer, meditation and reflective writing. There are many forms of attentiveness and we will explore the ways that are most fitting for you.

Our conversations are always confidential but I ask your permission to occasionally share information (not your name) with my supervisor. Regular supervision is a vital part of my spiritual & professional growth.

Practical matters: We may meet more often while getting acquainted, then once a month. Appointments: 24-hour notice is requested for change of date or cancellation. Fee: Sliding scale ranges from $25 to $150 with a current norm of $85. Obligation to report: State law requires reporting abuse. Ethics require intervention in suspected self-endangerment or harm to others. Evaluation: After three sessions we will assess how well we match and choose either to continue meeting or referral to someone else. After one year we will review and notice where each is being led.

To see God more clearly, love God more dearly and follow God more nearly . . .

*In agreement*_____

Date _____

This is the practical side of companioning, but it must be attended too. It lays the ground work of the responsibility and accountability of not only the companion but the traveler as well. It discloses what mandatory reporting is and what is required of the traveler. The agreement also states the companion is responsible, as well, in maintaining a prayer life, seeking their own spiritual companion and, perhaps, consulting with a supervisor.

As companions, there is a great need for self-care. Before one can walk with another, one needs to know their failings. A companion must be aware of her own spiritual pitfalls and failings. "We must know ourselves well, both our dark corners and our airless places-the spots where dust collects and mold begins to grow. - Guenther."[11] This means having our own director and perhaps counselor to help us keep ourselves centered. "Anyone presuming to undertake this ministry without guidance of her own spiritual director is embarking on a dangerous path of self-deception, the spiritual equivalent of jamming all the junk into an out-of-the-way closet or shoving it down the cellar stairs to be dealt with later."[12] This is not healthy for the companion or the traveler, for no matter how deep we try to bury our own stuff it will arise and the traveler does not need the companion going off on their own path.

Often as spiritual companions, we make an effort to create a space that is welcoming and inviting. We practice the gift of hospitality "by paying attention to those who are unfamiliar to us, as well as to the mysterious dimension of our very selves."[13] Through this gift we find unique ways of companioning those within and from outside our own faith traditions. This also opens the opportunity for further self-discovery.

Through the process of companioning others, we may find that "we open ourselves to the possibility of our spiritual development and to the discovery that God is up to far more than we can think or imagine."[14] This is the reason that as a companion we must have our own relationship with a spiritual companion and/or supervisor. As Jean Stairs states:

> Once we acknowledge and welcome the stranger within ourselves, we will be more likely to develop an empathy for others who find themselves marginalized or confronting the reality of the being the outsider . . . Finding someone who can warmly welcome us and regularly and lovingly tell us the truth that keeps us honest is crucial to our credibility.[15]

As a person considering, or who actually is engaged as a spiritual companion taking the time to know yourself, is crucial. You must know where you have come from and where you may be going. I say may be going for God often surprises us when we discover we are on another path than that from which we believe we started out.

I believe that it is through knowing myself, my community, and the people I serve that allows me to enter into a companioning relationship honestly and openly. In the *Dictionary of Pastoral* care in the section on "Philosophy of Self," it states: "It is also essential in all personal relations to be deeply sensitive to the genuine inner existence of the one another."[16] This is why it is important as a companion to take the time to know yourself, know your social location, and be aware of your life experiences and spiritual history for they will arise in sessions. The ideal spiritual companion is: "transparent rather than translucent, serving as an instrument of the Spirit's workings and modeling a centered serenity. Put another way, wounded people are best healed by directors (companions) who have known themselves as wounded."[17]

This requires self-knowledge, working on issues from ones past, knowing limitations, and an awareness that the work is never done. This is why there are so many programs that offer training to a would-be companion. I recommend going to the Spiritual Directors International website and seek out a program that may suit you in your area.[18]

A practice that is essential to spiritual companioning is that of Sabbath-keeping. This practice is defined by each individual and each individual must find their own way of keeping Sabbath. "The practice of Sabbath-keeping is another way to connect with God."[19] This is setting time aside to take rest in the spirit, to find moments between God and you. Sabbath-keeping means a daily ritual, a weekly ritual and, perhaps even, a quarterly ritual. For me, this is a mixture of journaling, quiet prayer, painting, and quarterly retreats. Each must find their own path and be aware that self-care is crucial.

As spiritual companions we need to take the time to really explore our lives, the lenses through which we encounter the other and the paths we are on. Once a companion is aware of self, it allows one the freedom to step away and be open to the travelers' experience, offering a truly honest and nonjudgmental view of their spiritual journey. With spiritual companions of our own and a practice of Sabbath-keeping we become whole and holy caregivers to fellow travelers that allow us to welcome the traveler as a holy gift themselves.

SPIRITUAL COMPANIONING WITHIN THE LGBT COMMUNITY

As an openly gay man serving as a spiritual companion and as a pastor, I bless the opportunity to address the care and compassion of the LGBTQ community. To companion a LGBTQ person on his or her spiritual journey requires some attention. One must be prepared to hear, as in any companioning relationship, pain and joys. But most importantly one must listen; listen intently to what is said and what is not said for in the story, that is our lives, lays the truth behind the words.

Often times the first thing someone may address is how they live in the world. LGBTQ people have several worlds they walk in and in each world there may be a different level of outness. Be aware that LGBTQ people are always in a process of coming out and that to come out is a healthy and timely event that is different for each person. "Coming out is a profoundly spiritual act. Coming out means letting go—letting go of fear; letting go of intimidation; letting go of anything that has held us back, or anything we have been grabbing onto" in that letting go there is sorrow and a sense of loss and yet abundant joy of the freedom to be who we are called to be as God's children.[20]

Often times a coming-out story is a great place to start a companioning relationship. These stories that shape the lives of LGBTQ people are stories of "rejecting feelings of shame or embarrassment . . . It's about coming out of the quagmire of our lives-freeing ourselves from our neurotic patterns- and emerging as liberated whole beings."[21] The coming-out process doesn't happen all at once but over time and over and over again. As a companion we will listen openly and lovingly affirm a process that one will see time and time again. These stories are sacred and must be treated with the respect and the awe that they deserve.

A cry often heard in the life of the LGBTQ person is the cry of being identified as the expert. For some reason, in life, the LGBTQ person who has chosen to come out and live openly, he or she is suddenly the expert on all things LGBTQ. In the book *Tender Fires*, Ferder and Heagle, the authors, share a story that expresses a sentiment that may or may not be discussed but many times it is experienced; "sometimes when sexual orientation is discussed, I wish I could feel less like a laboratory subject and more like a regular person. I keep hoping people will stop asking 'What causes homosexuality?' and instead say, 'Please tell us about your loving.'"[22] This is a gift that needs to be affirmed, to allow the traveler to tell their companion of their loving and the way that spirituality is expressed in and through that loving.

While companioning the LGBTQ person, one will be confronted with stories of rejection or a sterilization of the person's sexuality. "My way of loving is talked about as an entity in itself; as though it has no necessary connection to me . . . It is as though our collective hormones and genes are more important than our thousands of stories of loving."[23] This type of continuous nonattached clinical approach to a loving person leads to an internalized dichotomy of object versus person. As the daily news and people discuss the LGBTQ community as objects and not people it allows for that feeling of nonhumanness to internalize. This detachment or objectivity will come up in sessions and the companion should be prepared to hear it.

When the companion hears or notices these internalized world views whether it be the objectification of the self, or, perhaps, internalized homophobia, or just the tapes in our heads that run every day from our childhood of rejection, dejection, and or failure, the spiritual companion has a unique opportunity for a loving gentle approach to help the traveler see, identify, and then heal these internalized falsehoods whatever they may be. The skills required for this and any spiritual companioning are many. Here are a few as listed by David J. Kundtz and Bernard S. Schlager:

- Deep sensitivity;
- active listening skills;
- an understanding of the most basic aspects of the coming-out process;
- openness to learning about LGBTQ sexualities and queer identities;
- the ability to speak comfortably and knowledgeably about issues relating to faith and sexuality;
- an awareness of the deep alienation that many LGBTQ people feel from churches, synagogues, and other communities of faith; and
- a willingness to recommend appropriate resources and support systems.[24]

The willingness to recommend support systems and to make appropriate referrals is essential in the role of the companion. This was stated earlier in this section but I believe it bears repeating for with the LGBTQ person there may be a greater need to make a referral. Therefore it is important to acknowledge that in the midst of the relationship of companion and traveler there may arise the need of that which is more than the companion can offer.

An area of particular focus for a companion working in an LGBTQ context is that of sexuality. Through the experience of the spiritual sexuality is often expressed not strictly with the LGBTQ community. However, because of the nature of coming out and living as open loving people there may a deeper awareness of the ecstatic, even erotic, experience in the spiritual walk. As companions one must be aware and prepared for such revelations. "Only if we are comfortable with the sexual and spiritual and truly appreciate the confusing, troubled, guilt-ridden, intense, ecstatic, deceptive, revelatory, fluid, tender, joyful, powerful, and intimate quality of these stories can we help."[25] The companion must make their own awareness and how they may stand around sexuality and spirituality issues is a priority. If a topic comes up and one finds themselves uncomfortable it will show and it will do neither the traveler nor the companion any good to ignore this. Be honest of the emotions that arise in you, make a note to discuss it with a supervisor, and continue to offer a loving presence to the traveler.

If, as a spiritual companion, one finds topics that make them uncomfortable, say so. It is fine to say, "I am uncomfortable with this topic." Or "this topic makes me uneasy." However, in my opinion, this must go a step further to say "let's explore this together and see where it takes us, perhaps we both can grow from this experience." Remember honesty and the willingness to listen with compassion is the greatest gift the spiritual companion brings into this relationship. In the companion and traveler relationship within the LGBTQ community the companion should be committed to continue to study, learn, and be compassionate and open. By doing these, both the companion and the traveler are served and served well.

INTERFAITH SPIRITUAL COMPANION

Spirituality and the sacred journey allows for the traveler to create their own path. In this day and age a person from a faith tradition not of the companions own may come seeking. Even those who are in the mainstream traditions often find their spirituality crossing outside the lines of their own traditions allowing for a blended spirituality. Today "the formal practice of interfaith spiritual direction is still in its infancy. This contemporary practice has its roots in American religious pluralism and in the postmodern appeal of an integrative spiritual life."[26] The opportunity to be exposed to many different faith traditions and practices along with the freedom to create a blended spirituality has brought forth a call for interfaith skills.

Working with spiritual travelers from a wide range of backgrounds brings certain challenges to the foreground. Charles Burack lists them as follows:

1) Learning, in as comprehensive a way as possible, about the worlds spiritual traditions; (2) entering as fully as possible into the diverse spiritual worlds of the directees; (3) refraining from imposing my own spiritual views, values, and practices on spiritual directees; (4) finding spiritual language that works for each spiritual directee that is also comfortable for me; and (5) discerning when it is appropriate to share a spiritual teaching or practice from my own spiritual path.[27]

As the spiritual companion holds these challenges in mind I encourage them to take them and actually apply them across all practices. You can never know too much about any one tradition, especially your own. One should always enter into the companion or traveler relationship as fully as possible. Whatever the companion's experience and/or their views they should try to keep them to themselves as they are here to be present to the traveler, yet use discernment when it is appropriate to share an experience or practice that one believes the traveler may benefit from. Finally, the use of language must be one that both the companion and the traveler are comfortable with.

For all travelers of the sacred path there is a sense of common ground where all are looking for the sacred in their lives. Norvene Vest states it best when she said that "the soil for this common ground is found in the sense of being 'drenched' in God, or surrounded by hints of the sacred."[28] To be drenched in God, to know that wherever one goes and or engages in the element of God, the sacred, is all around. If one enters into the interfaith companionship with this in mind, the road ahead will be all that more blessed.

In the Buddhist tradition, a spiritual companion is "One who can look into the heart and mind of the student in order for him to see himself."[29] This is about mirroring the behavior and the experience one hopes the student may achieve. Being a spiritual companion to the young Buddhist "is not about gaining knowledge from one who knows but rather about being in a living relationship with one who is knowing, which makes possible the ending of all dukkha (suffering and unsatisfactoriness) and fosters the experience of real liberation of heart and mind."[30] In this way, the Buddhist traveler may seek out one who has experience in the tradition so that the companion has the skill to reflect the practice the traveler needs.

Much in this way, some spiritual companions "do not feel that it is necessary to know much about the spiritual directee's spiritual tradition. Their goal is more centered on the moment-to-moment experience of the spiritual directee during the session; helping the spiritual directee notice, savor, and respond to the presence and movements of divinity in his or her life."[31] This allows the spiritual traveler to educate and inform the companion as they journey together. This allows the traveler what of their own tradition brings them joy and where they are finding movement in themselves as they travel their own personal path.

The reflecting of one's personal path rings true to the companioning relationship in Sufism. Fariha al-Jerrahi explains that the relationship of companion and traveler is that of a mirror and their relationship as it grows is a path unto itself. "In one sense, their relation is the path, for in the way of love the path is simply the bond of heart to heart. How we relate to our guide, who is a mirror for our self, is how we relate to our self and to God and how we relate to all beings. This is the principle of the Sufi mystic path."[32] In this relationship the spiritual companion mirrors what our relation to oneself and God should be.

As was stated earlier many travelers these days have spiritualities based on more than one tradition. Burack has stated that he "found it valuable to be familiar with the mystical writings of Augustine, Thomas Aquinas, Eckhart, and Hildegaard as well as those of Muhyiddin Ibn Al-Arabi, Jalal ad-Din Rumi, Hafiz, and Hazrat Inayat Khan."[33] I would add to this list by suggesting Richard Rohr, Mary Catherine Bateson, and Parker J. Palmer. The spiritual companion should seek out that which inspires the mind and opens their heart so that they may better serve the spiritual traveler who comes to their door.

SILENCE IN THE COMPANIONING RELATIONSHIP

Another element in the companion or traveler relationship is one of silence. In this, a world full of noise and movement, a world in which we have become accustomed to quick responses and easy to find answers, there is a need to respect and honor silence. We expect to type a word into a search and have pages and pages of definitions and explanations. We can twitter an emotional response in 140 characters or less. Our phones keep us constantly bombarded with updates, tweets, emails, and even tell us where to go when we are lost.

The freeways, airplanes, boats, and trains are ready and willing to whisk us off to anywhere. Often our homes and apartments are nearby one of these venues and the roar of the planes, honks of the horns, or whine of the train whistle is in our ear. As we enter our home we collect the mail, grab our newspaper, and either turn on the radio or the television for the six o'clock news. There are billboards, posters, bulletin boards at the laundry mat, and advertisements all vying for our attention. Marquees, and traffic lights, headlights, and streetlights all add to the background noise of the modern world.

Do not be surprised when a traveler walks into a sacred space that you believe to be calming, quiet, and serene and they start running at full speed ahead without even hesitating to take a breath. Often times our lives and our internal motion reflect the world around us. Take time to ask the person to stop and breathe. Take time to be still with God and the traveler and hold open a loving space before any companioning session starts.

As a companion offers a safe and still space for a traveler to collect their thoughts and emotions this is a place for a companion to do the same. I would also offer that as a companion we sometimes want to move through a silent moment too quickly. If there is a pause in the conversation and you find yourself thinking about saying something count to seven very slowly in your head allowing for that extra time when the traveler may just need to collect for a moment.

There will be a day when the world may have been just too much, may have pushed the traveler too far, and all they need or want is a safe quiet space. Allow for that. Not every session has to be spoken. There is a gift, there is sacredness, and there is Sabbath in silence. The word Sabbath means, very simply, to rest. There may be time when a traveler needs to rest in a safe and sacred space. It is a great opportunity and blessing for the companion to allow for that to happen. To rest in sacred silence allowing the spirit to do what needs to be done and rest as a witness for the traveler.

As Psalm 46:10 says, "Be still and know that I am God." In the silence, in that sacred space of care and compassion the companion acts as the knower, knowing that the great I am is God and is present and allowing the traveler to find and connect to that through sacred silence. Do not fear the silence nor shy away from it, embrace it as a center of practice. Hold it sacred as an opening moment and a closing moment to allow that stillness to penetrate and bless the traveler who must emerge from the silence back into the throng of everyday life. If we as companions can mirror the peaceful stillness of God then the traveler may be able to take just a little with them to last till the next time you sit down to honor them again with the sacred witness of the companion.

THE PERSONAL IN THE COMPANION

Finally, as one enters into the companioning relationship, the spiritual companion must be aware that no matter what you have read, what you have studied, and what you may practice, you will always have your beliefs. They will come out in subtle ways no matter how hard you try.

> Perhaps in a "perfect spiritual direction situation" I would be able to completely set aside my beliefs in spiritual pluralism, unity, and omnipresence. But I am unable to do so and really don't want to do so. I handle this "bias" by letting spiritual directees know that my orientation is pluralistic and unitive.[34]

Simply, by being open and honest about who you are and where your spirituality approaches from this will lessen the odds of misunderstanding, misguidance, and mistrust. The rules are laid out I will tell you who I am openly and lovingly and I will listen to who and where you are openly and lovingly.

The essentials to becoming a good spiritual companion, whether that is a pluralistic spirituality or a more traditional form of faith, is to remember to love the traveler and show that love through authentic presence, concern, and care. Do not shy away from the opportunity to point out awe and mystery along the spiritual path and choose to challenge the traveler to look back over the path so we all have a clear vision of who we are and where we may be going.

All of what has been written here about the companion and the traveler comes to one place, a place of humility. "A Humble Heart is hospitable. It accepts people as they are—a mix of familiar and unfamiliar, good and bad."[35] This will allow whoever the companion meets to ease into a space of comfort for you will see that the one you greet along their own journey is actually the face of God and you are no more than a traveler yourself meeting God again for the first time.

NOTES

1. MCC in the Valley, Our Vision, http://www.mccinthevalley.com/ (accessed October 17, 2011).

2. Stillpoint; The Center for Christian Spirituality, http://stillpointca.org/ (accessed October 17, 2011).

3. Spiritual Directors International, http://www.sdiworld.org/ (accessed October 17, 2011).

4. Margaret Guenther, *Holy Listening: The Art of Spiritual Direction* (Cambridge, MA: Cowley Publications, 1992), ix.

5. W. Paul Jones, *The Art of Spiritual Direction: Giving and Receiving Spiritual Guidance* (Nashville: Upper Room, 2002), 18.

6. Ibid.

7. Ibid.

8. Ibid.

9. HungryHearts News Presbyterian Church (USA), *Spiritual Direction as Choosing Life.* http://seventhavenuechurch.org/home/wp-content/uploads/2009/08/Spiritual-Direction-What-Is-It-1.pdf

10. Guenther, *Holy Listening*, x.

11. Ibid.

12. Ibid., 11.

13. Ibid.

14. Jean Stairs, *Listening for the Soul: Pastoral Care and Spiritual Direction* (Minneapolis: Fortress Press, 2000), 114.

15. Ibid.

16. H. D. Lewis, "Philosophy of Self," in *Dictionary of Pastoral Care and Counseling*, ed. Robert J. Hunter et al. (Nashville: Abingdon Press, 2005), 1126.

17. Jones, *The Art of Spiritual Direction*, 12.

18. Their website is www.sdiworld.org.

19. Stairs, *Listening for the Soul*, 112.

20. Christian de la Huerta, *Coming Out Spiritually: The Next Step* (New York: Tarcher, 1999), 158.

21. Ibid., 159.

22. Fran Ferder and John Heagle, *Tender Fires: The Spiritual Promise of Sexuality* (New York: The Crossroad Publishers, 2002), 173.

23. Ibid., 175.

24. David Kundtz and Bernard Schlager, *Ministry Among God's queer Folk: LGBT Pastoral Care*, The Center for Lesbian and Gay Studies in Religion and Ministry (Cleveland: Pilgrim Press, 2007), 139.

25. Janet K Ruffing, "Flesh More than Flesh: Sexuality and Spirituality Direction," in *Still Listening: New Horizons in Spiritual Direction*, ed. Norvene Vest (Harrisburg, PA: Morehouse Publishing, 2000), 178.

26. Charles Burack, "Meeting the Challenges of Interfaith Spiritual Direction," *Presence, An International Journal of Spiritual Direction* 17, no. 3 (2011): 39.

27. Ibid.

28. Norvene Vest, ed. *Tending the Holy: Spiritual Direction Across Traditions* (Harrisburg, PA: Morehouse, 2003), viii.

29. Burack, "Meeting the Challenges," 39.

30. Vest, *Tending the Holy*, 6.

31. Ibid., 6.

32. Burack, "Meeting the Challenges," 40.

33. Vest, *Tending the Holy*, 29.

34. Burack, "Meeting the Challenges," 43.

35. Marjorie J. Thompson, *Soul Feast: An Invitation to the Christian Spiritual Life* (Louisville, KY: Westminster John Knox Press, 2005), 134.

20

Queer Hymnody: Celebrating Lesbian and Gay Poets and Composers

Jim Mitulski, Donna Hamilton, and Nancy Hall

The festival began with the organ prelude Magnificat—My soul magnifies the Lord, composed by Gerald Asheim for a gay friend who loves organ music, followed by a solo, "Sometimes I feel like a motherless child," arranged by H. T. Burleigh, and sung by Charles Lynch.

"Sometimes I feel like a motherless child"—that's how many gay and lesbian people have felt throughout the ages. Particularly in the last century, and especially in the past 30 years, gay and lesbian people have been presented as an issue, a "church-dividing issue," to quote some. And yet, for those of us who are gay and lesbian, we know that we are not motherless children. We know that the church is also there for us. We know that people who have tried to say we don't belong in the church are wrong, and that we have always been in the church. And in fact, even when churches say they don't want us in the pews, here we are in the hymnbooks.

Our festival title recalls the words of a prolific, historic hymn writer and a hymnal editor, Charles Wesley and his brother John Wesley. Charles Wesley's text, which we have paraphrased, refers to the humble

This hymn festival was presented on July 18, 2011, at First Congregational Church in Colorado Springs, Colorado, as part of The Hymn Society's Annual conference. This hymn festival includes materials presented at two previous festivals, held in Berkeley, California, at Epworth United Methodist Church, June 2010, and First Congregational Church of Berkeley, June 2011. With some modification, this festival could be presented in many other settings. We are grateful to the publishers, authors, and composers who granted permission to reprint their hymns here.

and contrite heart of Psalm 51. John Wesley was famous for welcoming persons into the Methodist Movement with only one condition, "If your heart is as my heart, give me your hand," a model of welcome and inclusiveness well suited to the subject of this hymn festival.

At the end of Radclyffe Hall's 1928 classic literary novel, *The Well of Loneliness*, is a prayer for vindication by God and by the church, spoken by the lesbian heroine of the story. This book was considered obscene when first published. It was banned both in the United States and in Great Britain, where it was written, because it did not present homosexuals as repenting of their sin. This is an excerpt from the prayer that closes Hall's novel in which her character imagines all the gay people throughout time:

> They possessed her. Her barren womb became fruitful. It ached with its fearful and sterile burden. It ached with the fierce yet helpless children who would clamor in vain for their right to salvation. They would turn first to God and then to the world and then to her. They would cry out, accusing, "We've asked for bread. Will you give us a stone? Answer us. Will you give us a stone? You, God, in whom we the outcasts believed. You, world, into which we are pitilessly born." . . . And then there was only one voice, one demand, her own voice, into which these millions had entered. A voice like the awful, deep rolling of thunder.
>
> . . . "God," she gasped, "we believe. We have told you we believe. We have not denied you. Now, rise up and defend us. Acknowledge us, O God, before the whole world. Give us also the right to our existence."[1]

This hymn festival is intended as an answer to Radclyffe Hall's prayer. As she recognized, all that gay or lesbian people have ever asked is to be acknowledged.

Tom Sopko, then a member of the Metropolitan Community Church (MCC) in Boston, wrote "Once we were not a people" for a gay pride service in 1987. This is one of the earliest hymns written specifically for gay people, and including the words "gay" and "lesbian." The first line sounds like the lament of an entire people as bereft of acceptance and comfort as a motherless child. But then the line continues, "God's people now are we." The hymn is an expansion and restatement of 1 Peter 2:9–10: "But you are a chosen race, a royal priesthood, a holy nation, God's own people, in order that you may proclaim the mighty acts of him who called you out of darkness into his marvelous light. Once you were not a people, but now you are God's people; once you had not received mercy but now you have received mercy" (NRSV). It's a strong statement of affirmation and encouragement, calling those once rejected to stand with Christ, the cornerstone, in their full personhood as people of God.

HYMN 1

Once We Were Not a People

For this festival presentation it was not easy to nail down precisely what we mean by a gay hymn. What makes it so—a gay or a lesbian poet or composer? Does it make it gay if gay people sing it? And who, precisely, is gay or lesbian? These questions are vibrant ones within academic contexts, where gay studies, gender studies, women's studies, and queer studies examine what it means to be gay or lesbian, bisexual, transgender, or queer. For this festival we tried our best to assemble words and music written by those who could probably be described as gay, though we certainly can't provide proof for this in every case. We mean no offense. I myself am gay and I like to be called gay. It's not an offense for me, and I hope it is not for others.

I think of what George Litch Knight, FHS, said to me. In 1976, I was a freshman at Columbia University and would take the train to Fort Green in Brooklyn, where Knight was pastor of the Lafayette Avenue Presbyterian Church. There he taught me so much about hymns. And drawing on his own experience, he assured me it was OK to be gay. Tonight I remember this mentor, who was the first editor of THE HYMN, along with his other many achievements.

In planning this festival we have worked to find the hidden histories that aren't necessarily where one would expect. Musicologists and hymnologists haven't always looked at gay, lesbian, or queer literary texts. And people in the literary world aren't always interested in religion. It has taken some cross-disciplinary study to discover these texts and tunes and the stories that go with them.

"These things shall be" was written by John Addington Symonds in 1880 as a reflection of his utopian vision. The four stanzas of the hymn are drawn from a larger poem of 15 stanzas, "A vista."

Symonds was a scholar who studied homosexuality; in fact, he was one of the first people to use the word "homosexual." His study of the New Testament led him to believe that Jesus did not condemn homosexuality. This poem reflects Symonds's values: "Nation with nation, land with land, unarmed shall live as comrades free." Some hymnals changed "inarmed" to "unarmed," as if two soldiers are facing each other. But

Symonds's vision was of soldiers as comrades, their arms locked, as those who could never fight each other or any others. He talks about "High friendship, hitherto unknown, or by great poets half divined," and portrays in the larger poem an egalitarian vision where "woman shall be man's mate and peer."[2]

HYMN 2

These Things Shall Be

These things shall be: a loftier race
inarmed shall live as comrades free;
with flame of freedom in their souls
and light of knowledge in their eyes.

Nation with nation, land with land,
than e'er the world hath known shall rise
in ev'ry heart and brain shall throb
the pulse of one community.

High friendship, hitherto unknown,
or by great poets half divined,
shall burn, a steadfast star, within
the calm clear ether of the mind.

New arts shall bloom of loftier mold,
and mightier music thrill the skies,
and ev'ry life shall be a song,
when all the earth is paradise.

J. Addington Symonds (1840–1893), alt.
Tune: TRURO

Samuel Longfellow, a 19th-century Unitarian minister, was a hymn writer often joined in his efforts by his fellow Unitarian clergyman, Samuel Johnson, who had been his classmate at Harvard Divinity School. In the emerging Unitarian movement these two perceived a need for hymns that could be sung in a more liberal faith context, and so, besides writing hymn texts of their own, they became known for revising Calvinist hymns to express Unitarian theology. One of Longfellow's most familiar hymn texts, "Now on land and sea descending," was one of several written in 1859 for vesper services at Second Unitarian Church in Brooklyn Heights. Longfellow's and Johnson's relationship was described by close relatives as the most significant of their lives. They never lived together, but they vacationed together, and they put hymnals together on their vacations.

"I look to thee in every need" is the complete text of Longfellow's poem "Looking unto God," who is named only with the pronoun "thee" in the course of the four stanzas. Longfellow said in a letter, "My two favorites among my hymns are the vesper hymn, 'Again as evening's shadow falls,' and one beginning, 'I look to Thee in every need.'"[3] It reflects a close, affectionate image of relating to God, through phrases such as "I feel thy strong and tender love" and "embosomed deep in thy dear love," and offers confident, encouragement of spiritual strength to the weary, troubled soul.

HYMN 3

I Look to Thee in Every Need

I look to thee in ev'ry need,
and never look in vain;
I feel thy strong and tender love,
and all is well again:
the thought of thee is mightier far
than sin and pain and sorrow are.

Discouraged in the work of life,
Disheartened by its load,
Shamed by its failures or its fears,
I sink beside the road;
But let me only think of thee,
And then new heart springs up in me.

Thy calmness bends serene above,
My restlessness to stil;
Around me flows thy quick'ning life,
To nerve my falt'ring will:
Thy presence fills my solitude;
thy providence turns all good.

Embosomed deep in they dear love,
Held in thy law, I stand;
Thy hand in all things I behold,
And all things in thy hand;

Thou leadest me by unsought ways,
and turn'st my mourning into praise.

Samuel Lonfellow (b. 1819–1892)
Tune: O Jesu

The question of what makes a hymn gay or what makes a composer gay often yields an ambiguous answer. One thing I do know is this: the work of changing the church, of liberation, could not happen were it not for allies who share the gay and lesbian struggle. Daniel C. Damon is a widely published hymn writer and United Methodist pastor in Richmond, California.

He has long been an ally and supporter of the Gay and Lesbian struggle for inclusion in the church.

Dan once asked if he could write a hymn that reflected gay people's particular terminology for talking about Jesus. Since lover was the word that gay people frequently used in 1960s, 1970s, and 1980s to describe one's life partner, Dan included this in a beautiful healing hymn called "Jesus, partner, lover, friend," which he dedicated to the MCC of San Francisco.

Damon continues to write hymns that are cutting edge in every way. He was one of the first to write a hymn for a holy union ceremony, "True union is a gift from God." Last year we commissioned Dan to write a hymn for our gay and lesbian hymn festival in Berkeley, using feminine imagery for the divine. He presented us with "Goddess of love."

HYMN 4

Goddess of Love

Al Carmines was better known for his theater music compositions than for his church music. His 1973 musical, *The Faggot*, won a Drama Desk award for outstanding lyrics and music. Less known is that he was the assistant pastor at Judson Memorial Church, an American Baptist congregation in New York's Greenwich Village. Carmines, who had been invited by the church's longtime pastor, Howard Moody to do an outreach ministry to "people who didn't like church," accepted the challenge, bringing together both his musical theater style and his religious context. Eventually, Carmines started his own church, the Rauschenbush Memorial United Church of Christ in New York City. He died in 1985, and was survived by his partner Paul Rounsaville.

Carmines wrote a number of hymns; "Many gifts, one spirit" is perhaps the best known of these. "Praise the Lord" is from a collection called *Go to Galilee*, and was the first hymn we could find anywhere that actually used the word "gay." Al Carmines said before he died, "If you want to know how to live, go to church. If you want to know, how your life is at its deepest roots, go to the theater."[4] We are thankful that he found a way to blend both.

HYMN 5

Praise the Lord

Phebe Hanaford was among the first women to be ordained in the Universalist Church, and the first in New England (1868). After serving a pastorate in Hingham and Walton, Massachusetts, she accepted a call to the First Universalist Church in New Haven, Connecticut. Her husband declined to accompany her and so she kept a separate household with her children. In New Haven Hanaford formed a relationship with poet Ellen Miles, who assisted her in the work of running a parish; they also raised Phebe's children and spent the rest of their lives together. Hanaford later became the pastor of a Universalist church in New Jersey where—well into her tenure and although the church had grown significantly during this time—she was asked to dismiss "the minister's wife," Miss Miles. It was seen by the church as unseemly for them to be sharing the parsonage. Hanaford declined, formed a new Universalist church a few blocks away, and continued to live in partnership with her companion.

This is how Phebe Hanaford described her love for Ellen, in the verses of a poem:

> They marry not in heaven!
> And yet those earth-born ties, if true and fond,
> Uniting spirits in the true marriage-bond
> Will not be sadly riven:
> They who were one on earth henceforth shall rove
> Still wedded lovers in the world above.
> They marry not in heaven!
> But all the joy which glowing fancy paints,
> The gift of God, the heritage of saints,
> To ransomed souls is given,

Where kindred spirits meet to part no more,
And blend, like rivers, on Life's farther shore.[5]

"Cast thy bread upon the waters" demonstrates that Phebe Hanaford could construct an entire hymn—as surely she and many other experienced preachers construct an entire sermon—from one verse of scripture, in this case Ecclesiastes 11:1. She fills in much between the lines of that one verse, offering analogies, allusions, and examples to expand and emphasize its meaning.

HYMN 6

Cast Thy Bread Upon the Waters

Cast thy bread upon the waters,
thinking not 'tis thrown away;
God himself saith, thou shalt gather
it again some future day.

Cast thy bread upon the waters;
wildly though the billows roll,
they but aid thee as thou toilest
truth to spread from pole to pole.

As the seed, by billows floated,
to some distant island lone,
so to human souls benighted,
that thou flingest may be borne.

Cast thy bread upon the waters,
why wilt thou still doubting stand?
Bounteous shall God send the harvest
if thou sow'st with lib'ral hand.

Phebe A. Hanaford (1829–1921)
Tune: AGAWAM

Social historians note that the African American civil rights movement and the Black movement for self-determination led to the raising of other voices for liberation. In particular, the women's movement in 1960s, 1970s, and 1980s may well have awakened the voices for gay and lesbian liberation. The issues of gay inclusion and gender inclusion continue to be deeply entwined.

The book of Exodus is a rich source of imagery for understanding what it means to engage in a liberation struggle. In 1968, Troy Perry started a church for gay people, the MCC. It was for those who were leaving mainline churches but who were not giving up their religion. Gays and lesbians felt that they could no longer be dependent upon traditional churches as the source of their consolation or Christian identity. In 1971 Mary Daly, the great feminist theologian, was the first woman to preach in the Harvard Memorial Church. There she conducted what she called an "exodus" from the church—after preaching her sermon, she invited all the women present to walk out with her halfway through the service, as a symbol of liberation.

"When Israel camped in Sinai" was written by Larry Bernier, then the pastor of the MCC in Boston. The text draws on this exodus imagery while revealing a concern for gender parity and gay inclusion. It was common in those days for MCC to use evangelical hymn tunes and pair them with liberation texts. In this case the tune, WEBB, is one most often associated with "Stand up! Stand up for Jesus."

HYMN 7

When Israel Camped in Sinai

When people become aware that there are separate churches for the LGBT community, they are often surprised to find that evangelical church music has been the style most frequently sung in these houses of worship. The most popular hymnal used in gay churches in the 1970s and 1980s was Hymns for the family of God.[6]

Marsha Stevens wrote the song "For those tears I died," when she was 16. The words describe her inner turmoil around struggling with her emerging lesbian identity, although she did not disclose this motive until later. She sang with a group called Children of the Day, and has been described in numerous Christian publications as "the mother of contemporary Christian church music." When she came out as a lesbian, 10 years after this hymn became popular, Stevens was denounced by the Christian Right. For many years following, she received in the mail copies of her hymn torn out of *Hymns for the Family of God.* Subsequent editions of the hymnal did not include "For those tears I died." Nevertheless, Stevens persisted in her music and has had a successful career, founding her own publishing and performing ministry, Born Again Lesbian Music—BALM.

HYMN 8

For Those Tears I Died

In the United States, the history of AIDS and HIV/AIDS has been deeply associated with the history of gay and lesbian liberation. In the 1980s legislators stood up in Congress to oppose funding for research into and care for people with AIDS. They waved Bibles and said that AIDS was God's way of taking care of undesirable or expendable populations—hemophiliacs, intravenous drug users, Haitian immigrants, sex workers, and homosexuals. It's a sad history, but thankfully it was not the last word. Despite the condemnation of those with AIDS, there were people who wrote hymns about the epidemic, mindful that many gifted and significant musicians had died or were dying of the disease.

In 1986 Shirley Erena Murray, FHS, wrote "Through all the world, a hungry Christ"; in her hymn collection, "In every corner sing," she notes this about the hymn: "The Christ presence in the victims of the world, including the differently abled and AIDS sufferers, is the theme here."[7]

The tune, DE TAR is by Calvin Hampton, who was a distinguished organist and sacred music composer. At midnight on Friday nights in New York, from 1974 to 1983, Calvary Episcopal Church, Gramercy Park, would be packed with those who came to hear Hampton play the organ. DE TAR was composed in tribute to one of Hampton's colleagues and mentors, Vernon De Tar, who was music director at Church of the Ascension, a nearby congregation. Hampton composed music for solo organ, piano, orchestra, vocal solo, and chorus, as well as several dozen hymn tunes. In 1984, at the age of 45, Hampton died of AIDS.

HYMN 9

Through All the World, a Hungry Christ

It is so appropriate that we include "America the beautiful" in this festival at Colorado Springs, in the shadow of Pike's Peak. It was here that Katharine Lee Bates was inspired to write her 1893 poem. Describing her trip up the mountain, Bates wrote,

We hired a prairie wagon. Near the top we had to leave the wagon and go the rest of the way on mules. I was very tired, but when I saw the view

I felt great joy. All the wonders of America seemed displayed there with a sea-like expanse.

This breathtaking view yielded phrases such as "spacious skies" and "purple mountain majesties." Having earlier in her journey visited the World's Fair/Columbian Exposition in Chicago, Bates had been impressed by a magnificent array of white stucco structures there, built in the neoclassical style; hence, the "alabaster cities" of stanza 4.

Less known about Bates is that she shared her life with fellow Wellesley College faculty member Katharine Coman. They lived together for 25 years in a romantic friendship, and after her partner died, Bates wrote, "So much of me died with Katharine Coman that I am sometimes not quite sure whether I am alive or not."

These verses are from a poem, "If you could come," that Bates wrote about losing Coman:

My love, my love, if you could come again once more
From your high place,
I would not question you for heavenly lore,
But, silent, take the comfort of your face.
. . . .
One touch of you were worth a thousand creeds.
My wound is numb
Though toil-pressed, but all night long it bleeds
In aching dreams, and still you cannot come.[8]

"My love, one touch of you were worth a thousand creeds"—it's one of the most beautiful expressions of love in poetry that I've ever heard. And it allows us to see another side of Bates's many loves—God, country, nature, and the written word.

HYMN 10

America the Beautiful

found in most hymnals, is not reprinted here.

The Unitarian Universalist Association (UUA) deserves to be acknowledged—in a way that distinguishes them from other mainline churches—for their prophetic advocacy of gay and lesbian people in church and society. Their most recent hymnal, *Singing the Living Tradition* (1993), set a new standard for inclusive language and inclusion of a variety of texts. Mark Belletini is the openly gay chair of the hymnal committee that brought us *Singing the Living Tradition,* and he is pastor of the First Unitarian Universalist Church of Columbus, Ohio. Included in this hymnal are seven of Belletini's hymn texts. In "Earth is our homeland," he liberally uses images from the natural world; the text is also notable for its singular metaphor for inclusiveness. Rather than list humanity's various skin colors, ages, races, nationalities, castes, genders, or sexual orientations, he draws a circle wide enough to include everyone by naming the cardinal directions as forms of music that move the human soul: chants, psalms, jazz, and Brahms.

HYMN 11

Earth Is Our Homeland

The German Lutheran liberation theologian Dorothee Sölle once said that in order to find the spirituality of an oppressed people you sometimes have to look for it outside the church. "Singing for our lives," by Holly Near, is an example of liberation music that is sung with religious fervor by people who are not always found in church. Near was one of several women performers in 1970s and 1980s who sang from her Methodist church upbringing as well as from her feminist experience. She wrote this song—or rather, as Near has said, she received it—at a rally after the 1978 assassinations of Harvey Milk and George Moscone in San Francisco. Witnessing the sometimes violent protests that were taking place, Near wanted to see if music could bring peace that night. Sometimes called "Song to remember Harvey Milk," "Singing for our lives" is included in the UUA's *Singing the Living Tradition,* and is often sung outdoors at rallies and at parades—but not so often in church.

HYMN 12

Singing for Our Lives

"Ours the journey" could be called the anthem of gay and lesbian inclusion for churches; yet, although it has appeared in several versions published over the last quarter-century, this hymn was not printed in its entirety until last year, in the Hymn Interpretation column by Donna Hamilton in our society's journal.[9] Previously, when "Ours the journey" has been included in hymnals, the word "gay"—in fact, the entire stanza referring to "a people long despised"—has been taken out. Author and composer Julian Rush, a United Methodist minister, wrote the words and music for a 1985 service about inclusiveness held at the Rocky Mountain Annual Conference Session. The stanzas enumerate the many definable categories of human difference, but name several collectives into which they all may be gathered, "the pilgrim peoples," "your global village," "a rainbow coalition," but chiefly, as repeated in the refrain, "We, your people"—God's own people. These are the words that have given hope to so many people on this same journey.

HYMN 13

Ours the Journey

    can be found in full in the Summer 2010 issue of THE HYMN.

"We are the church alive" was written by Jack Hoggatt–St. John, an MCC minister, in the early 1980s—well before AIDS emerged as the struggle that it would become and continues to be. Yet the hymn was prophetic for its focus on healing and on the body.

In the late 1980s we frequently held AIDS healing services at our gay church in the Castro district of San Francisco. People would gather to sing the old gospel songs such as "Sing the wondrous love of Jesus," with its refrain "When we all get to heaven." It meant something to us to sing about when we would all be together again. Young people in their 20s and 30s were laying on hands for each other and praying in the name of Jesus Christ for healing. "We are the church alive" was a hymn we often sang. It is included in the book of feminist liberation theologian Letty Russell, The church with AIDS: Renewal in the midst of crisis.[10] Russell, a lesbian, wrote that the wider church had much to learn from the gay church with AIDS. The third stanza states this eloquently:

> We are the church alive,
> the body must be healed;
> where strife has bruised and battered us,
> God's wholeness is revealed.
> Our mission is an urgent one,
> in strength and health let's stand,
> so that our witness to God's light
> will shine in every land.

This became our AIDS hymn for years and years—and we still sing it, because AIDS isn't over.

HYMN 14

We are the Church

Georgia Harkness was a Methodist, initially ordained in the 1920s in the Methodist Episcopal Church. She was the first woman to become a full professor at any seminary in the country, at Garrett Biblical Institute (now Garrett-Evangelical Theological Seminary) in Evanston, Illinois. She later served as professor at Pacific School of Religion in Berkeley, California, until her retirement. The author of over 30 books, she was also a staunch advocate for ecumenism and for the rights of women. Once, at a meeting of the World Council of Churches, Harkness took on theologian Karl Barth for his sexist perspectives on women. Barth later said of her, "Remember me not of that woman!"

Harkness was introduced to Verna Miller, her life partner, by the minister of their Methodist church in Evanston. The forewords and dedications in many of Harkness's books give tribute to Miller—who typed all of the manuscripts—indicating how Harkness recognized Miller's vital contribution to her life and her academic career.

"Hope of the world" was written in 1953 for a hymn competition by The Hymn Society of America on the theme, "Jesus Christ, hope of the world," for the Second Assembly of the World Council of Churches (1954). The society chose Harkness's text as the winner, from over five hundred submissions. Each stanza acclaims the Christ—as Savior, God's gift, the victor over death, the conqueror of grief and pain—and also prays for the needs we have and the hopes to which we aspire. Christ is our companion on the way and the model for a life of faith and integrity.

HYMN 15

Hope of the World

This festival was never meant to be comprehensive, but rather representative. For every hymn we sang this evening there were two or three more writers or composers from the past two hundred years, whose works we did not have room to include on this occasion. There were also some we wanted to include, but who were fearful that being associated with this festival program could somehow hurt them. Let's all pray for a time when such fears need no longer apply. There are many openly gay and lesbian members of The Hymn Society whose careers have been marked by their honesty and candor. We salute you for your public witness.

We close by singing the refrain to Fanny Crosby's hymn "Blessed assurance." As you sing "This is my story, this is my song," put yourself in the place of gay and lesbian people who have found liberation and salvation in believing that these words apply to them too:

This is my story, this is my song,
praising my Savior all the day long.

NOTES

1. Radclyffe Hall, *The Well of Loneliness* (Paris: Pegasus Press, 1928).

2. John Addington Symonds, *New and Old; A Volume of Verse* (London: Smith, Elder, & Co., 1880).

3. Wilbur Tillett, *The Hymns and Hymn Writers of the Church*, annotated ed. (New York: Eaton & Mains, 1911), 251.

4. New York Times, Obituary, http://www.nytimes.com/2005/08/13/arts/13carmines. html.

5. Phebe A. Hana, *From Shore to Shore, and Other Poems* (San Francisco: A.L. Bancroft & Co., 1871).

6. Fred Bock, ed., *Hymns for the Family of God* (Nashville: Paragon Associates, 1976).

7. Shirley Erena Murray, *In Every Corner Sing: The Hymns of Shirley Erena Murray* (Carol Stream, IL: Hope, 1992).

8. Katharine Lee Bates, *Yellow Clover; A Book of Remembrance* (New York: E.P. Dutton & Company, 1922), 39.

9. Donna Hamilton, "'Ours the Journey,' Complete at Last," *The Hymn* 61, no. 3 (2010): 41–43.

10. Letty M. Russell, ed., *The Church with AIDS: Renewal in the Midst of Crisis* (Louisville, KY: Westminster John Knox Press, 1990), 204.

About the Editors and Contributors

EDITORS

Robert E. Shore-Goss is the Senior Pastor of MCC in the Valley, the first "Green" church within MCC and is active in environmental activism and Earth care and other justice issues. He holds a ThD in Theology and Comparative Religion from Harvard University. He is author of *Jesus ACTED UP: A Gay and Lesbian Manifesto* and *Queering Christ* and coauthor of *Dead But, Not Lost: Grief Narratives in Religious Traditions*. He is coeditor of *Take Back the Word: A Queer Reading of the Bible, The Queer Bible Commentator, Gay Catholic Priests and Clerical Sexual Misconduct,* and *Our Families, Our Values.*

Thomas Bohache has been clergy in the Metropolitan Community Churches for 25 years and has pastored congregations in California, Virginia, Delaware, and New Jersey. He has graduate degrees in religion from the University of Virginia and Georgetown University and a D. Ministry in feminist liberation theologies from the Episcopal Divinity School. He is the author of *Christology from the Margins* and coeditor of *The Queer Bible Commentary.*

Patrick S. Cheng is the Associate Professor of Historical and Systematic Theology at the Episcopal Divinity School in Cambridge, Massachusetts. He holds a PhD in systematic theology from Union Theological Seminary in the City of New York. He is the author of *Radical Love: An Introduction to Queer Theology; From Sin to Amazing Grace: Discovering the Queer*

Christ; and *Rainbow Theology: Bridging Race, Sexuality, and Spirit*. Patrick is an ordained minister with the Metropolitan Community Churches, and he writes for the *Huffington Post*.

Rev. **Mona West** earned a PhD in Hebrew Bible/Old Testament from Southern Seminary in Louisville, Kentucky, and has taught biblical studies at several colleges, universities, and seminaries throughout the United States. She also holds a Certificate in Spiritual Formation from Columbia Seminary in Decatur, Georgia. Currently she is the Director of Formation and Leadership Development for Metropolitan Community Churches and in April 2012 was affirmed as an Elder in MCC. She writes and speaks about spirituality and queer biblical studies and is a contributing editor of: *Take Back the Word: A Queer Reading of the Bible* and *The Queer Bible Commentary*.

CONTRIBUTORS

Nic Arnzen lives in Pasadena with his husband and two kids. He still directs and produces the International touring company of Corpus Christi now in its seventh year. Nic also writes for film and stage.

James Brandon has been an actor and producer in all mediums for the past decade. He has played the title role of Joshua in Terrence McNally's CORPUS CHRISTI internationally for the past six years. He is the cofounder of 108 Productions, the producing company of the revival tour, codirector of the documentary film, "Corpus Christi: Playing with Redemption," and cofounder of the antireligious bullying movement—I AM Love Campaign.

Lea Brown is the Senior Pastor of MCC of the Palm Beaches. She has been a clergyperson in MCC since 1996 and received a D. Ministry from the Episcopal Divinity School. She enjoys ministry, life, and leather in West Palm Beach, Florida with her partner Sarah-Helen.

Rachelle Brown holds a Master of Divinity from Eden Theological Seminary and Master of Communications from Missouri State University, and is currently a PhD Candidate at Chicago Theological Seminary. Her teaching and research focuses on North American religious traditions, using a queer lens to investigate the historiography of modern religious thought and practices. She is ordained with Metropolitan Community Churches and an active Intentional Interim Minister in the greater Chicago area.

Robin H. Gorsline serves as Pastor of Metropolitan Community Church of Richmond and as President of People of Faith for Equality in Virginia. He received the MDiv from Episcopal Divinity School and the PhD from Union Theological Seminary in the City of New York. He is the coeditor of *Disrupting White Supremacy from Within* and the author of articles on sexuality and religion.

Nancy Hall teaches at the American Baptist Seminary of the West and pastors the First Baptist Church of Berkeley. She is a member of the Hymn Society of the United States and Canada, and has served on its executive board and as editor of the Hymn. She is an outstanding ally for the inclusion of GLBT people in the American Baptist Convention.

Donna Hamilton was a lifelong United Methodist, proud to have been raised in a parsonage. She devoted her considerable talents helping the United Methodist Church grow into its capacity to include GLBT people, and was a tireless ally for GLBT causes. She was a member for over 40 years of the Epworth United Methodist Church in Berkeley and was a lifetime member of the Hymn Society of the United States and Canada and served on its executive board. She was a graduate of University of California at Berkeley, and was a member of the California Historical Society. She is survived by her husband Patrick.

Kerri Mesner is a minister with Metropolitan Community Churches, a scholar, artist, and activist. Kerri is currently a doctoral candidate at the Centre for Cross Faculty Inquiry in Education at the University of British Columbia, exploring queer theology, arts-based research, and anti-oppressive education.

Jim Mitulski started collecting hymnals before he knew was gay. He is Co-Director of Worship and Campus Pastor at Pacific School of Religion where he also pastors New Spirit Community Church, an ecumenical church affiliated with the United Church of Christ, The Christian Church/Disciples of Christ, the Metropolitan Community Churches, and the Fellowship. He has been a pastor at MCC Churches in New York City, San Francisco, Guerneville, California and Glendale, California over the past 30 years and was a senior denominational executive for MCC. He has degrees from Columbia University and Pacific School of Religion, was a Merrill Fellow at the Harvard Divinity School and an honorary doctorate from Starr King School for the ministry. He belongs to the Hymn Society of United States and Canada. His favorite question is "What's your favorite hymn?"

Megan More received a M. Divinity from Claremont School of Theology and is Clergy on Staff at MCC in the Valley. She is an openly transgender woman actively working to increase awareness of Christ in the Trans community through her sermons and internet outreach. Rev. More is also happily married to her wife of nearly 27 years and lives in the Los Angeles area.

Bryce E. Rich is a PhD student in Theology at the University of Chicago Divinity School and a member of the MCC Theologies Team. His interests include sacramental theology, theological anthropology, Eastern Orthodoxy, and queer theory.

Joan M. Saniuk is a clergy and codirector of MCC New England Ministries in Boston and Cambridge, Massachusetts. She is the author of *Come to the Water: The Queer Congregation as Healing Community*.

Axel Schwaigert is the Pastor of Salz der Erde MCC in Stuttgart, Germany. He received his Diplom in Ev. Theologie from the school of theological studies at Tubingen. He also spent a year in the Religious Studies Department at Temple University in Philadelphia, Pennsylvania studying inter-religious dialog, among other things. Axel received his D. Ministry from Episcopal Divinity School in Cambridge, MA.

Joseph Shore-Goss, Pastor of Congregational Care and Spiritual Life at A Church Alive MCC in the Valley North Hollywood, holds an M. Divinity and MA with concentration in Pastoral Care and Counseling from Claremont School of Theology and is currently studying for a PhD at Graduate Theological foundation. He holds a certificate in Spiritual Direction and currently serves as part of the teaching staff at Stillpoint, California, the center for Christian Spirituality. Rev. Joe has an alternate personality and ministry as Sister Atilla D'Nun Keeper of Bears, Bikers and Mayhem with the Los Angeles Sisters of Perpetual Indulgence.

Douglas Smith, a transplant from rural Kansas, makes his home in the San Fernando Valley. His love of language and poetry began at an early age; it has only been in recent years that he has explored spiritual themes in his work. Douglas enjoys politics, theater, and his beloved dachshund, Desi (Desdemona).

Neil Thomas is currently the Senior Pastor of Founders Metropolitan Community Church, Los Angeles, California where he has served for the past 11 years (February 2013). He received a D. Ministry in Queer Theology from San Francisco Seminary and has been active in social action and equality for most of his pastoral career in both the United Kingdom and the United States and has a particular interest in marriage equality, immigration equality, and interfaith relationships. He has been honored by Queen Elizabeth II, sung for President Obama, and has received many commendations and awards from Assembly, state, and local organizations.

Index